**SCHAUM'S
OUTLINE OF**

Theory and Problems of
COMPUTER
NETWORKING

ED TITTEL

Austin Community College

Schaum's Outline Series

McGRAW-HILL
New York   Chicago   San Francisco   Lisbon
London   Madrid   Mexico City   Milan   New Delhi
San Juan   Seoul   Singapore   Sydney   Toronto

ED TITTEL has been an instructor at Austin Community College since 1996, where he teaches markup languages and networking topics. The author of over 100 computer books, and the originator of the Exam Cram certification preparation series. Ed also teaches various Windows topics at the NetWorld + Interop trade show. Feel free to e-mail Ed at etittel@jump.net.

Schaum's Outline of Theory and Problems of
COMPUTER NETWORKING

1 2 3 4 5 6 7 8 9 10 11 12 13 14 15 16 17 18 19 20 VLP VLP 0 9 8 7 6 5 4 3 2

ISBN 0-07-136285-1

Sponsoring Editor: Barbara Gilson
Production Supervisor: Elizabeth J. Shannon
Editing Supervisor: Maureen B. Walker
Compositor: Techset Composition

Library of Congress Cataloging-in-Publication Data applied for.

McGraw-Hill

A Division of The McGraw-Hill Companies

2

SCHAUM'S
OUTLINE OF

Theory and Problems of
COMPUTER
NETWORKING

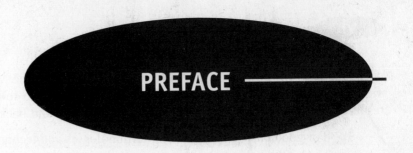

PREFACE

Today, the subject of computer networking embraces an ever-increasing body of knowledge. It spans a broad range of functions and capabilities, from the basic kinds of signaling and circuitry used to permit computers to exchange data, to the kinds of cables or wireless broadcast techniques used to transport data from sender to receiver.

Networking also embraces various sets of rules for communication between sender and receiver at various abstract levels of data exchange. These range from simple, limited streams of bits used to ferry data from a sender to a receiver, to various schemes for identifying, addressing, routing, and handling messages as they travel across various types of networking media. Likewise, protocols also apply to the kinds of services or activities that motivate data transmission across a network, be it to exchange e-mail messages, access remote files or file systems, access distributed databases of many kinds, and even to manage and monitor the behavior and characteristics of the networks that enable such communication to occur.

At first learning about networking involves mastering basic terminology and concepts. One a basic vocabulary is in place, it's a truism that the monolithic "big problem" of networking is best understood by breaking it down into a set of well-separated and mutually interdependent tasks and technologies. At this stage of learning, it's essential to understand various models for networking such as the International Standards Organization's Open Systems Interconnect (ISO/OSI) Network Reference model, as well as other models related to specific types of networking protocols. Likewise, important networking standards and technologies must also be digested and understood.

With a working understanding of how solving the problems inherent in networking depends on understanding how networking can be decomposed into a layered set of related (but technically and terminologically distinct) layers, it's possible to begin digging into some of the details involved in making networks really work. At this point, information about network naming and addressing schemes, network routing models and behaviors, and networked applications and services will begin to make sense. Thus, this represents the kind of developmental and evolutionary model that drives this book, and most of the networking textbooks, which this book seeks to supplement.

All students come to technical subjects with greater or lesser degrees of knowledge and understanding. Some may have to work harder to master basic concepts and vocabulary than others; likewise, some may have to spend more time and effort decoding and absorbing the structures and functions of the various networking models explored here. But all readers will benefit from the following networking resources online, no matter what their prior knowledge and backgrounds might be:

1. For good basic descriptions of terminologies and technologies, please visit www.whatis.com; this site provides encyclopedic listings for information technology terms, including most networking terms you'll encounter in this book and its companion texts.

2. For more detailed tutorials and overviews of general networking topics, tools, and technologies, please visit www.techfest.com; this site provides ample coverage of a broad range of networking topics from local area networks (LANs) to network cabling and management.

3. For middling levels of detail and information, and pointers to additional resources on networking terms and concepts, please visit www.techweb.com/encyclopedia.

Other networking resources and information is widely available on the Internet. Don't neglect to use your favorite search engines, such as Yahoo, Google, AskJeeves, AltaVista, and so forth, to find more information on topics where you might benefit from additional detail.

ED TITTEL

CONTENTS

Contents

SCHAUM'S
OUTLINE OF

Theory and Problems of
COMPUTER
NETWORKING

CHAPTER 1

Data Communications

The technologies used in moving data among computers involve many different components and methodologies. One primary goal of data communications is to allow different hardware and operating systems to communicate and understand each other. To accomplish these objectives, the transmission media involved in data communications have to meet certain hardware specifications. The software used by the computer's operating system to access the transmission media must also conform to standards. These are just two examples of the many components that come into play to allow data to be transmitted between devices. In this chapter, we introduce some of the terms and techniques used in data communications for networks, which range from telephones to the Internet.

Multiplexing

The transmission *media*, or link, refers to the devices used to carry information from one device to another. For example, the telephone line or cable that brings telephone service to your house is the transmission media for carrying voice communications. There may be different types of transmission media used between your house and the telephone company. Your house and the surrounding houses typically use copper wires encased in protective materials to carry the signals into and out of your house. Thus, for each house in your immediate neighborhood, there is a separate cable going to each house that carries the phone conversations for that house. Imagine there are 50 houses in your neighborhood and outside the neighborhood is a junction box or switch managed by the phone company. Switch boxes are used to connect adjacent junction boxes along the physical path or route to the phone company's central office. For our 50-house neighborhood example, the phone company would have to lay 50 individual cables between each of the junction boxes to carry the conversations from the houses to the central office. In addition, if other neighborhoods between yours and the central office use the same junction boxes, then additional cables would need to be added to handle all the neighborhoods' conversations. By the time the cables reached the central office there may be hundreds or even thousands of cables! To say nothing of the expense of all these cables, imagine the work involved when a new house is built or when one or more of the cables physically fails. To eliminate the need and cost of all these cables, conversations from several houses are *multiplexed*, or bundled, together and then transmitted over a single cable between the junction boxes.

Multiplexing technology is used on computer networks and especially over *wide area network* (WAN) exchanges. On computer networks, different carrier frequencies enable the use of multiple, simultaneous computer conversations over the same transmission media. When different carrier frequencies are used to carry different signals, they can use the same transmission media without interfering with each other. The techniques used to modulate the carrier wave for different frequencies are similar to how television stations modulate the carrier wave to broadcast video. Let's take a closer look at how television transmissions work to handle multiple channels at the same time.

Each television station that transmits a signal is assigned a channel number over which the station can broadcast its information. The numbers assigned to channels are actually an abbreviation of the frequency at which the television station's carrier oscillates. To receive a television station's signal, the receiving hardware must be able to select or tune to the same frequency or channel. Thus, when you change channels on your television, you are changing the frequency of the receiver component of the television. By using different channels, or frequencies, for different television stations, several television stations can transmit at the same time in the same geographic region. Cable television uses the same principle except the transmission media is wire instead of the atmosphere. Each cable station is assigned a different frequency, and many different channels can be transmitted simultaneously on the same transmission media. Computer networks use these same types of principles by using different frequencies or channels to carry multiple conversations over the same transmission media.

FREQUENCY DIVISION MULTIPLEXING

Techniques must be used to allow the simultaneous transmission of different carrier frequencies to travel through the media. One method, called *Frequency Division Multiplexing* (FDM), is designed for networks that use multiple carrier frequencies to permit the independent signals to pass through the transmission media. Because the *bandwidth* of the transmission media exceeds the needed bandwidth for a single signal, FDM is designed to take advantage of this bandwidth difference. FDM technology is used on networks that send signals over wire, radio frequencies, or optical fiber. The end of the network that generates the data to be transmitted uses a hardware device called a *multiplexor*, which combines the different frequencies so they can be transmitted along the single channel. At the destination, a *demultiplexor* device separates the different frequencies and routes them to the proper recipient.

For two-way conversations where each end can both transmit and receive, a multiplexor and demultiplexor pair are required at each end. Another hardware requirement for the multiplexor may be the ability to generate the carrier waves that will be propagated down the transmission media. Although multiplexing provides the capability of transmitting signals of different frequencies at the same time, there are problems if the frequencies used are too close or are multiples of another frequency. In these situations, interference between the different signals exists, which makes the transmitted data useless. To prevent these types of issues, the engineers who design FDM networks specify a minimum frequency separation between the different carriers. This minimum frequency difference also applies to radio and television station broadcasts.

A common usage of FDM is AM radio broadcasts. The permitted range of frequencies for AM radio is 500 to 1500 kHz. Different frequencies are assigned to the different logical channels, or stations. There is sufficient separation between the different frequencies to prevent interference between the various stations. Another area where FDM is used is on voice-grade telephone channels. The usable bandwidth is about 3000 Hz per voice-grade channel, and these limits are controlled by filters. When several of these voice-grade channels are multiplexed, 4000 Hz is assigned to each channel to provide sufficient separation, so interference does not occur between the channels. Before transmission, each of the voice-grade channels is raised in frequency by different amounts with a 4000-Hz frequency separation. The FDM schemes used around the world are somewhat standardized where twelve 4000-Hz voice channels are multiplexed into the 60- to 108-kHz band. This collection of voice channels on a specified range of frequencies is called a group. Each of the 12 voice channels includes 3000 Hz for the user plus two 500-Hz guard bands for each voice channel. These guard bands help reduce the interference from items such as spikes because the filters do not produce waves with sharp edges. In some environments, another group exists in the 12- to 60-kHz band. Five groups, or 60 voice channels, can be multiplexed together to form what is called a supergroup. A mastergroup is the collection of five supergroups for the CCITT standard or the assembly of 10 supergroups for the Bell system standard. Other standards exist that allow up to 230,000 voice channels.

Another purpose for using FDM is to provide high throughput on the transmission media. To allow a higher throughput, the hardware is designed to use a large part of the electromagnetic spectrum. Using a larger part of the electromagnetic spectrum generates a larger bandwidth, which gives more "space" for signals to travel. The term *broadband* is used to define technology methods that use larger portions of the electromagnetic spectrum. Methodologies that use small parts of the electromagnetic spectrum and only permit one signal at a time over the medium are referred to as *baseband* technologies.

An example of FDM usage is the phone system, which uses full-duplex *frequency-shift keying* (FSK) transmission. FSK transmission encodes the binary values with different frequencies near the carrier frequencies. *Full-duplex* means that the voice conversation can occur in both directions at the same time on the transmission media.

WAVE DIVISION MULTIPLEXING

Wave Division Multiplexing (WDM) is the term used to specify multiplexing techniques on optical transmission systems. Instead of using different frequencies, different optical wavelengths are used for different signals on the same transmission media. As with electrical signals, light signals at different wavelengths or frequencies do not interfere with each other. When many different wavelengths are used, *Dense Wave Division Multiplexing* (DWDM) is used. Engineers working on WDM systems sometimes use the term *color division multiplexing* and humorously refer to red, purple, orange, and other colors for the carriers. These informal terms arise from the fact that humans see visible light as colors. WDM functions by sending multiple light waves on a single optical fiber. A prism, or diffraction grating device, at the transmission source combines the different light waves and transmits the combined signal over the fiber-optic cable. At the receiving end, another prism is used to separate the light into separate wavelengths, which are then passed on to the recipient.

An issue that is important on multiplexing systems is reliability. Over the course of time, there may be sporadic interference that affects some, but not all, of the frequencies. For example, radio broadcasts can be affected by the movement of large objects in the space between the transmitter and the receiver. Across the available frequencies, broadcast of the radio signal may be better on one frequency at certain times of the day and better at other frequencies during other time frames. The special technique of using FDM on multiple carriers or frequencies to transmit data is called *spread spectrum*. The transmitter using spread spectrum transmits the same signal on different frequencies, and the receiver is designed to check the different frequencies and choose one that is presently working. A form of spread-spectrum technologies is used on some *analog* modems to improve reliability. These modems use a range of carrier frequencies and send the data on all the frequencies. The receiver uses one of the frequencies and, if interference occurs, the data can be "read" from the other frequencies.

One of the reasons why WDM is popular on long-distance fiber-optic lines is that the energy used is typically only a few gigahertz wide. In addition, because the bandwidth of a single fiber band is about 25,000 GHz, the possibility exists for multiplexing many channels together over long-distance runs. Figure 1-1 illustrates a typical WDM system.

In Fig. 1-1, the information coming from Computer A on Fiber A and from Computer B on Fiber B at the source end are multiplexed together and transmitted over the shared fiber-optic cable. At the receiving end, the signal from Computer A is extracted and placed on Fiber Y and the signal from Computer B is placed on Fiber Z. In this type of system, the signal from Computer A will always end up on Fiber Y, and Fiber Z will always carry the signal from Computer B. WDM systems can also be built that incorporate switching technologies. In a switched WDM system, the signal from Computer A on Fiber A can be placed on any of the fibers at the receiving end. In fact, any signal from any device at the source end can be put on any of the input fibers and can arrive on any of the output fibers. Spreading the signals across multiple fibers may reduce the amount of the signal's energy.

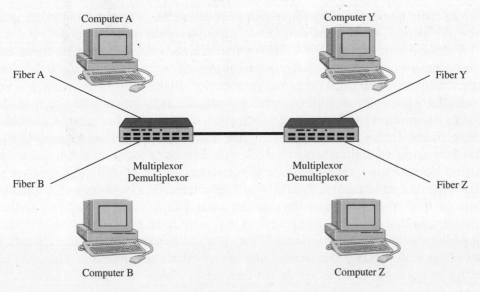

Fig. 1-1.   Typical Wave Division Multiplexing system.

However, these types of switched WDM systems are useful in environments that need hundreds of channels.

TIME DIVISION MULTIPLEXING

Time Division Multiplexing (TDM) is an alternative to FDM. In TDM, the transmitting sources use *time* slices, or take turns at using the transmission media. Each chunk of data for each time slice device is referred to as a frame. TDM methodology takes advantage of the fact that the bit rate of the transmission media is greater than the needed rate of a single transmission. There are two forms of TDM: *Synchronous Time Division Multiplexing* (STDM) and *Statistical Multiplexing*. STDM is also referred to as Slotted Time Division Multiplexing.

In STDM, each transmitting source gets access to the transmission media for a specific time where each time slice is the same size. Each transmitting device gets a turn at the transmission media and does not get another turn until all the other devices have had their turns to transmit. For example, imagine there are three devices that need to transmit: Computer A, Computer B, and Computer C. The first device that has access to the transmission media is Computer A. When Computer A is finished transmitting, Computer B gets its time and when Computer B is finished, Computer C gets access. Sometimes this type of media access is referred to as *round-robin*. The interleaving of data at different times can be done in bits, bytes, or for other groupings of data. TDM multiplexing is well-suited for telephone conversations because each telephone call on the shared transmission media generates data at the exact same rate. One problem with STDM is that even if Computer A and Computer B do not have any information to transmit, Computer C still must wait until the allocated time has passed for Computer A and Computer B before it can transmit. To use the media more efficiently, statistical multiplexing can be used when some systems don't have anything to transmit.

Statistical multiplexing still allocates time for each device to transmit, and each device must go in order. But if a device has nothing to transmit, the multiplexor skips the device and goes on to the next device. Statistical multiplexing is a very cost-effective way for multiple systems to share the same transmission media. Most computer networks use some form of statistical multiplexing because the devices on the network do not need to transmit data all the time and they generate data at different rates. Communicating devices on a network tend to transmit for a short period of time and then wait for a response. Because of this burst type of transmission, statistical multiplexing is preferred over synchronous multiplexing because time is not wasted on devices that are not transmitting. To make sure that a transmitting device allows other devices that want to transmit to get their time, an upper limit is placed on the amount of data that can be transmitted at a given time. In statistical multiplexing, this limited amount of data is referred to as a *packet*.

An example of TDM usage is the method in which AM radio is broadcast in some countries. In addition to each channel using an assigned frequency, each channel has two logical subchannels. One of the subchannels is used for music, and the other is used for advertising. Using TDM, the two subchannels alternate in time on the same channel.

On individual computer systems, TDM is not practical for copper wire or microwave channel transmissions because of the overhead of the needed analog circuitry. Instead, performing TDM can be done entirely by *digital* electronics and has become much more widespread in use. However, when digital techniques are used for TDM, it can only be used for digital data.

When modems are used to communicate between two different systems across the telephone company's transmission media, the analog signals on the copper wires must be converted to a digital form so they can be multiplexed by TDM. The multiplexed signal is then transmitted over fiber-optic cables used by the telephone companies between junction locations. The analog signals are digitized by a device called a *codec* (coder-decoder). The codec takes 8000 samples per second to produce a 7- or 8-bit number. The Nyquist theorem states that 8000 samples per second are sufficient to capture all the information from a 4-kHz telephone channel. If the sampling rate were lower, data would be lost and if the sampling rate were higher, no additional information would be gathered from the analog signal. The main concept in digitization is to compare the amplitude of an analog signal with a small set of numbered amplitude thresholds called *quantization levels*. The spacing between the quantization levels is logarithmically spaced because this scheme produces better resolution at low signal levels. The digital representation of the amplitude of an analog signal is the number of the quantization level closest to the sample. The 8000 sampled amplitudes per second are compared against 256 quantization levels to produce 8-bit samples. This results in the standard voice bandwidth of 64 Kbps. There are two implementations of quantization levels that are in common use. The μ-law form is used in the United States and Japan, and the A-law variant is used throughout the rest of the world. Unfortunately, this does not allow direct connections between different quantization levels so telephone conversations have to be remapped to fit the sender's and receiver's quantization scheme.

On telephone systems, the sampling of analog data is called *pulse code modulation* (PCM). The 8000 samples per second translate to a 125 µsec/sample and because of this, essentially all time intervals within the telephone system are multiples of 125 µsecs. When PCM was being developed, the CCITT organization was not able to reach an agreement on an international standard. As a result, PCM exists in different implementations in different countries, which does not allow a seamless connection between different PCM systems. To permit international hookups, expensive "black boxes" are used to convert the signals between different PCM systems.

One implementation of PCM that is used a lot in North America and Japan is *T1*. The T1 carrier is composed of 24 voice channels that are multiplexed together. When T1 is being used entirely for data, 23 channels are used for data and the twenty-fourth channel is used for a special synchronization pattern to allow recovery of the information if the transmission gets out of synchronization. The analog signals at the source end are sampled on a round-robin basis to produce an analog stream of data that is processed through the codec. The purpose of the round-robin approach is to reduce the need for 24 separate codecs at the source end. During creation of the round-robin analog data stream, each device inserts 8 bits of data, in which 7 bits are for data and 1 bit is for control. If you multiply 7 bits of data by the sample rate of 8000 samples per second, you arrive at the value of 56,000 bps (bits per second). Taking into account that a frame of information consists of 192 bits (24 channels × 8 bits) plus an additional bit for framing, there are 193 bits every 125 µsecs. These values produce a data rate of 1.544 Mbps. The *framing bit*, 193, uses the pattern of 0101010101 ..., which the receiver checks periodically to make sure transmission is synchronized. If things do get out of synchronization, the receiver can scan for the framing bit and get back into sync. The framing bit is added by the digital circuitry because if the pattern were in the analog signal, it would produce a sine wave at 4000 Hz, which would be filtered out.

The CCITT did finally come to an agreement about PCM and decided that the sampling rate of 8000 was too high. Consequently, the CCITT 1.544 Mbps standard is based on 8 bits for data instead of the 7 bits of data described previously. Because of these differences, there exists two incompatible variations. To handle these differences, one method, called *common-channel signaling*, assigns the extra bit the value of 10101010 ... in the odd frames and contains signaling information in the even frames for all the channels. The other approach for handling the differences is called *channel associated signaling*. In this technique, each channel has its own private signaling subchannel. This private subchannel is created by allocating one of the 8 data bits in every sixth frame for signaling purposes. Therefore, five out of six samples are 8 bits in length and the remaining sample is 7 bits in length.

The CCITT also specifies a PCM standard for 2.048 Mbps, which is referred to as *E1*. Usage of E1 is widespread outside of Japan and North America. The E1 carrier has thirty-two 8-bit data samples per 125 µsec frame. Two of the channels are used for signaling and the remaining 30 channels are used for data. Sixty-four signaling bits are provided by each group of four frames where 32 bits are used for channel-associated signaling and the remaining 32 are used for either frame synchronization or are reserved by each country to use as they wish.

TDM multiplexing also allows multiple T1 carriers to be multiplexed onto a *T2* or *T3* channel. Multiplexing T1s into T2s or T3s is done bit-for-bit instead of byte-for-byte for the 24 channels in each T1. Four T1s at 1.544 Mbps each would generate 6.176 Mbps, but the T2 implementation is actually 6.312 Mbps. The difference is caused by the addition of extra bits used for framing and synchronization recovery. In the United States, the T3 level is composed of six T2s that are multiplexed bit-by-bit and seven T3s are *bitwised* multiplexed to form a T4. The CCITT standard defines multiplexing of four carriers for each level—that is, four T2s combine for a T3 and four T3s combine for a T4. The CCITT specifications are listed in Table 1-1.

Table 1-1   CCITT Channel Specifications

Number of Channels	Mbps
32	2.048
128	8.848
512	34.304
2048	139.264
8192	565.148

Signaling

When discussing data communications, the terms analog and digital are frequently encountered. Analog refers to information that is in a continuous form, and digital refers to information that has discrete states. For example, an analog clock that has hour, minute, and second hands reports the information in a continuous form by the constant movement of the clock hands. A digital clock has discrete units of information. Digital clocks that report the hours and minutes will suddenly change from 29 minutes past the hour to 30 minutes past the hour. The minute value in the digital clock does not gradually change from 29 to 30 but instead makes a discrete change from 29 to 30.

The terms *analog* and *digital* are used in three different contexts when referring to data communications: data, signaling, and transmission. The word *data* when used in the context of networks refers to information that conveys or contains something of meaning to the source and/or the recipient. The information in the data may be the raw information or contain the interpreted results from raw data. Data is encoded in some electrical or electromagnetic form to produce analog or digital signals. The process by which a computer interacts with the network transmission media and sends the signal down the media is referred to as *signaling*. In addition to the data that will be transmitted, signaling also requires the transmission of network control messages. These control messages are sent as units of information across the same connection used by the transmission of the data. Typically, the control information is sent on a separate channel from the data or voice and may be referred to as *out-of-band signaling*. Telephone networks typically use out-of-band signaling that is called the *Common Channel Interoffice Signaling* (CCIS) network. Transmission is the propagation and processing of signals down the transmission media so that exchange of information occurs.

Transmission of data over transmission media can be propagated in analog or digital energy forms and the type of energies used can be electrical or optical. A continuously changing electromagnetic wave that is propagated over the transmission media is an analog signal. For example, a signal of varying frequencies traveling down an unshielded twisted-pair cable, a coaxial cable, a fiber-optic cable, or through the atmosphere, is an analog signal. If the signal is a series of voltage pulses traveling down the communication hardware, the form is a digital signal. Digital signaling has some advantages over analog signaling. Digital systems are usually more cost-effective and suffer less from noise interference. However, digital signals tend to attenuate more than analog signals. *Attenuation* is the reduction or loss of the signal strength as the distance of the transmitted signal increases. Furthermore, signals at higher frequencies suffer more from attenuation than lower frequencies. As digital signals travel farther and farther down the media, the strength of the wave is not as distinct as the initial signal. The wave shapes begin to become more rounded and it becomes more difficult for the receiver to differentiate between high and low values.

Analog data transmitted over analog hardware is typically expressed as a function of time within a limited frequency range. A good example of analog data is voice data. The frequency range of the human voice is between 20 Hz and 20 kHz, but most of the speech energy is in a small portion of that range. Typically, a 300- to 3400-Hz electromagnetic signal is quite sufficient to adequately propagate speech so that it is clear and understandable. This range of frequencies is what the standard telephone uses for both the speaker and microphone components. Information that is in digital form, such as from a computer, can be represented by analog signals. A good example of using analog signals to transmit digital data is a modem. The modem converts the binary voltage pulses from the computer into an analog signal that uses different frequencies to represent the digital data. The frequencies that are used by the modem occupy a certain range around the frequency of the carrier or channel. Thus, the modem uses a range of frequencies in the human voice range to send the signals down a voice-grade telephone line. Analog data can also be represented by digital signals with a codec (coder-decoder). In addition, digital signals can be used to carry digital data.

The techniques used to allow signaling on a computer network are often the most complex portion of the entire network. Take, for example, the telephone system with all the telephone switches located around the world and all the conversation features such as conference calls, call screening, and accounting. Each of these takes many lines of code to produce all the features and functions, but a good portion of the code is involved in handling the signaling requirements. The software must provide the services in a fast and reliable environment, and updating the software is a major undertaking involving hundreds of programmers on a daily basis.

Encoding and Decoding

When analog and digital signals are used to transport the information down the transmission media, the properties of the signals must, in some way, represent the data. The role of encoding is to define the properties of the signal to represent the information. Decoding is used by the recipient of the transmitted signal so the signal patterns are converted back into meaningful data. One of the simplest ways to communicate data in a computer network is to use a small electrical signal to represent the data. For example, the voltage on a wire connecting two devices can be changed so that a positive voltage level, such as 5 V, represents a binary one (1) and a negative voltage level (-5 V) represents a binary zero (0). To transmit a binary 1, the sending device places a positive voltage on the wire for a short period of time and then returns the voltage level to 0. The receiving device detects the positive voltage and records that a binary 1 has arrived. To send a binary 0, the sending device places a negative voltage on the wire for a short time period and then sets the voltage level to zero. The recipient senses the negative voltage and records that a binary 0 has arrived. Figure 1-2 is an example of how the voltage in the wire may vary over time to represent the binary information transmitted by the sender.

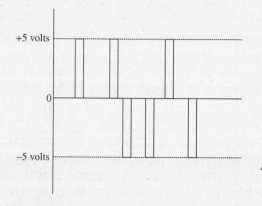

Fig. 1-2.   Example of voltage changes on a wire to represent binary information.

The graphic representation of the voltage values as shown in Fig. 1-2 is referred to as a waveform diagram. In addition to showing the voltage levels, the diagram also shows the length of time between changes in voltages. To ensure that the signals placed on the transmission media can be properly interpreted by the recipients, standards exist that define parameters, such as how long the change in voltage exists, the maximum rate at which the voltage can be changed, and so on.

Research into signal transmission has revealed that a continuously oscillating signal travels the farthest when compared to other signals. To take advantage of this fact, most signals for long-distance communication systems send a continuously oscillating signal called a *carrier*. These waves are usually sine waves and the carrier oscillates even when no data is being transmitted. To send data when there is a continuous signal, the transmitter modifies the carrier slightly to reflect the information. This type of modification of the carrier signal is called *modulation* and these techniques have been in use for radio, telephone, and television signals—well before computer networks. On computer networks, modulation of the carrier signal is used on copper wire, optic fibers, microwaves, and radio transmissions. There are different ways in which an analog carrier signal can be modulated to represent digital data.

AMPLITUDE MODULATION

Amplitude modulation is used by AM radio and it can be used on computer networks. In amplitude modulation, the strength of the carrier wave is modified to represent, or encode, the data. For example, a higher amplitude may represent a binary 1 and a lower amplitude encodes a binary 0. Figure 1-3 is an example of an amplitude-modulated carrier wave and how it can represent data.

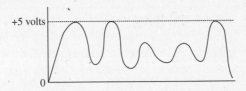

Fig. 1-3.   An amplitude-modulated carrier wave representing data.

Amplitude modulation has a tendency to suffer from sudden gain changes and is not a very efficient modulation technique for computer networks. However, it is used to transmit digital data over fiber-optic cables. Modulation of the amplitude of the carrier signal is also referred to as *amplitude-shift keying* (ASK).

FREQUENCY MODULATION

Frequency modulation is used by FM radio and computer networks and involves the modification of the frequency of the carrier wave to represent data. For example, an increase in the frequency of the carrier wave could be used to encode a binary 1. Similarly, a decrease in frequency would encode or represent a binary 0. Figure 1-4 is an example of a frequency-modulated carrier wave and how it can represent data.

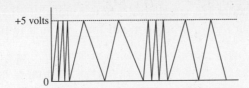

Fig. 1-4.   A frequency-modulated carrier wave representing data.

Frequency modulation is not as susceptible to the errors found in amplitude modulation techniques. It is commonly used in high-frequency radio transmissions.

Modulation of the frequency of the carrier signal is also referred to as *frequency-shift keying* (FSK).

PHASE-SHIFT MODULATION

Amplitude and frequency modulations work well for audio signals but they both use at least one complete wave cycle to encode a binary 1 or binary 0. If, however, you could encode multiple bits of data on a single wave cycle, then the number of bits sent per second would increase. This capability is described by the Nyquist theorem and is implemented on computer networks through phase-shift modulation. In phase-shift modulation, the timing of the carrier wave is modified to encode data. Once a phase shift has occurred, the carrier continues to oscillate but jumps to a new point in the wave cycle. Figure 1-5 illustrates a carrier wave that contains three phase shifts. Modulation of the phase of the carrier signal is also referred to as *phase-shift keying* (PSK).

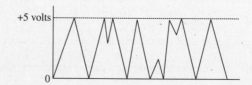

Fig. 1-5. Phase-shift modulation of a carrier signal.

To encode multiple bits of information on a single wave cycle, the amount of the phase shift is used in the calculations. In Fig. 1-5, the first two phase shifts are the same amount and each jumps half of a complete cycle. The third shift jumps three-quarters of a cycle. The phase shifts that are used in a phase-shift modulation system are usually selected to represent a power of two possible values. In a system that can shift the amount of the phase by eight different amounts, the number of bits that can be encoded on one phase shift is three. Examining the representation of decimal 8 as 2^3 means that any combination of three bits can be encoded by different amounts of phase shifts. That is: 000, 001, 010, 011, 100, 101, 110, 111. The maximum data rate that can be handled by a phase-shift modulation scheme is based on T, the number of bits used to create a phase shift and R, the number of signal changes per second. Using the variables R and T, the maximum data rate is $2RT$. The number of signal changes per second, R, is called the baud rate of the hardware so the number of bits per second that the environment can transmit is a multiple of the baud rate.

MULTILEVEL SIGNALING

The usage of amplitude, frequency, or phase-shift modulations can be combined to form what is called *multilevel signaling*. The effect of combining different modulation techniques allows more bits to be represented by each element of the signal. A common modulation combination involves amplitude and phase-shift modulation. In this combination, the phase shifts can occur at different amplitudes.

NRZ-L

Nonreturn to zero level (NRZ-L) encoding uses negative voltage to represent a binary 1 and positive voltage to represent a binary 0. Figure 1-6 illustrates an example of NRZ-L encoding.

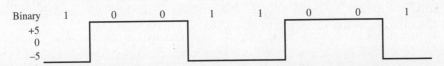

Fig. 1-6.   Example of how NRZ-L encoding represents binary data.

The use of the term *nonreturn to zero* means the voltage never returns to a value of zero and the value of the voltage during a bit time is level. *Bit time* is the amount of time one bit of data occupies. NRZ-L is typically used on very short connections, such as between a computer and an external modem or from a dedicated terminal to the main unit located a short distance away. One of the problems with NRZ-L is that for long strings of 1's or 0's, the signal's voltage remains positive or negative for extended periods of time. This can lead to the situation referred to as *baseline wander*, which makes it difficult for the receiver to properly decode the information. The second problem is that in order for the sender and receiver to remain in synchronization, frequent changes in the signal need to occur. When there are long runs of high or low voltages, the sender and receiver's clocks may begin to wander so that the two devices are no longer in synchronization. To prevent the loss of synchronization, a separate clock signal could be used on another channel but this takes up valuable data transmission space. To help overcome the problems with NRZ-L, NRZI encoding can be used.

Note: In some references, NRZ-L is defined where a high or positive voltage represents a binary 1 and a low or negative voltage represents a binary 0.

NRZI

NRZI or NRZ, invert on ones, is related to NRZ-L except the data is encoded by either the presence or absence of a voltage change at the beginning of the bit time. Figure 1-7 is an example of NRZI encoding.

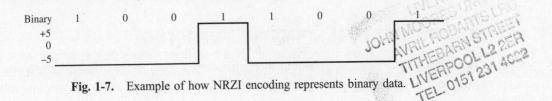

Fig. 1-7.   Example of how NRZI encoding represents binary data.

When the signal changes from a high to low voltage or from a low to high voltage, a binary 1 is encoded. When there is no change in the voltage at the beginning of the current bit time from the last bit time, a binary 0 is encoded. The mechanism by which NRZI encodes data is an example of a differential encoding technique. NRZI is also referred to as non-return to zero inverted.

In the amplitude and frequency modulation examples just mentioned to demonstrate changes in the carrier signal to represent data, the value of the amplitude or frequency was used to represent a binary 1 or binary 0. Information can also be encoded by using the change in the carrier signal instead of the absolute value of the signal. In general, hardware can detect changes in voltage levels more easily than monitoring voltages at fixed values. Manchester Encoding, or biphase encoding, uses the change in the property of the wave to encode data.

MANCHESTER ENCODING

In Manchester Encoding, the point at which the signal changes is used to represent data. For example, in Fig. 1-8, the locations at which the voltage changes from zero to a positive value represent a binary 1, and when the voltage changes from positive to zero, a binary 0 is represented.

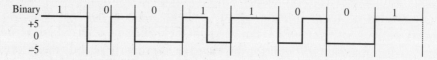

Fig. 1-8.   Example of how Manchester Encoding represents binary data.

The hardware used in Manchester-encoding schemes is said to be edge triggered and the changes or transitions are known as rising or falling edges. When the leading edge rises to a positive voltage, a binary 1 is encoded and when the leading edge falls to zero voltage, a binary 0 is encoded. With this type of structure, each bit period is divided into two equal intervals. Every bit period has a transition in the middle that makes it easier for the receiver to synchronize with the sender. To ensure there is proper synchronization of the time slots used when sampling the signal by the receiver, Manchester Encoding uses a preamble to permit synchronization by the receiver. The preamble is composed of 64 alternating 1's and 0's, which is sent before the frame of data. A pattern of alternating 1's and 0's produces a square wave from which the receiver can determine the value of the time slots. The combined effect of the preamble and the transition in the middle of the bit period eliminates the need for an external clock to synchronize the sender and receiver. Manchester Encoding is used in Ethernet and other LAN specifications.

DIFFERENTIAL MANCHESTER ENCODING

A variation on standard Manchester Encoding is referred to as *Differential Manchester Encoding*. In this form, a binary 1 is represented by the lack of a transition or voltage change at the beginning of the sampling interval. A binary 0 is encoded when a transition occurs at the beginning of the sampling interval. The differential form of Manchester Encoding requires hardware that is more complex, but it offers better immunity to influences from outside noises. Figure 1-9 illustrates an example of Differential Manchester Encoding for the same binary data found in Fig. 1-8. Differential Manchester Encoding is used in token ring networks.

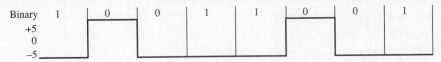

Fig. 1-9.   Example of how Differential Manchester Encoding represents binary data.

A problem with Manchester Encoding schemes is that the methodology doubles the rate at which the signal transitions are made on the transmission media. This means that the receiver has only half the time to detect the signal in each bit time. The baud rate of a transmission media is the rate at which the signal can change on the media. So, in the case of Manchester Encoding, the bit rate is half the baud rate, which means the encoding is only about 50 percent efficient. To help overcome some of the problems with Manchester Encoding, 4B/5B encoding can be used.

4B/5B

One of the principal functions of 4B/5B is to reduce the problems related to extended stretches of high or low signals. To provide relief from this problem, 4B/5B inserts extra bits into the stream of bits to break up long sequences of ones or zeros. The methodology of 4B/5B is that every four bits of data are encoded in a 5-bit code (code group), which is then delivered to the receiver. The selection of the 5-bit codes is done so that each one does not contain more than one leading zero and ends with no more than two trailing zeros. Therefore, when these 5-bit codes are sent in sequence, no more than three consecutive zeros are encountered. The 5-bit codes are transmitted by NRZI encoding and the result of the 4B/5B scheme results in 80 percent efficiency of data transport. Table 1-2 lists the 4B/5B 5-bit codes that correlate to the possible 4-bit combinations of data.

There are 16 sets of 4-bit combinations, and a 5-bit pattern can encode 32 different 4-bit combinations. This means that there are sixteen 5-bit codes that are not used for data, Some of these "leftover" codes are used for other purposes. For example, 11111 indicates the transmission media is idle and nothing is being transmitted. The sequence of five zeros means the line is dead and 00100 means there is a transmission error and to halt. This leaves 13 remaining 5-bit codes but of these, seven cannot be used because they include too many leading or trailing zeros, which would violate the rules for 4B/5B. The remaining six can be used to represent control symbols, which are used in some technologies, such as FDDI and 100BASE-FX.

Table 1-2 Correlation of 4- and 5-Bit Bit Codes

Data Code		Definition
(4-bits)	(5-bits)	
0000	11110	data 0
0001	01001	data 1
0010	10100	data 2
0011	10101	data 3
0100	01010	data 4
0101	01011	data 5
0110	01110	data 6
0111	01111	data 7
1000	10010	data 8
1001	10011	data 9
1010	10110	data A
1011	10111	data B
1100	11010	data C
1101	11011	data D
1110	11100	data E
	00000	line is dead
	11111	line is idle
	00100	halt, transmission error
	11000	delimiter for part 1 start of data stream
	10001	delimiter for part 2 start of data stream
	01101	delimiter for part 1 end of data stream
	00111	delimiter for part 2 end of data stream

MLT-3

The 4B/5B encoding scheme works well for fiber-optic transmissions but it does not work well for copper-based media, such as twisted pair. This is because the concentration of the signal energy in 4B/5B creates emissions which are radiated from the copper wire. To help overcome this emission problem, MLT-3 can be used. The encoding scheme is designed to concentrate most of the transmitted signal's energy to below 30 MHz because at those levels, the amount of radiated emissions drops, which results in fewer problems due to interference. The encoding on the voltage uses three states: positive, negative, and zero voltage. The following list outlines the MLT-3 encoding scheme.

- When the next input bit is zero, the next output bit is the same as the preceding output bit.

- When the next input bit is one and the last output bit is either a positive or negative voltage, then the next output bit is a zero.

- When the next input bit is one and the preceding output bit was zero, the next output value is non-zero and has the reverse sign of the last non-zero output voltage. For example, if the last non-zero output bit was a negative voltage, then the next output bit is a positive voltage.

The MLT-3 encoding scheme is used on 100BASE-FX and on the twisted-pair version of FDDI.

8B6T

The signaling used in 8B6T encoding is ternary, which means that the signal can have one of three possible values. A positive, negative, or zero voltage correlates to the three possible signal stages. Information on an 8B6T encoding scheme is grouped together in 8-bit data blocks where each chunk of data is mapped to a code that consists of a code group of six ternary symbols. The reasons why this type of encoding to a code group of six was done is to provide synchronization and to produce dc balance on the transmission media. When the average voltage on the line is zero, then dc balance has been obtained. To produce the dc balance, the combination of signals grouped as a collection of six contains either an equal number of positive and negative values or contains one extra positive voltage value. The 8B6T encoding mechanism is used on 100BASE-T4 transmission media.

8B/10B

In the 8B/10B encoding scheme, each chunk of 8 bits of data is mapped to a 10-bit code group. The 8B/10B method provides more error-detection capabilities than 4B/5B and provides for easier clock recovery when the sender and receiver start to drift out of synchronization. The 8B/10B encoding mechanism is used for Fibre Channel and the different Gigabit Ethernet implementations except those using twisted-pair cables.

4D-PAM5

The 4D-PAM5 encoding scheme is used on 1000BASE-T transmission media. The term *4D-PAM5* stands for four-dimensional, five-level pulse amplitude modulation. The encoding methodology takes advantage of the techniques used to provide high-speed communications over Category 5 copper cable. The implementation of 4D-PAM5 uses four twisted-pair links where each link provides a 250-Mbps data rate. Each of the four twisted-pair cables function at full duplex so signals can be transmitted in both directions at the same time. On each of the cables, 2 bits represents a symbol and the PAM5 encoding scheme uses five different voltage levels. Four of the five voltage levels are used to encode the 2-bit data chunks and the fifth is used for error correction. 4D-PAM5 is very complex and incorporates scrambling techniques to improve the signal quality by producing balanced patterns of ones and zeros.

Error Detection and Recovery

Errors can be introduced into transmitted data by many means such as physical interference with the transmission media to errors in coding of network drivers and router software. In this section, we concentrate on the errors that can be introduced during the transmission of data across the media and devices used to propagate the information.

External physical factors such as power surges, lightning, or interference from electromagnetic sources can alter the electrical signal traveling down the transmission media. These types of interferences affect signals passing down copper-based cable systems but other factors, such as rain, can interfere with wireless transmissions such as microwaves. Light traveling down a fiber-optic cable is not susceptible to external electromagnetic interferences or the weather.

Outside electrical forces can change the signal traveling down the copper transmission media, which results in changed data when the receiver decodes the signal. A small change in the signal can cause the receiver to improperly interpret multiple bits of data that can significantly modify the meaning of the data or render the data completely unusable. On the other hand, electrical interferences can introduce a signal on an idle transmission link that causes the receiver to believe there is data when in fact there is no information. In some cases, severe electrical activity, such as lightning, can permanently damage hardware. When data is lost, changed, or when signals appear that do not represent data, a transmission error occurs. Because of transmission errors, a good portion of the complexity of networks involves techniques to help account for, and correct, errors introduced during propagation of signals. Fortunately, most transmission errors occur infrequently, and communication links may operate for long periods of time without any problems. However, there is always the possibility of transmission errors so techniques have been designed to help detect and recover from errors.

Most of the error-detection schemes attach the error-detection information to each frame of data before it is transmitted down the media. In general, a transmitted frame that includes error-detection information looks like Fig. 1-10.

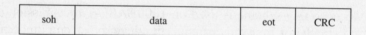

soh	data	eot	CRC

Fig. 1-10.   Generic frame format with error-detection information.

In Fig. 1-10, the portion labeled soh refers to start of header and eot represents end of transmission. The error-detecting code portion of the packet is referred to as a *frame check sequence* (FCS).

There are basically two methods for dealing with errors and correcting them. Error-correcting codes use redundant information with the data so the receiver has enough information to figure out what the lost information was. Error-correcting codes are sometimes referred to as *forward error correction* (FEC), and include quite a bit of overhead in the packets. The second approach, error-detecting codes, adds some redundancy with the data but only enough so the receiver knows when an error has occurred but not what the error actually is. With error-detecting codes, when the receiver realizes an error has occurred, it requests a retransmission of the information. *Cyclic Redundancy Checks* (CRCs), checksums, and parity checking are examples of error-detecting codes. Figure 1-11 is an example of a captured packet that contains an FCS element used for error detection.

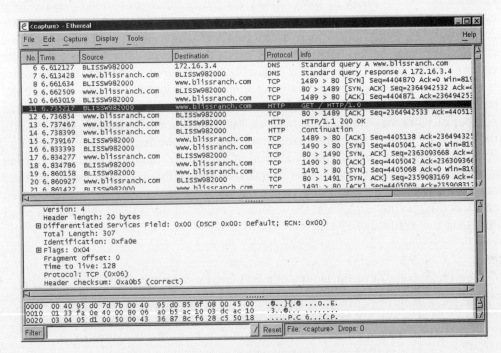

Fig. 1-11. Captured packet showing an FCS entry.

PARITY CHECK

The receiver on a serial communication link, such as a modem, starts a timer when signals begin to arrive and uses the timer to check the bits of the incoming information. The receiver expects to receive the signal at a constant voltage for a specified period of time and if this condition is not met, the hardware indicates that an error has occurred. Likewise, if a stop bit in the incoming signal does not occur at the proper time, the hardware declares an error. In addition to using expected signal durations, a second mechanism is typically used to assist in verifying that the arriving information is complete and nothing is missing. The second technique has the sender computer attach an additional bit to the data, called a parity bit, before it is transmitted. The use of a parity bit to detect errors is called a *parity check*. When the receiver gets the data with the parity bit, it removes the parity bit from the data, executes the same computation performed by the sender and uses the results to determine if the information arrived intact. The parity calculations are designed so that if one bit of the incoming data is modified, the receiver knows that the contents were damaged and reports that an error has occurred.

There are two types of parity checks, and both the sender and the receiver must agree and use the same type throughout the length of the data conversation. If the sender and the receiver use different types of parity checks, then nothing is gained and most likely more errors would be reported. The two types of parity are odd and even parity. The even parity calculation is to count the number of ones in the bit stream and if the number of ones is odd, the parity bit is set to 1 so that the total number of bits in the data and parity bit is an even number. For example, if the data is 0100110, then the parity bit is 1 to bring the number of even bits to 4. If the number of 1 bits in the data stream is even, then the parity bit is set to 0. For example, if the data is 0110110, the parity bit to produce even parity is 0. Odd parity is the opposite of even parity where the number of calculated bits in the data and parity bit is odd. For example, if the data is 0100110, the parity bit is 0 since the number of 1's in the data is already an odd number. If the data pattern was 0110110, the parity bit for the odd parity scheme is 1 to bring the total number of 1's to 5.

When either even or odd parity is used, if any one of the bits in the data portion changes from a 0 to a 1 or from a 1 to a 0, then the parity calculated by the receiver does not agree with the parity bit sent by the sender. For example, in Table 1-3, even parity is used by the sender and the receiver. Notice, in the second row, the effect of changing one bit in the data.

Table 1-3   Effects of a Bit Change with Even Parity

Original Data	Sender Parity Bit	Transmitted Information	Receiver Calculated Parity Bit	Agree?
0100110	1	10100110	1	Yes
0100110	1	10100100	0	No

Parity schemes perform properly in the event of a single bit change, but what happens if 2, or an even number of bits are changed? In Tables 1-4 and 1-5, observe the effect at the receiver's end when 2 and 4 bits are changed.

Furthermore, what about situations where the parity bit itself is changed? For example, take a look at Table 1-6. In Table 1-6, the data is intact but the receiver

Table 1-4   Effects of a Two-Bit Change with Even Parity

Original Data	Sender Parity Bit	Transmitted Information	Receiver Calculated Parity Bit	Agree?
0100110	1	10100110	1	Yes
0100110	1	10100000	1	Yes

Table 1-5   Effects of a Four-Bit Change with Even Parity

Original Data	Sender Parity Bit	Transmitted Information	Receiver Calculated Parity Bit	Agree?
0100110	1	10100110	1	Yes
0100110	1	10101001	1	Yes

Table 1-6   Effects of a Parity Bit Change with Even Parity

Original Data	Sender Parity Bit	Transmitted Information	Receiver Calculated Parity Bit	Agree?
0100110	1	10100110	1	Yes
0100110	1	00100110	1	No

cannot determine where in the bit pattern the error occurred so the entire received information is considered faulty.

To summarize, parity checking is effective in detecting transmission errors when an odd number of bits have changed, but it cannot properly indicate errors when an even number of bits have been modified.

CHECKSUMS

Checksums are another error-detecting method that provides more reliability than parity checks. However, more overhead is needed when compared to parity checking to generate the checksum by the sender and to process the checksum at the receiver. In practice, most computer networks do use checksums and attach the checksum to the information packet before it is placed on the transmission media.

The checksum calculation is a relatively easy computation that requires the sender to add up the binary integers that make up the data to generate a sum. This type of calculation can be used on data that is composed of numbers, images, characters, and floating-point numbers. For example, let's generate the 16-bit checksum for the word *Networks*. For clarity's sake, we will use the value of the ASCII characters in hexadecimal for the calculation. Figure 1-12 illustrates the ASCII codes for the letters and every two letters are paired together to produce groups of 16 bits.

N	e	t	w	o	r	k	s
4E	65	74	77	6F	72	6B	73

Fig. 1-12.   ASCII code equivalents for the string *Networks*.

To generate the checksum for the word *Networks*, add up the pairs of ASCII codes. For example:

$$4E65 + 7477 + 6F72 + 6B73 = 19DC1$$

If the resulting sum is greater than 16 bits, the value of the additional numbers is added to the 16-bit portion of the number. For example, the value 19DC1 is greater than 16 bits so the value outside the number 9DC1 is added to the number. That is, the checksum is $9DC1 + 1$, which equals 9DC2. The numbers that are outside the 16-bit portion of the summed values are sometimes referred to as the *carry bits*.

Checksums used by networks can be either 16-bit or 32-bit and typically generate a checksum for an entire packet of information. However, checksums cannot detect certain types of errors that modify multiple bits that create the same checksum. For example, consider the example in Table 1-7, which uses 4-bit data chunks.

Table 1-7   Data in 4-Bit Chunks
Used for Calculating a Checksum

Binary Value	Decimal Value
0101	5
0110	6
0100	4
0001	1

The calculated checksum for the data in Table 1-7 is decimal 16. Observe what happens in Table 1-8 when the last bit in each number is reversed:

Table 1-8   Data with Last Bits
Reversed

Binary Value	Decimal Value
0100	4
0111	7
0101	5
0000	0

The calculated checksum for the modified data with the reversed last bit is also 16. Thus, under this type of change in transmitted information, the checksum calculated at the receiver would indicate no errors. The type of errors that modify the bits in a specific position or pattern are referred to as *vertical errors*.

CYCLIC REDUNDANCY CHECKS

A Cyclic Redundancy Check (CRC) is able to detect more errors than either checksums or parity checks. CRCs implement a mathematical formula to produce the result. However, most implementations use CRC hardware because it is simple and cheap to build. CRC hardware uses two components: a shift register and an exclusive or (xor) device. Table 1-9 lists the results of the exclusive or operation for two inputs.

Table 1-9 Exclusive or Operation Results
for Two Inputs

First Input	Second Input	xor Output
0	0	0
0	1	1
1	0	1
1	1	0

The shift register in the CRC hardware holds only a fixed number of bits and the bits can move, or shift, from right to left. For example, a 16-bit shift register contains 16 bits so when a bit enters from the right, the left-most bit in the register is shifted or moved out of the register. Thus, the output of the shift register is the value of the left-most bit before a bit enters the register on the right. The shift register is capable of two operations. When the register is initialized, all the bits in the register are set to zero. The second operation is a shift and when this occurs, all the bits in the register move to the left by one position, or bit. In addition, in a shift operation, after all the existing bits have been shifted to the left, the right-most bit in the right-most register is set to the value of the input. For example, Fig. 1-13 illustrates the contents of the shift register prior to a shift and the results of the shift operation. Note that the value of the right-most position in the right register does not change until the shift operation occurs.

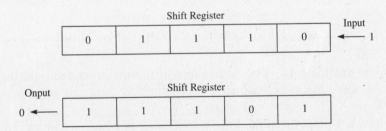

Fig. 1-13. Example of a shift register before and after a shift operation.

The hardware to compute a 16-bit CRC consists of three shift registers that are connected together by three exclusive (xor) elements. Figure 1-14 is a diagram of the hardware and the movement of bits for a 16-bit CRC system.

The output from the left-most shift register enters the three exclusive or units when a shift occurs. In Fig. 1-14, the right register contains 5 bits, the middle contains 7 bits, and the left register contains 4 bits to give a total of 16 bits. There are several CRC algorithms that can be used, and their differences are in the number of bits specified for each of the three registers. Looking at the CRC mathematically,

Fig. 1-14. An example of a 16-bit CRC device.

a CRC uses a polynomial expressed as powers of X to divide the message. The polynomial for the device shown in Fig. 1-14 is:

$$p(X) = X^{16} + X^{12} + X^5 + 1$$

X^{12} reflects the number of bits in the middle and right register and X^5 represents the number of bits in the right register. The following are common CRC polynomials:

- CRC-8 $X^8 + X^2 + X^1 + 1$: used when the character length is 4 bits
- CRC-10 $X^{10} + X^9 + X^5 + X^4 + X^1 + 1$: used when the character length is 5 bits
- CRC-12 $X^{12} + X^{11} + X^3 + X^2 + X^1 + 1$: used when the character length is 6 bits
- CRC-16 $X^{16} + X^{15} + X^2 + 1$: used when the character length is 8 bits
- CRC-CCITT $X^{16} + X^{12} + X^5 + 1$: used when the character length is 8 bits
- CRC-32 $X^{32} + X^{26} + X^{23} + X^{22} + X^{16} + X^{12} + X^{11} + X^{10} + X^8 + X^7 + X^5 + X^4 + X^2 + X + 1$: used when the character length is 16 bits

To compute a CRC, the following steps are performed:

1. The three registers are initialized so all the bits in the registers are set to zero.
2. The incoming bit is placed as one of the inputs in the right register.
3. All three registers are instructed to shift, at the same time, one bit to the left.
4. The left-most bit in the left-most register is placed as an input in all three exclusive or units.
5. The results of the exclusive or operation in the right-most exclusive or unit is entered into the right-most position of the register on the right.
6. The left-most bit shifted out of the middle register is placed as the second input to the left-most exclusive or unit.
7. The left-most bit shifted out of the right register is placed as the second input to the middle exclusive or unit.
8. The results of the exclusive or operations for the two left exclusive or units are placed in the right-most bits of the two left registers.
9. Steps 2 through 8 are repeated until all of the bits in the data have been shifted into the CRC device.

When all the CRC steps have been completed, the contents of the three registers in the CRC unit contain the 16-bit CRC for the data. The CRC is attached to the data before it is transmitted to the recipient. At the receiver's end, the data is processed using the same CRC algorithm as the sender and if the receiver's calculated CRC agrees with the CRC attached to the received data, then the receiver indicates that the data is intact.

A variation on the preceding CRC algorithm has the sender attach an additional string of 16 zeros to the message before it is sent. The receiver then computes the CRC on the data and the attached CRC. In this case, if all the bits arrive intact, the receiver's computed CRC results in zero. This scheme is better because the hardware can compare to a string of 16 zeros very efficiently.

CRCs can detect more errors than either checksums and parity checks because the modification of any one bit or multiple bits in the data changes the computed CRC. There are two types of transmission errors where a CRC can detect more errors than a checksum. The first situation is where a specific set or pattern of bits in the data is changed. The two examples used in the checksum section that showed how the checksum could not detect vertical errors will produce different CRC numbers. CRCs are very successful in detecting vertical errors. The second type of errors where CRC is very effective are burst errors. Burst errors usually occur on a small set of bits near the same location in the string of transmitted bits. External interference such as lightning or when a motor starts up, such as an elevator, often creates burst errors.

Note: In some references, the term checksum is used generically to refer to error-detecting codes and you may see the term *checksum* used to include CRCs. This is technically incorrect because checksums and CRCs are not the same.

CORRECTING ERRORS

Most computer networking protocols that incorporate error correction schemes implement requests to the sender to retransmit the missing information. To ensure that the information arrives, acknowledgment techniques are used so the sender has some type of feedback from the receiver that the information did or did not arrive. Acknowledgments are usually special control frames that contain either positive or negative acknowledgments about the incoming information. To ensure that retransmitted packets of the same information are not all processed, sequence numbers are assigned to outgoing packets so the receiver can tell which are the originals and which are the retransmissions.

The methods used for error control include combinations of the following mechanisms:

- *Error detection:* Packets arriving at the receiver that do not pass the error-checking routine are discarded.

- *Positive acknowledgment:* When the receiver determines that a packet has passed the error-checking routine, a positive acknowledgment is sent back to the sender.

- *Negative acknowledgment and retransmission:* When the receiver determines that a packet has failed the error-checking routine, a negative acknowledgment is sent back to the sender.
- *Retransmission after timeout:* If the sender has not received an acknowledgment within a certain time frame from a packet it has sent, the sender retransmits the packet.

As a group, these methods are referred to as *automatic repeat requests* (ARQ). There are two implementations of ARQ found in network communication protocols. The first is called Stop-and-Wait ARQ. In this scheme, the sender transmits a packet, waits for the acknowledgment, and then sends the next packet. The sender will not send any additional packets until an acknowledgment is received. In the second procedure, Go-back-N ARQ, the sender transmits a series of packets that contain sequence numbers. The receiver analyzes the transmitted packets and if any fail the error-checking routine, the sender retransmits the damaged packet and the packets following the damaged packet. For example, the sender transmits 10 packets numbered 1 through 10. The receiver's error-checking routing determines that packet number 7 is bad. The receiver sends back a negative acknowledgment to the sender and the sender retransmits packets 7, 8, 9, and 10.

Flow Control

Devices that communicate on a network do not all "talk" and "listen" at the same rates. If a sending device system transmits faster than the receiving system, data overrun occurs at the receiver's end and data is lost. Therefore, there needs to be some way of throttling back the sender so that it does not transmit information any faster than the receiver can accept. There are several mechanisms available for managing the rate of data communications that are known as flow control. At the end of the previous section, "Correcting Errors," we mentioned ARQ, which is also a simple method of flow control. In the Stop-and-Wait, or Stop-and-Go, technique, the sender does not send any more information until the receiver has indicated that it is ready to accept the next packet. This form of flow control prevents overrun at the receiver's end but is very inefficient and reduces the capacity of the network. As an example, consider Table 1-10, which shows a sample network's properties:

Table 1-10   Properties
for a Sample Network

Item	Value
packet size	100 bytes
capacity	200 Kbps
delay	50 ms

The sender on the sample network sends one packet to the receiver and then has to wait 100 ms for the acknowledgment. The 100-ms wait is the 50-ms transit time from sender to receiver plus the 50-ms time for the transit time of the acknowledgment packet. Therefore, the transmission rate is one packet per 100 ms, which translates to 10 packets per second. Each packet is 100 bytes so the transmission rate is 1000 bytes per second or 8000 bps. If the capacity of the network is 2000 Kbps, the actual data rate of 8000 bps means that the transfer rate is 4 percent of the actual capacity, which is very low. To overcome the problems associated with ARQ procedures, sliding window techniques are used.

Sliding Window

The sliding window technique defines a window size, which is the maximum amount of data the sender can transmit before an acknowledgment must be sent by the receiver. The size of the window is agreed on by both parties, the sender and receiver, before the transmission of the data occurs. For example, consider a sample network that uses a window size of six packets. The sender "bundles" together six packets and transmits them to the receiver without waiting for any acknowledgments for each individual packet. The sender then waits for an acknowledgment from the receiver that the entire six packets were successfully received. The acknowledgment includes the sequence number of the next expected packet. Once the sender receives the acknowledgment, the sender then transmits the next six packets. Without using a six-packet-size sliding window, the amount of time to send six packets would be $12N$ where N is the time it takes to send the packet in one direction. Using a six-packet-size sliding window, the time it takes to send the six packets is $2N$. Using the same six-packet-size window example, take a look at the amount of time it would take to send 600 packets when the time to send in one direction is 3 ms:

$$ARQ \text{ (no sliding window)} \quad (12 \times 3) \times 600 = 21,600 \text{ ms}$$
$$\text{Sliding window (6 packets)} \quad (2 \times 3) \times 600 = 3600 \text{ ms}$$

In this simple example, there is a significant difference when a sliding window is used to send the data. Note that these calculations are approximate because there is some delay between sending packets but over the course of time, the delay is insignificant. On networks that have high throughput and large round-trip times (RTT), such as satellite transmissions, implementing a sliding window can greatly improve performance.

In some implementations of sliding windows, the size of the window is fixed while in others the size can change as packets are being sent and received. The possibility also exists that the packets or frames in the sender's current window may be damaged or lost during transit. Therefore, in most sliding window implementations, the sender keeps the sent frames in memory in case of retransmission. Therefore, the sender needs a buffer that is at least as big as the window size to hold the transmitted packets in memory. On the receiver's end, any packets that arrive that are outside the size of the window are discarded. Figure 1-15 is a step-by-step illustration of a one-way transmission using a window size of five frames or protocol data units (PDU).

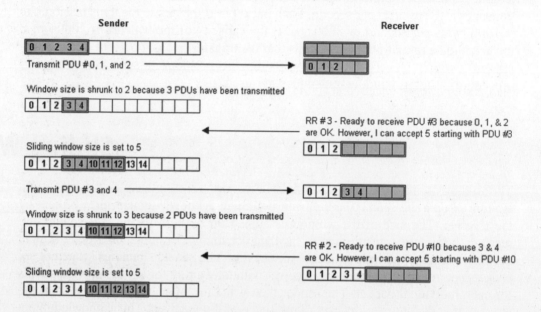

Fig. 1-15.   Sliding Window example.

An example of a protocol that uses a form of sliding window mechanism, called credit allocation, is Transmission Control Protocol (TCP). This form of flow control uses a sequence number, an acknowledgment number, and a window size. Figure 1-16 shows portions of a captured TCP packet.

```
 10 6.663019 BLISSW982000 www.blissranch.com TCP 1489 > 80 [ACK] Seq=4404871 Ack=2364942533 Win=8760 Len=0
⊞ Frame 10 (54 on wire, 54 captured)
⊞ Ethernet II
⊞ Internet Protocol, Src Addr: BLISSw982000 (172.16.3.220), Dst Addr: www.blissranch.com (172.16.3.4)
⊟ Transmission Control Protocol, Src Port: 1489 (1489), Dst Port: 80 (80), Seq: 4404871, Ack: 2364942533
     Source port: 1489 (1489)
     Destination port: 80 (80)
     Sequence number: 4404871
     Acknowledgement number: 2364942533
     Header length: 20 bytes
   ⊞ Flags: 0x0010 (ACK)
     Window size: 8760
     Checksum: 0x3bf5 (correct)

0000  00 40 95 d0 7d 7b 00 40  95 d0 85 6f 08 00 45 00   .@..}{.@ ...o..E.
0010  00 28 f9 0e 40 00 80 06  a2 c0 ac 10 03 dc ac 10   .(..@... ........
0020  03 04 05 d1 00 50 00 43  36 87 8c f6 28 c5 50 10   .....P.C 6...(.P.
```

Fig. 1-16.   A captured TCP packet.

Taking into account the features of the sliding window scheme, there are three roles in which sliding windows can participate. The first is the ability to reliably deliver frames to the receiver over a transmission connection that is not reliable due to interference or other factors that create transmission errors. Secondly, through the use of sequence numbers, the receiver can determine that all the packets have arrived before sending the information on to another protocol for processing. The last area that the sliding window technique provides is a flow control mechanism for the receiver to slow down, or throttle, the sender.

Congestion Management

Congestion on a network is like congestion on roads. The more cars there are on the road, the longer you must wait for an open space to enter the flow of traffic. When there is a lot of network traffic on the transmission media, packets attempting to enter the transmission media will experience delays as they wait at the end of a line (buffer). As the current capacity of the network begins to approach the maximum capacity possible of the transmission media, congestion occurs and data throughput drops. Even though delay and congestion are two different topics, there is a relationship between the two and you can estimate the amount of delay from the percentage of the network capacity that is being used. The current capacity of the network that is in use is referred to as *utilization* and is typically expressed as a percentage. The effective delay on a network can be determined using the following formula, where I is the delay when the transmission media is idle, U is the utilization expressed as a decimal, and D is the effective delay:

$$D = I(1 - U)$$

When there is no traffic on the network, the value of U is 0, so the effective delay (D) is equivalent to the delay of the network (I). As the amount of traffic increases, utilization goes up, the value of the denominator of the equation gets smaller, and the effective delay gets larger. For example, if I is 10 ms and utilization is 5 percent, the effective delay is 10.53 ms. At 25 percent utilization, the effective delay is 13.33 ms. At 50 percent utilization, the effective delay is 20 ms and, at 75 percent utilization, the effective delay has grown to 40 ms. An acceptable utilization, and therefore effective delay, depends on the needs of your network and the associated monetary costs. However, in general, a network should not be operating at a 90 percent utilization level or higher. On high-demand networks where low delays are needed, the maximum acceptable utilization may be 50 percent.

On packet-switched networks, congestion is a problem because packets can begin to build up in the buffers at the packet-switching device, or router, The backup of packets occurs because the router cannot send the packets out at the same rate they are arriving at the router. There are other reasons why the routers cannot transmit the packets in a timely fashion. For example:

- The processing power of the router may not be sufficient to handle the routing tasks.
- The size of the incoming buffers, or memory, may be too low to hold all of the packets that are arriving at the router.
- The outbound links' bandwidth(s) may be too low to handle the traffic.

If there is no mechanism to notify the other devices that the router is congested, packets that continue to arrive at the router will be discarded. Since packets are being dropped, the senders are not receiving acknowledgments from the receivers so the senders then begin to retransmit the dropped packets. Since the router is still congested, the retransmitted packets are also dropped, the senders again retransmit the dropped packets, and eventually the entire network becomes unusable and congestion collapse occurs. To overcome this problem, techniques are available to monitor the network and to respond to congestion once the problem begins. There are two methods that can be implemented to indicate congestion:

- Once the routers become congested, let the senders know so they will halt transmission until the condition clears.
- Determine that congestion has occurred when packets begin to get lost.

The first mechanism can be implemented by directing the routers to send a special message to the senders or modify one of the packet's header bits in delayed packets. In some implementations, these special messages are called *choke packets*. The choke packets sent out when congestion first occurs tell the senders to reduce their transmission rate by 50 percent. If the problem still persists, the second round of choke packets may tell the senders to reduce the rate to 25 percent. This type of notification scheme can produce a long delay between the time the congestion occurs and when the senders find out about the problem.

The second approach using packet loss is a reasonable solution on current networks because most network hardware works well and the loss of packets is primarily due to congestion. Packet loss can be determined quite easily by observing the amount of retransmissions the sender is experiencing. By implementing what is called rate control, the rate of retransmissions is reduced temporarily when congestion occurs. Protocols that use sliding windows can produce rate control by temporarily reducing the size of the window so less data is transmitted.

TCP is an example of a protocol that uses packet loss as a means of detecting congestion and temporarily reduces the rate at which information is retransmitted. When TCP determines a packet has been lost, the protocol sends a single packet instead of the number of packets that is acceptable by the receiver's window size. If the sender receives an acknowledgment from the single packet, TCP doubles the number of packets sent, which means two packets are transmitted. If the sender receives acknowledgments from the two packets, then TCP doubles the number of packets again, so now four packets are sent. TCP will continue to double the number of transmitted packets upon receipt of acknowledgments, until half the receiver's window size has been reached. At this point, TCP slows down the rate of increase in the number of packets transmitted. The dynamically changing size of the number of packets that TCP will transmit is called the Congestion Window. By implementing this method of congestion control, TCP is sometimes said to be self-clocking. This approach to congestion works well because the sender reduces the rate of transmission quickly when packets are lost and prevents congestion collapse.

TRAFFIC SHAPING

Networks that experience traffic that is bursty tend to have congestion problems. *Bursty traffic* is defined as idle transmission moments intermixed with sudden increases in traffic for short periods of time. One way to help overcome congestion under these conditions is to force the packets to be transmitted at a managed rate. This methodology is called *traffic shaping* and is used on ATM networks.

One way to implement a regulated rate of traffic is with the use of the leaky bucket algorithm. Imagine a bucket that has a small hole at the bottom. When you begin to fill the bucket with water, the water begins to leave the bucket at a nice steady drip. If you begin to rapidly fill the bucket with water, the amount leaving the bucket through the hole stays the same—a steady drip. If you reduce the rate at which you add water to the bucket, the water exiting through the hole maintains its steady rate. You can translate this concept to a network where a router has a buffer or queue that accepts packets—the bucket—and sends the packets on at a steady rate (the hole in the bucket). If the queue gets full—the bucket is full—arriving packets are dropped (the bucket overflows).

A second approach to regulating traffic is with the use of the token bucket algorithm. This is similar to the leaky bucket except that as the rate of incoming packets rises, the output of the system speeds up slightly—the hole in the bucket gets larger. The bucket in the token bucket scheme holds tokens and in order for a packet to leave the bucket, it must have a token. If the network is idle, the number of tokens in the bucket grows (up to the maximum size of the bucket) so if a burst of packets arrives, there are more tokens available for the packets to use to leave the bucket. Once the tokens are all used up, the packets must wait until tokens are regenerated before they can leave the bucket. Thus, you have controlled the rate of traffic but the rate can vary somewhat, depending on the rate at which packets arrive.

LOAD SHEDDING

Load shedding is usually a last-ditch effort by routers when other congestion control methods are not alleviating the congestion problem. Load shedding simply means that the routers will dump packets they cannot process. However, routers can be selective in which packets they discard instead of just dropping ones at random. In some types of applications, such as an FTP service, an old packet is more valuable than a new one. For example, if packets number 3, 4, and 5 have arrived and the router can accept only one, it makes more sense to keep packet number 3 instead of 4 or 5. If the router decided to keep packet number 5 instead, then packets 3 and 4 are missing from the data so the sender may need to resend packets 3, 4, and 5. On the other hand, for some types of data, such as multimedia information, new packets are more valuable than older packets. Often the term *wine* is applied to the "old-is-better-than-new" approach and *milk* refers to the "new-is-better-than-old" method.

JITTER CONTROL

For some applications it is important that the information arrive at the destination at a constant rate. The actual time it takes to transfer the information is not as important as the rate of information delivery. For example, with video and audio data, it is important that the information arrive at a constant rate; otherwise, the information will "jump" and cause jitters. To accomplish this, the amount of congestion must be taken into account when the rate at which the information will be transmitted is calculated. The anticipated transit time at each router in the path from sender to receiver is used to determine the overall transmission time. When a packet arrives at a router in the path, the router checks to see if the packet is ahead or behind its "delivery time." If it is behind, the router attempts to pass it on as quickly as possible. If the packet is ahead of its schedule, the router will hold it back a little so the packet gets back on its timetable.

Review Questions

1.1 TDM is designed to take advantage of what property of the transmission media?
  a. The bandwidth of the media is greater than the bit rate of the combined signals.
  b. The bandwidth of the media is less than the bandwidth of a single signal.
  c. The bit rate of the media is less than the bandwidth of the smallest signal.
  d. The bit rate of the media is more than the bit rate of a single signal.

1.2 FDM is commonly used on what types of broadcasts?
  a. Satellite transmissions
  b. FM radio
  c. AM radio
  d. Bursty

1.3 What is the CCITT mastergroup standard?

1.4 What is the Nyquist theorem?

1.5 What is WDM?
  a. Multiplexing on fiber-optic cable
  b. Multiplexing using the density of the transmission media
  c. A form of flow control that monitors WAN delays
  d. A form of congestion management for WANs

1.6 What does PCM stand for and where is it commonly used?

1.7 What is the CCITT standard for a T3?
  a. 2 multiplexed T1s
  b. 4 multiplexed T1s
  c. 2 multiplexed T2s
  d. 4 multiplexed T2s

1.8 What is the primary purpose of multiplexing?

1.9 Define signaling?

1.10 Describe statistical TDM.

1.11 Why do digital signals attenuate sooner than analog signals?

1.12 Define encoding.

1.13 What is the advantage of spread spectrum?

1.14 How are the individual signals kept separate in a multiplexed transmission link?

1.15 How can retransmission add to an existing congestion problem?

1.16 What is/are the purpose(s) of acknowledgments?

1.17 Describe even and odd parity checking.

1.18   Forward error correction implementations are:
   a.   Error-detecting codes
   b.   Error bytewise codes
   c.   Error bitwise codes
   d.   Error-correcting codes

Problems

1.1   What is the binary code from the Manchester-encoded wave shown in Fig. 1-17?

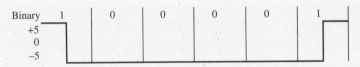

Fig. 1-17.   Manchester-encoded wave.

1.2   In an odd parity checking scheme, what is the value of the parity bit for the following sequence?

0101101

1.3   What is the 16-bit checksum for the following phrase?

giGGle

1.4   Describe how TCP implements congestion control.

1.5   Imagine a communication link that is experiencing interference so every 18th bit is changed from 0 to 1 or from 1 to 0. Does a parity check detect all the errors?

1.6   CRC computations can be performed with software but most implementations use hardware for CRCs. Explain why.

1.7   Why would a protocol that uses Stop-and-Wait (Stop-and-Go) have low throughput over a satellite communication link?

Answers to Review Questions

1.1   d.   TDM methodology takes advantage of the fact that the bit rate of the transmission media is greater than the needed rate of a single transmission.

1.2   c.   The other types of broadcasts do not use FDM technologies.

1.3   A mastergroup is the collection of five supergroups for the CCITT standard.

1.4   The Nyquist theorem states that 8000 samples per second are sufficient to capture all the information from a 4-kHz telephone channel.

1.5 **a.** Wave Division Multiplexing (WDM) is the term used to specify multiplexing techniques on optical transmission systems.

1.6 On telephone systems, the sampling of analog data is called PCM, or Pulse Code Modulation.

1.7 **d.** The CCITT standard defines multiplexing of 4 carriers for each level—that is, four T2s combine for a T3.

1.8 Multiplexing is used to reduce the cost associated with sending multiple signals over the same physical path.

1.9 The process by which a computer interacts with the network transmission media and sends the signal down the media is referred to as signaling.

1.10 Statistical Multiplexing allocates time for each device to transmit and each device must go "in order." However, if a device has nothing to transmit, the multiplexor skips the device and goes on to the next device. Statistical multiplexing is a very cost-effective way for multiple systems to share the same transmission media. Most computer networks use some form of statistical multiplexing because the devices on the network do not need to transmit data all the time and generate data at different rates.

1.11 As digital signals travel farther and farther down the "line," the "crispness" of the wave is not as distinct as the initial signal. The wave shapes begin to become more rounded, and it becomes more difficult for the receiver to differentiate between high and low values when the "edges" are smoothed instead of being square.

1.12 The role of encoding is to define the properties of the signal to represent data.

1.13 The special technique of using FDM on multiple carriers or frequencies to transmit data is called spread spectrum.

1.14 When different carrier frequencies are used to carry different signals, they can use the same transmission media without interfering with each other.

1.15 As more and more packets are not acknowledged in a congested network, the senders keep retransmitting the information, which adds more packets on the wire and the router's buffers fill up.

1.16 Acknowledgments are usually special control frames that contain either positive or negative acknowledgments about the incoming information.

1.17 The even parity calculation is to count the number of 1's in the bit stream and if the number of 1's is odd, the parity bit is set to 1 so that the total number if bits in the data and parity bit is an even number. Odd parity is the opposite of even parity where the number of calculated bits in the data and parity bit is odd.

1.18 **d.** Error-correcting codes are sometimes referred to as forward error correction, or FEC.

 # Solutions to Problems

1.1 100001: Whenever the leading edge is high, a binary 1 is encoded and when the leading edge is low, a binary 0 is encoded.

1.2 The parity bit would be 1 to bring the number of 1's in the data and the parity bit to 5—an odd number.

1.3   The 16-bit checksum for giGGle is 1B16. gi = 6769; GG = 4747; le = 6C65

$$6769 + 4747 + 6C65 = 11B15$$

The left-most 1 is the carry bit so the checksum = 1B15 + 1 = 1B16.

1.4   When TCP determines a packet has been lost, the protocol sends a single packet instead of the number of packets that is acceptable by the receiver's window size. If the sender receives an acknowledgment from the single packet, TCP doubles the number of packets sent which means two packets are transmitted. If the sender receives acknowledgments from the two packets, then TCP doubles the number of packets again, so now four packets are sent. TCP will continue to double the number of transmitted packets upon receipt of acknowledgments, until half the receiver's window size has been reached. At this point, TCP slows down the rate of increase in the number of packets transmitted.

1.5   No, because parity checking is effective in detecting transmission errors when an odd number of bits have changed but it cannot properly indicate errors when an even number of bits have been modified.

1.6   Most implementations use CRC hardware because it is simple and cheap to build.

1.7   In the Stop-and-Wait scheme, the sender transmits a packet, waits for the acknowledgment, and then sends the next packet. Satellite transmissions have long delays and the time the sender has to wait for the acknowledgment is twice the delay, which further degrades throughput on a satellite link.

CHAPTER 2

Communications Networks

Introduction to Networking

Communication between people and devices is critical to the success of many of today's business activities. To facilitate communication, we deploy networks. The meaning of the term *network* varies greatly by context, but it can include the physical devices and cables, the PCs and servers and their network operating system (NOS) software (such as Netware or Windows), and everything in between. It can also mean a natural class of IP addresses, such as the 10.0.0.0 network or the 192.168.0.0 network. In some contexts, network is used to describe a data-link segment (which you'll learn about shortly) such as a single Ethernet or an FDDI ring. However, in other contexts, the term *network* refers to all the cables, switches, hubs, routers, and related equipment of a single company or a geographic area. When you combine several such networks, it's called an *internetwork*. An example of this network of networks is the Internet, which is discussed later in this chapter. However, the Internet is certainly not the only internetwork. Because there are many different types of information, such as voice, video, computer data, and others, there are many types of networks. This chapter introduces several network types and the models and protocols that define them.

TELEPHONE NETWORKS

Although largely taken for granted by data networking folks, the telephone network is by far the largest network in the world, and probably the most important. Invented by Alexander Graham Bell in 1876, the telephone network began very simply by converting sound into an analog signal and transporting it down a wire, then converting it back into a similar sound at the other end. Since then, the telephone network has steadily grown larger and more complex.

Today, there are many major telephone technologies in use. The plain old telephone system (POTS) uses a single analog circuit consisting of a pair of copper wires to connect a residence or business to the Public Switched Telephony Network (PSTN) via the ubiquitous telephone network infrastructure (telephone poles, underground lines, etc.). The wires in a pair are often called Tip and Ring (T&R) or Ear and Mouth (E&M).

Digital circuits, such as the T-carrier systems and ISDN, are frequently used by business to carry multiple phone conversations across a single cable. These systems connect to both the PSTN and private telephone networks. Circuits that carry many simultaneous conversations are called trunks.

Finally, cellular systems allow analog and digital signals to be transported without wires, between phones and cellular towers. Telephone networks often employ multiplexing to allow several phone calls to cross their network at a time. The most common method is Time-Division Multiplexing, which was explained in Chapter 1. Recently, there has been a trend toward transporting voice over networks that were traditionally used only for data. To accomplish this, a Digital Signal Processor (DSP) is used to convert the analog wave forms of voice into digital signals and back into analog on the other end. They use a set of rules defined by a CODEC (for coder-decoder). Examples of common CODECs are G.711, G.726, G.729, and G.723.1. These are based on algorithms such as Pulse Code Modulation (PCM) and Code-Excited Linear Prediction (CELP), and all of these are defined under the umbrella recommendation of H.323. Again, the CODEC is the standard set of rules, whereas the DSP is the hardware that implements it. A DSP is typically a chip that is put inside a device, such as a phone or gateway, although a DSP can also be implemented in software. An example of that would be Microsoft's NetMeeting software.

All of these methods of transporting sound (typically voice) are combined to form the telephone network. The network is responsible for determining how to send signals from one telephone to another, which is accomplished by dialing a telephone number, which is, in fact, an address. The number, from left to right, precisely pinpoints the receiver's address. In a typical telephone number, such as 01-614-555-1212, the 01 is the country code, which represents the United States. As soon as the network receives these digits, it begins routing the call to the appropriate country. In the United States, the next three digits represent the area code, which is a collection of telephone switches in a large geographic area. In this case, 614 steers the call toward central Ohio. The next three digits are called the exchange, which identifies a specific switch inside the telephone company that serves a local area. The last four numbers identify an individual telephone line, which leads to the recipient. Many countries administer these numbers differently, and the length of a telephone number outside North America may vary greatly.

In addition to the public network, there are many private telephone networks. These systems are generally owned by large companies and are centered around a Private Branch Exchange (PBX), which is a telephone switch designed for enterprises rather than the much larger systems used by the telephone companies themselves.

Some readers may already be familiar with TCP/IP, which will be discussed in detail in later chapters. As an analogy, much as TCP/IP keeps track of how to get from one IP address on the Internet to another, Signaling System 7 (SS7) routes telephone calls from one phone to another across and between the various telephone companies' networks.

Because the installation of telephone wires to every house and business creates a natural monopoly, the telephone industry has been the subject of much political and legal attention, and continues to be highly regulated in most countries worldwide. Recent efforts to introduce competition and deregulation into this market have resulted in a host of new acronyms, if nothing else. Some of these are as follows:

- *BOC (Bell Operating Company):* One of the companies that was created as a result of the breakup of AT&T in 1983.

- *RBOC (Regional Bell Operating Company):* A holding company with at least two BOCs. There are seven RBOCs in the United States: Ameritech, Bell Atlantic, Bell South, NYNEX, Southwestern Bell, Pacific Bell, and US West.

- *LEC (Local Exchange Carrier):* One of 100 or so companies that once held a monopoly on phone services in a region of the United States.

- *ILEC (Incumbent Local Exchange Carrier):* A telephone company that provided local service when the Telecommunications Act of 1996 was enacted. ILECs include the BOCs.

- *CLEC (Competitive Local Exchange Carrier):* A company that the FCC has approved to compete against the ILECs. Some examples are Covad, Northpoint, and Rhythms.

- *IXC (Interexchange Carrier):* These provide long-distance services between local telephone companies, such as AT&T and Worldcom (which acquired two former IXCs: MCI and Sprint).

OSI MODEL FOR NETWORKING

Unlike telephone technology, which was created largely by a single company and not intended to be compatible with any other company's systems, data network technologies were created by groups of many different companies, standards organizations, and governments. These technologies were created with the expectation that they would be compatible not only with other network equipment manufacturers but also with other systems, from personal computers to mainframes, and with many different types of operating systems and application software. All these requirements would be impossible to meet without standards. Although IEEE specifies the majority of data communications technologies, these standards are created following guidelines from a conceptual model called the OSI (Open Systems Interconnection) Network Reference Model (OSI Standard 7498), which is divided into seven layers:

- *Layer 7:* Application
- *Layer 6:* Presentation
- *Layer 5:* Session

- *Layer 4:* Transport
- *Layer 3:* Network
- *Layer 2:* Data-Link
- *Layer 1:* Physical

Note: The organization of this list is critical to understanding most modern communication networks and should be committed to memory by anyone who intends to work with computer networks.

This seven-layer model consists of categories (layers) that represent functions required to communicate. The purpose of layering the model is to make the functions as discrete and independent as possible, so that changes to one layer do not necessarily require changes to any other layer. Also in this model, individual layers are said to provide services to the layers above them, and to consume data from the layers beneath them (when applicable).

It is important to note that not all technologies fit cleanly into the seven layers identified in the OSI model. Some technologies combine a few layers, whereas others skip unneeded layers. Still others may use a completely different model that has no relation to this model. Don't lose sleep trying to match technologies precisely to this model.

Starting at the top, the Application layer provides a consistent interface to the network for all computer software. These are often called application programming interfaces (APIs), and they allow a program to be written once, without regard to the type of network involved, and then used on any network, whether it's using TCP/IP, IPX, AppleTalk, Ethernet, Token Ring, or FDDI, just to name a few examples.

The next layer is the Presentation layer. It is responsible for data translation into a standard format. Examples are ASCII text, JPEG pictures, and MP3 music formats. This layer is also responsible for encryption and decryption for security purposes, as well as data compression.

The Session layer (layer 5) is responsible for establishing, maintaining, and ending sessions across the network. This layer manages name recognition, synchronization, and some access features, such as when a device can transmit and how long it can transmit. As an example of this, you can use your computer to open a browser window to your favorite Web site, then open a second window to the same server and follow different links in each browser. The windows can act independently because the Web server and your computer have two independent sessions.

Note: Layers 5, 6, and 7 are frequently referred to as the upper layers.

Layer 4 is the Transport layer, which is responsible for preparing data to be transported. Among other activities, the Transport layer manages flow control, error correction, and divides chunks of application data into segments appropriately sized for the layers below it. TCP and UDP are examples of layer 4 protocols. The Protocol Data Unit (PDU) at the Transport layer is called a datagram. (A PDU is a unit of data that consists of a header, which is defined by the protocol in use, followed by various application data. Some PDUs end in a footer, which is usually just a checksum to verify that no errors occurred during transmission.)

Note: Typically, hosts are the only devices that operate at OSI layers 4 through 7.

Layer 3 is the Network layer, which is responsible for assigning a globally unique address to every device and providing directions from any point on the network to any other point. To achieve this, there are two types of protocols employed at layer 3: routed protocols and routing protocols. IP, IPX, and AppleTalk are examples of routed protocols, whereas RIP, OSPF, and BGP are examples of routing protocols. The former are responsible for addressing; the latter are responsible for providing a loop-free path across a network. The devices that operate at this layer are called routers. The PDU at the Network layer is called a packet.

The Data-Link layer (layer 2) packages the data from the upper layers into frames and then transmits them onto the media. To do this, it must define a set of rules for flow and error control and assign physical addresses to each device on the link. To this end, layer 2 is commonly split into two sublayers: Logical Link Control (LLC) and Media Access Control (MAC). Each LAN and WAN protocol, such as Ethernet, Token Ring, ATM, and HDLC, have different methods and protocols for the LLC and MAC sublayers, but a common example of LLC is LLC1, LLC2, and LLC3, as defined in IEEE 802.2. An example of MAC is Carrier Sense Multi-Access/Collision Detect (CSMA/CD), which is the foundation for Ethernet. MAC addresses, such as 00-90-27-BD-03-D9, are also part of this layer. Bridges and switches operate at layer 2 and the PDU is called a frame.

The bottom layer is the Physical layer, which is responsible for defining a bit (a binary digit: 1 or 0). An example of this could be that the presence of a voltage on the line for a certain time period will be recognized as a 1, and the absence of a voltage will be interpreted as a 0. Alternately, a transition from a higher voltage to a lower voltage and vice versa could represent 1's and 0's, or various patterns of light pulses could represent 1's and 0's. The frequency and length (in time) of the bits are also important and thus are also defined in layer 1. The Physical layer also includes the media types, including the minimum and maximum cable lengths, the connecting interfaces, such as cable jacks, and, of course, voltages. As an example of why these characteristics and many more are necessary for compatibility, consider a network where everyone gets to pick a voltage at which to operate. Obviously, bad things would happen when you put those devices together, from melting down hardware to extended hospital stays for network administrators.

To make the OSI Network Reference Model a little clearer, the following example shows how each layer is related. In this example, a user sends a file from a PC to a server.

Once the user instructs the application to perform the file transfer, the application contacts the network APIs (layer 7) and relays those instructions. The data is then converted to ASCII text (layer 6) and compressed (layer 6). The user's PC then requests a connection to the host, using its host name (layer 5), which is resolved to an IP address. To establish the session, a session request is segmented (layer 4) and encapsulated in a UDP datagram (layer 4). Then the network driver software receives the datagram and, in turn, encapsulates it in an IP packet, which includes the source and destination IP addresses, along with other fields. It then determines the location of the target server (layer 3) and hands the packet to the Ethernet driver, which encapsulates the packet with an Ethernet header and footer, called a frame. Finally, the Physical layer reads each bit in the frame and generates the appropriate electrical voltage pulses and sends them down the network media.

As the server receives those voltage pulses, the server translates them into bits, and passes the 1's and 0's to the Data-Link layer, where they are put back together to form frames. The Ethernet header includes a protocol field that tells the driver into which memory buffer on the server it should place the packet. The IP driver reads the protocol field in the IP header and hands the contents of the packet (which is the datagram) to UDP. UDP reassembles the application data and hands it to the Session layer, which the server then uses to establish the session. It then hands the data to the corresponding application, which decrypts it and converts it back into a form the application understands.

Although Ethernet, IP, and UDP were used as examples here, the point of the model is to provide interoperability, so that it could just as easily be Token Ring, IP, and UDP or FDDI, IP, and TCP.

(*Note:* Although the OSI model can be used to explain TCP/IP (in fact, TCP/IP is most often compared to it), TCP/IP actually predates the OSI model and is based on a four-layer Department of Defense model.)

INTERNET

The Internet began in the 1960s as an Advanced Research Projects Agency (ARPA) project. It first came on-line in 1969 with four nodes connected via 56-Kbps circuits. After proving itself, similar networks were created by the military (MILNET). Universities and various government agencies began connecting to this network, and ARPANet was created. Commercial use was against the Acceptable Use Policy (AUP) for the ARPANet, which was decommissioned in 1989.

In the mid-1980s, the National Science Foundation created NSFNet, which had a three-tier architecture that was far more robust than ARPANet. In 1988, the NSFNet backbone was upgraded from 56 Kbps to T1 (1.544 Mbps) due to congestion. In 1991 it was again upgraded to T3 (45 Mbps). In 1995, NSFNet was decommissioned. A few years prior to that, Merit, IBM, and a few other companies began creating a separate network that evolved into the Internet we know today. These networks were all based on a protocol suite known as TCP/IP, which is discussed in Chapter 6. This protocol handles addressing and routing packets of information all over the network.

Today, the Internet is a massive collection of private networks. Each of these networks is connected to other networks, forming internetworks. Much of the Internet uses the same technology (T1s, ATM, Ethernet, TCP/IP, etc.) as typical enterprise networks, but there are some major differences.

One of the primary differences is administrative. Different organizations have different needs. For example, NASA might need a high level of security, whereas a university might need flexibility. A business might need stability whereas a multimedia site may need bandwidth. Those in charge of the Internet quickly discovered that it was impossible for a single administration to cater to each of these requirements. The solution was to separate the Internet into Autonomous Systems (AS), where each AS would have its own policies that didn't interfere with the policies of others. A special routing protocol, known as Border Gateway Protocol

(BGP), was developed to handle the exchange of Network Layer Reachability Information (NLRI) between multiple autonomous systems.

To understand how traffic on the Internet gets from one network to another, two terms are particularly important. The first is *Network Access Point* (NAP). Originally, four NAPs were commissioned and supported by the National Science Foundation. These were in New York, Washington D.C., Chicago, and San Francisco. These NAPs provide switching facilities for the general public. In other words, physical ports for all the network service providers (private companies) connect to the "Internet backbone." Since then, several more NAPs have been created.

The second term is *peering arrangement*, which is when two network service providers, IXCs, or ISPs directly connect their networks rather than going through the public facilities. The advantage here is fewer hops to get from one location to another, and less congestion in the NAPs. Peering arrangements are completely voluntary and follow strategic relationships set by the companies.

These two concepts are important because the Internet backbone literally consists of the networks of these companies that connect to the NAPs and peer with each other. Figure 2-1 shows six network service providers (NSPs) connected to a NAP, with a peer arrangement between NSP 1 and 6. In reality, for redundancy, efficiency, and revenue, many of these companies may be peered with many other companies in a partial mesh topology, which is explained at the end of this chapter.

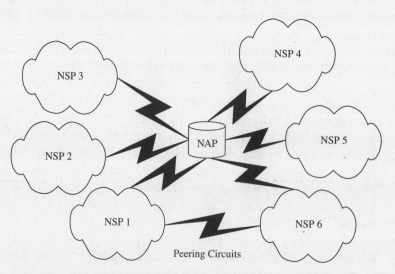

Fig. 2-1.   Network connections to a NAP.

Note: In network diagrams, a cloud is often used to represent a group of devices that you don't own or administer, or that you can't document because it's highly volatile. In other words, it changes so fast that your documentation is out of date before you've even finished it. These networks often belong to the telecom vendors, or technologies that use virtual circuits, such as ATM and Frame Relay.

Further, the Internet today is a very complicated place that continues to defy taxonomy. Terms like *network service provider* don't adequately describe these companies because the pace of mergers and acquisitions in the telecommunications industry is so fast. Some ISPs are so large that they have their own connections in the NAPs and their own peering arrangements. Almost all of the NSPs are also Internet service providers (ISP) for residential and commercial access to the Internet. In addition, several are also offering local phone service such as CLECs, and other telecommunications-related products. The point is that trying to apply labels to companies in this arena is often as futile as trying to fit technologies into the layers of the OSI Reference Model.

ATM

Asynchronous Transfer Mode (ATM) is a special type of network. At the same time, it is a layer 2 technology that anyone can employ, and it is a public network like the Internet, with a well-regulated address space, so that each device in the network can be uniquely identified. Unlike the Internet, which uses 4-byte IP addresses, ATM uses a 20-byte address. This means it will be a long time before there is any talk about running out of addresses.

As a layer 2 technology, ATM is immensely popular as a LAN and WAN backbone because it was designed to accommodate telephony, video, and data traffic simultaneously. It also is the most common technology used over SONET, which is commonly deployed at OC-48 (2.5-Gbps) and OC-192 (10-Gbps) speeds, making ATM one of the fastest networks money can buy. Although a 10-Gbps Ethernet specification was recently developed, at the time of this writing, no products are expected to ship for many months. That makes the ATM/SONET combination 10 times faster than Gigabit Ethernet (its nearest competitor) and 100 times faster than FDDI.

ATM also spans an unusually large number of layers. The ATM specifications include the network layer, where ATM handles the routing of ATM addresses across the entire network, irrespective of any IP or IPX addresses that may be encapsulated in its payload. ATM's standards explicitly list categories of service, in order to allow hardware to be optimized to fit an application. These classes are as follows:

- *Constant Bit Rate (CBR):* Emulates a physical line, no error checking or flow control, no jitter.
- *Variable Bit Rate: Non-Real Time (NRT-VBR):* Designed for services that have some variance in bandwidth needs and some toleration for jitter, commonly used for less important multimedia.
- *Variable Bit Rate: Real Time (RT-VBR):* Designed for services that have some variance in bandwidth needs but no tolerance for jitter; commonly used for video teleconferencing when quality is important.
- *Available Bit Rate (ABR):* Designed for services with highly variable, and usually unknown, bandwidth needs; provides rate feedback to the sender.
- *Unspecified Bit Rate (UBR):* Provides no guarantees or feedback whatsoever; generally cheaper than other classes; most commonly used for IP and other data services.

Going a little farther up the OSI model, ATM adaptation layers handle the concerns of the Transport layer. However, nine out of ten network gurus disagree about whether ATM actually has a transport layer or not. The confusion stems from the fact that the adaptation layers perform many services similar to UDP and TCP, but that another transport layer protocol rides on top of the adaptation layer. For example, if you had a Web browsing session going over an ATM link, you might have HTTP over TCP over IP over AAL5 over ATM, as shown in Table 2-1.

Table 2-1   Mapping Protocols to the Layers of the OSI Reference Model

Protocol	OSI Reference Model Layer
HTTP	Layer 7, Application
TCP	Layer 4, Transport
IP	Layer 3, Network
AAL5	Layer 4, Transport
ATM	Layer 2, Data-link and Layer 3, Network

This is another good example about how real life doesn't always fit the model. However, there is no question that the adaptation layers perform some of the same functions commonly attributed to the Transport layer. The adaptation layers themselves are designed to allow a single network to provide real-time and non-real-time service, constant bit rate and variable bit rate service, and connection-oriented and connectionless services. Each layer was designed to provide service for one of the classes mentioned above, but after much revision, the number of adaptation layers shrank to four. These are listed as follows:

- *AAL1:* Used for Class A traffic, real-time, constant bit rate, connection-oriented. Sample applications are uncompressed video and voice.

- *AAL2:* Designed for variable rate traffic, such as compressed video, but still real-time.

- *AAL3/4:* Originally designed as two connection-oriented and connectionless protocols, then combined into one, where reliable and unreliable transport are both available. Offers ability to multiplex traffic, sensitive to data loss, but not to time, supports message mode and stream mode.

- *AAL5:* Designed by the computer industry and originally called Simple Efficient Adaptation Layer (SEAL) in response to the previous four layers, which were designed by the telecommunications industry. Provides several choices, including reliable and unreliable, unicast and multicast, message mode and stream mode.

ATM itself operates much differently than most protocols because it uses cells instead of frames. The difference between a cell and a frame is that a cell is always 53 bytes long, whereas a frame is variable in length. As an example, an Ethernet frame can be between 64 and 1518 bytes in length and a Token Ring frame can be up to 4096 bytes.

The reason this is so important is efficiency versus the ability to prioritize network traffic. Consider that in the 53-byte cell, five of those bytes are overhead (headers that don't carry data), which only leaves 48 bytes of data. In other words, almost 10 percent of your bandwidth is tied up in the overhead of just the first layer.

You still have the AAL header, the IP header, the TCP header, etc., before you manage to put the first bit of actual data on the wire. This overhead is commonly known as the *cell tax*.

In contrast, Ethernet has 18 bytes of overhead in each frame, but 18 bytes out of 1518 is a fraction of the overhead of ATM. The downside of all that efficiency comes when you have a very important 64-byte frame (e.g., real-time voice) that is waiting behind a much less important 1518 frame. By the time the larger frame is finished transmitting, the voice packet is no longer relevant. Delivering it will only distort the conversation. So as always, flexibility comes with a price.

Next, ATM is what is known as a Non-Broadcast Multi-Access (NBMA) media, whereas Ethernet and Token Ring both use broadcasts. For compatibility, ATM uses LAN Emulation (LANE) in order to allow traffic to seamlessly cross from Ethernet or Token Ring to ATM and back. When the ATM network meets a non-ATM network, you configure a LAN Emulation Client (LEC). The client then uses the following three types of servers to facilitate this communication.

- *LAN Emulation Server (LES):* Manages Emulated LANs (ELAN) that are the ATM version of VLANs. Each ELAN bounds a broadcast domain.

- *Broadcast/Unknown Server (BUS):* Facilitates one-to-many communication, much like broadcasts in Ethernet or Token Ring.

- *LAN Emulation Configuration Server (LECS):* Much like DHCP, it provides a well-known ATM address for LECs to find their LES and BUS.

ATM is sometimes said to be cell-switched as opposed to circuit-switched or packet-switched. This means that instead of each cell having the MAC address of its destination, each cell has a number that identifies it as belonging to a Virtual Circuit.

Virtual Circuits are used to multiplex different types of data over a given link. A Virtual Path Indicator (VPI) and a Virtual Channel Indicator (VCI) define a virtual circuit. The VPI is an 8-bit number and the VCI is a 16-bit number. Thus, ATM can multiplex 2^{24} virtual connections over a single physical link.

So when a cell arrives on a port in an ATM switch, the switch reads the VC information and compares it to its list of PVCs and SVCs. If there is a match, it switches the cell on to the next link in the PVC or SVC.

In Fig. 2-2, there are four ATM switches, labeled A, B, C, and D. The switches connect two PCs, a server, and a video camera. The dotted lines represent PVCs. ATM allows all three PVCs to have different levels of service. For instance, the PVC between the PC and the video camera could be a constant bit rate service, and the two PVCs connecting the servers to the computers could be an unspecified bit rate. The advantage of this system is that large file transfers or print jobs would not trample the highly time-sensitive traffic from the video camera.

There are two types of Virtual Circuits: PVCs and SVCs. Permanent Virtual Circuits (PVC) are manually configured paths through the network that do not change unless manually reconfigured. Switched Virtual Circuits (SVC) are dynamically established when needed and dynamically torn down when no longer needed. These circuits use various ATM routing mechanisms, such as PNNI, to determine the best path through the network from source to destination.

Another important advantage is that ATM has specifications that use almost any physical medium. Although the most common is SM and MM fiber using SONET,

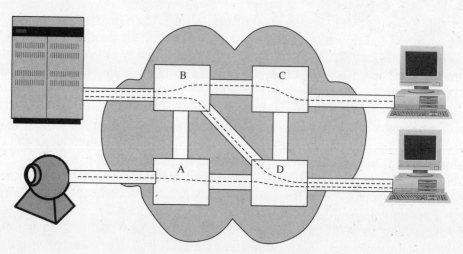

Fig. 2-2.   The operation of Virtual Circuits.

ATM can also run at 155 Mbs on CAT5 copper cabling, and 25 Mbs over CAT3. ATM is commonly run over T1 and T3 circuits as well.

Despite the advantages of ATM, its complexity and expense have caused it to fall out of favor in modern LANs, although it still enjoys a strong presence in the WAN space. ATM is also the technology behind most of the xDSL Internet connections.

For more information about ATM, visit www.atmforum.com/.

Network Components

Almost all modern networks are created by connecting various physical devices to establish a path from the sending device to the receiving device. The OSI Model layer at which they operate generally classifies these devices, as shown in Table 2-2. In this chapter, we focus on the most common groups: cables, hubs, bridges, switches, and routers. There are other components, such as protocols, software, etc. Many of these are covered in other sections and chapters.

Table 2-2   Mapping Network Components
to the OSI Model

OSI Model Layer	Network Component
Layer 3: Network	Routers
Layer 2: Data-link	Bridges and switches
Layer 1: Physical	Hubs and cables

CABLES

Cables carry the signals discussed in Chapter 1 from one location to another. This could be across a room, or across the country. The maximum length of a cable is an important design criterion and is generally bounded by a factor called attenuation.

Attenuation is a measure of the strength of the signal as it travels over an increasingly long segment of cable; the longer the cable, the greater the attenuation.

Shielding is another important design criterion. Some cables are shielded to prevent outside interference, like that caused by motors or fluorescent lights, from changing a signal as it passes through a cable.

The cable medium is also important. Most cables are either copper, which carries an electrical signal, or fiber-optic, which carries a beam of light. Copper-based cables are generally more durable, cheaper and easier to use, whereas fiber-optic cables can go much greater distances and support much higher frequencies, which translates into more bandwidth than copper cables.

In the absence of great distances, or high interference, many of these features, such as shielding, are overlooked in favor of lowest-cost cables.

Cables are terminated by plugs. Plugs plug into jacks (hence the name). Plugs and jacks are typically plastic or metal pieces that allow the individual wires inside a cable to be easily connected to the corresponding wires of another cable or device, such as a PC.

The cables used in most computer networks are specified by one of the following bodies:

- American National Standards Institute (ANSI)
- Electronic Industry Association (EIA)
- Telecommunications Industry Association (TIA)

Note: The last two are frequently seen together as EIA-TIA.

Cables are also classified for building codes. Such things as how much smoke or flame is emitted during a fire generally determine these classifications. These classifications include:

- *Restricted Cable:* Must be enclosed in conduit
- *General Purpose Cable:* For general connections
- *Riser Cable:* For use between floors
- *Plenum Cable:* For use in ceilings and air ducts

The most common type of copper cable is unshielded, twisted-pair (UTP). This cable is specified in Categories 1 to 6, with Category 7 expected soon. These are commonly abbreviated CAT1, CAT2, etc. The most common categories are as follows:

- *CAT2:* Commonly used for telephone wiring inside a building and is rated for a maximum frequency of 1 MHz. An RJ-11 plug commonly terminates this cable. This is the plug seen on residential telephones.
- *CAT3:* Commonly used for Ethernet 10Base-T networks (discussed in Chapter 3) and is rated for 16 MHz. CAT3 cable is most often terminated by RJ-45 plugs, which are similar to RJ-11, but have eight wires (four pair) instead of four wires (two pair).
- *CAT5:* The minimum specification for Fast Ethernet 100Base-T. It also supports 10Base-T, Token Ring, and telephones. Because of this, it is the most common wiring used in modern networks. CAT5 also uses RJ-45 plugs.

Another type of copper cable is coaxial, which is used by cable TV systems. It is made of concentric rings of conducting material, separated by an insulating layer of some kind, rather than individual pairs of wires twisted together. A BNC connector typically terminates coaxial cable.

Fiber-optic cable comes in several flavors as well. The two most common types are called Single Mode (SM) and Multimode (MM). Unlike copper cable, the specification for fiber-optic cable includes the diameter of the core, which is where the light travels, and the diameter of the cladding. These values for multimode fiber are usually 62.5 and 125 μm, respectively. (In Europe, a 50-μm core is often used.) Single-mode fiber has a much smaller core, typically 5 to 10 μm. Fiber-optic specification also typically includes the wavelength supported. This is typically 850 nm or 1350 nm. Note that the primary difference between single mode and multimode is that an actual laser is used for single mode, making it very expensive; a Light-Emitting Diode (LED) is used for multimode. This allows single-mode fiber to support much greater distances (typically greater than 20 miles), whereas multimode fiber is used almost exclusively inside buildings and small campus networks.

Another important difference between fiber-optic and copper cable is that copper cable often has several pairs of wires; fiber optic just has a single pair (one to transmit and one to receive).

Fiber-optic cables are generally terminated with SC or ST plugs. These are similar, but the ST plugs are round and the SC plugs are square. Most older communications systems, such as telephony and Token Ring networks used the ST jacks, whereas newer systems, such as Ethernet, use the SC jacks. One drawback of these connectors is that each fiber in the pair gets a separate connector, so terminating one circuit (two wires) requires quite a bit of space relative to typical copper connectors. This limits the number of connections that can be easily terminated into a device. Recently, the MTRJ connector was developed to compensate for this deficiency. It terminates both fibers in a single connector and is much smaller, although somewhat fragile.

Other points of interest include the following:

- All cables have a minimum bend radius because kinks in the cable affect the signal. Fiber-optic cable is much more sensitive to tight curves than copper.

- Fiber-optic cable is not susceptible to electromagnetic interference.

- To learn more, visit the Data Communications Cabling FAQ at the following Web site:

  ```
  www.faqs.org/faqs/LANs/cabling-faq/preamble.html.
  ```

HUBS

To connect several computers in a building, cables are typically run from the PCs on people's desks back to wiring closets. Here, a special device is required to connect all the cables together. This device is typically a hub. *Hubs* are devices that provide a physical path for a signal to travel from one cable to another. Although their behavior is specified by a technology, such as Ethernet or Token Ring, that is generally considered layer 2 of the OSI Model, hubs are considered to operate at layer 1, which is the Physical layer. This is because they act as multiport repeaters. In other words, they simply regenerate an electrical signal received on one port out one or more other ports, with no changes whatsoever.

Because a hub simply repeats a signal without modifying the information, every port on a hub is part of the same network segment or data-link. This means that in an Ethernet network (which we'll cover in Chapter 3), all ports on a hub are part of the same collision domain. This means that for the entire hub, only one computer can send data at a time. In a Token Ring network (also covered in Chapter 3), all ports on a hub are part of the same ring.

BRIDGES

Once the number of users began to push the limits of a single network segment, there was a need to create a new segment to link two networks together. A device called a *bridge* accomplished this. Originally, bridges had only two ports, one for each network. However, unlike hubs, bridges actually inspect the data that passes through them and make decisions about whether to send it to the other network or not. This decision is based on the MAC address in Ethernet networks, and on the ring number in Token Ring networks. Because of this behavior (specifically, that bridges read and act on the data in the layer 2 headers of each frame), we say that bridges are layer 2 devices.

Ethernet bridges listen to traffic sent by computers and other network devices, and then they record the MAC address of the computer, which is located in the Source Address field of the Ethernet frame header, and the port from which the address was learned. If the bridge then receives a frame from the other network that is destined for the MAC address it learned from the first network, it will send the frame to the first network.

Token Ring bridges operate by ring numbers. Each bridge is assigned a bridge number and a ring number. Token Ring frames contain a Routing Information Field (RIF), which is a list of the ring numbers and bridge numbers that a frame must traverse to get to its destination. When a Token Ring bridge sees a frame on one ring destined for another ring that is also attached to the same bridge, it will retransmit the frame on that ring.

SWITCHES

As networks grew even larger, and the amount of data transmitted by each computer increased, segmenting networks became even more important. Two-port bridges were no longer sufficient. Although they have much more functionality now, switches began as multiport bridges and are considered layer 2 devices. Most switches have 12 or 24 ports, but many are modular and can have several hundred ports.

Another distinction is that switches can handle several conversations at the same time. Each 100Base-TX port on a switch can send and receive frames at the same time (called Full-Duplex, as opposed to hubs, which are Half-Duplex). This means that switches have to have a fairly complex backplane (often called a switch fabric) that allows each port to talk to every other port. Although the details of this are often published, they are not part of any technology standard, but are proprietary for each switch type.

Switches also employ buffers. These buffers are memory that can be used to store frames until the frame can be transmitted. This is useful when many devices converse with a single device, and collectively send more data than the link can support in a given time. In this case, the frames would wait in the buffer until there is enough available bandwidth on the link to transmit the frame.

There are two types of switches that are commonly used:

- Store and forward switches receive the entire frame into the buffer before transmitting it. This allows a switch to read and calculate a checksum at the end to ensure that the frame is not corrupted.

- Cut-through switches read only the destination address field from the layer 2 header before beginning to transmit. Cut-through switches do forward frames with errors and frame fragments, but are somewhat faster than store and forward switches.

ROUTERS

Although segregating network segments was helpful, all the devices attached to hubs, bridges, and switches are still in the same broadcast domain, and there are practical limits to the number of devices that can exist in any broadcast domain. So to segregate broadcast domains, routers were created. Routers act as the boundary between broadcast domains. Similar to the way bridges and switches read and act upon the layer 2 headers, routers read and make decisions based on the layer 3 headers, such as the TCP/IP or IPX headers. Therefore, we say that routers are layer 3 devices.

A router's job is to inspect each packet sent to it and determine if it belongs to the local IP or IPX network or to a remote network. If the destination of the packet is a remote network, and the router knows how to reach that network, the router forwards the packet; otherwise the packet is discarded.

Routers are also used almost exclusively to connect remote networks via WAN links, but this is unrelated to the actual function of routing. It is possible to use bridges or other devices, such as PCs, this is to connect WAN links, but rare.

Routers often use sophisticated algorithms and routing protocols to communicate with other routers to discover the best way to reach remote networks. This is discussed in detail in Chapter 7.

Network Topologies

As mentioned previously, there must be a physical path connecting the sending and receiving devices (even if that path is wireless). However, there are many different types of paths that can be created. These types of paths are called *topologies*. A given topology can describe several different network protocols. For example, FDDI and Token Ring are both rings. The types of paths are typically divided into several categories as shown below, but before we discuss the categories, we need to define the terms *physical* and *logical*.

In this context, *physical* is what it normally means and does not refer to the Physical layer of the OSI model. Physical attributes of a network describe things you can put your hands on, whereas the Physical layer describes the behavior of electrons and light waves. They do overlap somewhat in the area of cable and jack specifications.

By comparison, the term *logical* in the context of network topologies describes the behavior specified in layer 2. (See the section "OSI Model for Networking" earlier in this chapter.)

This is important because a given technology, such as Ethernet or Token Ring, can be one topology physically, but another topology logically.

SHARED MEDIUM

A shared topology is capable of having more than two devices share the network at a time. Unlike others, shared mediums must deal with contention. In other words, only in shared mediums is it possible for multiple conversations to take place simultaneously. This means that the medium must have some method of controlling access.

Although this will be described in Chapter 3 in much greater detail, we use Ethernet and Token Ring as an example in this section. Ethernet is a shared medium and its MAC layer protocol is CSMA/CD. Recall that "MA" stands for Multiple Access. This term has two meanings. The much more common definition is that MA means many devices can share the same data-link. In other words, MA means it is a shared medium. The other, and more accurate, definition is that MA refers to Ethernet's ability to have access to the network multiple times in a row. This means an Ethernet card in a computer could transmit several frames in a row. By contrast, Token Ring devices may only transmit one frame at a time. After that, they must relinquish the token to their downstream neighbor. Even if no other devices have frames to transmit, the token must make its way completely around the ring before the first station may transmit its second frame.

Ethernet's method of controlling access is collision detect (CD). In simple terms, CD means the device listens for other devices on the network. If no one else is transmitting, the device is free to transmit as much as possible.

Shared mediums also must deal with addressing. With only two devices on a network, it is obvious in other topologies that the other device will always be the recipient of your traffic and vice versa. Once a third device is added, you need some way to identify with which device you want to communicate.

Although it is implemented differently, almost all modern network technologies use some form of MAC addressing. Shared media come in many types, but the two most prevalent are bus and ring.

Bus

A bus topology is similar to the bus architecture that connects the main memory to the CPU and disk drives in your computer. It is a simple data path that connects all devices on the network to itself, so that only one device can use it at a time. This path can be either physical or logical (see Fig. 2-3).

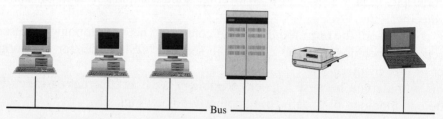

Fig. 2-3.   The bus topology.

For instance, logically, Ethernet is always a bus. However, physically, Ethernet can be a bus (10Base2) where each computer is connected to the next computer and the ends of the bus are terminated. Ethernet can also be a star topology physically (10BaseT), where each device has its own cable that runs back to a central hub, forming a hub-and-spoke or star topology.

Ring

Logically, a ring topology is one where each device transmits only to its downstream neighbor and receives only from its upstream neighbor. In other words, if you want to receive a frame from your nearest downstream neighbor, the frame would have to travel all the way around the ring, through every other device before you receive it (see Fig. 2-4).

Physically, a ring topology is the same concept. Each device is connected to exactly two other devices (unless, of course, there are only two devices on the network) so that they form a circle. As another example of the difference between physical and logical, Token Ring is logically a ring, but is physically a star, just like twisted-pair Ethernet, where each device is connected to a central hub.

PEER-TO-PEER

A peer-to-peer network, often abbreviated P2P, is the simplest network type when there are very few peers, but if you have several devices that need to talk to more than one other device, it can quickly become unmanageable. This network is made up of a single link between two peers. These peers could be two PCs with a serial cable or two routers connected via a point-to-point T1 circuit. The important

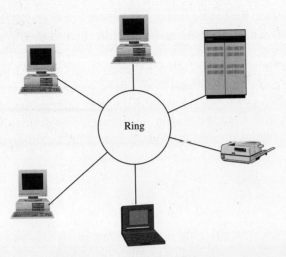

Fig. 2-4.   The ring topology.

distinction is that there are only two devices and one connection. Although they sometimes do use MAC addresses, it is unnecessary (see Fig. 2-5).

Another important point is that the term *peer-to-peer* in the popular media usually refers to the relationship of two computers above the application layer: client-to-server, server-to-server, or client-to-client, which is another way of saying peer-to-peer. A very old example of this is Windows for Workgroups. More recent examples of peer-to-peer would be the music-swapping services like Gnutella. The point is that those are totally unrelated to peer-to-peer in the context of networking topologies.

When many devices are involved and several need to communicate with multiple other devices, several peer-to-peer networks are often combined to form one of these configurations:

Star

In a star configuration, one central device has connections to all other devices, and relays communication between them. The star configuration is also commonly called *hub and spoke* because it resembles a wagon wheel.

Mesh

To connect all devices to all other devices, you need $n(n-1)/2$ connections. If you only have 10 devices in the network, that would be 45 physical links, and each

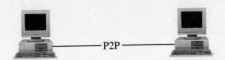

Fig. 2-5.   A simple P2P network.

device would have to have nine interfaces to connect to its neighbors. The advantage of this is that no data ever has to travel more than one hop away; therefore, this network can be incredibly fast.

A common compromise is called a partial mesh. In a partial mesh, you simply remove some of the links. The reality of traffic patterns in your network is that each device in the network will spend most of its time talking to only a handful of other devices. So by eliminating the seldom-used links, you eliminate a great deal of cost and complexity. Partial meshes are very common in technologies such as ATM and Frame Relay.

HYBRID

No matter how well your rules are defined, someone is always going to want to bend them. It's not surprising then, that a number of companies try to take the best parts of each topology and merge them. One very old example of this is IBM's baseband technology, which is a combination of a bus and a star. In this topology, each bus can have up to eight devices and several buses can be connected together in a star configuration, as shown in Fig. 2-6.

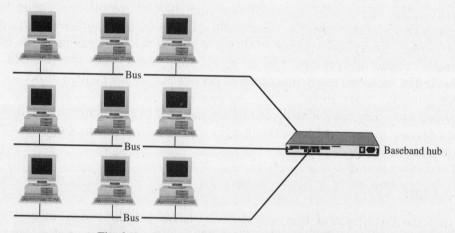

Fig. 2-6.   Buses connected in a star configuration.

There are a number of logical examples of hybrid networks, such as ATM and Frame Relay. These will be covered in more detail in later chapters.

 # Review Questions

2.1   List the components required to connect two PCs using an Ethernet hub.

2.2   What is the least number of components required to connect two PCs using the Ethernet technology?

2.3   How many power cords are required in Question 2.1?

2.4   How many power cords are required to connect two PCs using two Token Ring NICs and a Token Ring hub?

2.5   Two PCs are located in adjacent rooms and a third PC is in a building 300 yards away. Explain how you could connect the three PCs to create a single network.

2.6   You have three more PCs at an office on the other side of town. What is the most common way of connecting these devices with those in Review Question 2.5?

2.7   You have a network of 10 PCs. Five PCs are connected to one Ethernet hub and five PCs are connected to a second Ethernet hub. Both hubs are connected to a switch. A router connects your switch to a remote office with an identical configuration. How many MAC addresses will your switch learn?

2.8   You have a single PC in Alabama, and another PC in Tennessee. Not counting any components provided by the telecommunications provider, what is the least number of components required to connect the two PCs?

2.9   There are 20 PCs in your network. Five PCs are connected to one Ethernet hub, and five PCs are connected to another hub. Each hub is connected to a separate switch and both switches are connected to a separate router. The routers are connected via an Ethernet bridge. The remaining 10 PCs are directly connected to one of the two switches. How many Ethernet segments are there?

2.10 Using the scenario in Review Question 2.9, how many broadcast domains are there?

2.11 Using the scenario in Review Question 2.9, how many cables are required?

2.12 Your Ethernet NIC has one 15-pin connector marked AUI. Your hub has an RJ-45 jack. How do you connect them?

2.13 Do wireless networks have a physical layer?

2.14 Do wireless networks have physical components?

2.15 You are experiencing difficulty getting a connection between two devices and you suspect the single-mode fiber-optic cable. Your friend suggests you unplug one end and look inside it to see if it is sending any light. Choose two of the following to describe this idea:
   a. It is a good idea because you can see if the other device is transmitting any light.
   b. It is a bad idea because the laser doesn't use a frequency in the visible spectrum.
   c. It is a bad idea because the laser will burn your retinas out.
   d. It's OK. The laser isn't powerful enough to hurt you.

2.16 How many networks can a router connect?

2.17 If an ATM-connected PC using LANE needs to broadcast a frame to all the other devices on the network, how does it accomplish this on a nonbroadcast network?

2.18 Once the layer 2 component of your network driver software receives a frame, how does it know what to do with it?

2.19 How is data handed up to the next layer for further processing?

2.20 At what layer does Fast Ethernet operate?

2.21 Computer A is on a Token Ring network, connected to an Ethernet network by a router. This Ethernet network is in turn connected to another Token Ring network by a translation bridge. Computer B resides on the second Token Ring network. Explain what happens to the data sent by Computer A to Computer B.

2.22 In what layer of the OSI model does TCP/IP reside?

2.23 What is a LAN?

2.24   Can a LAN have routers?

2.25   What's the difference between a packet and a frame?

2.26   How are frames routed through the network?

2.27   If ATM has a layer 3 component, why is it necessary to run TCP/IP over ATM?

Problems

2.1   What factors enter into the selection of network topology?

2.2   What happens when a computer in a ring becomes unplugged and breaks the ring?

2.3   What happens when a computer in a bus becomes unplugged and breaks the bus?

2.4   How do ring networks control media access?

2.5   How do mesh networks control media access?

2.6   Figure 2-7 shows four connected ATM switches, labeled A, B, C, and D. The white lines between them represent fiber-optic connections. The dotted lines represent PVCs. Physically, what type of topology is this?

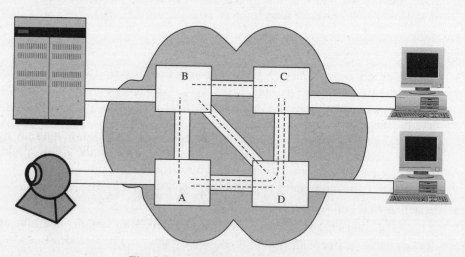

Fig. 2-7.   A sample fiber-optic network.

2.7   Figure 2-7 shows four connected ATM switches, labeled A, B, C, and D. The white lines between them represent fiber-optic connections. The dotted lines represent PVCs. Logically, what type of topology is this?

2.8   In Figure 2-7, show all possible paths for a PVC to travel from the top PC to the video camera.

2.9   The analog (POTS) phone lines and telephones in your house are not connected to any electrical power source. How does the phone ring and light up?

2.10 You are starting a CLEC, but the telephone lines are all owned by the ILEC. How do you connect to your customers' residences and businesses to provide service?

2.11 You have two offices and want to put a PBX in each and connect the two so that your employees in one office can call the employees in another office without being charged for each call by the telephone company. How can you do this?

Answers to Review Questions

2.1 Components: Two PCs with network interface cards (NICs), two CAT5 cables with RJ-45 connectors on each end, one Ethernet hub. One end of each cable would be inserted into the PC's NIC and the other end into the hub, as shown in Fig. 2-8.

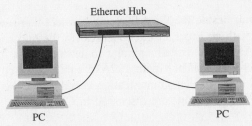

Fig. 2-8. Hub connections.

2.2 Three components: Two PCs and a crossover cable. The CAT5 crossover cable would be connected to the NIC in each PC. The crossover cable is like a normal cable in all respects, except the transmit (Tx) and receive (Rx) pairs of wires are reversed, so that what one PC sends is received on the correct wire by the other PC. If a normal cable is used, one PC would send a signal to the Tx wire on the second PC, which would be ignored. The ports on hubs have the crossover built in, so normal cables are straight through (see Fig. 2-9).

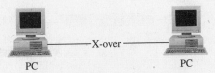

Fig. 2-9. Network crossover.

2.3 Three: One for each PC and one for the hub.

2.4 Two or Three. Token Ring hubs that use the IBM Type-1 cables do not require power. They do not repeat the signal like Ethernet hubs. They contain a relay that closes to complete a circuit when it detects that a device has been plugged in (this is responsible for the clicking noises often heard in TR wiring closets). Once this relay is closed, the device essentially is a single wire connecting one PC to the next in the ring. The PC's NIC is responsible for generating a signal strong enough to reach its next or downstream neighbor. However, many newer Token Ring hubs that use RJ-45 jacks do require power.

2.5   Purchase a hub that has both UTP and fiber-optic ports. Place the hub close to the two PCs and connect them via CAT5 cables. Run fiber-optic cable (either MM or SM) between the remote computer and the hub. At the remote end, use a media converter to connect the UTP to the fiber-optic cables. This is shown in Fig. 2-10.

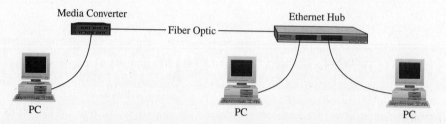

Fig. 2-10.   UTP and fiber-optic hub connections.

2.6   Place another hub beside the three PCs and connect them with three CAT5 cables. Install a router with an Ethernet interface next to the hub and connect it to the hub with another CAT5 cable. Install a similar router beside the hub in Review Question 2.5, and connect it to that hub with a CAT5 cable. Last, connect the routers via a circuit provided by your telecommunications vendor (such as an ISDN link or a T1) (see Fig. 2-11). WAN circuits are discussed in Chapter 3.

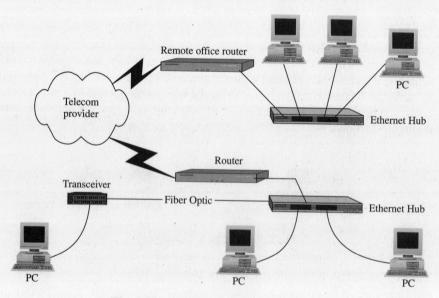

Fig. 2-11.   A wide area network connection.

2.7   11. The switch will learn the MAC address of all 10 PCs, plus the MAC address of the router. Hubs are not layer 2-aware devices, so they do not have MAC addresses. Also, the switch only operates on the local network, so it will not learn any MAC addresses from the other side of the local router.

2.8   Four. Connect the PC in Alabama to a router using a CAT5 crossover cable and connect the PC in Tennessee to a router using a CAT5 crossover cable. Connect the two routers to the equipment provided by the telecom vendor, as shown in Fig. 2-12.

Note: A more common solution would be to place a hub at each site, and connect the router and the PC to the hub using a regular CAT5 cable.

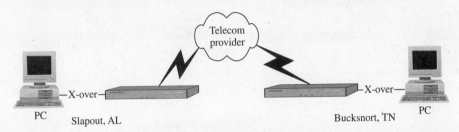

PC   Slapout, AL   Bucksnort, TN   PC

Fig. 2-12.   Connecting routed networks.

2.9   16. The switches, bridges, routers, and PCs all bound Ethernet segments. The hubs do not. Thus, all the devices connected to a hub are in the same Ethernet segment. The easiest way to determine this is to start with the switches. There are seven devices plugged into each switch (5 PCs, a hub, and a router). Therefore, there are 7 Ethernet segments for each switch. Multiply by 2 switches gives 14 segments. Plus the connection between the routers requires 2 more segments, because of the bridge between them (see Fig. 2-13).

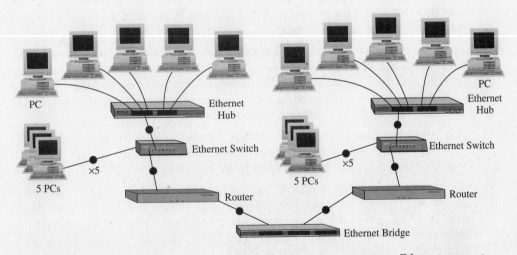

Fig. 2-13.   A sample network—each dot on the diagram represents an Ethernet segment.

2.10   Three. The routers are the only devices that operate at layer 3, and thus bound broadcast domains. Therefore, the two groups of PCs, hubs, and switches are each a broadcast domain. The connection between the two routers, across the bridge, is the third broadcast domain (see Fig. 2-14).

2.11   Twenty-four normal CAT5 cables and two crossover CAT5 cables. Each PC requires one cable to connect to either a hub or switch, for a total of 20 cables. Each router requires a cable to connect to the bridge and a cable to connect to the switch. That is

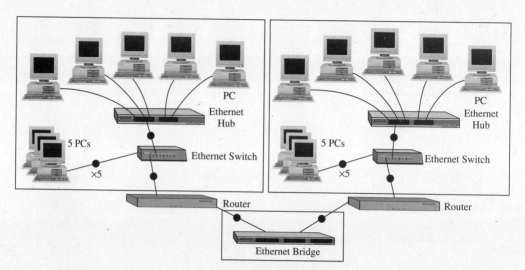

Fig. 2-14. Broadcast domains.

four more cables for a total of 24. Each of the two hubs is connected to a switch with a crossover cable.

2.12 Although most NICs have an RJ-45 jack, the AUI port allows much more flexibility. A device called a *transceiver* is attached to the AUI port. Transceivers can have many types of jacks, from fiber optic to thin net to RJ-45. This allows an administrator to use many different types of Ethernet, including 10Base-T, 10Base-2, 10Base-5, and 10Base-F, all without changing the NIC in the PC or the software drivers. Thus, the answer is that a transceiver with an RJ-45 jack can be installed and a normal CAT5 patch cable can be used to connect the transceiver to the hub.

2.13 Yes. The media is considered RF (Radio Frequency) and although you can't put your finger on it, you can observe and measure it with a number of tools. The physical layer is specified in IEEE 802.11b (among others), and it includes the same components as other physical media, such as frequency, signal strength and characteristics, theoretical distance limitations, etc.

2.14 Yes. Most wireless networks consist of adapter cards (typically in the PCMCIA form) with internal or external antenna, and base stations, which are actually hubs that merely convert from one physical layer to another (typically 10BaseT).

2.15 The correct answers are **a** and **c**. You can see the light (assuming the device is transmitting) but you may also lose your eyesight. Thus, it is a *very bad idea. Never* look into fiber-optic cable or any sort of laser, whether it's visible light or not. An alternative is to hold the end of the cable less than a centimeter away from your hand, or a sheet of paper. You should be able to see a little pinpoint of light. Multimode fiber-optic cable uses an LED instead of a real laser, so it won't, in theory, harm your eyes, but it's still not a good idea, much like playing with an unloaded gun. No point in taking chances.

2.16 There isn't a theoretical limit. Practically, the number of physical interfaces the router manufacturers allow limits this. Although most routers have only two or three interfaces, more expensive routers can have over 100 interfaces. However, this can also be a trick question, because you can have more than one network on a physical interface. This is common practice when using ATM or Frame Relay PVCs. In these networks, each PVC may represent a separate layer 3 network.

2.17 As part of each LEC's initialization, it establishes an SVC with both the LES and the BUS, which is the Broadcast/Unknown server. Figure 2-15 illustrates the BUS, which is actually a piece of software that typically runs on one or more ATM switches. Anytime a PC needs to broadcast a frame, its LEC simply sends this frame to the BUS, which then distributes it to all LECs that have registered with the BUS.

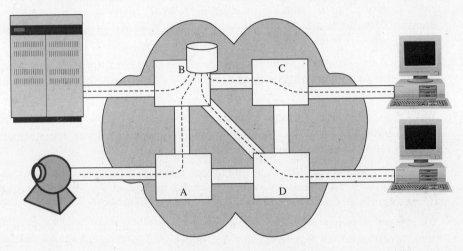

Fig. 2-15. BUS networking.

2.18 Most layer 2 protocols define a header that includes a field, which indicates the next highest layer. For instance, the Ethernet header includes a field called Ethertype. If this value is set to 0800h, the data portion of the frame, which is the packet from layer 3, is handed to the TCP/IP software for further processing. If the value is 0806h, the contents of the data field belong to the Address Resolution Protocol (ARP).

2.19 Usually, when a protocol such as IP is initialized, a number of memory buffers are created for sending and receiving packets. When the protocol is bound to a network adapter, the adapter's device driver (which is the layer 2 software) is assigned a memory address at which to place its incoming data. Once it places the data in the specified memory address, the IP software can begin processing the packet.

2.20 For most exams, the correct answer to this question is simply "Layer 2." However, it's important to realize that these technologies don't exist in a vacuum.

2.21 The sending application on Computer A passes the data down through the upper layers until it reaches layer 3, where it is placed inside a packet. This packet is in turn placed in a Token Ring frame (layer 2). The frame is then turned into electrical signals and placed on the wire. (layer 1)

Because the first Token Ring and Ethernet segments are separated by a router, which operates at layer 3, the router must discard the Token Ring headers and footers, then read the header for the packet (layer 3). Once the location of Computer B is determined, the router then creates a new Ethernet frame by placing an Ethernet header and footer around the packet (layer 2), and sends the frame on its way by again converting the 1's and 0's into electrical signals (layer 1).

Once the frame arrives at the bridge, which operates at layer 2, the bridge determines that Computer B resides on the second Token Ring segment. Since the bridge is oblivious to the contents of the packet (again, it only operates at layer 2) and the Ethernet frame it received cannot be transmitted across the Token Ring network, the bridge must strip the Ethernet header and footer and apply a Token Ring header and footer (layer 2), and then transmit the frame (layer 1).

2.22 Again, the short exam answer is "Layer 3." However, in reality, TCP/IP is a suite of many separate protocols. Included in this suite are TCP and UDP, which operate at layer 4, as well as IP, which is a layer 3 protocol. Many of these protocols are designed to perform management functions, such as ICMP, or to facilitate communication between layers, such as ARP and DNS.

2.23 A Local Area Network (LAN) is a common acronym used to describe a group of devices that share a geographic location. Usually, this is limited to a single building or campus.

2.24 Yes. LANs often contain many routers to segment the LANs into many smaller broadcast domains, but the term LAN describes a geography rather than distinctions between layers 2 and 3 of the OSI model.

2.25 A frame is the PDU at the Data-Link layer, whereas a packet is the PDU at the Network layer. Put another way, a data-link header and footer are added to a packet to create a frame. A frame is therefore said to encapsulate a packet.

2.26 They aren't. A frame only exists inside a broadcast domain. If the packet inside the frame is destined for a remote network, the router copies the packet to its buffers, and then discards the frame. Once the router determines the outbound interface, it creates a new frame, places the packet inside it, and sends them both on their way.

2.27 It isn't. It is certainly possible to write applications that request the ATM services directly and use the 20-byte ATM addresses instead of IP addresses and allow ATM's routing to provide a loop-free path through the internetwork. In fact, one of the reasons ATM was so popular was this capability. Everyone assumed that "they" were writing killer-apps to take advantage of ATM's inherent quality of service and that a host of next-generation multimedia applications would drive the whole world to convert from Ethernet to ATM. Unfortunately, there was no "they" and the applications never appeared. In the absence of any burning need, few companies could justify the cost of ATM, and so it is rapidly being replaced with Ethernet once again.

Solutions to Problems

2.1 Many years ago, these decisions were based on the physical arrangement of the PCs and servers, and how much bandwidth was required and what kinds of traffic patterns were most common on the network. However, modern LANs are almost exclusively Ethernet, which is a star topology. This is largely because most businesses also require telephones, and it is easy to run both telephone and data cables at the same time (and, in fact, they're often identical cables). It's also based on cost and availability of support, because there is almost no competition. On the WAN, these decisions are usually made based on cost, because the monthly costs for maintaining data circuits can be very expensive. Thus, although it may be technically beneficial to have an ATM or Frame Relay full mesh between remote offices, it is usually difficult to justify financially.

Because of evolution, star networks are also common in the WAN. These begin with a small company that needs to connect two sites. A point-to-point network is configured. As the company grows and adds sites, they add point-to-point circuits. These are usually run from the headquarters to the remote sites, creating a star.

2.2   If the path around the ring is broken, none of the devices on the ring can communicate. However, many ring technologies, such as SONET and FDDI, use "dual, counter-rotating" rings, which offers some redundancy. Token Ring, however, does not. Fortunately, it does provide a mechanism to prevent disruption of all network services every time a computer on the ring is turned off or on.

2.3   In most bus networks, the computer itself may be powered down or unplugged without affecting the other devices, but if the link to the next device is disconnected, the entire network will be disabled. This is because most bus networks must be terminated on either end by a device appropriately called a *terminator*. Terminators are typically a resistor with an Ohm rating specified by the technology. A resistor is necessary to keep the signal from bouncing back and affecting other signals.

2.4   Most ring networks use token passing. A token is a special frame that is sent from a computer to its nearest downstream neighbor on the ring, who in turn sends the token to the next device on the ring, and so on. Only the device that has the token is allowed access to the media. In other words, if you want to send some data, you have to wait until your upstream neighbor sends you the token, then you send your data. After you've sent your data, you pass the token to the next computer, so it has a chance to send.

2.5   They typically don't. Since there are only two devices on each link, and the connections are generally full-duplex, which means both devices can speak and listen simultaneously, there is no need to control media access.

2.6   Physically, this is a partial mesh of peer-to-peer networks. If the A and C switches were directly connected, this would be a full mesh.

2.7   Logically, this is a full mesh, because all switches have a direct connection to all other switches via a PVC. It is not important that there is no physical connection between switches A and C.

2.8   The possible paths are via the following switches:

- C, D, A
- C, B, A
- C, B, D, A
- C, D, B, A

There are four possible paths from the computer to the video camera and neither the computer nor the video camera has any way of knowing what path the data is taking through the network. This lack of visibility is why ATM networks and other virtual circuit-based networks, such as Frame Relay, are referred to as clouds.

The primary benefit of using these connections is that traffic may be routed around congested or broken links. For instance, if an SVC is carrying data via path C, D, A and the physical link between switches A and D breaks, the traffic can quickly and automatically be rerouted to take path C, B, A. If the link between B and C is congested, such that the ATM network cannot guarantee that the constant bit rate can be maintained, it could choose path C, D, B, A instead. Although this flexibility is very valuable, it is also quite complicated, both to configure and troubleshoot.

2.9 The Central Office telephone switch supplies power through the same pairs of wires that carries voice conversation. The power supplied is 48 VDC. Although the amperage and voltage are both very small, you will feel a shock if you touch the wires and complete a circuit.

2.10 Federal law mandates that the ILEC must provide space in its facilities and access to the shared infrastructure for you, once you've been approved by the FCC. You will have to install your own telecommunications equipment, however, and pay fees to the ILEC.

2.11 Lease a dedicated circuit, such as a T1 or an ISDN-PRI (Primary Rate Interface) from the phone company. Then connect this circuit to each PBX. This will allow up to 23 simultaneous telephone conversations between the offices.

Although there is a physical connection, the T1, or DS1, is a virtual circuit, so that no matter how many devices it travels through physically, it appears to your PBXs as if they are separated only by one wire. In other words, if your offices were several states apart, the circuit may physically connect your PBX to the CO's facilities, and then the CO may connect to another switch, which connects to another switch, etc. This connection may pass through the equipment of several different companies, including IXCs (long-distance carriers) and the LEC at the remote office, before it finally arrives at the remote office. However, all of that appears as only a single link to the PBXs. This is because the PSTN is circuit-switched.

CHAPTER 3

Network Technologies

A technology is the process, method, and knowledge involved in accomplishing a task. In the field of communication networks, that task is getting data from one device to another, and to some extent there are separate technologies at quite a few layers of the Open Systems Interconnection (OSI) model that all interact to accomplish this task. But when people in the field speak of a networking technology, they are commonly referring to the classical use of the term *network*, which typically means a Data-link protocol combined with a Physical layer medium.

The process, methods, and knowledge for a network technology are detailed in a specification. A specification can be a public standard, such as the IEEE 802.x series, or it can be proprietary to a single company. Proprietary standards often exist because a company obtains patents on the results of its research. Additionally, proprietary standards are created because the official standards are occasionally ambiguous, or companies modify or extend the standard to take advantage of features in their legacy products or hardware.

This chapter covers a few of the more common technologies. For the sake of comparison, we have divided them into categories based on their most common use. The section on local area networks (LANs) includes the most popular technologies used to connect devices in a limited geographic area (typically a single building or campus), even though some of these technologies can span 20 or more miles. The section on wide area networks (WANs) includes the most popular technologies typically used to connect two or more geographically diverse LANs, even though some of these technologies are used in LANs as well. Finally, the section on wireless technologies looks at the Physical layer of wireless technologies and how they differ from their wired counterparts.

Local Area Network Technologies

We discuss LAN technologies in order of relevance to today's enterprise networks. Some of these technologies are increasing in popularity, while others are waning, but the most important thing to realize about these technologies is that the specifications represent a snapshot in time. In reality, network equipment manufacturers often release working products in anticipation of a specification, just to be the first to market. And, of course, these technologies are always being improved, especially the Physical layer, where the bulk of research is aimed, so the specifications are intended to be just restrictive enough to ensure compatibility, without preventing continuous improvements to hardware and software implementation of these technologies.

ETHERNET TECHNOLOGIES

Ethernet is by far the most popular LAN technology in use today and for the foreseeable future. Its popularity has more to do with the cost per port to manufacture than with any practical advantages. In fact, there are faster, more secure, technologies that are capable of communicating over much greater distances, but nothing is cheaper than Ethernet. Nevertheless, Ethernet has a distinguished history.

Bob Metcalfe originally created Ethernet in 1976, at Xerox's famed Palo Alto Research Center (PARC). It was designed to connect a PC to a laser printer. Figure 3-1 shows the original Ethernet drawing by Metcalfe. Among many other things, Metcalfe acquired his undergraduate degree from MIT, a Ph.D. from Harvard, founded 3Com, and was the editor of *InfoWorld* magazine.

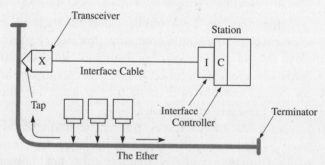

Fig. 3-1.   An artist's rendering of Bob Metcalfe's original conception of Ethernet. Metcalfe created his drawing in 1976.

Ethernet Frame Types

Because of its long history, there are many versions of Ethernet frames and many specifications for Physical layer implementations. If you're running Ethernet in an enterprise network today, there is a good chance you will find two or more of the four common frame types. These types are more than a little confusing because different organizations refer to them by different names. Table 3.1 clarifies this matter.

All four frame formats are very simple and lightweight. They all provide the following features:

- A destination address field
- A source address field

- A mechanism for identifying the contents of the payload
- A payload field, which carries the data (for example, a TCP/IP packet)
- A checksum

Table 3-1   Ethernet Frame Types

Frame Type	Cisco	Novell	Notes
Version II IEEE 802.3 IEEE 802.3 SNAP Novell's format	ARPA LLC SNAP NOVELL	Ethernet II Ethernet 802.2 Ethernet SNAP Ethernet 802.3	Often called DIX Includes the 802.2 LLC header Used for compatibility Proprietary

Version II Ethernet

The first version of Ethernet has been completely replaced by Version II and is no longer relevant. Version II is the first specification that had any widespread use. It is commonly called DIX, which comes from the initials of the three companies that backed the Ethernet standard: DEC (Digital Equipment Corporation), Intel, and Xerox. Version II is specified by the DIX consortium and uses the frame format shown in Table 3-2.

Table 3-2   The Version II Ethernet Frame Format

6 Bytes	6 Bytes	2 Bytes	Variable	4 Bytes
Destination address (unicast, broadcast, or multicast)	Source address	Ethertype	Payload	FCS

The destination and source address fields carry the six-byte MAC address of the recipient and sender, respectively. This is fairly straightforward, but there are three types of destination addresses:

- Unicast, which identifies a single node on the network
- Broadcast, which is sent to every node on the network
- Multicast, which is sent to a group of nodes on the network

A unicast destination address begins with the Organizationally Unique Identifier (OUI) field, which is the first three bytes of the MAC address. These three bytes are assigned by the IEEE to uniquely identify a network hardware manufacturer. The manufacturer determines the last three bytes of the MAC address. This scheme makes it possible to ensure that all network interface cards (NICs) worldwide have a unique hardware address.

A broadcast destination address consists of all ones in binary (11111111-11111111-11111111-11111111-11111111-11111111), which is commonly displayed as FF-FF-FF-FF-FF-FF in hexadecimal. A node on the network may send a broadcast packet when it wants to share or request information from all other nodes on the network.

A multicast address always begins with a one in the first byte. This is because the first bit of the MAC address is called the Individual/Group (I/G) bit. If the I/G bit is a zero, the address is an individual adapter. If the I/G bit is a one, it is a group address. The OUI portion is always 0x01.00.5E. The remainder of the MAC address maps to the multicast IP address. Unfortunately, only 23 bits of space are available in the MAC address, and there are 28 bits in a multicast IP address (remember that the first four bits in a Class D IP address are always set to 1110). This means that you cannot map the entire IP multicast address into a multicast MAC address.

The Internet Assigned Number Authority (IANA) maintains this list of protocols that ride on top of Ethernet, a current list of which can be found on-line at www.iana.org. Some common example values are 0x0800 for IP traffic, 0x0806 for Address Resolution Protocol (ARP), and 0x8137 for Novell's IPX/SPX (Internetwork Packet Exchange/Sequenced Packet Exchange). When the Ethernet driver software sees one of these values in the Ethertype field, it knows to which software process or memory location to deliver the contents of its payload. The payload is the packet being transported, which contains the layer 3 header (for example, IP or IPX) and the data.

The source Ethernet adapter calculates a complex polynomial, called the Frame Check Sequence (FCS), using the Ethernet header and payload as input. The result of this calculation is a 32-bit number, which is appended to the payload. When this process is complete, the frame is sent across the wire to the destination. The destination adapter collects all the bits it sees in its receive buffer. When it detects that the voltage on the line returns to zero (in the case of 10BaseT) or an idle signal (in the case of 100Base-TX), it calculates the same complex polynomial based on all but the last four bytes in its buffer. It then compares the result with the contents of the buffer, and if the values are identical, it sends the payload to the process specified in the Ethertype field. If the values are not identical, the adapter assumes that the frame is corrupt and discards it.

IEEE 802.3 and 802.2 Ethernet

The next frame type is IEEE 802.3. The format is shown in Table 3-3.

Table 3-3   **IEEE 802.3 Ethernet Frame Format**

6 Bytes	6 Bytes	2 Bytes	3 Bytes	Variable	4 Bytes
Destination address	Source address	Length	LLC header	Payload	FCS

The Logical Link Control (LLC) header that appears after the Length field is defined in IEEE 802.2 and has the format listed in Table 3-4:

Table 3-4   The 3-Byte LLC Header

1 Byte	1 Byte	1 Byte
Destination Service Access Point (DSAP)	Source Service Access Point (SSAP)	Control

The fields in the IEEE 802.3 header operate exactly like the Version II fields of the same name, with two exceptions. The first is that the Ethertype value has been replaced with a Length field that holds a value equal to the length of the payload. Second, an additional LLC header has been added before the payload. The LLC field operates like the Ethertype field, except that it carries information about the source protocol in addition to the destination protocol. This function is defined in IEEE 802.2 Logical Link Control.

SNAP Frame Format

The SNAP frame format is identical to the IEEE 802.3 header, except that a SNAP header follows the LLC header. See Table 3-5.

Table 3-5   SNAP Frame Format

3 Bytes	2 Bytes
Vendor Code	Local Code

The SNAP header contains two fields: a vendor code and a local code. These fields provide backward compatibility between IEEE 802.3 and Version II. To accomplish this, the vendor code is generally set to the first three bytes of the source address, which is the OUI part of the MAC address of the transmitting adapter. The local code is set to the Ethertype value that would have been used if this were a Version II frame.

The Novell proprietary format of the SNAP frame type is nearly identical to the IEEE 802.3 format as well, except it does not include the LLC header. For this reason, this format is often called RAW. The other differentiator is that it begins the payload field with an optional checksum, which by default always is turned off (set to FF-FFh).

ETHERNET VERSIONS

Not only are there four frame types, but there are several different versions of Ethernet. These are commonly called 10-Mbps Ethernet (plain old Ethernet), 100-Mbps Fast Ethernet, and 1000-Mbps Gigabit Ethernet. Although they are all "Ethernet," they are actually quite different at the Physical layer, because they used different encoding schemes.

10-Mbps Ethernet

There are several Physical layer specifications with 10-Mbps Ethernet. These specifications started in the following format: a number representing the speed in Mbps followed by the word *Base* for "baseband" or *Broad* for "broadband" and then a number, which originally represented the maximum distance in hundreds of meters. The four types of 10-Mbps Ethernet covered here are 10Base2, 10Base5, 10BaseT, and 10Base-F.

- *10Base2*. Commonly called thin Ethernet or thinnet, 10Base2 operates at 10 Mbps and has a maximum distance of 200 m. This specification uses a thin coaxial cable and is physically a bus topology, where each node on the Ethernet has a single connection (sometimes called a tap) at some point on the coaxial cable. Thin Ethernet specifies a 50-Ohm resistor to terminate each end of the coaxial cable, which prevents signals from bouncing (that is, reflecting off the end of the cable and back down the segment and subsequently being misinterpreted as a different signal from another device). The connectors used for 10Base2 are called BNC T-junctions.

- *10Base5*. The 10Base5 standard, called thick Ethernet or thicknet, also uses similar but much thicker coaxial cable. This cable is less suitable for connecting PCs in a typical office environment because the cable is much more rigid than that for thinnet. Because this specification has a 500-m maximum distance, it was often used as a backbone to connect closets in a building or sometimes to connect buildings in a campus.

- *10BaseT*. Both 10Base2 and 10Base5 were almost completely abandoned by the mid-1990s in favor of the 10BaseT specification. In this case, the "T" stands for "twisted-pair cable." 10BaseT deviates substantially from the other two 10-Mbps Ethernets in that it is physically a star topology. Instead of nodes being connected to each other in series, every node is connected to a central device called a "hub." This setup was discussed at length in Chapter 2. The 10BaseT specification usually uses CAT3 or CAT5 unshielded twisted-pair cables. One of the major advantages of this specification is that a cable can be plugged and unplugged from the hub without disrupting other devices' communications.

- *10Base-F*. The last Ethernet standard that merits mention is 10Base-F. In this case, the "F" stands for "fiber optic," which is the physical medium this specification uses. 10Base-F also uses a star topology, but in practice most hubs will contain 8, 16, or 24 10Base-T ports and one or two 10Base-F ports. This combination makes possible several cheaper, local runs to PCs with the capability for very long-distance runs between closets or buildings.

Note: Although the term *broadband* is commonly misused to differentiate fast and slow connections (for example, cable modems are broadband, and the implication is that slower connections are baseband), the term actually refers to whether multiple signals are used simultaneously on a wire or only a single signal is used. Cable modems are broadband because both data and cable television can use a single coaxial cable segment at the same time. Likewise, Digital Subscriber Loop (DSL) connections are broadband because you can send and receive data and use your phone over the same copper pair simultaneously. Although Ethernet is much faster than cable and DSL, it is a baseband technology because it can't share the physical media with any other signal.

Fast Ethernet

Much like 10-Mbps Ethernet, Fast Ethernet has several specifications for different physical ... optional modes of operation. The ... ...seT. At this Physical layer, however, ... Fast Ethernet breaks the Physical

... 2, but here we will go into more ... ...eded.

...rks is that high-frequency signals ... Worse, Ethernet uses Manchester ... ...hester Encoding works by changing ...e. A change from a higher voltage ... ...ge from a lower voltage to a higher ... regular transitioning enables the ..., even when several ones or zeros ... ...rly doubles the frequency required. ... ...to a 20-Mhz waveform.

... 00 Mbps would require almost 200- ... ...cy requirements, the 100Base-TX ... ...ns with three levels (MLT-3) and

... wo constant voltages (for example, ...n a one bit is sent, the transmitter ... voltage remains constant for the ... ...her level to this procedure, so that ... ...e voltage can now be used. The ... ...w be represented in a single clock ... ...n order. For example, if a byte that ... ...ge would be 1, 0, −1, 0, 1, 0, −1, 0.

If a byte with a value of 11001100 is sent, that would be represented electrically as 1, 0, 0, 0, −1, 0, 0, 0. Both of these examples assume the last voltage was zero. Because several transitions can now be contained in a single clock cycle, a lower frequency can be used.

There is one challenge left with MLT-3 and NRZI: If a large number of zeros are sent in a row, there would be no change in voltage. That, in turn, means that the receiving clock could become unsynchronized. To solve this, the 4B5B encoding is used. The 4B5B encoding simply creates a table of all the possible values of a nibble (that is, half of a byte, or four bits) and then maps those values to a corresponding five-bit value, where every five-bit value includes at least two one values (see Table 3-6). This means that no combination of actual data values will ever allow more than a few bit-times to pass without transitioning the voltage.

Table 3-6   4B5B Encoding

Nibble of Data	Five-Bit Code Used to Replace Nibble
0000	11110
0001	01001
0010	10100
0011	10101
0100	01010
0101	01011
0110	01110
0111	01111
1000	10010
1001	10011
1010	10110
1011	10111
1100	11010
1101	11011
1110	11100
1111	11101

There are three more important code values:

- 11111 is used when the line is idle
- 00000 is used when the line is dead
- 00100 is a halt signal

The end result is that MLT-3, NRZI, and 4B5B allow the 100Base-TX standard to use a maximum frequency of 31.25 Mhz, which is easily accommodated by CAT 5 cabling.

The 100Base-T4 specification uses an alternate method to deal with the high-frequency problem. First, the data is "fanned out" over three pairs of wires instead of one pair. Second, instead of using 4B5B, an 8B6T scheme is used that maps each octet to a pattern of six ternary or tri-state symbols. The result is that only a 12.5-Mhz frequency is now required, which means that the cheaper CAT3 cabling can be used to transmit 100 Mbps. Recall that CAT3 is rated to 16 Mhz.

100Base-FX is the Fast Ethernet specification that uses multimode fiber optics. 100Base-FX is identical to 100Base-TX, except that it doesn't use MLT-3, which means it requires twice the frequency, or 62.5 Mhz. Its maximum distance is 2 km.

Gigabit Ethernet

The Gigabit Ethernet standard also has many specifications. Gigabit Ethernet operates in two primary modes: full duplex and half duplex. These will be explained later in this chapter, but for now you should know that the half-duplex mode operates much like Ethernet and Fast Ethernet, using CSMA/CD (which is also explained later in this chapter). Full duplex mode uses a frame-based flow control defined in IEEE 802.x.

One of the most common specifications for Gigabit Ethernet is IEEE 802.3z. This includes 1000Base-CX, 1000Base-SX, and 1000Base-LX. The "C," "S," and "L," stand for "Cluster," "Short," and "Long," respectively. The differences are primarily in the type of fiber used (that is, single or multimode) and the type of light source (that is, LED or laser). Another popular specification is IEEE 802.3ab, which includes 1000Base-T, which uses CAT5 cabling. These specifications are all part of the PHY sublayer of the Physical layer.

At the PCS layer, Gigabit Ethernet uses 8B10B encoding, which is somewhat similar to 4B5B. The 10-Gigabit Ethernet is specified in IEEE 802.3ae. This standard operates on existing multimode fiber at 850 nm with a maximum distance of 65 m. On newer multimode fiber, it operates up to 300 m. There are several single-mode implementations, which range from 1300 nm with a maximum range up to 300 m, using a technology called Wide Wave Division Multiplexing (WWDM) to 1550 nm with a maximum range of 40 km.

Most of these frame formats and physical specifications share a common protocol at the MAC sublayer of the Data-Link layer. This protocol is Carrier Sense, Multiple-Access/Collision Detect, more commonly abbreviated CSMA/CD. This was discussed briefly in Chapter 2. The purpose of this protocol is to manage flow control and contention. Since Ethernet defines ones and zeros by transitions of the relative voltage on the wire, if two devices are putting voltage on the wire at the same time, the bit will be corrupted. To prevent two devices from transmitting at the same time, all half-duplex specifications employ a mechanism to detect collisions (which is Ethernet jargon for the change in voltage as two signals meet on a wire, which corrupts both frames). The receive circuit listens while the transmit circuitry begins sending, and when a collision is detected, both nodes cease transmitting data and begin transmitting a 32-bit jam signal. A short while later, both nodes execute the "truncated binary exponential backoff" algorithm, and then begin transmitting again. The truncated binary exponential backoff algorithm means the node waits a random amount of time from the collision and then attempts to transmit again. If another collision occurs, both nodes execute the truncated binary exponential backoff algorithm again. This process is repeated until both nodes successfully transmit their frames, or 16 attempts are made, in which case, the adapter will report that an error has occurred.

The algorithm used to determine that time is as follows:

$$0 < r < 2^k$$

where
$$k = \min(n,\ 10)$$

In this equation, r is the number of timeslots (bit-times) to wait before retransmitting, and n is the number of retransmission attempts.

Despite all the options and technologies and protocols, Ethernet excels in ease of installation and operation. For the most part, it is as simple as plugging one end of a cable into a hub, and the other end into a computer.

ETHERNET MODES OF OPERATION

The two primary modes of operation for Ethernet are called "full duplex" and "half duplex." The difference is simply that a half duplex connection supports traffic moving in both directions, but only one direction at a time. (A simplex connection, such as a radio, only supports data moving in a single direction.) That is, a node can either send or receive, but it cannot do both at any given time. Full duplex, on the other hand, can transmit and receive at the same time, effectively doubling the transmission rate. As far as the specifications are concerned, both 10BaseT and 100BaseTX can support full-duplex mode, but in practice it's only implemented in 100BaseTX. Even then, it's only supported between a node and a switch. You cannot use full duplex when connecting a node to a hub. Also note that full duplex does not have collisions.

The second operational option is auto-negotiation, auto-sensing, or manually configured. Because many different forms of Ethernet can be run over a twisted-pair cable, many manufacturers enable a single adapter to support more than one specification. For example, most NICs support both 10BaseT and 100BaseTX. Further, at 100BaseTX, they support both full- and half-duplex modes. So when these cards are plugged into a hub, the hub and the NIC have to agree on which specification they are going to use to communicate.

The auto-negotiation process is defined in IEEE 802.3u section 28 and allows the node and hub or switch to automatically determine the highest common denominator. IEEE 802.3 section 28B.3 lists the following modes that auto-negotiation supports (in order of preference):

- 100BaseT Full-duplex
- 100BaseT4
- 100BaseT Half-duplex
- 10BaseT Full-duplex
- 10BaseT Half-duplex

(Note that 100BaseT4 does not support a full-duplex mode.)

The process uses a test signal specified in 10BaseT. This signal is called a Normal Link Pulse (NLP). If a node receives this signal, it assumes the sender is only capable of 10BaseT. If it receives a Fast Link Pulse (FLP), which is a special group of these signals arranged to form a code word, then the node knows the sender is capable of whatever the code word indicates.

In auto-negotiation, both the node and the hub or switch exchange these signals. In auto-sensing, the device only listens and configures itself to match its peer node. Manual configuration, of course, is set by a human and overrides any negotiation.

TOKEN RING TECHNOLOGIES

In a Token Ring architecture, data flows in only one direction. If a station wants to send a frame to its upstream neighbor, it must actually send it to its downstream neighbor, which in turn sends it to its downstream neighbor, and so on, until it eventually wraps all the way around the ring and is finally received by the destination. But the frame has not finished its journey because only the sender can remove the frame from the ring. The destination node regenerates the token just like the other nodes on the ring and sends it on around, except it flags a single bit in the header that indicates the frame was successfully received. When the source receives the frame, if this bit is checked, it knows the frame was delivered successfully. If not, it can continue retransmitting the frame. This is effectively a built-in acknowledgment.

Fiber Distributed Data Interface (FDDI)

Fiber Distributed Data Interface (FDDI) is an ANSI standard that uses a token-based, ring access method. The FDDI's topology is logically and physically a ring, but physically it can also be a star configuration. Yet instead of one ring like IBM's Token Ring, FDDI uses dual, counter-rotating rings. The secondary ring is only used if the primary fails. The rings operate at a rate of 100 Mbps, but they can connect up to 500 dual-attached stations in a 100-km network. Because of the expense of two rings, it is possible to attach a station to an FDDI network by only one cable. This setup is referred to as a *single-attached station*.

Note: By segmenting the ring, two rings can be combined, enabling 1000 stations to be attached, so be sure to clarify whether the ring is segmented if you are asked what the maximum number of stations is.

In a token-based system, only the node with the token may transmit data onto the network. When an FDDI-attached station wants to transmit, it waits until the token arrives. Once it arrives, it removes the token from the ring, stopping the token passing process. This way, it knows that no other device on the network will attempt to transmit. There is no such thing as a collision in a token-based network. The FDDI setup handles contention for network resources by using a timed-token protocol. When a station is inserted into the ring, it negotiates the amount of network access it will have. It is guaranteed this time. In the timed-token scheme, the station can begin transmitting as soon as it captures the token. It can continue transmitting until the timer expires or it has no more frames to transmit. It then sends the token to its downstream neighbor.

The FDDI system also uses MAC addresses and the IEEE 802.2 LLC sublayer, just like Ethernet and Token Ring. One difference, however, is that the MAC specification calls for two reserved bits. Even though Ethernet implements only the I/G bit, FDDI implements both the I/G bit and the U/L bit. The U/L bit indicates whether an address is locally administered or universally administered. This enables network administrators to change the MAC addresses to some internal scheme, at which point they are responsible, instead of the IEEE and the manufacturer, for making sure that no duplicates exist.

In the source address field, where Ethernet always starts the MAC address with a zero, FDDI uses the first bit as a Routing Information Indicator (RII). The RII field indicates whether source routing information is present in the Routing Information Field (RIF). FDDI rarely uses source routing.

A major caveat with FDDI (and Token Ring) is that these setups transmit bytes in a different order than Ethernet does. Specifically, FDDI and Token Ring transmit the bits in a byte in the order in which they appear, whereas Ethernet reverses the bits, sending the right-most bit first. This can cause major problems when you are trying to bridge frames between FDDI and Ethernet because the MAC addresses will be reversed.

Another important distinction is that an FDDI frame can hold up to 4500 (4472) bytes of data. This can make FDDI much more efficient than Ethernet, but it can also cause a significant amount of delay while other stations wait on this frame to be processed. And, of course, if an FDDI frame is bridged onto an Ethernet network, whose maximum size is 1500 bytes of data, fragmentation can be a problem.

Token-based networks, including FDDI and Token Ring, use a Ring Monitor to perform management functions on the ring; however, FDDI differs from Token Ring in that FDDI distributes the Ring Monitor role amongst a number of devices, whereas a single node on each Token-Ring network is designated the Active Monitor.

Unlike Ethernet, each FDDI node employs several timers, including:

- *Target token rotational timer* (TTRT), which is set during ring initialization and represents the delay of the ring

- *Token rotational timer* (TRT), which measures the time it takes the token to traverse the ring

- *Token holding timer* (THT), which sets the amount of time a node can hold the token before releasing it to the next station

- *Valid transmission timer* (TVX), which is calculated from the time it would take to send the largest possible frame (4500 bytes) around the largest possible ring (200 km). This timer is used to allow nodes to reinitialize faster.

These timers are used to reinitialize the ring in the event it takes more than twice the TTRT for a frame to traverse the ring. FDDI also uses 4B5B encoding, like Ethernet, but does not use Manchester. As a technology, FDDI was well received and generally implemented as a backbone or to connect a number of high-bandwidth, mission-critical servers because of its speed, distance limitations, and inherent redundancy. However, FDDI has been all but replaced by Gigabit Ethernet and other technologies.

IBM's Token Ring and IEEE 802.5

Token Ring was originally created by IBM and later standardized in IEEE 802.5 in 1985. As the name suggests, it is a token-based technology that is logically a ring, although it can be somewhat confusing physically. This is because the electrical circuit used is physically a ring, in that it must pass through each device, in a big loop. But it looks like a star because all the cables are typically run from each node back to a hub. It is generally acceptable to refer to it as a ring or a star topology for this reason.

Like Ethernet and FDDI, Token Ring uses the MAC system of addressing, and, like FDDI, bytes are transmitted in the order in which they are written. Originally,

Token Ring supported ring speeds of 4 Mbps and 16 Mbps. Recent work has been done on 100-Mbps Token Ring, but this has not been widely adopted, given that it's almost two orders of magnitude slower than ATM and Ethernet.

Token Ring uses differential Manchester Encoding, which is slightly different from the Manchester Encoding used by Ethernet. In differential Manchester Encoding, it is possible to transition the voltage at the beginning of the bit-time, just like regular Manchester does at the middle of the bit-time. The presence of a transition indicates a one, while the absence of a transition indicates a zero. The direction of the transition at either the beginning or middle of a bit-time does not matter.

The format of a Token Ring frame is considerably more complex than Ethernet because several fields are allowed to vary in size (see Table 3-7) and the format supports Source Routing information.

Table 3-7   Token Ring Frame Format

1 Byte	1 Byte	1 Byte	6 Bytes*	6 Bytes*	2–18 Bytes	1 Byte
Starting Delimiter	Access Control	Frame Control	Destination Address	Source Address	Optional Routing Information	Destination Service Access
1 Byte	1 or 2 Bytes	Variable	1 Byte	4 Bytes	1 Byte	
Source Service Access	Control Fields	Payload	Ending Delimiter	Frame Check Sequence	Frame Status	

* The specification allows both the destination and source addresses to be two bytes or six bytes, but the two-byte source address is never used. The token itself only has three fields, as shown in Table 3-8.

The maximum size of a Token Ring frame is also complicated. The maximum is usually 4096 bytes or 4500 bytes or 4472 bytes. But, in reality, the maximum frame size is a function of the speed of the ring and the Token Hold Time (THT). Thus on a 16-Mbps ring, with the maximum hold time, it is possible to have a 17,800-byte frame.

Although Token Ring uses a Ring Monitor concept, like FDDI, a Token Ring network will designate only one station to be the Active Monitor and one station to be the Standby Monitor, in case the Active Monitor fails. This station acts as a source of timing information and provides a number of ring-maintenance functions.

Table 3-8   The Three Fields of a Token

1 Byte	1 Byte	1 Byte
Starting Delimiter	Access Control	Ending Delimiter

An example of this would be the removal of a continuously circulating frame and token generation. Another function, which is done by all stations, is called *beaconing*. This happens when any station detects a problem with the network, such as a broken cable. The beaconing process is used to define a failure domain and send the rest of the network into an auto-reconfiguration process.

For the auto-reconfiguration process to work, each station has to know its Nearest Active Upstream Neighbor (NAUN). To get this information, a process called *ring polling* occurs once every 7 seconds. Like Ethernet and FDDI, the IEEE 802.5 standard uses the IEEE 802.2 LLC protocols. Token Ring also has a prioritization process that allows some stations access to the token more often than others. Part of this process requires that the token itself has a priority, and every station on the ring has its own priority. Stations can capture the token only if the current priority of the token is lower than their priority. Once a station is finished with the token, it adjusts the priority back to what it was originally.

The source routing feature of Token Ring enables several rings to be connected via bridges. Each bridge and each ring is given a number. If a node wishes to communicate with another node, it sends out an All Routes Explorer (ARE) frame, which is picked up by the bridge and placed on all adjacent rings. As it does this, it records the ring number and its bridge number in the ARE frame. This process repeats until the destination eventually sees the frame. The destination marks the frame and reverses the process. When the ARE finally makes it back to the source, it will have a record of every bridge and ring that was crossed to make the round-trip. If there are multiple paths, the source will receive an ARE for each possible path. When the source is ready to send its data to the destination, it evaluates all the AREs it received and places the shortest one in the Routing Information Field (RIF) of the Token Ring header. When the bridge receives this frame, it reads the RIF field and forwards the frame to the next ring recorded in the RIF field.

Although somewhat cumbersome and not very scalable, this source routing feature enables hosts to be very explicit with respect to how they want their frames handled. Also note that this entire process is bridging and not routing. Source routing is typically used with nonroutable protocols, such as IBM's NetBIOS and SNA.

OTHER LAN PROTOCOLS

Although more than 99 percent of the LAN protocols in use are of the types discussed in the preceding sections, there are many others. Some standards, such as IEEE 802.4 Token Bus, never made it off the drawing boards, whereas others, such as IBM's Baseband, Bus & Tag, and ARCNet, lacked the ability to expand and were subsequently abandoned. Many newer technologies, such as Universal Serial Bus (USB) and Firewire (IEEE 1394) are gaining acceptance rapidly. Of course, there are many older technologies still in use, such as serial links (the COM port in your PC) and Fibre-Channel, which is primarily used in storage area networks. And there are technologies such as Enterprise Systems Connection (ESCON), which are used almost exclusively in mainframes. This section briefly describes a few of these technologies.

ARCNet was a briefly popular baseband protocol during the 1980s. It used a frequency-shifting method of encoding. Basically in a given bit time, one complete cycle represents a one whereas two complete cycles represent a zero. ARCNet is also a token-based protocol that is extremely simple. Logically, it is a ring, and it is deterministic, like IBM's Token Ring. Packet sizes range from 0 to 507 bytes.

IEEE 802.4 Token Bus is very similar to ARCNet in that it was created in the 1980s (primarily by General Motors), is a token-based protocol, and it uses the same frequency-shifting encoding method, except that it is a broadband protocol instead of a baseband protocol. But, unlike ARCNet, 802.4 is extremely complex, with several hundred pages in the specification. Further, it behaves like a logical ring but is a bus. It supported speeds of 5 and 10 Mbps. General Motors gave it the name Manufacturing Automation Protocol.

Enterprise Systems Connection (ESCON) technology is a channel attachment technology created by IBM in 1990 to replace the company's copper-based Bus & Tag (for IBM, Enterprise = mainframes). ESCON uses fiber-optic cable with a maximum single link of 3 km (without repeating). ESCON provides two main types of channels called *byte-multiplexor* and *block-multiplexor*. The maximum bandwidth of a single channel is 18.6 Mbps (or 148.8 Mbps) and can be maintained up to a distance of 8 km.

Wide Area Network Technologies

Most wide area network (WAN) technologies differ dramatically from their LAN counterparts in several ways:

- They are typically designed with the carriers in mind—who often need to connect tens of thousands of customers—so they are extremely scalable.
- The Physical layer usually has a maximum distance between 2 and 40 mi.
- They are specified at many different speeds, from 56 Kbps or less up to 10 Gbps.
- They often use multiplexing to carry several logical circuits over a single physical circuit.

As you read about these technologies, a little perspective may help you understand the decisions the designers have made. Specifically, where most of the LAN technologies are sold by the box—that is, a customer buys an Ethernet or Token Ring hub, some cables and adapters for their PCs, and is free to do what he or she wants—the WAN technologies were designed to be leased by the circuit—where the customer pays monthly for the circuit, plus pays a usage fee based on the amount of traffic sent over the carrier's network.

FRAME RELAY

Frame Relay began in 1988, when ISDN developers realized that the Link Access Protocol-D (LAPD), which was used to provide signaling for the D channel of an ISDN circuit, could be used for far more. This resulted in the ITU-T-approved recommendation I.122 "Framework for additional packet mode bearer services." Several ANSI and ITU-T standards make up this protocol, and half of these are shared with ISDN, so there is no single place to view the entire standard as with the IEEE protocols. But a good place to start is with the Frame Relay Forum and the ITU-T standards Q.922 and Q.933. The Frame Relay Forum (www.frforum. com) is a nonprofit organization made up of approximately 300 companies, which promotes Frame Relay and publishes Implementation Agreements. These agreements detail how certain problems will be handled, such as Switched Virtual Circuits (SVCs), fragmentation, voice traffic, and more.

Frame Relay is based on a concept called a virtual circuit (VC). A virtual circuit is a bidirectional path through the network that is defined in software. Virtual circuits were explained briefly in the ATM section of Chapter 2. The primary benefit of Frame Relay is that many virtual circuits can be used across a single physical connection.

For instance, as shown in Fig. 3-2, a company's headquarters needs to communicate with three remote offices. Instead of leasing three point-to-point circuits to connect each of these three offices, a single circuit connects each to the Frame Relay network, and three virtual circuits are used. From layer 3 up, the virtual circuits are completely transparent so that as far as the hosts on the network are concerned, there really are three physical circuits.

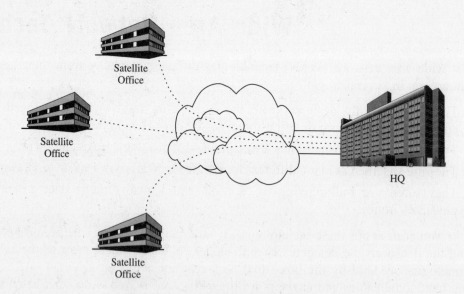

Fig. 3-2.　A sample Frame Relay Network.

Frame Relay accomplishes this feat by using Data Link Connection Identifiers (DLCI)—10-bit numbers that are locally significant. That means that the DLCI on one of the virtual circuits at the headquarters in Figure 3-2 could be the same number as the DLCI on that virtual circuit at the satellite office, or it could be a completely different number. It doesn't matter. But each of the three virtual circuits on the link at the headquarters must be different. The Frame Relay header is shown in Table 3-9.

Table 3-9   A Frame Relay Header

6 Bits	1 Bit	1 Byte	4 Bits	1 Bit	1 Bit	1 Bit	1 Bit
DLCI	CR	Ext. Bit	DLCI	FECN	BECN	DE	EA

These fields are:

- The first part of the DLCI.
- A Command/Response bit indicates whether this is a command or a response.
- An Extension Bit allows a three- or four-byte header for expanding address space if required.
- The second part of the DLCI.
- The Forward Explicit Congestion Notification bit tells the device receiving this frame that congestion was encountered.
- The Backward Explicit Congestion Notification bit is set by a switch in the Frame Relay network to let the receiving device know that frames the receiver is transmitting are causing congestion.
- The Discard Eligible bit indicates that this frame should be discarded first in the event of congestion.
- The Extension bit allows a three- or four-byte header.

Virtual circuits come in two flavors: Permanent Virtual Circuit and Switched Virtual Circuit. A Permanent Virtual Circuit, or PVC, is manually configured. In a Switched Virtual Circuit, or SVC, when a node has data to send, the Frame Relay network sets up a virtual circuit on the fly (the SVC) and then data is transmitted across it. When it is done, after a period of inactivity, it is torn down or removed. In this way, the Frame Relay network can be extremely flexible because devices can be moved without having to manually reconfigure the virtual paths.

SWITCHED MULTIMEGABIT DATA SERVICE (SMDS)

Switched Multimegabit Data Service (SMDS) is a public, packet-switched network that is primarily used for sending large amounts of data sporadically. Switched Multimegabit Data Service resembles the Public Switched Telephone Network (PSTN) in that companies are assigned addresses that are unique, 10-digit numbers. Unlike Frame Relay, there are no Virtual Circuits. The path through the network is completely dynamic, so that any company can send to any other company without configuring circuits. Because SMDS packets contain up to 7168 bytes, most common LAN frames can be sent without fragmentation.

INTEGRATED SERVICES DIGITAL NETWORK (ISDN)

Integrated Services Digital Network (ISDN) is a set of ITU-T standards for the transmission of digital data, primarily over standard copper telephone line. This service is quite complex but very flexible. ISDN has two service levels: Basic Rate Interface (BRI) and Primary Rate Interface (PRI). These services use two types of channels: "B" channels and "D" channels. The B channels provide 64 Kbps and are used to transport either voice or data. In a Basic Rate Interface, there are two B channels and one D channel, which is 16 Kbps. The D channel is used to carry control and signaling information. In the Primary Rate Interface (PRI), there are 23 B channels at 64 Kbps each, and 1 D channel at 64 Kbps.

In fact, there are several channel types, including A, B, C, D, E, and H, but B and D are by far the most commonly used in the United States.

Note: Although most medium-sized or larger organizations in the United States have at least one PRI, it is very common to hear the term "an ISDN connection" used to refer only to a BRI.

In a typical environment, a BRI is used to carry one voice and one data circuit into a small office or home, and a PRI is used to carry 23 channels of voice or some combination of 23 channels of voice and data. BRIs are usually used in a "dial-up" capacity, where an ISDN modem only connects to the service provider (and generates toll charges) when there is data to send. The PRI is usually a permanent connection.

ISDN is implemented in a complex series of devices. The devices are connected with interfaces that are labeled "reference points." Starting from the carrier's network working backward to the end user, we have an ISDN switch connected to a Network Terminating device 1 (NT1) via the U interface. The NT1 connects to an NT2 via the T interface. The NT2 connects to a data terminal (TE1) or an ISDN phone (TE1) using the S reference point. In practice, the S and T reference points are often combined in a piece of hardware and labeled S/T. The interfaces are:

Data Terminal–S–NT2–T–NT1–U–ISDN Switch

There is actually one more reference point: the R reference point, which is used to connect a non-ISDN capable device to an ISDN Terminal Adapter (TA). The terminal adapter has an S reference point that allows a non-ISDN device to communicate across an ISDN network as follows:

Non–ISDN Terminal–R–TA–S–NT2–T–NT1–U–ISDN Switch

SYNCHRONOUS OPTICAL NETwork (SONET)

Synchronous Optical NETwork (SONET) is a set of standards defining the rates and formats for optical networks specified in ANSI T1.105, ANSI T1.106, and ANSI T1.117. The Synchronous Digital Hierarchy (SDH) is a similar standard defined by the ITU-T and used primarily in Europe. The frame format used by SONET is Synchronous Transport Module (STM). STM-1 is the base level signal, which is 155 Mbps and is carried in an OC-3 signal. This is said to be hierarchical because smaller signal levels can be multiplexed together to form larger ones.

An STS-1 frame is nine rows by 90 bytes. The first three bytes of each row are overhead that contain framing bits. Line overhead is transmitted inside the payload at a floating position determined by the pointer in the Section overhead. A single

STS-1 frame is transmitted in 125 µsec, which is 8000 frames per second. (At 810 bytes per frame×8000 frames per second = 51.84 Mbps.)

There are many higher levels, such as STS-3, which is eight rows by 270 bytes, with nine bytes of overhead bytes per row. SONET is primarily used in Metropolitan Area Networks (MAN), where the Local Exchange Carrier (LEC) runs fiber-optic cable in loops around the city. This network technology is ideal because the ring may run at a speed of OC-12 (622 Mbps), and four businesses may each lease a circuit, which appears to them as an OC-3 (155 Mbps). The action of carving out bandwidth from a circuit to create another circuit is called "provisioning."

SONET has an additional benefit in that it has inherent redundancy very similar to FDDI. By employing a dual, counter-rotating ring architecture, the ring can immediately compensate for a fiber cut or single equipment failure. This property is sometimes referred to as "self-healing."

POINT-TO-POINT PROTOCOL (PPP)

The Point-to-Point Protocol (PPP) is a very significant piece of the networking puzzle. Originally designed to encapsulate IP over serial point-to-point links, PPP now supports many other protocols, such as Novell's IPX and DEC's DECnet. It also has a host of options and features, including IP address management, authentication multiplexing, and like management features, such as configuration, testing, error detection, and so forth. It is commonly used by PCs with modems to dial either the Internet or a corporate network. It is also commonly used in enterprise WANs for 56 K through T1 (1.544 Mbps) links.

PPP consists of a High-level Data Link Control (HDLC), Link Control Protocol (LCP), and a set of protocols called Network Control Protocols (NCPs). High-Level Data Link Control is used to encapsulate datagrams over serial links; it is discussed in the following section. Link Control Protocol establishes, configures, and tests the data-link connection. Network Control Protocol is used to establish and configure one or more network-layer protocols. Point-to-Point Protocol operates between Data Terminal Equipment (DTE) and Data Communications Equipment (DCE) interfaces. The link between these devices must be duplex, and it may operate in either synchronous or asynchronous mode. A PPP frame is shown in Table 3-10.

Table 3-10   A PPP Frame

1 Byte	1 Byte	1 Byte	2 Bytes	Variable	2 or 4 Bytes
Flag	Address	Control	Protocol	Data	FCS

The flag simply marks the beginning of a frame. It is always 01111110 binary. The address field is always 11111111, which is a broadcast address because PPP doesn't define station addresses. The control field is always 00000011, which indicates a connectionless link service similar to LLC1. The data field, of course, contains the datagram, which is theoretically a max of 1500 bytes, but can be changed in some circumstances. The Frame Check Sequence (FCS) is a 16- or 32-bit calculation used to detect errors in the frame. It works just like FCS fields in nearly every other data link protocol described above.

PPP uses the ISO HDLC procedures (ISO 3309-1979), as modified by ISO 3309:1984/PDAD1 "Addendum 1: Start/stop transmission." ISO 3309-1979 is for use in synchronous environments. ISO 3309:1984/PDAD1 is for use in asynchronous environments. ISO 4335-1979/Addendum 1-1979 contains the control procedures and encoding.

HIGH-LEVEL DATA LINK CONTROL (HDLC)

High-level Data Link Control (HDLC) is a derivative of Synchronous Data Link Control (SDLC), which was developed by IBM in the mid-1970s for SNA. SDLC was the first synchronous, bit-oriented link-layer protocol. IBM submitted SDLC for standardization and in typical fashion, ISO modified it and called it HDLC, and the ITU-T modified it and called it Link Access Procedure, Balanced (LAPB). Then the IEEE modified HDLC for LAN environments to create IEEE 802.2.

Understanding HDLC is important because many things, such as PPP, use it. And many others use IEEE 802.2 LLC, including Ethernet, Token Ring, FDDI, and more.

Fundamentally, HDLC's frame format is identical to SDLC's; it is shown in Table 3-11.

Table 3-11   HDLC's Frame Format

1 Byte	1 or 2 Bytes	1 or 2 Bytes	2 Bytes	Variable	2 or 4 Bytes	1 Byte
Flag	Address	Control	Protocol	Data	FCS	Flag

These fields should look familiar from the PPP discussion above. But, unlike PPP, in SDLC and HDLC these fields are actually meaningful. The address field contains the address of the secondary station, which can be a specific address, a group address, or a broadcast address. The control field uses three different formats: I, S, and U. The I, or information, frame carries upper-layer information and control information. The I frame's format is shown in Table 3-12.

The operation of the sequence numbers in these frames is similar to TCP's. A primary station uses the Poll/Final bit to poll the secondary station, which tells it

Table 3-12   The Control Field's I Frame Format

7 Bits	1 Bit	7 Bits	1 Bit
Receive Sequence Number	Poll/Final bit	Send Sequence Number	0

that an immediate response is expected. The secondary station uses this same bit on frames traveling the opposite direction to tell the primary station whether or not this frame is the last frame in its response.

S frames are supervisor frames that provide more control information, such as suspending transmission and acknowledging receipt of I frames. Their format is shown in Table 3-13.

Table 3-13   The Control Field's S Frame Format

7 Bits	1 Bit	7 Bits	1 Bit	1 Bit
Receive Sequence Number	Poll/Final bit	Function code	0	1

U frames (see Table 3-14) are unnumbered. They support control, such as initializing devices. These frames are not sequenced.

Table 3-14   The Control Field's U Frame Format

7 Bits	1 Bit	7 Bits	1 Bit	1 Bit
Function code	Poll/Final bit	Function code	1	1

Whereas SDLC only supports one transport mode, HDLC supports three: Normal Response mode (NRM) is used by SLDC, where the secondary cannot communicate with the primary until given permission. Asynchronous Response Mode (ARM) allows secondaries to initiate communication sans permission. In Asynchronous Balanced Mode (ABM) a given node can be both a primary and a secondary at the same time. This is called "combined mode."

LOGICAL LINK CONTROL (LLC)

Although IEEE's 802.2 Logical Link Control (LLC) specification is primarily used in LANs by IEEE 802.2, IEEE 802.4, IEEE 802.5, and more, we felt it would be better understood after SLDC and HDLC had been explained. LLC provides three types of service called LLC1, LLC2, and LLC3. These service classes offer a wide variety, from fast, low-overhead links with little flow control to slower, reliable, connection-oriented links. The service classes are as follows:

- LLC Type 1 is an unacknowledged, connectionless service. It relies on protocols such as TCP to do any error correcting. Because of this, it is the most common protocol. Essentially, it only provides the Destination Service Access Point and Source Service Access Point fields, which function similar to the Ethertype field in version II Ethernet frames.

- LLC Type 2 is an acknowledged, connection-oriented service. This means that a reliable connection is established between two nodes before any data is transmitted, and once transmitted, every bit is acknowledged. If a bit is missed, LLC Type 2 will resend the frame. This type of service is rarely used.

- LLC Type 3 is a compromise between type 1 and 2. It is acknowledged, but is not connection-oriented.

Wireless Networks

Although wireless networks in the form of AM, FM, and short-wave radio have been around for quite some time, duplex wireless networks supporting voice and data are relatively new and are gaining popularity quickly. As in wired networks, the number of oscillations per second of a wave is called "frequency" and is measured in hertz (Hz). The distance between two adjacent peaks or two adjacent valleys in the wave is the "wavelength," typically represented with the Greek letter lambda (λ).

This section is organized by the type of transmission these networks employ.

RADIO FREQUENCIES

Radio waves are very common in networking because they can travel long distances, pass through walls, and are relatively inexpensive to generate. The behavior of radio waves is also frequency-dependent, such that at high frequencies the waves tend to travel in straight lines and be reflected off obstacles. At low frequencies, however, the waves tend to pass through walls, but they have much shorter distance limitations, so the medium is fairly flexible.

One problem with radio networks is that two devices using the same frequency will interfere with each other. In an attempt to prevent this, the governments of most countries regulate frequencies. In the United States, the FCC is responsible for regulating frequencies. Governments license certain frequency bands to the highest bidder and reserve other bands for low-power public use.

These bands are described in the Table 3-15.

Table 3-15   Radio Frequency Bands

Band Name	Low End	High End
Very Low Frequency (VLF)	3 kHz	30 kHz
Low Frequency (LF)	300 kHz	3 MHz
High Frequency (HF)	3 MHz	30 MHz
Very High Frequency (VHF)	30 MHz	300 MHz
Ultra High Frequency (UHF)	300 MHz	3 GHz

There are many bands with lower frequencies, but these are seldom used because lower frequency translates to lower bandwidth. See Table 3-16.

Table 3-16 Low Radio Frequency Bands

Band Name	Low End	High End
Subaudible (below human hearing range)	1 Hz	30 Hz
Subaudible (audible, but below typical speech range)	30 Hz	300 Hz
Audible (typical speech range)	300 Hz	3000 Hz
Ultrasound (above human hearing, but dogs can still hear)	3 kHz	30 kHz
Ultra High Frequency (UHF)	300 MHz	3 GHz

The bands actually continue above UHF, as listed below, but are seldom used:

- Super High Frequency (SHF)
- Extremely High Frequency (EHF)
- Tremendously High Frequency (THF)

MICROWAVE FREQUENCIES

Microwave is a subset of radio frequencies that is generally considered to begin at 1 GHz and end around 18 GHz. Bands above 18 GHz are typically referred to as "millimeter" wave bands. Most professional and military personnel associate letter designations with bands in the microwave range. These are shown in Table 3-17.

Table 3-17 Microwave Frequency Bands

Band Name	Low End	High End
L-band	1 GHz	1 GHz
S-band	2 GHz	4 GHz
C-band	4 GHz	8 GHz
X-band	8 GHz	12 GHz
Ku-band	12 GHz	18 GHz

The millimeter bands also have letter designations, including K, Ka, W, and others. There is one important type of band to note: the Industrial/Scientific/Medical bands. These do not require government licensing and are open worldwide. These bands fall into the 2.400 to 2.484 GHz frequency range. In the United States and Canada, there are also bands from 902 to 928 MHz and from 5.725 to 5.850 GHz. If you own a cordless phone, it will probably say 900 MHz or 2.4 GHz on it.

One of the most popular wireless LAN technologies is IEEE 802.11b, which operates in the 2.4 GHz range. This standard is very similar to Ethernet at layer 2 but uses Direct Sequence Spread Spectrum (DSSS) at the Physical layer.

INFRARED WAVES

Infrared waves exist between the visible spectrum (that is, the rainbow) and microwave. Infrared technology is typically used in very local settings, such as in remote controls on televisions and VCRs and the infrared ports on most laptop computers. This is because infrared is directional (it has to be pointed in the general vicinity of any device it is communicating with), and because infrared cannot pass through solid objects, notably walls.

On the positive side, these characteristics make infrared technology more secure than the radio and microwave technologies, and the government does not regulate it. The IEEE 802.11b standard also includes a specification using infrared, but this is limited to a distance of 10 m and cannot pass through walls.

Review Questions

3.1   An Ethernet host joins the multicast group 225.128.47.81. The arrival of a frame with what MAC address will cause the NIC to interrupt the CPU?

3.2   A second Ethernet host joins the multicast group 224.1.47.81. The arrival of a frame with what MAC address will cause the NIC to interrupt the CPU?

3.3   How can two adapters, each of which has its own clock, make sure that its clock is exactly the same frequency as the other adapter so that it knows when each bit ends and the next one begins?
   a.   Quantization scheme
   b.   Manchester scheme
   c.   Odd parity scheme
   d.   Timed-token scheme

3.4   How do adapters synchronize their clocks to recognize the first few bits of each frame?
   a.   Using a prefix
   b.   Using a preamble
   c.   Using a synchronization bit

3.5   It is possible for a Token Ring network to have collisions.
   a.   True
   b.   False

3.6   How does Token Ring's differential Manchester Encoding differ from Ethernet's regular Manchester Encoding?

3.7   What is the maximum number of connections that can be multiplexed on a 1.544 Mbps T1 link with Frame Relay using the ANSI Frame Relay encapsulation standard?

3.8   What happens when a frame arrives with the BECN bit set to 1?

3.9   If ISDN is switched, like SMDS, how does data know how to get from one point on the network to another?

3.10   How does ISDN support both voice and data?

3.11   Why do SDLC and HDLC use the terms *primary stations* and *secondary stations*?

3.12   What is the difference between bit rate and baud rate?

Problems

3.1 Demonstrate how the FCS field is populated.

3.2 Calculate the number of bit-times an adapter will wait if it experiences five consecutive collisions.

3.3 Create a diagram of the NRZ, NRZI, and Manchester Encodings for the bit pattern 11010011.

Answers to Review Questions

3.1 01-00-5E-01-2F-51. The first bit of the first byte is always a one. The OUI portion is always 01-00-5E. The last 23 bytes of the IP address (given in decimal in the question) are converted to hex for the answer.

3.2 01-00-5E-01-2F-51. The first bit of the first byte is always a one. The OUI portion is always 01-00-5E. The last 23 bytes of the IP address (given in decimal in the question) are converted to hex for the answer.

3.3 **b,** Manchester scheme

3.4 **a,** using a preamble. The IEEE 802.3 specification includes a preamble that precedes each frame. This preamble is a series of 7 bytes of alternating ones and zeros (that is, 10101010×7) followed by a Starting Delimiter, which is the same as the preamble, but ends with two one bits (that is, 10101011). This series of ones and zeros gives the receiving circuitry time to acquire and synchronize its clock before the real frame begins. When it sees two ones, it knows that the next bit is the first bit of the frame.

3.5 **b,** false. It is impossible to have collisions on a Token Ring network.

3.6 Regular Manchester Encoding uses a transition from a higher voltage to a lower voltage to represent a one, and a transition from a lower voltage to a higher voltage to represent a zero. In differential Manchester Encoding, the presence or lack of a transition at the bit-time boundary represents a zero or one, respectively.

3.7 The DLCI field is 10 bits. That means the total number of Virtual Circuits on a link is 2^{10} or 1024. The link speed or type is irrelevant. Other vendors have proprietary formats that may hold more, and the address extension field can also be used to add a second byte to the header.

3.8 In theory, the device would reduce its transmission rate until incoming frames no longer had the BECN bit set to one. However, this behavior is optional and most Frame Relay equipment manufacturers allow administrators to decide whether the device will respond to BECNs or not.

3.9 ISDN uses addresses like SMDS (and the telephone network) as well. Each B channel on a BRI gets a SPID. This identifies the interface to the ISDN switch. The interface is then configured to dial a number that is used to route the data through the ISDN network.

3.10 Conveniently, an ISDN B channel is exactly the size required by Pulse Code Modulation (PCM), which is 64 Kbps. This extremely simple and low-latency method of converting analog audio signals to a stream of binary ones and zeros allows a single call to occupy a single channel.

Because ISDN is digital, packetized data traffic can also easily traverse the network as well. And since each channel has a fixed bandwidth, the channels don't interfere with each other, so data from one channel will not delay data or voice on another channel.

3.11 These terms date back to the terminal/host days. Recall that IBM created this protocol for communication between the host, which is typically an enterprise-class mainframe, where all the processing was done, and the dumb terminals or other devices such as printers, which had no intelligence of their own. Because of this, control was definitely centralized, which is reflected in the protocol's design.

3.12 Baud rate is the number of pulses per second that are sent on a given wire. The bit rate is the number of bits (ones or zeros) of data that are transmitted on a given wire per second.

Solutions to Problems

3.1 The Frame Check Sequence field stores the result of the Cyclical Redundancy Check (CRC) calculation. The CRC is based on a polynomial code with coefficients of 0 and 1 only. For example, in a frame with k number of bits, the bits represent the coefficients of a polynomial with k terms ranging from x^{k-1} to x^0. The byte 10110010 would result in the following:

$$1x^7 + 0x^6 + 1x^5 + 1x^4 + 0x^3 + 0x^2 + 1x^1 + 0x^0$$

or
$$x^7 + x^5 + x^4 + x^1$$

Modulo 2 polynomial arithmetic is then performed. First, the sender and receiver agree on a generator polynomial, which we'll represent as $G(x)$. This value is determined in the protocol's specification. For instance, in some protocols this number is 16 bits, whereas in others it is 32 bits.

The objective is to take a frame and calculate a checksum. This checksum is then appended to the frame (in the FCS field) and when received, it is divided by $G(x)$. If there is a remainder, an error has occurred in the frame. If not, then the frame is delivered to the next layer.

3.2 The formula for this is as follows:

$$0 < r < 2^k$$

where:
$$k = \min(n, 10)$$

In this case, $n = 5$, so $k = 5$ (because $5 < 10$), so $2^k = 32$. Therefore a random amount of time will be chosen in the range of 0 to 32. If more collisions occur, the range grows exponentially, all the way up to the range of 0 to 2^{10}, which is 1024 bit times.

3.3   This diagram is shown in Figure 3-3.

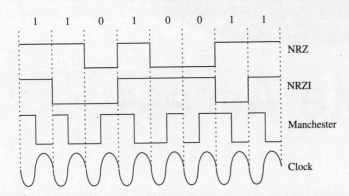

Fig. 3-3. A diagram of the NRZ, NRZI, and Manchester Encodings for the bit pattern 11010011.

CHAPTER 4

Multiple Access

One of the critical needs of a network is the coordination and management of communication between the different devices. Imagine sitting in a room with 50 other people who are all talking at the same time. Maybe you have already experienced something like this at a party or gathering. You might be able to communicate with one or two people at a time by shouting, or perhaps there is too much interference and your conversation ceases. If you extend this analogy to a network, there would be no effective throughput of information, and the network would be essentially useless. Furthermore, on a network, if two or more packets encounter each other at the same place on the transmission media, a collision occurs and the information is lost. Since signals travel at about 70 percent of the speed of light, two signals transmitted by different devices on the media will eventually reach the same point and collide. When packets collide, the information in either packet is no longer useful. Technologies need to be in place that reduce the number of collisions while at the same time maximizing the number of messages sent per second without introducing delays for the devices attempting to transmit. How to accomplish these network communication goals is called the *multiple-access problem*. One of the primary roles of the Open Systems Interconnection (OSI) Data-Link layer is controlling access to the media and coordination of communicating entities so all devices get a chance to communicate.

Design Issues

During the initial development and implementation stages of networks, connections and communications were point-to-point or mesh. In a point-to-point network there is a dedicated transmission link between two devices. This type of design has several advantages. First, the capacity and other physical properties of the connections can be different between each point-to-point link. Because the two devices on a point-to-point connection have exclusive access to the media, they can decide how and when to transmit without the need for negotiation or contention within the transmission media. The remaining details on a point-to-point network, such as the format of the packets, the maximum packet size, and error detection or correction schemes, can be quickly decided upon by both parties. Finally, it is much easier to secure and protect the information on a point-to-point network than on a shared network. However, point-to-point connections are not practical on today's networks. For instance, the expense of physically installing the necessary cables to connect every device to every other device with a dedicated line would be enormous. In addition, there are limits to the number of physical connections that could be made to a system. This means you would be able to be connected to only a handful of other devices. For example, take a look at Figure 4-1 and notice the number of cables (and connections) that are necessary between a three-, four-, and five-device point-to-point network.

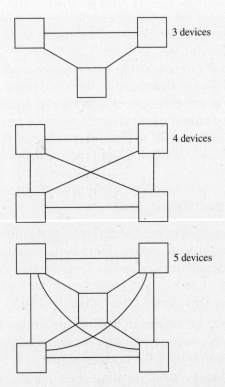

Fig. 4-1.   Point-to-point network physical cable connections.

The number of connections required for a point-to-point network can be expressed by the following equation:

$$\text{Number of direct connections} = (N^2 - N)/2$$

The value of N in the above equation is the number of devices on the network. For example, a network with five systems requires 10 connections and a 10-device network needs 45 connections. In fact, for each system added to the network, the number of additional connections required rises by $N - 1$. So to go from a 10-node network of 45 connections to an 11-node network requires 10 more connections.

Can you imagine what the Internet would look like if it was a point-to-point network?

Because of these issues, network transmission media used on today's local networks is shared. The terms *broadcast*, *multi-access channels*, and *random channels* are all used to refer to transmission media that is shared among multiple devices. The evolution from the original point-to-point networks began in the late 1960s and the early 1970s with the development of the local area network, or LAN. The new designs created an environment where the transmission media is shared. Once you introduce a shared media, there needs to be some method to determine which device has access to the media, at what time, and for how long. In addition, each device needs to have a chance to transmit so all devices can communicate in a timely fashion. These problems gave rise to several different LAN types that primarily differ in physical aspects such as modulation techniques and voltages, and schemes such as how the media is shared. The protocols that have been defined that determine how devices gain access to the media are found at the Media Access Control (MAC) sublayer of the OSI Data-Link layer.

Overall, point-to-point transmissions are typically used on wide area connections (except satellite), and long-distance connections and point-to-point links are used on LANs. Although there are economic advantages to sharing the same media on a LAN, this is not necessarily the best choice for a wide area network, or WAN, link. For example, methodologies used to determine access to shared media take time and bandwidth, which on a WAN link can add considerable delays and reduce bandwidth.

The multiple-access problem appears in several different communication areas that are identified in the following list:

- *Wired local networks*. Wired local networks typically use a twisted-pair copper cable as the transmission media. Fiber-optic cables are also used on local networks. The different devices on the network share the same cable or "ether." Two common solutions to allow multiple access for wired local networks are Ethernet and Fiber Distributed Data Interface (FDDI).

- *Cellular telephony*. In cellular telephony networks, cellular phones that are within the same cell communicate with the same base station and therefore share the "space" and portions of the radio spectrum.

- *Wireless local networks*. Wireless local networks are becoming more common, especially among laptop and notebook computer users. The wireless network has fixed transceivers, and all the devices within the range of the transceiver share the same radio or infrared frequency "spaces." One solution to the wireless network multiple-access problem is the IEEE 802.11 standard.

- *Packet radio*. Packet radio can be used for distance links between wired local networks. Packet radio's distance is greater than the distances found on wireless local network devices.

- *Satellites*. Satellites are primarily geostationary, and all communicating devices transmit in the same "space" to the stationary satellite. There are also low-earth satellites, which do not stay at a fixed point above the earth, but transmitting devices in the same area will communicate simultaneously to the current low-earth satellite that is within range.

The two main design schemes for addressing communications on a broadcast media are as follows:

- Distributed and centralized design
- Circuit-mode and packet-mode-design

In the following sections we discuss both of these design strategies.

DISTRIBUTED AND CENTRALIZED DESIGN

In a centralized design, one of the systems on the network acts as a moderator that polls each device in order to determine what device needs to send data on the transmission media. This method provides a very ordered access to the media, but it also introduces delays because even if a device does not want to communicate, the moderator must still ask each device its status. In addition, if the device that is providing the polling service should fail, then none of the devices can communicate. An example of a centralized system is cellular telephony. Each cell phone's transmission is coordinated by the base station.

The second design employs a distributed environment where a device that needs to communicate does so as soon as the current communicating device stops sending data. But devices that are waiting to communicate and are "listening" for the end of the current conversation are not aware of other devices that are also listening. If two listening devices "jump" onto the transmission media at the same time, their packets of data will collide. The entities attempting to communicate will continue to collide because they are not receiving acknowledgments, so they will continue to resend the information. An example of a distributed design is Ethernet.

CIRCUIT-MODE AND PACKET-MODE DESIGN

The second design category addresses the type of workload carried by the transmission media. There are two types of traffic patterns experienced on a network—continuous and bursty. *Continuous data stream* means a smooth, constant rate of traffic, such as voice conversations on a telephone network. *Bursty transmissions* refer to sudden, unpredictable increases in network traffic. For continuous traffic patterns, allocating a portion of the transmission media to the devices makes sense. In those cases, you don't need to involve the devices in negotiating access to the media. This multiple-access design method is referred to as circuit mode. This approach does not work well for bursts of transmissions, which need as much of the communication link as possible. If the transmission media is divided into dedicated portions for each device, when a device is not communicating, its portion of the media is not used and stands idle. Therefore when bursts of traffic appear, these idle segments cannot be used, and the transmission media is not efficiently used. Bursty traffic could be better handled if the access method provided a means for the devices to negotiate use of the transmission media. This type of multiple-access design approach is referred to as packet mode.

Implementation Issues

The actual development and usage of a multiple-access method is determined by the network environment. There are three constraints to consider for multiple-access implementations: spectrum scarcity, radio link properties, and the so-called "a" constraint.

The spectrum scarcity issue is applicable to wireless networks, cell phones, and packet radio links. The entire electromagnetic spectrum is not available for network communications. A good portion of the available frequencies are already in use by other systems, and government regulations specify what frequencies are permitted for network transmissions. For example, there are only a few frequencies that can be used for radio transmissions of 1 to 10 mi. Therefore there are a limited number of frequencies that can be used for multiple-access designs.

The second consideration, radio link properties, addresses the physical issues of radio waves and the environment. A condition called "fading" occurs when interference from items such as thick trees and brush, hills and mountains, and moving obstacles like trains causes the signal to be degraded. There is also the condition called "multipath interference," which arises when a receiving antenna gets the same signal from multiple sources. This causes a lot of bit errors at the receiver, which must have error-control mechanisms in place to handle this condition. Another problem, called the "hidden terminal problem," can cause multiple devices to transmit at the same time. This problem is created when a transmitting device is "heard" by only some of the devices in the same area. Thus, if a device is transmitting and another device does not hear the transmitting device, it may deduce the media is clear and begin to transmit. Another category of radio link problems is called the "capture" or "near-far" problem. In this situation, the receiver is getting information from more than one device, but one of the transmitting devices is so "loud" that the other devices' signals are "drowned" out and the receiver does not get the "soft-spoken" device's information. Sometimes the term *capture* is used when a strong transmitter "captures" the "attention" of the receiver. In some cases, this is good if the data received from the different devices is the same. But if the information is different, mechanisms need to be in place to allow equal access to the media for all transmitting devices.

The third constraint, which is referred to as "a," has an impact on packet-mode networks. The parameter a is defined as

$$a = D/T$$

In the equation, D refers to the maximum transmission propagation delay in seconds. The element T is the travel time in seconds of an average-sized packet. Examining the equation reveals that a represents the number of packets, or the portion of a packet, that can be placed on the communication media by the transmitting device before any of the bits are received by the device that is the farthest away. On wired and wireless networks, cell phones and packet radio links, a is usually small at around 0.01. As the speed of the transmission path increases, the value of T decreases, resulting in larger values for a. On some fast wired networks, the value of a may be 1, which means the transmitting device has sent out an entire packet before the receiver gets any of the transmitted packets. On other networks that are very fast, such as satellite links where the speed may be 500 Mbps, the value of a may reach 100. The value of a comes into play when we are dealing with collisions. When a is small, the different transmitting devices realize "quickly" that collisions are occurring and can rapidly react to the situation. But on networks where a is large, it takes much longer for transmitting devices to realize that collisions are happening. In these cases, it makes more sense to create a solution that helps stations avoid collisions instead of only helps detect them.

Performance Considerations

As multiple-access schemes are being designed, it is important to measure their performance to determine if the solutions are practical. The different performance parameters that are measured include

- Normalized throughput or goodput
- Mean delay
- Stability
- Fairness

Goodput, or normalized throughput, is the portion of the capacity of the transmission link that is carrying non-retransmitted packets. When time is lost to overhead introduced by the protocols that are in use, packet collisions and retransmissions are not counted toward the goodput performance value. If there were no loss of packets on the media owing to congestion or other factors, the goodput value for an ideal environment would be 1.0. Most protocols and systems in use on today's networks have between 1.0 and 0.95 goodput values. To calculate the goodput value you need the following information:

- Speed/bandwidth of the communication link
- The size of an average packet
- The functioning peak throughput of the transmission link

As an example, we will calculate the goodput of a 10-Mbps network that has an average packet length of 125 bytes whose peak throughput is 8500 packets per second. These values produce a carrying capacity of 10,000 packets per second. This is derived from

$$10,000 \text{ packets/second} = 10,000,000 \text{ bps}$$
$$(125 \text{ byte packet} \times 8 \text{ bits/packet})$$

At a peak throughput of 8500, the goodput value of 0.85 is calculated as follows:

$$0.85 \text{ goodput} = 8500 \text{ packets/second}$$
$$10,000 \text{ packets/second}$$

The mean delay is the mean time that a packet waits at the sender before it can be transmitted, plus the time it takes to transmit the packet. Factors that affect this value include the workload of the sending device and the transmission media characteristics.

The stability of a multiple-access technique refers to the ability of the method to handle increases in the amount of traffic without affecting the throughput. As more and more devices communicate on the transmission media, the chances of collisions increase, and when a threshold is reached, the system becomes unusable and is no longer stable. If the multiple-access technique includes the ability to adjust to situations reaching an overload, then the method can successfully handle traffic increases.

The final performance item is fairness, which means that every device that wants to transmit has equal access to the media within a specified time frame.

Base Technology

Base technology is one of the steps used to solve the multiple-access problem. The role of this portion of the solution is to isolate traffic from the other devices on the same communication channel. Two approaches to traffic isolation are time domain and frequency domain. The second role of base technology is to provide methods for allocating the time or frequency transmission resources to each of the devices on the network.

FREQUENCY DIVISION MULTIPLE ACCESS (FDMA)

Frequency division (or domain) multiple access (FDMA) incorporates dividing the available frequencies among the devices so each entity transmits and receives on a frequency different from that of the other devices. This is a fairly simple technology, and it works well on analog communication links. Each frequency band is separated by guard bands, so there is some separation between the transmissions in the event of slight variations in frequencies. In a wireless environment, such as cell phones, there may be hundreds and thousands of communications occurring, and there are not enough frequencies to divide among all the devices. To get around this problem, the size of the cell or geographic area is reduced, the power of the transmissions is reduced, and the same frequencies are reused in different, nonadjacent cells. Although this technique makes more communications possible, it also introduces the problem of how to handle an active communication when the sender moves to another cell. In this case, the sender must change to a different frequency that is used in the adjacent cell. The process of moving from cell to cell is called a "handoff," and the techniques to provide uninterrupted conversations across cell boundaries are complicated.

Frequency division duplex, or FDD, is a frequency division technique that permits two-way or duplex communications. The two communicating devices use different frequencies to obtain the duplex conversation.

TIME DIVISION MULTIPLE ACCESS (TDMA)

In the time domain (or division) multiple-access (TDMA) approach, all stations use the same frequency, and each device is given a time slot and transmits in "order." That is, Computer A transmits, then Computer B, then Computer C, and so on. This is also referred to as a "round-robin" approach. The time allocated for each device can be fixed or variable in length and is called a time slot. At any instance a transmitting device can use only one time slot to send its data, and then the device must wait until its "turn" comes around again. By coordinating station access to the time slots and with proper time synchronization among all the devices, a single communication frequency can be used by all the entities. To achieve proper time synchronization, one of the communicating devices produces a synchronization signal at specific intervals. Most computer networks incorporate TDMA technologies.

Time division multiple access has some advantages over FDMA, which makes TDMA more feasible for computer networks. With TDMA, devices can be dynamically assigned multiple time slots when other devices are idle and do not need the time slot. This method provides for increased throughput on behalf of the transmitting devices. On the other hand, TDMA devices must be properly time synchronized, and a portion of the bandwidth is used for synchronization events instead of for data communications. Approximately 20 to 30 percent of the bandwidth is used for time synchronization and other management processes, such as handling the guard bands. Time division multiple access systems also include handoff issues in wireless implementations.

Time division duplex, or TDD, allows for two-way conversations to exist in a time division scheme. Each communicating device uses alternating time slots to create the duplex conversation.

CODE DIVISION MULTIPLE ACCESS (CDMA)

Another approach to the multiple-access problem is to combine time domain and frequency domain technologies. There are two possible combinations, and we will first discuss frequency-hopping CDMA or FH/CDMA. In this technique, the transmitting device begins sending information on one frequency and then after a short period of time changes to another frequency. Thus the transmitting device hops from frequency to frequency throughout the duration of the conversation. The receiving device must use the same frequency-hopping pattern to be able to properly understand the conversation. In this CDMA scheme, the devices are using both time slots and frequency technologies. The time slot is the amount of time used on a specific frequency, and the frequency element is the usage of different frequencies.

Direct sequence CDMA, or DS/CDMA, is more complicated than FH/CDMA. In this technique, a code word is assigned to represent a binary 1, and each device uses a different code word. For example, one device may use 00101101 to represent a binary 1, while another device uses 10110110 to indicate a binary 1. Each of these code words is transmitted for the same time duration and across different frequencies. Because each of the recipients uses a different code word "dictionary," the recipient's message can be extracted from all the bits spread across the different frequencies. The term "smearing" is used to indicate that a single bit of the sending device has been smeared across different frequencies by using a code word. Each bit in the code word is called a "chip," and the bit rate of the code word is measured in chips/second. The code words used in this scheme must be carefully selected so confusion does not exist among the different devices. Sets of compatible code words that can be used together are said to be "orthogonal."

Because of the nature in which CDMA technologies work across different frequencies, they are also called *spread spectrum transmission methods*. You may wonder why hopping between frequencies and using more bits in a code word to represent a single bit would be advantageous. The answer resides in protecting the data from being picked up and understood by an unauthorized party. If a recipient does not know the different frequencies and code words used, the information cannot be properly deciphered. The first use of spread spectrum techniques was in the military, but the technique is now used on civilian wireless communication channels for the same protection reasons. On the other hand, there are some issues with CDMA. The first issue is the level of complexity needed to implement the features. Second, proper power management is required, and, last, a large band of contiguous frequencies is needed.

Centralized Access

Now that we have covered the different base technologies that can be used in multiple-access solutions, we can address some of the schemes developed for multiple access. The centralized-access method involves a master device that controls access to the transmission media. The other devices in a centralized-access technique are referred to as slaves because they cannot do anything until the master device says so. This type of media access control provides for very ordered and coordinated communications. But if the master device is unavailable or fails, the entire network ceases to communicate. This disruption could be overcome by allowing the slaves to "elect" a new master when the original master fails or is no longer available. But this strategy adds much more complexity to the solution. Another factor to consider is the added delay to each transmission because of the involvement of the master device in each transmission.

Some network physical topologies lead to a centralized-access scheme. A good example is wireless networks, where the transceiver or base station for an area is the centralized device that controls communications. There are three centralized schemes found in usage: circuit mode, polling (packet mode), and reservation (packet mode). Circuit mode is used primarily for cellular and cordless telephone networks.

CIRCUIT-MODE ACCESS

Cellular telephone networks divide each broadcast area into several cells to provide more conversations for the same geographic area. A registration message sent on a control channel is sent to a cell's base station when a cell phone is turned on. The first task encountered by the cell phone is gaining access to the control channel because other phones are also being turned on or need access to the control channel. The multiple-access protocol a cell phone uses to access the control channel is called ALOHA. ALOHA is a packet-mode multiple-access protocol. (ALOHA is discussed in more detail later in this chapter.) Once the registration message is properly interpreted by the base station, circuit-mode multiple-access protocols come into play. Recall that circuit-mode technologies work well for transmissions that operate at a constant rate. Depending on the vendor, the base station will create a communication circuit for the cell phone by using either FDMA, TDMA, or CDMA technologies. Once the cell phone gets its channel, it uses the same channel for the entire conversation and does not need to continuously go through the process of gaining access to the channel.

POLLING OR PACKET-MODE ACCESS

Packet-mode technologies are well suited for environments that experience constant traffic flows intermingled with spells of bursty traffic. In these situations, each device must contend for access to the media for each packet it wishes to transmit. In the polling methodology, the master device asks (polls) each station if it needs to transmit. If the station has data to send, it will send it directly to the recipient or to the master, which then sends it on to the recipient. If the polled station has nothing to transmit, the master continues to the next device, asking each in turn until all devices have been queried. The master then begins the process over again and continues polling each device in turn. One of the disadvantages of a polling system is the time delay at the device that wants to transmit. The delay is the time it takes the master to poll all the other devices that are "in line" before the one that wants to transmit. For example, if a device has multiple packets to transmit and none of the other stations has any data to send, the single active station must wait for all devices to be polled between each packet it wishes to send.

A variation on the polling method, "probing," assigns each device a consecutive address. Each device has a turn, in sequence, at the transmission media. This technique is a bit better than standard polling because the master device is not involved in each transmission. Yet each device must be able to receive information sent to its address and messages sent to the group as a broadcast or multicast.

RESERVATION-BASED ACCESS

On networks that have a large value for *a*, such as fast, long-delay networks as in satellite transmissions, polling and circuit-mode techniques are not effective. In these situations, a reservation-based system may be a good solution. In a reservation-based system, there are two types of time slots used. One type of time slot carries reservation messages that are generated by a device that has data to transmit. The remaining time slots are used to carry the data. The reservation time slots are smaller than the data time slots and are called *reservation minislots*. When a station needs to transmit, it sends a reservation message using a reservation minislot to the master device. The master device then determines a time schedule for the devices to transmit and informs the slave devices of the transmission schedule. Since multiple devices may wish to send data, access to a reservation minislot must also be addressed. There are two mechanisms available to provide a reservation minislot to a device that needs to send a reservation message. In the first approach, fixed priority-oriented demand assignment (FPODA), a reservation minislot is assigned to each device, and there is no contention for a minislot. The other technique, packet-demand assignment multiple access (PDAMA), the devices that need a minislot contend for access by using a distributed packet-based system such as ALOHA.

Reservation-based systems allow priority scheduling for environments that include systems that need preferred access to the transmission media. In addition, the effect of collisions is minimal because collisions in a PDAMA system occur only when the stations contend for a minislot. Since most of the available bandwidth is dedicated to data, collisions on the minislots do not have an impact on data transmissions.

Distributed Access

In a distributed-access network, all the devices follow specific processes and work together to gain access to the transmission media. Distributed-access systems are primarily used with packet-mode technologies, but they can also be used with circuit-mode methods. A primary reason for not using circuit-mode methods in distributed-access systems is the overhead involved, with access negotiation occurring for each packet that needs to be transmitted. The principal packet-mode distributed-access schemes are discussed in this section.

DECENTRALIZED POLLING

The decentralized polling approach is essentially TDMA, where each device is allocated a particular time slot. If a station needs to transmit, a device gains access to the media when its time slot arrives, and if it has nothing to transmit, the station is idle during that device's time slot. In order for this method to work well, time has to be synchronized among all the devices, and the value of the parameter *a* must be small. For environments that have a lot of devices of which only a few at any time are active, decentralized polling is not efficient, since a lot of time will be wasted on all the idle systems.

CARRIER SENSE MULTIPLE ACCESS (CSMA)

Carrier sense multiple access, or CSMA, methodologies incorporate a mechanism that devices can use to detect if the transmission media is in use. If a station that wants to transmit "hears" packets on the media, the station must wait before transmitting. Otherwise, if the station began to transmit, collisions would occur. In a CSMA scheme, each device contains carrier-sensing techniques to determine if the transmission media is in use. The absence or presence of electrical or other energy on the transmission media is used by the carrier-sensing system to determine if the communication channel is available or is in use. There is an important factor to consider in a sensing system—the propagation delay. *Propagation delay* is the time it takes for a device to detect a message that has been sent by the most distant device. To handle this issue, CSMA designs assume that the propagation delay is small when compared to the time it takes to transmit a packet.

A device that is ready to transmit can sense traffic on the transmission media via two mechanisms. The first is called *persistent*; the station that wants to transmit waits until the media is idle and then transmits. This type is referred to as *1-persistent*. The second approach, *nonpersistent*, has the device set a timer, wait for a period of time, and check again if the media is free. If the media is free, the station will immediately transmit the data. A problem with the persistent approach is that if two stations "hear" the same idle time at the same moment, they will both transmit and a collision will occur. The probability of collisions increases as the number of devices that want to transmit increases. In order to help overcome this problem, persistent methods can incorporate p-persistent CSMA or binary exponential backoff.

In *p-persistent* CSMA, the device wanting to transmit does not immediately send data when it detects that the media is idle. Instead it uses a random scheme that gives it a fifty-fifty chance to either send the data immediately or to wait and then repeat the process. The reasoning behind this concept is that if two stations detect the same idle moment, the chance of a collision is reduced. The p value—the p in p-persistent—in this technique is 0.5, and it can reduce the chance of a collision from 100 percent to 33.33 percent. Instead of using a fifty-fifty approach, you can use different values where the range of p is between 0 and 1.

Binary exponential backoff systems incorporate a collision-detection scheme in addition to the carrier-sensing techniques. In the backoff algorithm, if the transmitting device realizes that a collision has occurred, it backs off and remains idle for a random period of time. This random time is chosen from a time interval calculated by multiplying the maximum propagation delay by two. After this random time has elapsed, the device retransmits the data that was originally lost in the collision. If the transmitting station detects another collision from this retransmission, it again backs off for a random time. However, on this second collision detection, the time interval is four times the maximum propagation delay. The device retransmits again after the second idle time period has passed. Each time the station detects a collision after retransmitting data, the time interval length is doubled. The effect of doubling the time interval gives rise to an exponential backoff timer. In most implementations of the backoff routine, once the number of attempts to transmit has reached 16, the station gives up and reports an error.

CARRIER SENSE MULTIPLE ACCESS/COLLISION AVOIDANCE (CSMA/CA)

On some networks, such as wireless LANs, the system cannot detect collisions because the power of the transmitting device is much stronger than the receiver's power. In these situations, where collision detection is not practical, it makes sense to try to devise a system that can help prevent collisions. Thus the *CA* in CSMA/CA refers to "collision avoidance." CSMA/CA is essentially a p-persistent scheme with the addition of idle time management. When a device detects that the transmission media is idle, the device must wait for a specified time before it can contend for access to the media. This specified waiting time is called *interframe spacing*, or IFS time. Interframe spacing can also be used for prioritizing transmissions. If a device is given a smaller interframe value, then it has more chances of gaining access to the transmission media. After the IFS time has elapsed, the device that wants to transmit sets a contention timer. The value of the contention time interval is randomly selected from a predefined contention window length value. After the contention timer has expired, the device transmits the data onto the media and waits for an acknowledgment. If the sender does not receive an acknowledgment, then the device assumes a collision has occurred. The device then selects another contention timer value, waits for the timer to expire, and retransmits the information. In this second attempt, the time interval from which the contention time is derived is twice as long—thus implementing binary exponential backoff. If the station that is waiting to transmit senses the media is in use while the contention timer is counting down, the contention timer stops. When the media becomes idle again, the contention timer continues its countdown. The reasoning behind stopping the timer versus restarting the timer is to allow the stations that have been waiting the longest to get a higher priority at the next contention cycle.

CARRIER SENSE MULTIPLE ACCESS/COLLISION DETECTION (CSMA/CD)

CSMA systems that use collision-detection schemes are referred to as CSMA/CD, where *CD* refers to collision detection. A collision-detection mechanism compares the amount of energy on the media after a packet is transmitted. If the value is greater than the energy used by the transmitting device, then a collision has occurred. If there is no difference in the two measured values, then a collision has not occurred. One of the reasons for the maximum length specifications for transmission media is to ensure that the strength of the signal on the transmission media will be strong enough to be detected. If the devices are too far apart, the signal strength will be too weak to be able to detect a small change in energy levels, so collisions would go undetected. Other collision-detection schemes work at the hub or concentrator on a physical star network. In these environments, if the hub detects activity on more than one input at the same time, then a collision is assumed. The hub then sends out a special signal called the *collision presence signal* to all the ports. The hub will continue sending the signal as long as the multiple activity occurs. When the remaining devices on the hub receive the collision presence signal, they interpret the information as if a collision has occurred.

In addition to detecting collisions, CSMA/CD can also recover from collisions. Once a collision has occurred it makes no sense for the two sending devices to immediately transmit again. If they do, their packets will collide again, and the two devices will get into an endless loop of transmit–collide–transmit–collide, and so on. To alleviate this issue, CSMA/CD issues a short jamming signal when a collision is detected. When all the stations detect the jamming signal, they immediately stop trying to transmit. The devices then wait for a period of time by using a binary exponential backoff routine before attempting to transmit again.

Probably the most common implementation of CSMA/CD is in Ethernet and IEEE 802.3 networks. Both of these use a 1-persistent scheme with binary exponential backoff routines. The combination of these technologies produces an efficient network over a wide range of traffic loads and patterns.

BUSY TONE MULTIPLE ACCESS (BTMA) AND MULTIPLE ACCESS COLLISION AVOIDANCE (MACA)

Busy tone multiple access (BTMA)/(MACA) and multiple access collision avoidance are two approaches that are used in environments that suffer from the hidden terminal and exposed terminal situations. In the hidden terminal situation illustrated in Figure 4-2, Computer A can "hear" Computer B and Computer C, so it can

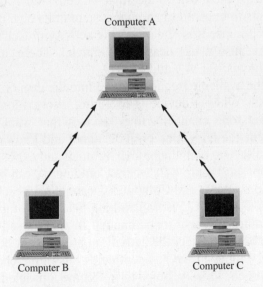

Fig. 4-2. Hidden terminal.

properly detect activity on the media. But Computer B cannot "hear" Computer C, and Computer C cannot "hear" Computer B. In this scenario, when Computer B is ready to transmit, it will not be able to detect if Computer C is transmitting. Collisions will occur if Computer B and Computer C transmit at the same time because they cannot "hear" each other.

The exposed terminal situation is the opposite problem, where a station that wants to transmit "hears" too much and thinks that the media is in use. Figure 4-3 is an example of an exposed terminal situation.

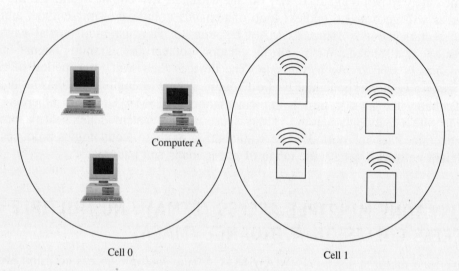

Fig. 4-3.   Exposed terminal.

The exposed terminal problem can occur on wireless networks where Computer A in Cell 0 is detecting the traffic in the adjacent cell, Cell 1. In this situation, when Computer A attempts to transmit to another system in its own cell (Cell 0), it detects the media is in use because it is "hearing" the activity in Cell 1. Thus Computer A will not transmit because it has heard "too much." There are two approaches to avoiding these problems: BTMA and MACA.

BTMA divides the available frequency band into the data or message channel and a busy tone channel. When a device is receiving information, it places data, or a "tone," on the busy tone channel. Other devices that want to send data to the receiving station hear the busy tone on its channel and know not to send the data. This scheme helps alleviate both the hidden terminal and exposed terminal situation. If we use the example in Figure 4-2, where Computer A can hear Computer B and Computer C, but Computer B and Computer C cannot hear each other, with BTMA, Computer B knows Computer C is transmitting because Computer B can sense the busy tone on Computer A's busy tone channel. In an exposed terminal situation, a device in one cell does not detect the activity in an adjacent cell's media because it cannot hear the busy tones in the adjacent cell's busy tone channels.

The second approach, MACA, helps to overcome a problem with BTMA. Since BTMA requires the frequency to be subdivided, there is the chance of cross-talk or interference between the data and busy tone channels. If this occurs, then a station may detect a busy tone when there isn't any data, or a device may detect data but without an associated busy tone so it cannot determine who is using the media. In MACA, the busy tone concept is used, except the busy tone is sent as a special message so that all the stations know that a receiver is busy and the media is in use. This approach also helps solve the hidden terminal and exposed terminal problem in the same manner as just described.

TOKEN PASSING

One of the issues of distributed polling networks is the need for all the devices to maintain the same time base. This necessity requires that some of the bandwidth be used for synchronization signals and events, and this requirement impacts the overall throughput of the media. Token passing schemes reduce the time synchronization needs because when a device has completed its transmission, it informs the next station that it is finished sending. This design reduces the need for devices to "fight," or contend, for access to the transmission media. In order for token passing to function properly, each device must know who its immediate neighbors are so it knows what station to expect the signal to come from and what station to inform when it is finished transmitting. This methodology of token passing is the basis for Token Ring networks.

One of the requirements of a Token Ring network is that the devices be arranged in a logical connection ring. In order to determine what device can transmit, a token travels around the ring. If a device wants to transmit, it waits until the token arrives and then it can transmit. The token is like a "permission slip" that allows the device with the token to send data. When the device is finished transmitting, the token is passed to the next device in the ring. This type of approach gives all devices equal access to the media and eliminates collisions. In a Token Ring network, the physical topology of the transmission media does not have to be in a ring. But in order to pass media access from device to device, the communication path between the devices must be a ring. The term *logical connection ring* refers to the communication path between the different devices. There are four types of physical topologies that can support a logical ring communication. Figure 4-4 illustrates the four physical topologies.

One possible physical topology for a Token Ring network is a physical ring of devices [see (a) in Figure 4-4]. Each station has a transmitter and receiver, and when the token arrives at a device that wants to transmit, it "grabs" the token and sends the data. There are two ways in which the sender can be notified that the recipient received the information. Since the data is going in a ring, the sender will eventually receive the data that was sent. Using this feature, the recipient can "mark" the data it received so when the sender examines the packet it originally transmitted, the mark indicates the receiver got the information. The sender then discards the transmitted packet so it does not go around the ring again. The second approach is to modify the token itself. When there are no devices transmitting, the token traveling around the ring has an idle flag set. When a device needs to transmit, it detects the idle flag in the token, modifies the flag to indicate the media is busy, and then transmits its data.

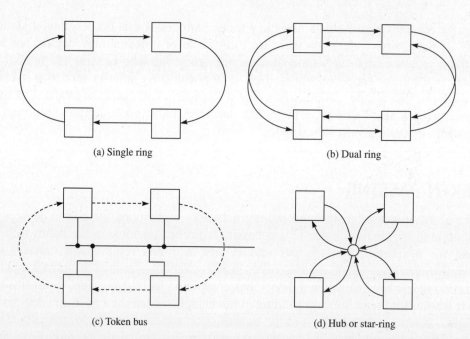

Fig. 4-4.   Four possible physical topologies for a Token Ring network.

The other devices see the busy flag in the token and know the media is in use and they cannot transmit. When the device is finished transmitting, it waits until the token returns, changes the busy flag to the idle flag, and then releases the token back onto the media.

One problem with a physical ring topology is that if any device on the ring fails, the entire ring is nonfunctional. In order to overcome this obstacle, another physical topology design introduces a second ring that runs in parallel to the first ring [see (b) in Figure 4-4]. The flow of data in the second ring is opposite the direction in the first ring. This concept of two parallel rings traveling in opposite directions is referred to as *dual counter rotating rings*. In order to accomplish this setup, each device has to have two transmitters and two receivers so it can communicate on both rings. In most implementations of dual counter rotating rings, only one of the two rings is used for data transfer. The other ring is used for management and as a backup in case of a failure on the data or primary ring. When a break occurs on the primary ring, a link between the two rings is formed so the data can travel around the break onto the secondary ring and then back onto the primary ring. Figure 4-5 is an example of the flow of data in a dual-counter rotating ring setup when a failure has occurred on the primary ring.

This type of arrangement requires each station to be aware of its immediate neighbors and to monitor them in case there is a change in normal ring activity. An example of an implementation of dual-counter rotating ring topology is FDDI.

Another type of topology is the token bus arrangement, where the devices are physically connected together as a bus but the data travels in a ring between the devices [see (c) in Figure 4-4]. The fourth possible physical arrangement of devices

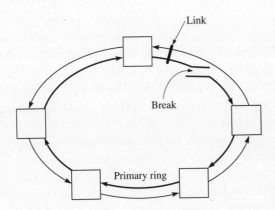

Link

Break

Primary ring

Fig. 4-5. The flow of data in a dual counter rotating ring topology after a break in the primary ring, when the link between both rings is in place.

is called a *hub* or *star-ring* topology [see (d) in Figure 4-4]. This topology makes it much easier to add and remove devices from the ring, and most implementations of a Token Ring network are a star-ring type topology. The hub device may be either a passive or an active device. For passive hub arrangements, the hub acts solely as a connectivity device and does not participate in any of the Token Ring protocols. Devices in a passive hub star-ring network are not aware of the presence of the passive hubs. Active hubs, on the other hand, do participate in the Token Ring protocols. These hubs can detect failures in the ring and shut out the offending device at the hub so it no longer participates in the ring.

Token Ring networks have several advantages over contention-based systems. By nature of a token, access to the media is explicit, collisions do not occur, and priority levels can be set. There is no need to include carrier-sensing or time-synchronization schemes, which makes the protocols easier to implement. Yet there are some limitations and disadvantages to token-passing systems. If the token becomes damaged or the station that is set to deliver a free token back onto the media crashes, the entire system becomes unusable. To overcome this single point of failure, Token Ring implementations designate one of the devices on the ring to act as a monitor. This device checks for the length of time an idle token has been circulating the ring. If the time is too long, the monitor device assumes the token has been corrupted or lost and a new token is generated and released onto the ring. The monitor will also generate a new token when a token is lacking. A token can be removed if a device that has a token receives a packet from another station. In this event, the station with the token removes all data and token(s) from the media so there is nothing circulating on the ring. Another item to consider about Token Ring networks is that all the devices on the Token Ring network must participate in the token-passing and token-release processes. If for some reason a station does not release the token or refuses to pass the token on to the next station in the ring, activity on the ring ceases. There is a level of complexity required to carry out the token-passing management routines and to maintain the integrity of the token through error detection routines.

ALOHA

ALOHA is the simplest of the multiple-access methods covered in this chapter. It was developed before the other schemes, but it is still useful in some of today's networks. ALOHA was developed at the University of Hawaii and was originally developed for packet radio networks. On an ALOHA multiple-access network, when a device needs to transmit data, it begins transmission without performing any checks. The sender then waits for an acknowledgment, and if it does not receive one after a period of time, the sender assumes the packet was lost. The sender then waits for a random period of time before retransmitting the packet. The ALOHA scheme is useful on networks that have a large "a," where it is not feasible to use polling or carrier-sensing techniques.

The ALOHA technique is very simple because there are no carrier-sensing, time-synchronization, or token-passing schemes to implement. On the other hand, ALOHA's performance does not stack up to the other multiple-access methods we have addressed. The peak possible goodput of an ALOHA implementation is only about 18 percent. But if there are only two devices using the media, the goodput reaches 100 percent. In addition, if the capacity of the media is high, the goodput increases and the simplicity of ALOHA may overcome any throughput issues. For example, on a cellular phone network, when a phone turns on, ALOHA is used to transmit the phone's information to the base station. Since the size of the information sent to the base station is small, ALOHA is a viable multiple-media access choice. An area where ALOHA does not perform well is with bursty traffic. When there is an increase in network transmissions, more collisions will occur, and the network may become unusable or unstable. One mechanism that can be used to overcome this problem is a binary exponential backoff scheme. There are two variations of ALOHA—slotted ALOHA and reservation ALOHA. Both of these schemes are used quite a bit in various networks.

Slotted ALOHA (S-ALOHA)

One of the problems with ALOHA is that as soon as a device transmits a packet, it can collide with another packet already on the media. The window of vulnerability to a collision is determined by the following formula:

$$2 \times L$$

L is the time it takes to transmit a packet, and the formula is based on an environment where all the packets are the same length. If the resulting value of this formula can be reduced, then the number of collisions will also be reduced. In slotted ALOHA (S-ALOHA), the time base for the environment is divided into time slots of the same duration. When a station wants to transmit, it waits until the beginning of the next time slot before it starts transmitting. The effect of this strategy is to reduce the size of the window of vulnerability by a factor of two, thereby doubling the effective throughput to about 36 percent. S-ALOHA is not as simple as plain ALOHA because the network needs a time-synchronization plan and some of the bandwidth is lost to synchronization activity. The best place for

S-ALOHA is in networks that already have a time synchronization system in place for other protocols.

Reservation ALOHA (R-ALOHA)

In this scheme, time is divided into slots, and each device has an assigned time slot, which is reserved for the exclusive use of the device. The time base is divided into frames that are composed of a fixed number of time slots. When a device gets access to a time slot by use of R-ALOHA, the device then gets all the time slots for the frame the original time slot came from. This scheme helps reduce collisions because once a device gets a time slot, no other device can transmit during the remaining time slots of the frame.

R-ALOHA is a bit different from the reservation system we discussed earlier (FPODA) in that there is no master, and each station examines the reservation requests and determines which device owns which reservation slot. One item to keep in mind with R-ALOHA is that priorities cannot be set.

Hardware Addressing

In this chapter and previous chapters, we have covered the physical structure and components of networks, the types of networks, and the methodologies devices can use to gain access and transmit on a shared network. Yet even with all these pieces in place, two devices cannot "talk" to each other if they don't know how to contact and "address" each other. In this section we discuss hardware addressing, which is used by devices on the same logical network to find and communicate with each other. In Chapter 6, we will cover other addressing issues that involve communication between different logical networks and naming schemes.

On a shared media network, such as Ethernet or IBM Token Ring, each device on the network "sees" all the packets or frames passing by on the media. In that type of environment, there needs to be some mechanism in place for the recipient to know which packet it is supposed to receive. In addition, the sender needs some way to be able to identify the recipient and to indicate where the information came from. On a LAN, each communicating device is assigned a unique number that is called a physical address, hardware address, or media access address (MAC address). One of the roles of the MAC sublayer of the Data Link layer is physical addresses—thus, the name MAC address. When the sender prepares to transmit a frame to a recipient, the physical address of the sender and recipient are attached to the information. Each station examines the frames passing on the media and checks to see if the "To:" or destination address matches its physical address. If it does, the device "captures" the packet, and if it finds that the packet is not addressed to the device, it simply "ignores" the packet. If there were no way for each station to identify packets destined for it, the systems would have to accept all packets and would soon be "flooded" with too much data.

There are three ways in which a hardware address can be assigned to a device. Some or all of these may be supported by network interfaces constructed by different vendors.

- *Static.* These hardware address types are assigned by the manufacturer and cannot be changed by the user. If you want to change the hardware address you will need to change the hardware device.

- *Configurable.* In this type of addressing, the hardware address can be set by the user. The mechanism for changing the address may range from jumpers and dip switches to setup software that saves the settings in EPROM.

- *Dynamic.* This address assignment type is designed around the boot-up or power-on sequence of a device. When the system starts up, the hardware begins self-assigning a random physical address. Before it actually accepts and starts using the self-assigned number, the device sends a message on the network to determine if the address is already in use. In dynamic implementations, there is the possibility of a device having a different address assigned each time it is started.

Each of these schemes has its benefits and disadvantages. For example, static addressing is the easiest one from the administration point of view. In addition, there are international entities such as the IEEE that assign address ranges to different vendors so conflicts should not appear in environments that use different manufacturers' hardware. On the other hand, if you want a numbering pattern for the devices, then the static solution will not satisfy that need. A configurable address requires careful documentation on the part of the administrator so that duplicate addresses are not generated. But if you have a need for numbering patterns, configurable addressing solutions may be beneficial. Dynamic addressing removes the need for long addresses that are unique between vendors, because the number of devices on a LAN is much smaller than the number of possible devices released by different vendors. At the same time, dynamic numbers do not allow devices to have permanent numbers, which may be necessary for some devices, such as service-providing components and servers.

Each frame of data that is constructed by the sender includes a header that has space reserved for the source (sender) and destination (recipient) addresses. As an example, we will examine the relevant portions of an Ethernet frame captured from a 10-Mbps copper-based network. Figure 4-6 shows the details of an Ethernet frame. Ethernet network interface components that are assigned static numbers from the vendor use a 48-bit hardware address. At the beginning of an Ethernet frame is a 64-bit preamble that contains a sequence of alternating 1's and 0's. The purpose of the preamble is to allow the recipient's hardware to properly synchronize so the frame is read properly. Following the preamble are three fields. The first two fields contain the destination device's and source device's physical addresses. The third field contains a 16-bit number that indicates the Ethernet frame type.

The physical address numbers in the capture utility are reported as hexadecimal values. In Figure 4-6, the destination (recipient) address is 004095D07D7B, and the source (sender) address is 004095D0856F. The Ethernet frame type is 0800, which indicates IPv4. For the Ethernet environment, the values of the physical addresses are managed by the IEEE organization.

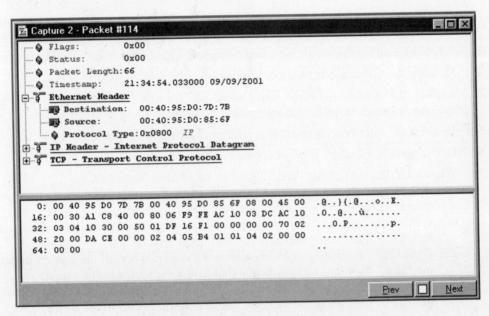

Fig. 4-6. Ethernet frame addressing details.

To "capture" network traffic on the transmission media, a network analyzer or network monitor is used. Network analyzers may be dedicated hardware devices that are expensive but yield a tremendous amount of information. There are also software network monitors that capture the traffic that is "seen" by the device running the monitoring software. In order for a software network monitor to capture packets that are destined for itself and the rest of the LAN, the network interface component must be capable of running in promiscuous mode. Most typical network interface components used on workstations and other network devices are capable of running in promiscuous mode. Keep in mind that a network monitor program in conjunction with a promiscuous mode network interface is a potential security issue. It is not recommended that you leave your software or hardware network analysis tools "lying around" unattended!

Review Questions

4.1 The term *goodput* is used to define the following characteristic of a transmission:

    a. The portion of the capacity of the transmission link that is carrying retransmitted packets

    b. The portion of the transmitted packets on the transmission link that is carrying nonretransmitted packets

    c. The portion of the capacity of the transmission link that is carrying non-retransmitted packets

d. The portion of the transmitted packets on the transmission link that is carrying retransmitted packets

4.2 What is meant by the term *chip* when discussing CDMA schemes?

4.3 Describe the difference between polling and probing.

4.4 Explain the reasoning behind using minislots instead of normal data slots in reservation-based media access schemes.

4.5 Describe the difference between p-persistent CSMA and nonpersistent CSMA.

4.6 Define what is meant by binary exponential backoff.

4.7 What is the function of the "jam" signal on an Ethernet network?
  a. CSMA/CA issues a "jam" when a collision is detected. When all the stations detect the "jam," they immediately stop trying to transmit.
  b. CSMA/CD issues a "jam" when a collision is detected. When all the stations detect the "jam," they immediately stop trying to transmit.
  c. CSMA/CD issues a "jam" when the media is idle. When all the stations detect the "jam," they immediately begin contending for access to the media.
  d. CSMA/CA issues a "jam" when the media is idle. When all the stations detect the "jam," they immediately begin contending for access to the media.

4.8 On a CSMA/CA network, Computer A has an interframe spacing of two slots, Computer B's interframe spacing is six slots, and the interframe spacing for Computer C is four slots. Which device has the highest priority?
  a. Computer A
  b. Computer B
  c. Computer C
  d. Priority cannot be assigned in a CSMA/CA network.

4.9 Define the usage of the term *exposed terminal*.

4.10 In a BTMA scheme, what is the purpose of the "busy tone"?
  a. When other devices do not hear the busy tone on a device's busy tone channel, they know not to send the data because the media is in use.
  b. Devices on the network that are not transmitting send out a busy tone so the other devices know the media is idle.
  c. Devices on the network that are not transmitting send out a busy tone so the other devices know the media is not idle.
  d. When other devices hear the busy tone on a device's busy tone channel they know not to send the data because the media is in use.

4.11 On a Token Ring network, what happens when the token gets corrupted?

4.12 What happens when two devices on the same LAN network have the same static MAC address?
  a. The device that boots first has exclusive use of the address, and the second device cannot communicate.
  b. The device that boots last has exclusive use of the address, and the other device cannot communicate.
  c. Neither device can communicate properly on the network.
  d. Both devices can communicate since they can read the entire contents of the packets and know which packets are for them and not for the other stations.

4.13 You have a four-node point-to-point network. What is the number of connections necessary to allow each device to communicate with another?

4.14 What is FDD?
  a. FDD is a frequency division technique that permits dedicated communications.
  b. FDD is a frequency division technique that permits dynamic media allocation.
  c. FDD is a frequency division technique that permits guaranteed delivery of information.
  d. FDD is a frequency division technique that permits two-way or duplex communications.

Problems

4.1 Discuss a method you could use to eliminate the multiple-access problem for a local area network.

4.2 What is the parameter "*a*" when we are discussing designs for solving the multiple-access issue?

4.3 What is meant by the "hidden terminal problem"?

4.4 What are the four performance parameters for a multiple-access scheme?

4.5 What is the value of "*a*" for a network where the average packet size is 400 bytes, and bandwidth is 10 Mbps, the propagation delay is 120 μs, and the travel time of a packet is 12 μs?

4.6 Why does the FH/CDMA scheme need to take both frequency and time into consideration?

4.7 Why was CSMA/CA developed?

4.8 Describe what is meant by dual counter rotating rings.

4.9 How can dual counter rotating rings help when there is a failure of the transmission media?

4.10 Describe the differences between S-ALOHA and R-ALOHA.

4.11 What criteria would change your design from a BTMA to a MACA scheme?

4.12 Assigning hardware addresses to devices can be accomplished by three different methods: static, configurable, or dynamic. For each of these types, define which device is in error when duplicate hardware addresses appear on the network.

4.13 You are using your workstation on an Ethernet network to access a Web site on the Internet. Using a network monitor or analyzer, how can you find out your machine's hardware address for the network interface card?

4.14 Calculate the goodput of a 10-Mbps network that has an average packet length of 110 bytes, whose peak throughput is 9500 packets per second.

Answers to Review Questions

4.1 **c.** Goodput is the portion of the capacity of the transmission link that is carrying nonretransmitted packets. If there were no loss of packets on the media owing to congestion or other factors, the goodput value for an ideal environment would be 1.0.

4.2 In DS/CDMA, or direct sequence CDMA, code words are assigned to represent the binary 1's. Each bit in the code word is called a *chip*, and the bit rate of the code word is measured in chips/second.

4.3 In the polling methodology, the master device asks (polls) each station if it needs to transmit. A variation on the polling mode method—probing—assigns each device a consecutive address. Each device has a turn, in sequence, at the transmission media.

4.4 When smaller minislots are used to handle the reservation requests and other management tasks, collisions occurring on the minislots do not have an impact on data transmissions.

4.5 In nonpersistent CSMA, when a collision occurs, the transmitting device sets a timer, waits for a period of time, and checks again to determine if the media is free. If the media is free, the station will immediately transmit the data. In p-persistent CSMA, the device wanting to transmit does not immediately send data when it detects the media is idle. Instead it uses a random scheme that gives it a fifty-fifty chance to either send the data immediately or to wait and then repeat the process.

4.6 In the binary exponential backoff algorithm, if a transmitting device realizes that a collision has occurred, it backs off and remains idle for a random period of time. This random time is chosen from a time interval calculated by multiplying the maximum propagation delay by two. After this random time has elapsed, the device retransmits the data that was originally lost in the collision. If the transmitting station detects another collision from this retransmission, it again backs off for a random time. But on this second collision detection, the time interval is four times the maximum propagation delay. The device retransmits again after the second idle time period has passed. Each time the station detects a collision after retransmitting data, the time interval length is doubled. The effect of doubling the time interval gives rise to an exponential backoff timer. In most implementations of the backoff routine, once the number of attempts to transmit has reached 16, the station gives up and reports an error.

4.7 **b.** CSMA/CD issues a short jamming signal when a collision is detected. When all the stations detect the jamming signal, they immediately stop trying to transmit. The devices then wait for a period of time by using a binary exponential backoff routine before attempting to transmit again. This is the scheme used on Ethernet networks.

4.8 **a.** Interframe spacing (IFS) can also be used for prioritizing transmissions. If a device is given a smaller interframe value, then it has more chances of gaining access to the transmission media. Of the three devices in the question, Computer A has the smallest interframe spacing value.

4.9 The exposed terminal situation occurs when a station that wants to transmit "hears" too much and thinks that the media is in use. The exposed terminal problem can occur on wireless networks where a system in one cell detects traffic in an adjacent cell. In this situation, the device "thinks" the media is in use because it is "hearing" the activity in the adjacent cell. The device will not transmit because it has heard "too much."

4.10 **d.** When a device is receiving information, it places data, or a "tone," on the busy tone channel. Other devices that want to send data to the receiving station hear the busy tone on its channel and know not to send the data.

4.11 If the token becomes damaged, the Token Ring network will cease to function because there is no available token for the stations to use. To help reduce the effect of this problem, the network assigns a device to act as a monitor that will generate a new token when the token is damaged or missing.

4.12   **c.** If duplicate hardware addresses occur on systems that are using static addresses, neither device can communicate. Each device on a LAN must have a unique hardware address.

4.13   The number of connections required for a point-to-point network can be expressed by the following equation:

$$\text{Number of direct connections} = (N^2 - N)/2$$

The value of N in the above equation is the number of devices on the network. For a four-node network, the required number of connections would be six.

4.14   **d.** Frequency division duplex, or FDD, is a frequency division technique that permits two-way or duplex communications. The two communicating devices use different frequencies to obtain the duplex conversation.

Solutions to Problems

4.1   One method to eliminate the multiple-access problem on a LAN is through the use of point-to-point communication links. In this type of connection solution there is no contention for the transmission because each link has only two devices.

4.2   The parameter "a" represents the number of packets, or the portion of a packet, that can be placed on the communication media by the transmitting device before any of the bits are received by the device that is the farthest away.

4.3   The hidden terminal problem can cause multiple devices to transmit at the same time. This problem is created when a transmitting device is only "heard" by some of the devices in the same area. If a device is transmitting and another device does not hear the transmitting device, it may conclude that the media is clear and begin to transmit.

4.4   • *Normalized throughput or goodput:* Goodput is the portion of the capacity of the transmission link that is carrying nonretransmitted packets.
      • *Mean delay.* The mean delay is the mean time that a packet waits at the sender before it can be transmitted, plus the time it takes to transmit the packet.
      • *Stability.* The stability of a multiple-access technique refers to the ability of the method to handle increases in the amount of traffic without affecting the throughput.
      • *Fairness.* Fairness means that every device that wants to transmit has equal access to the media within a specified time frame.

4.5   The parameter "a" is defined as

$$a = D/T$$

where D refers to the maximum transmission propagation delay in seconds, and T is the travel time in seconds of an average-sized packet. With a value of $120\,\mu s$ for the propagation delay and $12\,\mu s$ for the travel time of a packet, "a" is 10 (120/12).

4.6   In frequency-hopping CDMA or FH/CDMA, the transmitting devices begin sending information on one frequency and then after a short period of time change to another frequency. In this CDMA scheme, the devices are using both time slots and frequency technologies. The time slot is the amount of time used on a specific frequency, and the frequency element is the usage of different frequencies.

4.7   On some networks, such as wireless LANs, the system cannot detect collisions because the power of the transmitting device is much stronger than the receiver's power. In these type of situations where collision detection is not practical, it makes sense to try to devise a system that can help avoid collisions. Thus CSMA collision avoidance was developed.

4.8   Dual counter rotating rings are two physical parallel rings where the data is traveling in opposite directions on each ring. In order to accomplish this setup, each device has to have two transmitters and two receivers so it can communicate on both rings.

4.9   In most implementations of dual counter rotating rings, only one of the two rings is used for data transfer. The other ring is used for management and as a backup in case of a failure on the data or primary ring. When a break occurs on the primary ring, a link between the two rings is formed so the data can travel around the break onto the secondary ring and then back onto the primary ring.

4.10   In slotted ALOHA (S-ALOHA), the time base for the environment is divided into time slots of the same duration. When a station wants to transmit, it waits until the beginning of the next time slot before it starts transmitting. In the reservation ALOHA (R-ALOHA) scheme, time is divided into slots, and each device has an assigned time slot, which is reserved for the exclusive use of the device.

4.11   Busy tone multiple access (BTMA) requires the frequency to be subdivided, which introduces the chance of cross-talk or interference between the data and busy tone channels. If this occurs, then a station may detect a busy tone when there isn't any data, or a device may detect data but without an associated busy tone so it cannot determine who is using the media. In MACA the busy tone concept is used, except the busy tone is sent as a special message on the data channel so that all the stations know that a receiver is busy and the media is in use.

4.12   If duplicate hardware addresses occur on systems that are using static addresses, the fault lies with the manufacturer. The administrator cannot change the addresses. In a configurable environment, the fault lies with the administrator, who is responsible for documenting the current addresses in use. In a dynamic environment, duplicate addresses may result from different conditions. For example, if the transmission media has a problem, a device checking to see if an address is in use may receive faulty information. On the other hand, if the routines built into the device to determine hardware address duplication are not designed properly, the fault then lies with the vendor.

4.13   To determine your workstation's address on an Ethernet network, you will need to capture packets from the media that are being transmitted from your workstation. Once the packets are captured, examining the source address field of the Ethernet header will disclose the hardware address of your workstation's network interface card.

4.14   On a 10-Mbps network that has an average packet length of 110 bytes and whose peak throughput is 9500 packets per second, the carrying capacity is 11,364 packets per second. This is derived from

$$11,364 \text{ packets/second} = 10,000,000 \text{ bps}$$
$$(110 \text{ byte packet} \times 8 \text{ bits/packet})$$

At a peak throughput of 9500, the goodput value of 0.85 is calculated as follows:

$$0.84 \text{ goodput} = \frac{9500 \text{ packets/second}}{11,364 \text{ packets/second}}$$

CHAPTER 5

Switching

Every time you access the Internet or another network outside your immediate location, your messages are sent through a maze of transmission media and connection devices. The mechanism for moving information between different networks and network segments is called *switching*. For example, whenever a telephone call is placed, there are numerous junctions in the communication path that perform this movement of data from one network onto another network. There are different types of junction hardware involved in a multinetwork connection, and each is designed to perform a specific function or functions. In this chapter we concentrate on the nature of switching data around a network and switches, which are the types of hardware involved in switching.

The internal physical structure of a generic switch is composed of four primary elements—input buffers, a port mapper, a switch fabric, and output buffers. Each of these plays a role in the primary purpose of a switch, which is to forward data that arrives at its input buffers to one of the switch's output buffers. Before delving into the details of specific types of switching or switches, a brief description of the four basic components follows:

- *Input buffers*. Switches include buffers to store packets arriving at their input connections. Some switches have buffers for all the inputs, and others have small buffers that are only used to hold data when contention for the switch fabric is under way. If the buffers' capacity cannot keep up with the arrival rate of the packets, the switch becomes congested.

- *Port mapper*. This element is found only in packet switches and is not used on circuit switches. The packet switch contains a table that associates, or maps, each input to an output. The switch reads the destination address of the packet at the input, looks up the location in a table, and then assigns an output port to the packet. Circuit switches do not need a port mapper or table because the destination output is already known when the packet arrives at the switch's input.

- *Switch fabric*. The switch fabric is the hardware and software elements of the switch that move data from a switch input to a switch output. The complexity of the fabric may range from the simple technique of copying the data from the input port and writing it to the output port, to multiprocessor components that concurrently transfer thousands of packets to many output ports.

- *Output buffers*. These buffers hold the data that has been processed through the switch fabric. These buffers may be large or small and may include a scheduler that handles media access for the output connections. Systems that include a scheduler may be able to provide for different qualities of service levels.

Depending on the overall function of the switch, some of these basic components may be combined. For example, some switches omit input buffers, and others combine the input and output buffers. Other designs may implement a port mapper for each input line instead of a single port mapper for the entire unit.

The mechanism by which data is switched is grouped into two classifications—packet and circuit. Packets of information on a network contain data, and some may include meta-data, which contains descriptions or other information about the data. Circuit switching deals with packets on the media that do not contain any meta-data. A good example of a circuit switch is a telephone switch. Packet switching can handle data with or without any associated meta-data. Two good examples of packet switches are routers and Asynchronous Transfer Mode (ATM) switches.

Switching can also be categorized as being either connectionless or connection-oriented. In a connectionless switching environment, the packet contains all the information necessary for it to be delivered to its final destination. This type of packet is referred to as "self-contained"; the switch simply reads the packet's header, looks in its table for the proper output port, and the fabric moves the packet to the proper output buffer or port. A connection-oriented switch contains a switch controller that looks at the destination address in the incoming packet and assigns the appropriate data forwarding path for the packet. The packet is then moved to the proper output port by the switch fabric methods. Before any packets can be properly moved across a connection-oriented switching system, the switch must first contain all the appropriate data forwarding paths for the environment. Connection-oriented systems can provide admission control to incoming data and decide whether or not to allow the information to enter the switch.

There are several important services that a switch must be able to provide in order to make it a useful device. The capacity of the switch must be sufficient to handle all the potential traffic that can pass through the switch. The capacity of a switch, when reported in the specifications, indicates the maximum rate at which it can move information from the input to the output side. Another important factor is reliability. The device must be able to provide the rated capacity while maintaining the integrity of the data that passes through, accurate pathway assignments, and table maintenance. Circuit switches that do not contain input buffers must be able to perform call blocking. If the device does not have a path defined for an input to an output, the circuit switch will perform call blocking and reject the incoming data. On a packet switch that contains input buffers, the incoming information can be stored in the buffers. But, if a burst of traffic arrives at the switch, the input buffers become full and packets are dropped, leading to packet loss. Both call blocking and packet loss cause lower throughput of data through the switch, resulting in slowing down the movement of data. The switches must be able to minimize the use of call blocking and packet loss to provide better performance. Finally, switches ideally should not modify the order at which packets arrive at the switch and are sent to the output interfaces. Some implementations, such as ATM switches, do not allow reordering of data, while others do affect packet ordering. On the Internet, it is common for packets to be reordered as they navigate through the different segments between the sender and the receiver.

Circuit Switching

Probably the most common usage of circuit switching is the telephone system. When you initiate a telephone call, the entire path from your telephone to the recipient's telephone is determined when the call is made. It is up to the switching equipment between the two telephones to determine the physical communication path. Once this path is determined, the same path is used for the entire duration of the conversation. When another call is made to the same recipient at another time, the same physical path may or may not be used. The path used in a circuit-switching environment is also referred to as a *virtual circuit*. Figure 5-1 illustrates the concepts behind a circuit-switched telephone network.

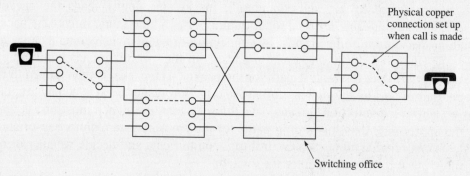

Fig. 5-1.   Circuit-switched network.

Once the end-to-end path has been established, data can begin traveling across the network. The time it takes to establish the path can be several seconds or more, depending on the distance and the number of different telephone companies involved. Once the connection is made, congestion will not occur on the link since only the sender and receiver are using the channel. Yet, during call establishment, contention may occur because there may not be an available channel. This situation results in a busy signal at the sender end.

In circuit switching, packets do not contain meta-data information, such as destination and source addresses. The source and destination are determined from the signals on the transmission media. The time at which the data packet was placed on the line corresponds to its position in a frame. Units of voice data traveling across the phone network are 8 bits long, each containing 125 μsec of sampled voice.

Recall from earlier chapters that multiple telephone conversations are multiplexed together at the telephone company's central office and are demultiplexed at the recipient's central office. Because of the way the multiplexors and demultiplexors function, the units of data do not need addressing information. The only item required is an accurate time base and the timing information of the data packets. In a circuit-switching environment, the switch must be able to take the incoming data, redirect it to the proper output port, and place the data in the correct time slot in the output frame.

If a circuit switch is said to be able to service a certain number of circuits, N, we can say that the number of inputs and outputs are each N, respectively. The value of N for circuit switches can be as large as 120,000. When the information is time multiplexed on the input connections, then many more telephone conversations can pass through the switch. For example, if each of the inputs can handle 672 voice calls, as in DS3 switches, then the number of physical input and output ports can be reduced by a factor of 672.

In telephone networks, there are two types of switches that are distinguished by the connection types. *Line switches* connect individual telephone lines and must connect a specific input to a specific output. *Transit switches* connect multiplexed links and must be able to connect an input to any one of the outputs that is going in the same direction. On both of these types of switches, a call may be blocked and prevented from being switched if there is no path between the input and the output. There are two types of blocking that can occur—*internal* and *output*. When internal blocking occurs, there is no path to an available output. Packets building up at the buffers waiting for the same output will prevent other packets further back in line from getting a chance at their output port. This is referred to as *head-of-line blocking*. In an output blocking situation, two inputs are in competition for the same output port, and one does not get access to the output. Evaluating these two types of blocking situations with the two types of switches, a transit switch will reduce the occurrence of blocking because a transit switch can use different outputs. There are two different methods in which the information can be switched through a circuit switch. Both of these techniques, "time-division" and "space-division," are discussed next.

TIME-DIVISION SWITCHING

In time-division switching, the packets appear in one order in the input buffer and in a different order on the output side. The switch has only one input and output, but the incoming and outgoing lines carry multiplexed data. The resulting effect of this order change is that at the demultiplexor, the individual packets are placed on different output links. This process is how a Time Slot Interchange (TSI) switch rearranges the order of packets on a multiplexed line. This technique, however, cannot handle a large number of conversations, because the speed required by the memory to process all the information is not fast enough to keep up with the amount of data flowing to the destination.

SPACE-DIVISION SWITCHING

Space-division switching mechanisms take each input packet on a different path through the switch. The path a specific packet will take depends on the destination of the packet. There are a couple of ways in which space-division switching can work. The first, called a *crossbar*, is the simplest method of providing switching for multiplexed data. The input and output lines are arranged as a grid perpendicular to each other. The intersection of an input and output line is called a *crosspoint*, and if the crosspoint is active, then data can travel from the input line over to the output line. If the crosspoint is not active, data on the input line cannot cross over to the output line. If the switch has eight input and eight output lines, then the crossbar switch is referred to as an 8 × 8 switch. If the input line coming into the switch is not multiplexed, then the input lines will always switch to the same output lines. If the incoming links are multiplexed, the individual elements entering will have different destinations. In this case, a controller is required to produce a schedule that specifies which crosspoints are active at each time unit of the multiplexed data. As the number of input lines increases, it takes longer for the controller to communicate to all the crosspoints to turn them off and on. This problem led to the development of *multistage crossbar switches*. For small switches that have 64 or fewer input and output lines, a crossbar switch is a viable solution.

A multistage crossbar provides for multiple paths between groups of inputs and outputs. The switch divides the input lines into groups, which are themselves switched internally by a crossbar. This arrangement creates a center stage that is shared by input and output groups to create multiple paths. This technique reduces the number of crosspoints. Crossbar switches are also said to be internally non-blocking because there is always an output available and data is not blocked in the switch.

TIME-SPACE SWITCHING

A time-space (TS) switch takes the outputs of several time-division switches, for example, TSI switches, and connects them as inputs to a space-division switch. The effect of this paired arrangement is that packets can be swapped between different output lines. Thus, if there were two inputs on a time-division switch contending for the same output, the space-division switch delivers one of the two outputs to another output path. This arrangement also reduces the number of crosspoints required.

TIME-SPACE-TIME SWITCHING

A time-space-time (TST) switch places two time-division switches each at the input crossbar and output crossbar points. One of the issues with the time-space switch is that if a different output is used for a packet that lost out to the output it was in contention with, the data may arrive at the wrong location. To overcome this problem, the TST switch places a time-division switch at the outputs of the space-division switch so the proper sequence of packets to the correct destinations is achieved. This design also reduces the chances of blocking occurring at the space-division switch.

Packet Switching

In contrast to circuit switching, packet switching does not entail predefined paths from input to output ports. Instead, the units of data in a packet-switched network contain source and destination addresses, which is referred to as meta-data. When a packet arrives at a packet switch, it is stored and then transmitted later. This means that the arrival time of a packet is not a factor in determining the destination of the packet, since the switch does not contain predefined delivery paths based on a timing scheme. In a packet switch, a port mapper component is used to determine the output port of the packets based on their address information. Packet switches are referred to as *store-and-forward switches* because the frames are stored in the switch before they are transmitted on to the other side. Figure 5-2 illustrates the concepts of a packet-switched network.

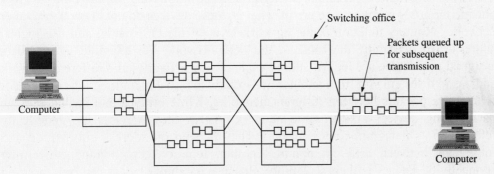

Fig. 5-2.   Packet-switched network.

The earliest implementation of packet switching was called *message switching*, and it was used for telegrams. Message switching does not put any limitation on block sizes, which makes message switching impractical for use in current networks. With unlimited block sizes, a long message could tie up a switch's buffers so that other messages are unable to pass through. This type of design cannot be used on interactive information communications such as today's computer networks. To overcome this problem, current packet-switching networks place limitations on the maximum size of packets that are passed through the switches. In contrast to circuit switching, packet switching makes better use of bandwidth. In circuit switching, the dedicated path holds on to a portion of the bandwidth as long as the connection is in place. Packet switching gains access to the transmission media when it is needed, and when the media is not in use, the media is available for other devices to use. These types of design features make packet-switching networks well suited for the exchange of interactive information. Nonetheless, there are some issues about packet-switched networks that can affect communications. For instance, packets can arrive at the recipient out of order. Because packets are stored in the switches and released at different rates, the recipient can receive them in the incorrect order. This is not an issue with circuit-switched networks because the path is dedicated between two entities, and packets are transmitted from switch to switch in the same order.

There are two classifications of packet switches—*virtual circuit ATM* and *datagram routers*. One of the principal differences between these two switches is the size of the packets. Asynchronous transfer mode switches work with fixed-size packets, and the virtual circuit identifier (VCI) information is used by the port mapper to determine the destination. Datagram routers can handle packets of variable sizes; they require the port mapper to read the destination address to determine the destination.

Before we get into the details of packet switches, we need to clarify the term *datagram routers* and its use in respect to bridges, switches, and routers. All three of these devices move data from their input ports to their output ports by examining the address information in the packets. But the types of addresses used by the devices depend on the level in the Open Systems Interconnection (OSI) model the devices participate in. Both bridges and switches use the datalink address to determine the destination. The datalink address is also known as the *physical* or *media access* (MAC) *address* and bridges and switches have no knowledge of any other devices outside the LAN segment they are in. That is, these devices do not know about other networks. Routers function at the network layer of the OSI model and use logical addresses to determine the route to the next network. For example, IP numbers assigned to a device are logical addresses, and each network has a different network address to distinguish it from another network. One of the main functions of a router is to move packets between different networks, while bridges and switches move data among devices on the same network. All of these devices are generically referred to as datagram routers because they depend on address information and route data between different points. Another item to keep in mind concerning connectivity devices is their scalability. Because datalink devices can only be used on the same network, datalink level connection devices are not scalable for large networks. Network layer devices scale to larger networks because of their ability to communicate between different networks. Scalability is an important issue when it comes to designing the types of devices used on LANs.

In this section we concentrate on the technologies and devices that route data using physical addresses—bridges and switches. Whenever the term *route* is used for datagram routers that function at the datalink layer, we are referring to moving data from point to point based on the packet's physical address information. Routers and routing functions that operate at the network layer of the OSI model are covered in Chapter 7.

PORT MAPPERS

Packet-switching bridges and switches must maintain a table of destinations that are associated with their output ports. It is the role of the port mapper to maintain these lists and to look up entries when packets arrive at the input side of the device. The matching function of the port mapper to get the packets to the correct locations is not an easy task. The device must perform the port mapping efficiently and provide the best path for the incoming packets. One simple approach for a best-match method is to have a list, or table, of the addresses of the input locations paired with an output location. In this design, when a packet arrives at the device, the source and destination addresses are read, the port mapper goes down the list of devices until it finds a match, and then it sends the packet on. This approach is very inefficient because as the number of devices increases, it takes longer to search the list. In order to overcome this type of problem, techniques are available that use different data structures to perform a faster best-match lookup. One common data structure for best-match situations is the "trie" arrangement. The trie organization is a hierarchy of arrays where each entry can have one of three values:

- If a better match exists elsewhere in the data, the entry will contain a pointer to another array.

- If no known better matches exist, the entry indicates this status with a special symbol.

- If the parent of the point in the tree contains possible valid arrays, the entry contains a null pointer.

When a packet arrives for a specific destination, it is assumed that other packets for the same destination will also be arriving. Thus, if the path information derived from the trie function for the first packet is stored in cache, paths for other packets with the same destination address are first checked in cache before the trie search is performed, resulting in an improvement in the trie's performance. A second approach assumes that most addresses that will be looked up are for devices that are local to the switch. Thus, if the addresses for local devices are placed high in the trie hierarchy, less time is needed to look up local addresses. When these two techniques are used together, the performance of the switch can be greatly enhanced.

BLOCKING

Both internal and output blocking can occur in a packet switch. In a circuit switch, since the paths are fixed, a path will always be available, or if a path is not available when a telephone call comes in to the switch, the call is rejected. Yet in a packet switch it is not possible to determine if packets will be blocked since the paths are not preestablished. To assist in reducing the loss of packets to blocking, the following methods can be used:

- *Overprovisioning*. In this approach, the internal links in the switch fabric perform faster than the input links do. This design can accommodate arriving packets that are contending for the same output to be carried by faster internal links in the switch fabric. This method frees up the input ports and reduces collisions.

- *Buffers*. If paths in the switch fabric are not available, then incoming packets will be lost. Buffers that are placed on the input side and in the switch fabric can store packets until a path or outbound link is available.

- *Backpressure*. In a multistage switch that contains different levels or stages to process the packets, one of the stages in the switching fabric may not be able to pass on any more packets. When this occurs, signals are sent back toward the input of the switch to prevent any more packets from entering the blocked stage. While backpressure is in effect, the switch can either buffer packets at the input or drop the packets at the inputs. With backpressure, packets may be lost, but the loss occurs at the input locations and not in the switch fabric. This design does not require the switch fabric to handle a lot of internal buffering activities.

- *Sorting and randomization*. In this scheme, a sorting or randomizing stage is placed before the switch fabric. This helps to reduce internal blocking by the switch.

- *Parallel fabrics*. In this design, there are multiple switch fabrics running in parallel between the inputs and outputs. This approach helps reduce contention by the packets to the switch fabric. But, in order for the method to function properly, the transit time from the input to the output side must be fast.

ATM SWITCHING

Asynchronous Transfer Mode (ATM) first began to appear in the 1980s and early 1990s. It is a cell- (packet-) switching technology that is connection-oriented and uses virtual circuits. The speed of ATM on fiber-optic links ranges from 0.6 to 2.4 Gbps. The connection phase of an ATM link is called *signaling*, and the most common protocol used is Q.2931. The Q.2931 protocol provides several features, such as discovering the route across the ATM network and allocating resources at the switches used by a connection. The primary purpose of these features is to provide quality of service (QoS) options.

When an ATM connection is established, the signaling message includes the address of the destination device. There are different formats for the signaling embedded address. This address is not the same as the MAC address. Because ATM is a cell technology, the packets have a specific length of 53 bytes. The cell or packet consists of 5 bytes for the header and 48 bytes for the data and remaining packet elements. The term *cell* is used on an ATM network instead of the term *packet* because the size of the packets (cells) is fixed in length. Most other packet-switching networks support variable-length packets, and the term *packet* is typically used to refer to networks with different length packets.

Using fixed-length packets has some advantages. For example, the amount of overhead used by other systems to accommodate variable-length packets is not needed. In addition, the fixed-length packet simplifies an ATM hardware switch. Fixed packet lengths also enable the switches to perform tasks in parallel because each of the systems takes the same time to do a task. This approach permits scalability of switch designs. The fixed-length cells also make possible more consistent management of buffers, or queues at the switches. Asynchronous Transfer Mode queues can still become filled when network traffic increases, but it is easier to handle buffer issues when packets are the same size.

ATM cells come in two formats: *user-network interface* and *network-network interface*. The user-network interface (UNI) format is typically used at the interface between the telephone company and the customer. The network-network interface (NNI) is found at the junction of two telephone companies.

Switching Fabric

The switching fabric is all the elements, links, and components that handle the transfer of packets from the input side of a switch to the output side. There have been, and continue to be, many designs proposed and used for switching fabric methodologies. Some are too expensive to implement with current technologies, and others are not sufficient to handle the increased growth in network traffic. In this section, we cover some of the switching fabrics and their schemes.

CROSSBAR

This style of switching fabric was covered earlier in this chapter in the section on space-division switching. The simplest style of crossbar is a one-to-one correspondence of the number of input and output ports. If the number of inputs is N (and, thus, the number of outputs is also N), the number of junctions or crosspoints is N^2.

The crosspoints may be either on or off, and, therefore, the switch is internal nonblocking. Because these crosspoints may be on or off, the device needs a switching schedule that indicates what outputs at a specific time are connected to the inputs. If the packets arriving at the input are entering at a constant rate, then the schedule can be determined in advance. But if the packets are not arriving at a consistent rate, the schedule cannot be calculated in advance.

If two packets arrive at the same input and they want to go to the same output, only one will make it to the output. This results in output blocking. To help overcome this, the crossbar component can be run faster than the inputs, or buffers can be placed in the crossbar to hold the packets that are waiting for an output. In another approach, a buffer can be placed at each crosspoint. But crossbar switches do not perform well for large switches even with some of these enhancements. Crossbar switches perform satisfactorily in small switches or as components in larger switches.

BROADCAST

A broadcast switch is physically like a crossbar switch in that the input and output lines are perpendicular, and crosspoints exist at each intersection. In the broadcast scheme, an incoming packet is assigned an output port, and the switch broadcasts the packet to all of the output ports. The output ports look to see if the output port ID of the packet matches their port, and if it does, the packet is stored in the output port's queue (buffer). On the output side, a scheduler handles packets contending for the same output connection. A broadcast switch does not need a scheduler for the crosspoints, but output port addresses must be matched at the output ports.

A problem with broadcast switches is scalability. As the number of input and output lines increases, the number of address comparisons at the output buffers rises dramatically, and the system cannot keep up with the demand.

SWITCHING FABRIC ELEMENTS

A technique for overcoming the limitations of crossbar and broadcast switches is to combine both methods in a switch. The switching fabrics are referred to as *switching fabric elements* because they use a combination of crossbar and broadcast schemes. A benefit of these types of designs is that once a packet has been assigned to the correct output port, the packet will automatically go from any input to the appropriate output port. This feature is called *self-routing*. Another feature of combining switching fabric methods is that the fabric can be either synchronous or asynchronous.

Bridges

Before we delve into the details of switches used on LANs in comparison to switches used on telephone networks or WAN links, we need to cover bridges. A switch is essentially a collection of bridges incorporated into a physical unit. Each of the ports on a switch functions in the same manner as a bridge. Several years ago, when LANs began to grow in popularity and size, bridges were developed to help divide up and balance the flow of traffic in a LAN. On current networks, the amount of traffic and the number of devices are much larger than in the bridge days. This has led to the development of switches to accommodate these increased demands. In general, whenever you come across a reference to a bridge for a LAN, the same concept holds true for a switch used on a LAN.

Throughout the development of local area networks, there have been several techniques developed to extend the physical capacity of a LAN. As we have seen earlier, there are limits to how far signals can travel down a copper, fiber-optic, or atmospheric media before the signal becomes too weak and/or noisy to be able to properly extract the data from the signals. This property, called *attenuation*, can be overcome, or reduced, through the use of other physical network devices. Repeaters, for example, can be used to boost the signal so it can travel further down the media. Although repeaters can help make the signal travel further, they do not help in situations where there is a lot of traffic. Bridges, on the other hand, can reduce the amount of overall traffic on a network segment by constraining traffic to portions of the network.

A bridge connects two network segments that are on the same logical network. That is, bridges do not connect two different networks that have different network layer addresses. Bridges operate at the MAC sublayer of the datalink layer and use physical or MAC address information. A bridge has no knowledge if the data packet is of type IP, IPX, or whatever, and the bridge treats all packets equally. In order for a bridge to be able to pass data from one side to the other, the bridge operates in promiscuous mode so it reads all packets. Before a bridge passes the packet on, it first checks to make sure the packet, or frame, has arrived intact. If the frame is damaged, the bridge will not pass the packet on. If the bridge determines that the frame is intact, the frame is passed on according to the bridging functions. One nice benefit of having a bridge evaluate the integrity of frames is that if one segment is experiencing problems, such as electrical interference that is producing bad packets, these problems will not be propagated to the other network segment attached to the bridge. In addition, if a collision has occurred on one side of the bridge, the fractured data packets will not be transferred to the other network segments.

For a bridge to play a role in managing traffic loads, it makes no sense for bridges to just blindly copy frames from one side to another. Instead, bridges perform what is called *frame filtering*; they will not pass a frame on to the other network segment unless the packet needs to go there. Bridges do forward all broadcast and multicast frames so the devices on the other side of the bridge receive the information.

TRANSPARENT BRIDGES

On some types of networks, such as IEEE 802.3 and related implementations (Ethernet), the presence of a bridge on the network is transparent to the other devices because they have no knowledge of its presence. This concept, along with the way the bridge works, leads to the term *transparent bridge*.

In order to keep track of where the different devices are on each side of a bridge, the bridge maintains a hash table of physical addresses of the devices that connect to each of its ports. For example, if the bridge is connected to Segment A that contains devices Computer 01 and Computer 02, the table will list those machines as accessible on port Segment A. Similarly, on the other port, Segment B, devices Computer 100 and Computer 200 are accessible, and the bridge table lists those two machines at port Segment B. Figure 5-3 illustrates an example of a bridged LAN and the bridge's table.

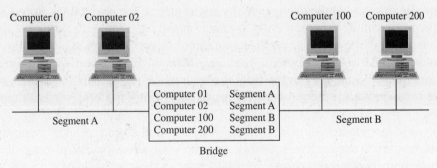

Fig. 5-3.   Example of a bridged LAN and the bridge's table.

When Computer 01 sends a frame to Computer 100, the bridge reads the destination address in Computer 01's packet, and since it knows Computer 100 is located on the Segment B port, the bridge forwards the packet to the Segment B port. On the other hand, if Computer 01 sends a packet to Computer 02, the bridge realizes the destination device is on the same side as the sending device, and the packet is not forwarded to the other side; that is, it is not forwarded to the network Segment B.

The question then becomes, how does the bridge know what devices are accessible through each of its ports? For most bridges, this is accomplished through a learning process. Learning, or adaptive bridges, start the learning process when the bridge is first turned on. When a bridge picks up a frame on the network, it performs two tasks. First, it reads the source address of the packet and adds that to its table along with the port from which it received the packet. For example, if the source address is Computer 100 and the packet was received on port Segment A, then the table lists Computer 100 as on the network Segment A. The second task is to read the destination address. If the destination address is already in the bridge's table, then the bridge will forward the packet, depending on the table's information. But if there is no entry in the table for the destination device, the bridge will send the packet out all ports, since it does not know where the destination device is. The process of sending packets out all ports is called *flooding*. Over the course of time, as frames from different devices travel around the network, the bridge builds a complete table for all the devices. This style of learning the location of devices by reading the packets is referred to as *backward learning*.

Once the bridge reaches the stage where its hash table has all the device entries, the bridge is functioning in its desired mode, or steady state, and is forwarding packets from side to side only when necessary. In this mode, the bridge's hash table is also referred to as a *filtering database*, since only certain packets can cross to the other side of the bridge. Because networked devices tend to be chatty, sending out packets when they start up and expecting replies from packets they send out, bridges can quickly learn the location of all the devices. The types of bridges that learn the environment are also referred to as *transparent* because their operation is transparent to the devices on the network, which have no knowledge of the bridges on the network.

An item to consider on a bridged network is what happens when devices are turned off and on, or when a device is moved to another location on the network. In order to handle changes in the environment, the hash tables stored in the bridges are dynamic. When an entry is made in the hash table, the time the frame arrives is noted in the table. At regular time intervals, the bridge looks at all the time stamps in the hash table entries. Any time stamps that are older than what is permitted by the bridge are purged from the hash table. This process also means that if there is no traffic on the network for a period of time, the bridge's hash table is emptied.

Knowing the nature of how bridges function and doing proper planning of network resources can improve performance on your network. By placing devices that communicate between themselves frequently on the same side of a bridge, their traffic on the other side of the bridge is eliminated. That is, each segment's traffic does not interfere with the other side's traffic. The effect is almost like running two networks in parallel. A good rule of thumb for device placement in respect to a bridge is that no more than 20 percent of the traffic should be bridged, and the remaining should be local.

So far we have been discussing bridges on a LAN where all the devices are in close physical proximity. But bridges can also be used to span large distances between network segments. For example, bridges can be used between two segments separated by a leased satellite link. The bridge at each segment's interface to the satellite link keeps local traffic from crossing over the satellite connection. This also helps to reduce delays because the amount of bandwidth necessary on the satellite link does not need to be as high as the local bandwidth because not all of the packets are sent to the other side. There is, however, another feature required by bridges that connect large distances. Since the speed of the local LAN is often quite a bit faster than the WAN link, the bridges must contain sufficient buffers to store all the packets that need to be sent to the other segment.

More than one bridge can be used on a network to create multiple segments. For example, Figure 5-4 illustrates an example of a network that consists of eight segments that are connected together by seven bridges.

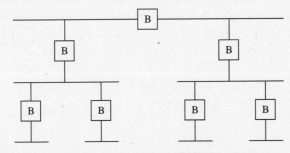

Fig. 5-4.   Multiple-segment bridged LAN.

At the same time, the physical placement of multiple switches in a network can lead to packets traveling in infinite loops through a cycle of bridges. To discuss how this can come about, we will use the example a multiple-segment bridged LAN shown in Figure 5-5.

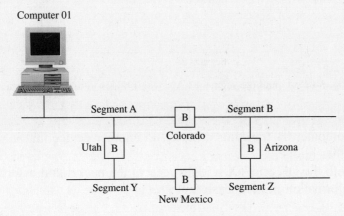

Fig. 5-5.   A multiple-segment bridged LAN design that creates infinite loops.

Let's go through the step-by-step process of how this problem develops when a system on Segment A sends out a broadcast:

1. The broadcast is delivered to Segment B and Segment Y.
2. The New Mexico bridge sends the broadcasts onto Segment Z.
3. The Arizona bridge sends the broadcasts onto Segment Z.
4. Segment Z now contains duplicate copies of the broadcasts.
5. The Arizona bridge sends the broadcasts delivered to Segment Z by the New Mexico bridge to Segment B.
6. Segment B now contains duplicate copies of the broadcasts.
7. The New Mexico bridge sends the broadcasts delivered to Segment Z by the Arizona bridge to Segment Y.
8. Segment Y now contains duplicate copies of the broadcasts.

This process continues forever, so there are potentially an infinite number of broadcasts circulating around the cycle of bridges. This type of problem can also develop when nonbroadcast packets are placed on the network with redundant bridges that do not know the location of the destination. As an example, we will go through the series of events that occur in redundant bridge locations that together produce a bridging loop. Figure 5-6 is an example of two network segments that are connected by two bridges that are in the learning stage. The device labeled Computer 01 is located on Segment A and sends out a packet for a device that is not known to the bridges. In addition, the bridges have not received any previous packets from Computer 01, so they will read the source address in the packet and place the information in their hash tables.

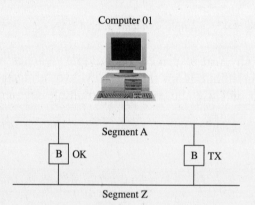

Fig. 5-6.   A multiple-segment LAN with bridges in the learning stage.

9. Computer 01 transmits a packet to another device that is not known by either bridge.
10. Both the OK and TX bridges receive the packet and enter the following information in their hash tables:

OK Bridge TX Bridge

Computer 01 on Segment A   Computer 01 on Segment A

11.   The frame is flooded (transmitted) by both bridges to Segment Z because the location of the destination device is not in the bridge's hash tables. Figure 5-7 illustrates the flow of the Computer 01 packet on Segment Z.

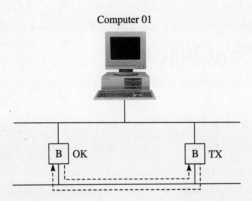

Fig. 5-7.   Flow of packet from Computer 01 onto the Segment Z section of the network.

12.   The flooded packets are read by the other bridge on the Segment Z network segment. That is, the Computer 01 packet forwarded by the TX bridge is read by the OK bridge, and the Computer 01 packet forwarded by the OK bridge is read by the TX bridge. The packets read by the two bridges indicate that Computer 01 is on Segment Z because that is the network segment from which the packets were received by the bridge.

13.   The bridges update their hash tables to reflect the new information:

OK Bridge TX Bridge

Computer 01 on Segment Z   Computer 01 on Segment Z

14.   Because the location of the destination device is not known, both bridges forward the packet back onto Segment A.

15.   The two bridges receive the new packets and determine that Computer 01 is on Segment A, since that is the device from which they received the packet.

16.   The bridges update their hash tables to include the new information:

OK Bridge TX Bridge

Computer 01 on Segment Z Computer 01 on Segment Z

The whole process starts over again, and the result is that the contents in the hash tables keep switching back and forth and the network comes to a standstill.

In order to prevent this type of looping from occurring, some of the bridges in a redundant bridge arrangement must be directed not to forward frames to their output port. One way to overcome this issue is through the use of the spanning tree algorithm.

SPANNING TREE ALGORITHM

Infinite loops occur in a network containing multiple bridges as a result of one of the following conditions:

- The bridges are forwarding all frames to all the segments.
- The arrangement of bridges is such that redundancy or cycling of bridges results.

Incorporating redundant bridges in a network is often a good idea, but processes must be in place to reduce infinite loops. To prevent these problems, some bridges in the network must be configured not to forward frames under normal operations. But if a bridge that is forwarding frames fails, the nonforwarding (redundant) bridges must be able to take over and keep the network running. Fortunately, the network administrator does not have to manually configure which bridges forward frames or intervene when a bridge fails. The spanning tree routine, which was developed by Radia Perlman, takes care of these tasks automatically.

When a bridge is powered on, it sends out special types of packets called bridge protocol data units (BPDUs) so the bridge can communicate with the other bridges on the network. All the bridges then execute the distributed spanning tree (DST) algorithm and decide which bridge does and which bridge does not forward frames. Bridges that are on redundant segments decide among themselves, through the DST algorithm, which bridge will forward the frames. The other bridges on a redundant segment do not forward any frames but are ready to take over if the bridge that is forwarding frames fails. Each bridge creates a map or tree of the bridged network.

When a bridge in a spanning tree configuration is first powered on, the bridge informs all the other bridges of its vital statistics by sending out the information in BPDUs. The vital statistics consist of the following information:

- The ID of the bridge.
- The ID of the bridge that the bridge sending out the BPDUs believes is the root bridge.
- The distance between the root bridge and the bridge sending out the BPDUs. The distance is measured in hops, where each hop represents a bridge.

The bridge ID value may be set by the vendor, or on some bridges it can be set by the administrator. From the collection of ID numbers, the bridges go through a decision process and determine which of the bridges has the lowest ID number. The one bridge in the collection of bridges that has the lowest ID number becomes the root bridge for the network. Once the root is determined, the remaining bridges calculate the shortest path to the root bridge. Within each group of redundant bridges, one of the bridges becomes the designated bridge and will forward frames between the two attached segments. The remaining bridges in the group will not forward frames. The map of the routes from the root bridge to the designated bridges is called the *spanning tree*. If a bridge fails, the entire process of determining the root, designated bridges, and the paths is recalculated. Similarly, if there are any topology changes or a bridge is powered on, the spanning tree algorithm will detect the change and determine a new root bridge and/or designated bridges, depending on what the change was. Figure 5-8 shows an example of a redundant bridge network without the implementation of the spanning tree protocol.

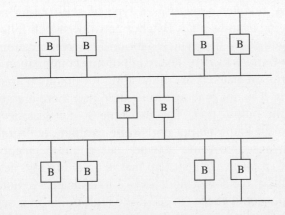

Fig. 5-8.   A redundant bridged network without a spanning tree.

Figure 5-9 shows the result of the spanning tree process on the same redundant bridge network shown in Figure 5-7.

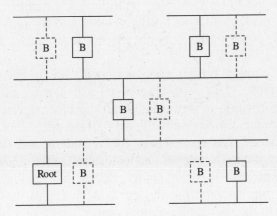

Fig. 5-9.   A redundant bridged network with a spanning tree configuration.

One drawback to the spanning tree configuration is that some bridges are idle and do not participate in frame forwarding. For example, during bursts of traffic, the single forwarding bridge between two segments may become congested, and the other redundant bridge(s) cannot be used to help alleviate the traffic load.

SOURCE ROUTING BRIDGES

Source routing bridges are used primarily by Token Ring networks and are not implemented in Carrier Sense, Multiple Access, Collision Detection (CSMA/CD) (for example, Ethernet) or token bus networks. When a packet is released onto the media by a device on a Token Ring network, it is assumed the device knows where the destination device is located. The location of the destination device is known because each device maintains a table of the locations of the other devices on the network. Thus the term *source routing* is used because each source device knows the path or route to each device. Source routing networks are also known as *self-routing networks*. In some references, self-routing networks are referred to as *banyan networks*. A *Batcher network* is a type of self-routing network that sorts packets in order. Some designs put a Batcher network switch followed by a banyan network switch together in the switch fabric. This combination creates what is known as a *Batcher-banyan switch*. The result of this combination is a non-blocking switch, and as long as the packets are all heading for unique output ports, there will be no collisions. But it is not practical to assume that there are no packets that are destined for the same output port. The Sunshine switch was developed to permit packets to switch to the same output port while avoiding collisions.

Every device on a source route network has a unique identification number. When a device sends a packet to a system that is on a different network segment, it sets the high-order bit of the source address to 1 to indicate a remote segment. When a bridge receives a packet, it checks to see if the high-order bit is set to 1, and if it is, the bridge will process the frame. If the high-order bit is not set to 1, the bridge ignores the frame. The bridge then searches the route contained in the packet for the same number of the LAN the frame arrived on. Once it locates the matching LAN number, the bridge checks to see if the bridge number following the LAN number in the packet is the same number as itself, that is, the same number as the bridge. If the bridge's number is found to be associated with the LAN number, the bridge reads the destination LAN number after its bridge number and forwards the frame on to the destination LAN. If the bridge's number is not associated with the LAN, the bridge does not forward the frame.

Devices on a source routed bridging network need a way to find the other devices to build their route tables. Discovery frames are sent out by each device on the network, and this information is forwarded to all the other devices. The discovery frame sent out by a source device essentially asks all the other devices where it is on the network. The devices send replies back to the source, and from the collected information the source device can determine its location in the bridged network. The idea behind this process is that the source device has enough information to determine the best route to get from device to device. But the discovery frame process also delivers to the source all possible routes. Every time a discovery frame passes through redundant bridges, duplicate copies of the discovery frames end up on the remote network segment. This extra information can lead to the condition called *frame explosion*, wherein the number of frames increases every time a bridge is traversed. To reduce this problem, once a device has discovered a route to a specific device, the path is stored in memory so the discovery process does not keep running.

Managing source routed bridging networks is more involved than managing transparent bridging networks. There is essentially no management or configuration of a transparent bridge since it learns the network automatically. If you have a transparent bridge that allows you to set the bridge number, then some management is required. Furthermore, if the bridge supports Simple Network Management Protocol (SNMP), some configuration is necessary so you can monitor the device, but a configuration is not required for the device to operate. On a source routed bridging network, the numbers of IDs of the LANs must be set, and it is very important there are no duplicate LAN numbers across the entire bridged environment. As with transparent bridges, if the source routed bridge supports SNMP and you wish to trap events, you may need to configure SNMP.

OTHER BRIDGE OPTIONS

A bridge can participate in priority-level traffic forwarding for LANs that support priorities. For example, token networks such as FDDI, Token Ring, and token bus support priority levels. The need to determine how to handle priority-level considerations at bridges has led to the development of traffic classes and quality of service, or QoS. Traffic classification pertains to bridges that operate at the datalink layer of the OSI model, and QoS impacts bridges, routers, and network layer switches. The idea behind these processes is to provide an effective method for bridges to handle time-sensitive data such as video or voice information. Frames that contain higher-priority values are transmitted before lower-priority buffered frames in a bridge.

VIRTUAL LANS (VLANS)

When you add more bridges to a LAN, the size of the network can become quite large and the traffic load increases. This growth and size become an issue when you are dealing with broadcast packets. Bridges forward any broadcast packets they receive to all of their ports except the port they received the broadcast from. In a large environment it may not be necessary for all devices to broadcast to all of the systems on the network. Instead there may be groupings of machines that need to see each other's broadcasts but no broadcasts from outside the group. One way to divide the LAN into logical groups is with VLANs. Virtual LANs (VLANs) make it possible for you to assign network segments to the same or different VLANs. The effect is like having individual separate LANs within the LAN. To distinguish each VLAN from another, a unique ID is assigned to each VLAN. Any device within a VLAN can communicate with any other devices in the same VLAN but not outside its VLAN. Figure 5-10 shows an example of a bridged LAN that contains three VLANs.

When the computer labeled Notebook 01 sends out a packet for Notebook 50, the OK bridge examines the VLAN number the packet came from. If the VLAN ID is the same as the VLAN number of the OK bridge, the packet is forwarded to the TX bridge. The TX bridge also inspects the VLAN number of the packet, and if it is the same as the bridge's VLAN ID, the packet is delivered to Segment Z. Packets sent

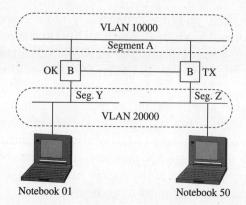

Fig. 5-10. A bridged LAN with three VLANs.

from devices on the two segments, Segment Y and Segment Z, will not go to Segment A because of the different VLAN numbers.

One of the nice features about configuring VLANs is the setup. Virtual LANs are logical sub-LANs inside the LAN, so cables or connections do not have to be physically modified. VLAN numbers are configured in the bridge's software by the administrator. If there is a topology change or address change, the administrator makes all those changes in the software configuration of the bridges.

Switches

The term *switched LAN* is used to refer to a network that contains a device that moves or transfers frames between multiple devices. The physical appearance of a LAN switch is similar to that of a hub or concentrator. Each port of the multiport switch can be attached to a single device or to a hub. But although the physical appearance may be similar, the functionality of a switch and a hub is different.

Each device attached to a hub shares the media with all the other devices on the same hub. For example, let's examine a hub on a contention-based network, such as Ethernet, that has six connected devices. When device Notebook 1 wants to send a message to Notebook 4, all the devices on the hubbed network see the packet, and all devices must contend for access to the common media. The same thing happens when device Notebook 3 sends a message to Notebook 2—packets from all devices are seen by all the other devices. Figure 5-11 illustrates the flow of packets in a hubbed network.

A switch, on the other hand, operates as a bridge at each of the connection ports. Using the same example of a network with six devices (Figure 5-11), let's see what happens when a switch is put in place of the hub (Figure 5-12). With a switch in place, when Notebook 1 wants to send a message to Notebook 4, a bridge is established in the path between the two ports that the two notebooks are attached to. The same happens for data exchanged between Notebook 3 and Notebook 2.

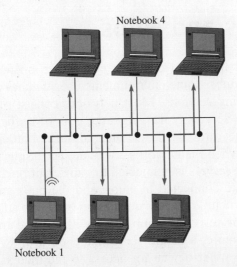

Fig. 5-11.   Flow of packets in a hubbed network.

When Notebook 1 transmits data destined for Notebook 4, none of the other devices attached to the other ports will see the packets. The same goes for Notebook 3 and Notebook 2—only the two ports with the two conversing notebooks will see the packets. This bridging function at each of the ports greatly increases the overall transmission of data from one side of the switch to another.

On a hubbed network, the fastest rate at which data can be transferred across the hub is the maximum throughput of a single system, since only one device at a time can use the media. On a switched network, the throughput rate is the maximum throughput of a single system times the number of ports that contain a connected system divided by two. In other words:

Switch throughput = rate of a single system × number of connected ports/2

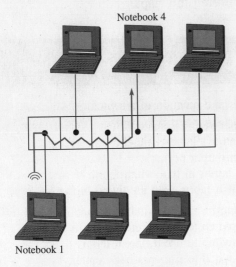

Fig. 5-12.   Flow of packets in a switched network.

Integrating Switches and Hubs

Combining switches and hubs is a common occurrence on today's LANs. Since switches cost more than hubs, some environments use switches at certain locations and hubs for the remaining sections. Most networks consist of a combination of servers and workstations. Servers typically get the bulk of traffic addressed to them because of the services they provide. Thus potential traffic bottlenecks can occur on a shared media network when many workstations are accessing the server. In these environments, each of the servers is connected to a different port on the switch. The remaining workstations are connected by hubs, and the hubs are connected to the remaining ports on the switch. While the devices on each hub attached to the switch see all the traffic on their respective hub, they will not see traffic on any other hubbed segment. Furthermore, a single server attached to a switch port does not have to contend with any other device for access to the media. In addition, some switches support full duplex mode on the ports. If the servers attached to the ports support full duplex, then the connection port to the server can be switched to full duplex mode, further increasing the throughput to and from the server.

Integrating Switches and Routers

Combining switches and hubs is a common occurrence in LANs that are not communicating with other networks. When there is a need to connect to another network, routers must be used at the junction between the different networks. In these combinations, switches assist in optimizing usage of the available bandwidth for devices communicating between themselves on the local network. When a system needs to access another device outside the network, routers handle the switching or routing of the packets to another network. Routers and routing functions and features are covered in Chapter 7.

 ## Review Questions

5.1   Define, in general terms, the function of a switch.

5.2   The role of a part mapper is to associate
   a.   An output port to an available channel on the media
   b.   An input port to an output port
   c.   An input port to a buffer in the switch fabric
   d.   A buffer in the switch fabric with an output buffer

5.3   The reduction of blocking in transit switches is accomplished by
   a.   The ability of the switch to use different outputs
   b.   The ability of the switch to use different inputs
   c.   The ability of the switch to use crossbar elements
   d.   The ability of the switch to reserve outputs

5.4   Define internal blocking.

5.5   Briefly define what a trie is used for.

5.6   Is it necessary for a broadcast switch to have a scheduler to arrange switching specifics?

5.7   Describe what is meant by head-of-line blocking.

5.8   What is the recommended division of devices in a bridged network?

5.9   Define the term *hop* when used in reference to a bridged network.

5.10 Briefly define the term *switch fabric*.

5.11 A telephone switch is a good example of which of the following types of switches:
   a. Packet
   b. Buffer
   c. Fabric
   d. Circuit

5.12 Define output blocking.

5.13 Define the term backpressure in the context of a multistage switch.

5.14 Explain the purpose of using VLANs on bridged networks.

5.15 Describe the advantages of combining switches with hubs and routers.

Problems

5.1   Given the following diagram of a spanning tree bridged network (Figure 5-13), which bridges would be used in forwarding packets?

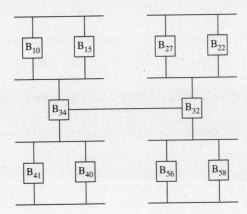

Fig. 5-13. Spanning tree bridged network before bridge selection.

5.2   Why would an attempt to implement the spanning tree protocol on repeaters fail?

5.3   Why do cell-switching networks use virtual circuits instead of packet switching?

5.4   A computer on a bridged network sends out a packet to a device that is not present on the network. What do the bridges do with the packet?

5.5   Most current networks that have sufficient financial resources usually prefer switches instead of hubs. Give a brief explanation for this preference.

5.6   A simple crossbar switch has five input lines and five output lines. How many crosspoints are present in the switch?

5.7   Give an example of packet meta-data.

5.8   Define time-division switching.

5.9   Explain time-space-time switching.

5.10   What is overprovisioning?

5.11   Explain the type of addresses used by switches to filter and pass packets.

5.12   Explain how bridging loops occur.

5.13   What is the formula for calculating the throughput of a switch?

Answers to Review Questions

5.1   **a.** switch is the hardware used to perform switching, which entails moving information between different networks and network segments.

5.2   **b.** A port mapper is found only in packet switches and is not used on circuit switches. The packet switch contains a table that associates, or maps, each input to an output. The switch reads the destination address of the packet at the input, looks up the location in a table, and then assigns an output port to the packet. Circuit switches do not need a port mapper or table because the destination output is already known when the packet arrives at the switch's input.

5.3   **a.** A transit switch reduces the occurrence of blocking because of the switch's ability to use different outputs.

5.4   When internal blocking occurs, there is no path to an available output. Packets building up at the buffers waiting for the same output will prevent other packets further back in line from getting a chance at their output port.

5.5   One common data structure for best-match situations is the trie arrangement. The trie organization is a hierarchy of arrays, where each entry can have one of three values:

- If a better match exists elsewhere in the data, the entry will contain a pointer to another array.
- If no known better matches exist, the entry indicates this status with a special symbol.
- If the parent of the point in the tree contains possible valid arrays, the entry contains a null pointer.

5.6   A scheduler is not needed in the broadcast scheme because the incoming packets are assigned an output port, and the switch broadcasts the packet to all of the output ports.

5.7   Head-of-line blocking occurs when packets building up at the buffers waiting for the same output prevent other packets further back in line from getting a chance at their output port.

5.8   A good rule of thumb for device placement in respect to a bridge is that no more than 20 percent of the traffic should be bridged and the remaining traffic should be local.

5.9   On a bridged network, each bridge a packet goes through from sender to destination is referred to as a hop.

5.10   The switch fabric is the hardware and software elements of the switch that move data from a switch input to a switch output. The complexity of the fabric may range from the simple technique of copying the data from the input port and writing it to the output port, to multiprocessor components that concurrently transfer thousands of packets to many output ports.

5.11   **d.**   A good example of a circuit switch is a telephone switch. Circuit switching deals with packets on the media that do not contain any meta-data.

5.12   In an output blocking situation, two inputs are in competition for the same output port, and one does not get access to the output.

5.13   In a multistage switch that contains different levels or stages to process the packets, one of the stages in the switching fabric may not be able to pass on any more packets. When this occurs, signals are sent back toward the input of the switch to prevent any more packets from entering the blocked stage. While backpressure is in effect, the switch can either buffer packets at the input or drop the packets at the inputs. With backpressure, packets may be lost, but the loss occurs at the input locations and not in the switch fabric. This design does not require the switch fabric to handle a lot of internal buffering activities.

5.14   VLANs are used to isolate traffic to subsections of the network. This is an important issue when you are dealing with broadcast packets.

5.15   Attaching devices, such as servers, to their own port on a switch helps reduce the server's traffic from the other network devices. Hubbed devices will see traffic from all devices connected to their hub. But when a hub is attached to a switch, the devices on the hub will not see traffic on other hubbed segments. Routers are used to connect one network to another network. Since switches do not deal with network layer, or logical, addresses, routers are necessary to go from network to network.

Solutions to Problems

5.1   The bridges with the lowest bridge number will be used in a spanning tree environment to prevent bridging loops. Based on the diagram used in the problem, bridge numbers 10, 22, 32, 34, 40, and 56 will be used.

5.2   Bridges and spanning trees use bridge numbers and the physical addresses of the network devices. Repeaters simply copy packets without any knowledge of packet addresses, and repeaters do not contain device IDs.

5.3   Cell switching networks use fixed length packets. This leads to predictable analysis of the signals on the transmission media so that addressing information is not needed. Thus it is more efficient for cell switching to use circuit switching instead of packet switching.

5.4   The bridge does not know that the device is not available. The only thing the bridge is aware of is that the destination device is not in the bridge's table. Thus, when the bridge receives the unknown destination packet, the switch will flood the packet— that is, send the packet to all of its connected network segments.

5.5 Switches can operate basically the same way that hubs do, except switches have the advantage of being more scalable as the network grows. Switches play a role in traffic management, whereas hubs have no such role.

5.6 If the number of inputs is 8 and the number of outputs is 8, the number of junctions or crosspoints is 8^2, or 64.

5.7 An example of meta-data information is the destination and source addresses contained in a packet's header fields. For bridges and switches, these addresses are the MAC or physical layer addresses.

5.8 In time-division switching, the order of packets in the input buffer is different from the order of packets on the output side. The switch only has only one input and output, but the incoming and outgoing lines carry multiplexed data.

5.9 A time-space-time (TST) switch places two time-division switches each at the input crossbar and output crossbar points.

5.10 In overprovisioning, the internal links in the switch fabric perform faster than the input links. This design can help arriving packets that are contending for the same output to be carried by faster internal links in the switch fabric. This method frees up the input ports and reduces collisions.

5.11 Switches operate at the MAC sublayer of the datalink layer and use physical or MAC address information. A switch has no knowledge if the data packet is of type IP, IPX, or whatever, and the switch treats all packets equally.

5.12 Bridging loops occur when redundant bridges continuously send the packets received from the other bridge in the redundant pair to all connected networks.

5.13 On a switched network, the throughput rate is the maximum throughput of a single system times the number of ports that contain a connected system divided by two. In other words:

Switch throughput = rate of a single system × number of connected ports/2

CHAPTER 6

Naming and Addressing

For devices to communicate on a network, they need some way to identify each other. Just as in conversations, where we refer to each other by name, network devices use names to locate and communicate with each other. In addition to names, network devices use addresses to send network packets through the network from the sender to the receiver. Network addresses are like the postal addresses we use to send letters and packages through the mail. In network systems, the names of devices and services are usually used when we interact with the system. That is, people use the names of devices when interacting with network systems and services, and network addresses are used by the devices and services to locate and communicate with each other. Overall, it is easier and less complicated for network devices to use addresses to interact with each other, but it is more difficult for people to use and remember addresses. It is much easier for people to remember words or phrases for network services instead of strings of numbers. For example, it is probably easier for you to remember a Web site by its name, such as www.packet sandpings.com, rather than its IP network address, 209.25.171.161.

To provide support for both names and addresses, the network needs a way to translate names to addresses and addresses to names. This type of functionality is the role of *name resolution services*. The design and methodology of network address names involve several important elements. For example, the addresses must be able to allow other network devices to send the packets onto other networks as necessary to get to the destination. In addition to the structure of network addresses, the addresses somehow must be assigned or associated with the different devices. The process of assigning unique addresses to the different network devices is called *addressing*. Similarly, devices must be assigned or receive a unique network name; this procedure is called *naming*. In this chapter, we explore the processes involved in network addresses and names. Details of services that provide address resolution and routing functions are covered in other chapters.

Hierarchical Naming

The structure of device names needs to include a way to determine the location of the system and the system itself. For example, if a network has two locations, the names of the devices need to indicate the network location and the specific system. To illustrate this, let's look at a fictitious company called Silverton Flags that has two network locations—one each in Loretto and Lancaster. At each site there are two Web servers and several workstations. The company has decided to name the Web servers at each location, Web01 and Web02. Yet using this design, there is no way to distinguish the servers at the Lancaster location from those at the Loretto site. To address this issue, an abbreviation for each location is added to each device's name. Now the servers at Lancaster are named Web01LAN and Web02LAN, and those at Loretto are named Web01LOR, Web02LOR. The company plans to make the Web servers accessible to other networks that also have Web servers. Once again, we need a way to distinguish the servers at the Silverton Flags company from the other Web servers on the network. One solution might be to add the name of the company to the end of each server's name. Now each device has a unique name on a shared network that identifies its location and specific system. This type of addressing scheme that includes information about the location of a system is called *hierarchical*.

A hierarchical naming system also makes it simpler and more efficient to route or move the packets from network to network. If a router in the Silverton Flags company is attached to both the Loretto and Lancaster networks, the router protocol can use a portion of the network address to determine on which network to forward the packets. Once the packets are on the appropriate network, each device can examine the remaining portion of the address to determine if the packets are for that device. In the example we have been using for the Silverton Flag company, each element that makes up the hierarchical name of the device is strung together in one continuous run of characters. This format introduces more complexity into the process of writing software and designing hardware to parse the name of the devices and extract the appropriate address element. Adding a delimiter to separate each address component makes the software and hardware less complicated. Most addressing schemes that use a hierarchical naming structure use a delimiter between each of the address pieces. In addition to using a delimiter, most schemes must specify the length of each portion of the address and acceptable characters. Again, this structure makes it easier for devices to properly read the address information and keeps the packet headers a reasonable size.

In the TCP/IP environment, a dot (period) is used between each address element of the name of a device. For example, the name Web01.Loretto.SilvertonFlags.com would indicate the server called Web01 at the Loretto location of the Silverton Flags company. This name structure is what is used by Domain Name Services (DNSs) for names of devices on a TCP/IP network. Another example of an IP protocol that uses a hierarchical naming structure is the Lightweight Directory Access Protocol (LDAP). In LDAP, commas are used to separate the different components of the name of directory objects. Domain Name Services are covered in more detail in Chapter 8, Services and Applications.

Another important consideration for a hierarchical naming structure that is used by different networks is the authority to catalog and control the different names. If each organization decided to independently create its own names, a high probability exists that the same name would be used for different, unrelated systems. Therefore, naming authorities exist that keep track of the names currently in use, and allow individuals and organizations to register their names. This type of structure prevents duplication of names and confusion on the network. The naming authority can also provide logical organization of names if it decides to implement categorization, such as types of users or companies.

For example, the naming authority may decide to divide the network name space into geographic regions, or domains, starting with continents. To further subdivide the network name space, countries are specified for each of the continents. Under this type of design, the continent level is called the *top-level domain*, and the country level is referred to as a *subdomain*. The name space could be further broken down along state or territory boundaries if more granularity is needed. Using the continent and country type model, the name for one of the Web servers at the Lancaster location in the United States, would be Web02.Lancaster.USA.NA. A Web server at the Loretto location in Canada would be Web01.Loretto.CANADA.NA.

Figure 6-1 shows the hierarchical structure of the system naming convention for the Silverton Flags company used in the examples.

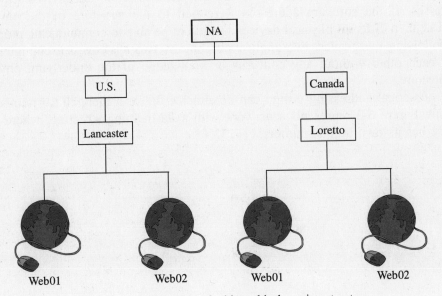

Fig. 6-1.   An example of a hierarchical naming structure.

Asynchronous Transfer Mode (ATM) networks typically use the same type of DNS system that is used on LAN IP networks. One difference is the correlation or mapping of a DNS name to the device's address. ATM uses a different addressing system, which we explore later in this chapter.

The standard telephone network for communicating voice information does not use naming services to identify the different devices. Because of this structure, the phone system uses only addresses to refer to the different communicating devices.

Addressing

Most networks rely on some type of addressing scheme to uniquely identify each of the communicating entities. Even on networks that use names to refer to systems, the various networking protocols and services rely on a numbering scheme to interact with the different network components. Naming systems, as we discussed above, are designed for human interaction with the network because it is more difficult for people to remember long strings of numbers. Numerical addressing schemes are used by the different network devices to communicate among each other. There are some important requirements that must be followed in creating addresses for systems. The first consideration is that each device on the network must have a unique address. Without this requirement, it would be impossible to distinguish between two devices that have the same number. Secondly, the software addressing scheme must be completely independent of any of the devices' physical addresses. If the software addresses were tied to the structure of the physical address, then different physical devices would not be able to communicate properly. By following these rules, two applications on any two systems can communicate with each other without any concerns or knowledge of the underlying physical architecture.

A numerical addressing design can be either a flat or a hierarchical numbering system. Figure 6-2 represents a network with a flat naming structure, where each device has its own unique number.

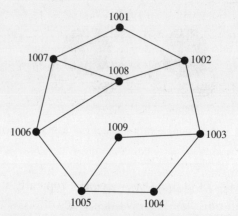

Fig. 6-2. An example of a flat naming structure.

In order for devices to be able to communicate with other systems on the network, each device must maintain a table that contains the route and distance, or hops and times, to each device. For example, the table of other systems that device 1009 uses would look like this:

Destination	Route	Hops
1001	1003-1002-1001	3
1002	1003-1002	2
1003	1003	1
1004	1003-1004	2
1005	1005	1
1006	1005-1006	2
1007	1005-1006-1007	3
1008	1003-1002-1008	3

In the example route and distance table used for device 1009, only the shortest routes between any two devices are listed. The table could also include all possible routes to provide information in case there is a problem along the route with the shortest path. One of the problems with a flat naming structure is that as more and more devices are added to the network, the size of the route tables in each device grows and becomes unusable and unmanageable. Imagine the size of the tables if the Internet used a flat numbering scheme! Tables would contain entries for thousands upon thousands of devices. Add to that the issues that would come up if one of the devices on the list were renumbered! To alleviate these problems, hierarchical numbering schemes are used.

In a hierarchical numbering scheme, portions, or segments, of the network are created along some type of common boundary. For example, the devices may be grouped together based on geographic areas or departments. Furthermore, once systems are grouped together, it is not necessary for all the devices in each area to maintain a complete table of all the other devices. Instead one system in each segment could be designated to hold the table of routes to the other segments. Using this design, the devices in each segment need only know the system in their group that will send messages to other networks. This type of configuration is what is typically used on most computer networks. The device in each group that handles the routing of traffic from that segment to other segments is referred to as a *border router* since it acts as the entry point, or border control, to and from the network segment. These border routers are also called *gateways*. Whenever a device wants to send a message to another system outside its segment, it sends the message to the border router, which then sends the message on to the destination network or route. To demonstrate this concept, the network shown in Figure 6-2 has been redesigned in Figure 6-3 to incorporate a hierarchical numbering scheme.

The network now consists of two segments: 400 and 800. Devices 1001, 1002, 1006, 1007, and 1008 are on network 400; systems 1003, 1004, 1005, and 1009 are on network 800. Using a dot (period) as a separator between the network number and device number, each device can be referred to as follows:

Device Number

400.1001
400.1002
800.1003
800.1004
800.1005
400.1006
400.1007
400.1008
800.1009

On each network, one device is designated as a border router. Devices 400.1002 and 800.1003 are the two border routers. All the other devices on network 400 use 400.1002 as their gateway, and the devices on network 800 use 800.1003 as their gateway. Using this type of hierarchical design, in conjunction with border routers and gateways, each border router needs only to maintain a table of where the other networks are in the environment. The border routers do not need to keep track of all the devices on each network segment. This scheme makes the size of the tables much smaller, easier to manage, and more quickly adaptable to changes in the network. At the same time, this design makes the delivery of messages between networks a little less efficient, but the overall gain in routing simplicity makes up for these inefficiencies. In Chapter 7 we go into more detail on routing protocols and functions.

The method of using a common number to represent a collection of devices is referred to as *aggregation*. This method works well for some solutions, but it does not fit with other scenarios. A good example of where address aggregation is not practical or feasible is with the hardware addresses of different vendors' network cards. For example, let's examine the addressing system used by Ethernet cards. Every device on an Ethernet network must have a unique physical address to distinguish it from all the other devices. The Ethernet hardware address is a 48-bit, or 6-byte, address. There are many different manufacturers of network cards, and in

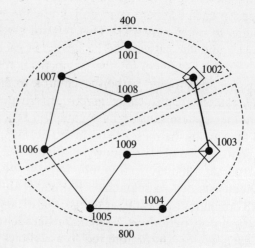

Fig. 6-3. An example of a hierarchical numbering structure.

order to distinguish the different vendors, a portion of the media access (MAC) address contains a vendor code. The IEEE organization controls the assignment of vendor codes, and the first 3 bytes of an Ethernet hardware address represents the manufacturer's number. The last 3 bytes, or adapter number, are assigned by the vendor, and it is up to the vendor to make sure the numbers it assigns for its adapter numbers are unique. This design, where half the number is controlled by an authority and the other portion is determined by the vendor, prevents address duplication. Even if two vendors use the same 3-byte adapter number, the vendor portion of the number makes the MAC numbers unique. Figure 6-4 shows the MAC addresses, of two different NIC cards from the same vendor in different systems. Notice that the first 3 bytes of the MAC addresses are the same for both network cards.

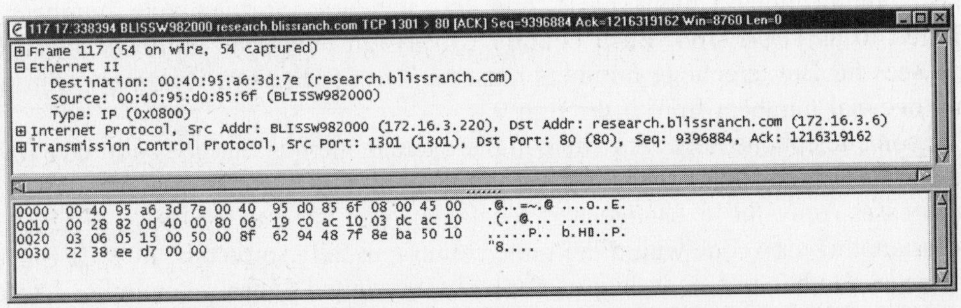

Fig. 6-4.   Same vendor's network cards MAC addresses.

Figure 6-5 is another packet capture, but in this example two different vendors' network cards are in the two systems. Notice that the first 3 bytes of the MAC address are different.

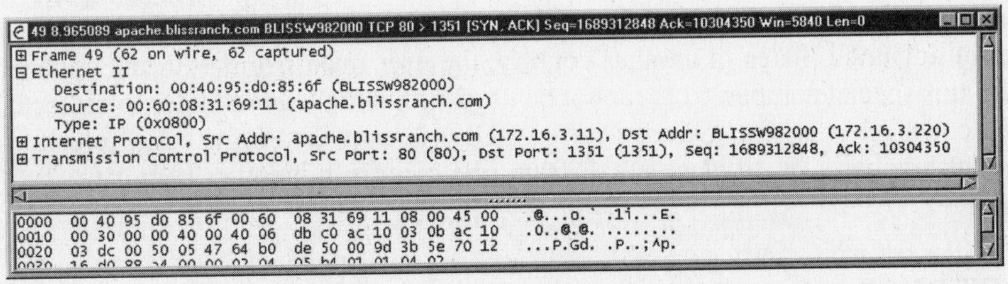

Fig. 6-5.   Different vendors' network cards MAC addresses.

In a network that contains network cards from different vendors, there is no portion of the address that is common to all devices. This style of addressing does not lend itself to incorporating Ethernet addresses into routing tables, since there is no aggregation of addresses. The primary reason for not using MAC addresses in router tables has to do with scalability. Since there is no common portion of the MAC addresses to distinguish which network segment the devices reside on, the tables would have to include the addresses of all devices, making the tables very large and unmanageable.

TELEPHONE NETWORKS

The addressing scheme used by telephones is a hierarchical system that makes it possible for every telephone in the world to have a unique number. The first major division of the telephone address space is by country. Each country is assigned a unique country code. Each country then divides up its areas into area codes, and within each area code the central offices assign different exchange numbers. Finally, within each exchange, all the telephones on the local loop are assigned a unique number. Each element of the telephone number is arbitrary in length, which makes it more challenging to parse the number. But the telephone number is used only when a call is initially set up and is not sent with every packet of voice information. Therefore the parsing complexity only occurs at the stage when the connection is first set up. The authority that governs the country codes is the International Telecommunications Union (ITU), and the standard for telephone numbers is referred to as ITU-E.164. Each country can assign telephone numbers internally as it sees fit. But telephone numbers must be 7 to 15 digits in length and can use only decimal numbers from 0 through 9.

In some telephone networks, the complete telephone number does not have to be used when one calls another telephone number from within the same area code. In these cases, only the exchange and local loop number need to be specified. To access another area code within the same country, usually some type of code is used to contact another area code. For example, in the United States, the number 1 (one) is used to indicate that the call is outside the area code from which the call is originating. With this type of rule, the number used to access another area code cannot be used as the first digit of an area code. For example, in the United States, there are no area codes that begin with the number 1. The term *National Direct Dialing* (NDD) is also used to refer to this special code used to access another area code. Similarly, there needs to be a way to specify when a call is destined for another telephone outside the country. This special code is necessary when complete and incomplete ITU-E.164 addresses are allowed to be used. For example, to place a call from the United States to another country, the user must begin with the code 011. Also this special number, 011, cannot be used within the United States to indicate an area code. *International Direct Dialing* (IDD) is another term used to refer to the special number used to place a call from one country to another country.

INTERNET

The numerical addresses used on Internet Protocol (IP) networks, such as the Internet, are used for each network interface that communicates on the network. For example, a server that has three network cards attached to the network has an IP number for each network card—not just one number assigned to the server. This is different from the numbering scheme for telephones, in which only one number is assigned to each device. Devices on an IP network that have more than one interface or connection to the same or different networks are called *multi-homed systems*. There are two forms of IP addresses that can be used on networks: IPv4 and IPv6. IPv4 is currently the most common form used on today's networks. IPv6 allows for many more devices, but most systems, hardware or software, are not currently equipped to handle the IPv6 addressing scheme.

For systems and devices that will be accessible and present on the Internet, their IP number must be registered with an authority. It is the responsibility of the authority to make sure that each device has a unique number. There are two primary methods by which an Internet-friendly IP number can be obtained. One is through the Internet Service Provider (ISP) that an organization is using. Many ISPs handle all the details of unique number assignment and registration. You can also communicate directly with the Internet Assigned Number Authority (IANA) to obtain a valid Internet IP address. Internet Service Providers also interact with the IANA to make sure the numbers they assign to customers are unique.

IPv4

The numbering scheme used for IPv4 addresses is a 32-bit number that incorporates a two-part hierarchical structure. The IP number contains a network portion that is shared by all devices on the same network segment, and a unique number for each interface. When IPv4 was initially designed, it was expected there would be only a maximum of 256 networks on the Internet. Starting in 1984, it became apparent that with the rapid growth of the Internet, changes in the IP addressing scheme were needed. This necessity led to the development of subnetting, classless interdomain routing (CIDR; pronounced *cider*), and Dynamic Host Configuration Protocol (DHCP).

The 32-bit IP address, as typically seen by humans, is a 4-byte address where each byte, or octet, is separated by a dot (period). For example, 172.16.3.4 is how the IP address typically appears when setting the address in software interfaces. This number format is also called *dotted decimal notation*. Figures 6-6 and 6-7 show two different server operating systems' IP configuration information. In the first example, Figure 6-6, the decimal value for the IP address is used. In the second example, Figure 6-7, the hexadecimal value for the IP address is used. Some operating systems permit the use of either decimal or hexadecimal values for the IP address.

Packets that are sent out on an IP network include an IP header that contains many items, including the source and destination devices' IPv4 header details displayed from a packet capture program. Notice that the fourth line from the top of the screen image indicates the version of IP as 4.

The design of the IP addressing scheme divides the addresses into five classes: A, B, C, D, and E. This separation of the address space into classes is referred to as *classful IP addressing*. To distinguish the different classes, specific bit patterns are used to indicate the class of the address. The bit pattern in the first portion of the first byte of the 4-byte address determines the IP address class. In the table below, the bit pattern of the first byte is listed for each class. Note that in the table, an *x* indicates that either a 1 or a 0 can be used because this portion of the IP number has no impact on the classification of the IP address.

Bit Pattern	Class

0 x x x x x x   A
1 0 x x x x x   B
1 1 0 x x x x   C
1 1 1 0 x x x   D
1 1 1 1 0 x x x   E

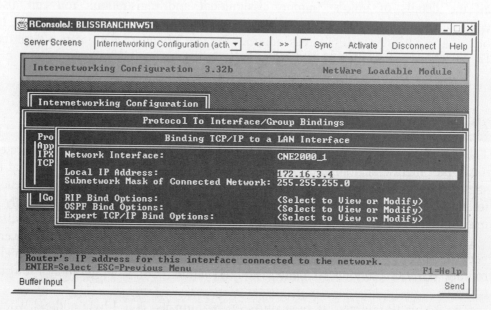

Fig. 6-6. IP address using decimal values.

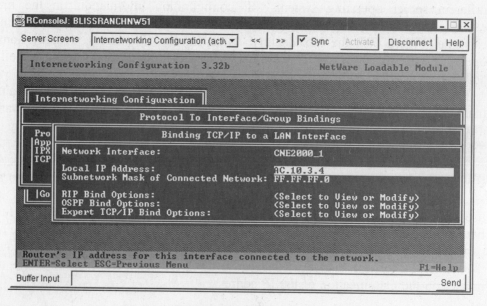

Fig. 6-7. IP address using hexadecimal values.

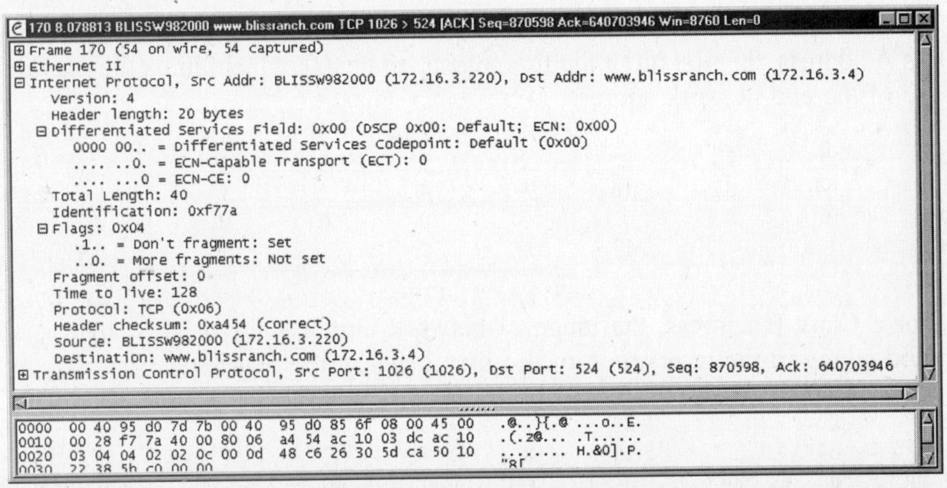

```
170 8.078813 BLISSW982000 www.blissranch.com TCP 1026 > 524 [ACK] Seq=870598 Ack=640703946 Win=8760 Len=0
⊞ Frame 170 (54 on wire, 54 captured)
⊞ Ethernet II
⊟ Internet Protocol, Src Addr: BLISSW982000 (172.16.3.220), Dst Addr: www.blissranch.com (172.16.3.4)
     Version: 4
     Header length: 20 bytes
  ⊟ Differentiated Services Field: 0x00 (DSCP 0x00: Default; ECN: 0x00)
        0000 00.. = Differentiated Services Codepoint: Default (0x00)
        .... ..0. = ECN-Capable Transport (ECT): 0
        .... ...0 = ECN-CE: 0
     Total Length: 40
     Identification: 0xf77a
  ⊟ Flags: 0x04
        .1.. = Don't fragment: Set
        ..0. = More fragments: Not set
     Fragment offset: 0
     Time to live: 128
     Protocol: TCP (0x06)
     Header checksum: 0xa454 (correct)
     Source: BLISSW982000 (172.16.3.220)
     Destination: www.blissranch.com (172.16.3.4)
⊞ Transmission Control Protocol, Src Port: 1026 (1026), Dst Port: 524 (524), Seq: 870598, Ack: 640703946

0000  00 40 95 d0 7d 7b 00 40  95 d0 85 6f 08 00 45 00   .@..}{.@ ...o..E.
0010  00 28 f7 7a 40 00 80 06  a4 54 ac 10 03 dc ac 10   .(.z@... .T......
0020  03 04 04 02 02 0c 00 0d  48 c6 26 30 5d ca 50 10   ........ H.&0].P.
0030  22 38 5b c0 00 00                                    "8[
```

Fig. 6-8. IPv4 header details.

Another component of the class definition involves the division of the IP address to represent the common network portion and the unique interface, or host, number. The devices on the same portion of a network must all use the same network number. This is necessary because the routers that are at the boundaries of the different networks, or subnets, use the network addresses to determine where to route packets. The second portion of the IP address must be different for all devices, or hosts, on the same network. Again, the designers of the IPv4 addressing scheme defined the following specifications:

Class	Number of Network Bits	Number of Host Bits
A	8	24
B	16	16
C	24	8

Notice that Class D and Class E are not included in the above table. The reason is that these two classes are not assigned to specific devices. Class D addresses are used for multicasting, and Class E is reserved for special and research uses.

Taking into account the number of bits for network and host portions of the IP address, we can also say that the first byte of a Class A address is the network number, the first 2 bytes of a Class B address are the network number, and the first 3 bytes of a Class C address are the network number. If we take into account the bit pattern in the first byte and the number of bits for the network address, we can list the network address ranges for the first byte in each class of IP addresses as follows:

Class	Beginning Address	Ending Address
A	0	127
B	128	191
C	192	223
D	224	239
E	240	255

To determine these address ranges, we need to look at the binary values. For a Class A address, the first bit of the first byte must be a 0, which limits the maximum value of the end network address.

2^7	2^6	2^5	2^4	2^3	2^2	2^1	2^0	
128	64	32	16	8	4	2	1	
0	0	0	0	0	0	0	0	= decimal 0
0	1	1	1	1	1	1	1	= decimal 127

For a Class B address, the range of network numbers for the first byte is also limited owing to the reservation of the first 2 bits in the first byte.

2^7	2^6	2^5	2^4	2^3	2^2	2^1	2^0	
128	64	32	16	8	4	2	1	
1	**0**	0	0	0	0	0	0	= decimal 128
1	**0**	1	1	1	1	1	1	= decimal 191

The Class C available network address for the first byte is restricted because of the first 3 bits set aside for the class definition.

2^7	2^6	2^5	2^4	2^3	2^2	2^1	2^0	
128	64	32	16	8	4	2	1	
1	**1**	**0**	0	0	0	0	0	= decimal 192
1	**1**	**0**	1	1	1	1	1	= decimal 223

If you take into account the remaining 3 bytes and the number of bits used for the network portion of an IP address, the number of available networks for classes B and C are greater than in a Class A address. You can determine the number of maximum networks for each class by counting the number of bits in the network portion of the address and then raising that value to the power of two. For example, for a Class A address there are 7 bits that can be used for the network address. Since the first bit must be a 0, we cannot manipulate that bit, which leaves 7 remaining bits in the first byte. When you convert 2^7 to decimal, the value returned is 128. Thus, in the total IP address space, there are a maximum of 128 Class A networks. Extending this to a Class B address, the number of bits that can be used for the network portion of the IP address is 14: 6 bits from the first byte and 8 bits from the second byte, because a Class B address uses the first 2 bytes as the network address. Converting 2^{14} to decimal gives us 16,384. Therefore, there are a maximum of 16,384 Class B networks in the IP address space. In the Class C network, there are a maximum of 2^{21} or 2,097,152 possible networks. This is calculated by adding the 5 bits in the first byte plus the 16 bits in the second and third byte to give us 21 usable bits for the network address. Note that there are some values that are not permitted, but we are not considering these at this point.

Class D IP addresses are reserved for multicasting, which is the ability to send a message to a group of devices that are members of the same multicast group. In the Class D address scheme, 28 bits are available for specifying multicast groups. This means there are over 268 million, or 268,435,456 to be exact, possible multicast groups. There are two types of multicast groups that are supported by the Class D address rules. Permanent multicast groups always exist and do not have to be set up or configured. Some examples of permanent multicast group addresses include the following:

IP Address	Group Definition
224.0.0.1	All devices on the local network
224.0.0.2	All routers connected to the local network
224.0.0.5	All Open Shortest Path First (OSPF) routers connected to the local network
224.0.0.6	All designated OSPF routers connected to the local network

The other types of multicast groups are temporary; they must be created before they can be used by any device. Once the group is defined, the multicast implementations can include procedures for hosts to ask to join a multicast group and to leave a multicast group. When all members of a multicast group leave the group, the temporary multicast group is no longer available.

The host, or unique, portion of the IP address is the bits that are not used for the network address. For a Class A address, the last 3 bytes of the IP address are available for host assignments. To determine the maximum number of hosts you can use on a particular class address, count the number of bits available for the host portion of the address and raise that value to the power of two. For example, in a Class A address, there are 24 bits available for the host address. The value 2^{24} translates to 16,777,216 decimal. This means that each Class A network can have a maximum of 16,777,216 hosts on the same network. A Class B network can have 2^{16} or 65,536 hosts per network, and a Class C network can have 2^8 or 256 hosts per network. Note that there are some values that are not permitted, but we are not considering these at this point.

Another element in the IP addressing scheme is a subnet mask. When a packet arrives at a router, or any device, the device needs to be able to determine the IP address's class. To efficiently determine this, an IP address is associated with a subnet mask. The subnet mask is used to determine which portion of the address is the network portion and which part is the host address. To accomplish this number separation, the router performs an AND operation of the IP address with the subnet mask. Each class of addresses has a default subnet mask; these subnet masks are listed in the following table:

Class	Subnet Mask
A	255.0.0.0
B	255.255.0.0
C	255.255.255.0

Converting the subnet masks to their binary equivalent reveals the following patterns:

Decimal	Binary
255.0.0.0	11111111.00000000.00000000.00000000
255.255.0.0	11111111.11111111.00000000.00000000
255.255.255.0	11111111.11111111.11111111.00000000

With both the IP address and the subnet mask, the routers can determine which portion of the IP address is the network address and which section is the host number.

SUBNETTING IPv4 NETWORKS WITH STANDARD SUBNET MASKS

In the early days of IPv4 usage, environments that were using Class A and Class B addresses rarely used all of the available host numbers that were possible for their network addresses. Instead of using another IP network address and wasting unused host addresses, the concept of subdividing or subnetting a network address to be used across networks was proposed. The first implementation of this concept was to use a Class C subnet mask with a Class B address, and a Class B subnet mask with a Class A address to produce more subnetworks. To see how this works, let's take a look at the Class B network address 172.16.0.0 and examine how a Class C subnet mask can produce subnets. Note that when an IP number ends with a zero, the IP number is referring to an IP network. So, for example, 172.16.0.0 refers to the network 172.16, and the 0.0 indicates the portion of the address that is used for host addresses. The Class A network, 10.0.0.0, shows that the last 3 bytes are available for host addresses. Before we delve into subnetting 172.16.0.0, let's first list some of the possible IP addresses using the standard Class B subnet mask of 255.255.0.0.

Network	Subnet Mask	Example IP Addresses
172.16.0.0	255.255.0.0	172.16.1.5
		172.16.1.46
		172.16.2.5
		172.16.2.46
		172.16.52.8
		172.16.52.72
		172.16.52.100
		and so on, for a total of 65,536 possible host numbers

By applying the Class C subnet mask 255.255.255.0, you can divide the Class B network 172.16.0.0 into 256 possible subnets, and each of those subnets would have a maximum of 256 hosts. The following table shows some examples of possible subnets and IP addresses.

Network Addresses	Subnet Mask	Subnet	Example IP
172.16.0.0	255.255.255.0	172.16.1.0	172.16.1.5
			172.16.1.46
			and so on, for a total of 256 possible host numbers
		172.16.2.0	172.16.2.5
			172.16.2.46
			and so on, for a total of 256 possible host numbers
		172.16.52.0	172.16.52.8
			172.16.52.72
			172.16.52.100
			and so on, for a total of 256 possible host numbers

Notice that we used the same example IP addresses in the previous table, but now with the Class C subnet mask we have three different subnets using the same range of numbers.

You can also apply this concept to a Class A address. That is, you can use either a Class B or a Class C subnet mask with a Class A address. The mask you decide to use depends on the maximum number of hosts you will be supporting on each subnet. If you have more than 256 hosts on some or all of the subnets, then you will need to use a Class B subnet mask. Using a Class B subnet mask with a Class A address gives you 256 subnets, with each subnet supporting the 65,536 possible hosts. Using a Class C subnet mask with a Class A address allows for 65,536 possible subnets with 256 hosts per subnet.

The technique of using another class's subnet masks for the different classes of networks worked well until about 1991, when it was apparent that the number of available Class B addresses was running out. At this point in the history of the Internet, blocks of Class C addresses were not in use because at the time most networks had more than 256 hosts, so Class A or Class B addresses were used. To better utilize some of these blocks of Class C addresses, classless interdomain routing (CIDR) was developed.

CLASSLESS INTERDOMAIN ROUTING (CIDR) FOR IPv4

As you recall, a standard Class C subnet mask is 255.255.255.0, and applying this to a Class C address, such as 192.168.1.0, produces 256 hosts on the network. You can also specify the subnet mask of a network by appending the number of bits in the mask to the end of the IP network number. For example, the 192.168.1.0 number with the standard Class C subnet mask can also be specified as 192.168.1.0/24, where the "/24" indicates the number of bits in the subnet mask. As another example, 172.16.0.0/16 specifies the standard Class B subnet of 255.255.0.0 for the Class B address. The network address of 10.0.0.0/8 indicates that the Class A subnet mask of 255.0.0.0 is in use for the Class A network of 10.0.0.0. Adding the number of bits in the mask to the IP address we create what is called a *CIDR mask*.

In addition to the IP number and mask naming format, CIDR makes it possible for contiguous Class C addresses to act together to produce fewer subnets but more hosts per subnet. This essentially produces the opposite effect of using a Class B or Class C subnet mask with a Class A address or using a Class C subnet mask on a Class B address. Let's examine how CIDR and a range of Class C addresses can produce more than 256 hosts per subnet.

For the first CIDR example, we have two Class C addresses that will be used to produce more than 256 hosts per subnet. For clarification, we will only show the binary portion of the third octet, since that is the only area where the two addresses differ. The two addresses we will use in the example are 192.168.20.0 and 192.168.21.0.

Decimal	Binary of Third Byte
192.168.20.0	00010100
192.168.21.0	00010101

Notice that the only difference between the two numbers, 20 and 21, is the rightmost bit of the third byte. The remaining portion of the address is the same for both addresses, 20 and 21. If we apply a subnet mask of 23 bits instead of the standard 24-bit Class C subnet bit, then we can have a total of 9 bits available for host addresses. That is, the 1 bit from the third octet has been masked off with the 23-bit subnet mask plus the 8 bits in the last byte. Translating 2^9 to decimal gives a value of 512. Thus the network 192.168.20.0/23 yields 512 possible host addresses. As another example, let's say the network numbers of 192.168.20.0 through 192.168.23.0 were available to be used with CIDR. Exploring the binary values of the third byte for these numbers reveals the following results:

Decimal	Binary of Third Byte
192.168.20.0	00010100
192.168.21.0	00010101
192.168.22.0	00010110
192.168.23.0	00010111

Analyzing this information, we see that the two rightmost bits of the third byte are the only bits that change among the four numbers. Thus, if we applied a 22-bit subnet mask instead of a 24-bit subnet mask, 10 bits are now available for the host addresses. Converting 2^{10} to decimal produces 1024. Therefore the IP network address of 192.168.20.0/22 could have 1024 possible hosts. As a final example, suppose the addresses from 192.168.20.0 through 192.168.31.0 are available. Listing the binary values for the third byte produces the following information:

Decimal	Binary of Third Byte
192.168.20.0	00010100
192.168.21.0	00010101
192.168.22.0	00010110
192.168.23.0	00010111
192.168.24.0	00011000
192.168.25.0	00011001
192.168.26.0	00011010
192.168.27.0	00011011
192.168.28.0	00011100
192.168.29.0	00011101
192.168.30.0	00011110
192.168.31.0	00011111

In this range of values, the four leftmost bits of the third byte are the same. Thus, we could implement a 20-bit subnet mask, which allows for 12 bits for the host addresses. This allows the maximum of 2^{12} or 4096 hosts across this contiguous range of 12 Class C addresses. The IP address of 192.168.20.0/20 is used to represent this scenario.

SUBNETTING IPv4 NETWORKS WITH NONSTANDARD SUBNET MASKS

Over the last several years, the proliferation of systems and users on the Internet has grown to the point where all Class A and Class B addresses are in use and very few

Class C addresses remain available. Because of this shortage of available addresses, the various IPv4 task force members implemented the use of nonstandard IP subnet masks to allow for more possible subnets. The usage of nonstandard subnet masks is also referred to as *classless addressing*. To demonstrate the use of nonstandard IP subnet masks, we will use the Class C address of 192.168.44.0 to provide more than one subnet. Recall that the standard subnet mask of a Class C address is 255.255.255.0, and the last, or fourth byte, is available for host addresses. By applying a nonstandard subnet mask to 192.168.44.0, some of the bits in the host portion can be used to create additional subnets. For example, let's say that we need to be able to provide different subnets for the 192.168.44.0 address. If we use the two leftmost bits of the fourth byte, we can produce four different subnets. Once again, we need to refer to the binary values, and in this example we are concerned only with the last byte.

Binary of Fourth Byte

00000000
01000000
10000000
11000000

Using 2 bits to create subnets leaves 6 bits that can be used for host addresses. That is, 2^6, or 64 hosts per subnet. In reality, not all of the possible numbers can be used for IP addresses. We mentioned this limitation previously, so now let's cover some of the rules that are important to know when designing an IP subnetting scheme for production networks.

1. The network 127.0.0.0 cannot be assigned to a network. Typically, the address 127.0.0.1 in the 127.0.0.0 network is used to refer to the interface or device itself. The address 127.0.0.1 is also called the *local host number* or *loopback address*.
2. A network address cannot consist of all bits set to zeros. When zeros are used in the network portion of the address, the IP number refers to the host number on the local network. For example, 0.0.0.68 means host number 68 on the network the device resides on.
3. A host address cannot consist of all bits set to zeros. When zeros are used in the host portion of the address, the IP number is referring to the network address. For example, 192.168.18.0 is referring to the network 192.168.18. Similarly, 10.0.0.0 is referring to the Class A network 10.
4. A host address cannot consist of all bits set to ones. When ones are used for the host portion of the address, the IP address is referring to all hosts on the network. For example, 192.168.18.255 means all hosts on network 192.168.18.0.
5. The number 0.0.0.0 refers to this host on this network.
6. The address 255.255.255.255 is a broadcast address and means all hosts on the local network. An early implementation of BSD UNIX used the IP address format of all zeros in the host portion as a broadcast. This form is referred to as the *Berkeley broadcast*. Some systems are designed to accept both address forms for broadcasts.

Taking these rules into account, we need to revise the actual number of subnets and hosts available on a network. For example, in the following table of possible IP subnet numbers, both the first and the last entries are not valid:

Binary of Fourth Byte

00000000
01000000
10000000
11000000

The reason the first and last entries cannot be used is the bits that will be used to produce the subnets are either all 0's or 1's. Thus, using 2 bits of the fourth byte produces only two subnets. We can express the number of possible subnets as a formula:

$$\text{Number of subnets} = 2^M - 2$$

where M is the number of bits used to define the subnet or the number of masked host bits. In our example, there are two bits that are used to define the subnets. Thus,

$$\text{Number of subnets} = 2^2 - 2 = 2$$

So now the number of legal subnets left when two host bits are used to produce subnets is as follows:

Binary of Fourth Byte

01000000
10000000

We can also calculate the number of hosts per subnet with a similar formula:

$$\text{Number of hosts per subnet} = 2^U - 2$$

where U is the number of remaining host bits or unmasked host bits. In our example, there are 6 bits available for the host addresses, so

$$\text{Number of hosts per subnet} = 2^6 - 2 = 62$$

Since we have used 2 bits of the last byte to create two subnets, the subnet mask is no longer the following:

```
Binary 11111111.11111111.11111111.00000000
Decimal 255.255.255.0
```

Instead, the subnet mask is

```
Binary 11111111.11111111.11111111.11000000
Decimal 255.255.255.192
```

We can also specify the subnet mask by using a CIDR naming notation. For example, using the subnet mask of 255.255.255.192 with the network IP address of 192.168.44.0, the CIDR address is 192.168.44.0/26.

Another item we need to define is the number of each subnet and the available host numbers on each subnet. Examining the binary value of the last byte of a Class C IP address where the subnet mask is 255.255.255.192, we see:

2^7	2^6	2^5	2^4	2^3	2^2	2^1	2^0
128	64	32	16	8	4	2	1
0	1	-	-	-	-	-	-
1	0	-	-	-	-	-	-

This reveals that we have subnet 64 and subnet 128. For subnet 64, the range of host numbers is

2^7	2^6	2^5	2^4	2^3	2^2	2^1	2^0	
128	64	32	16	8	4	2	1	
0	**1**	0	0	0	0	0	1	= decimal 65
0	**1**	1	1	1	1	1	0	= decimal 126

For subnet 128, the range of host numbers is

2^7	2^6	2^5	2^4	2^3	2^2	2^1	2^0	
128	64	32	16	8	4	2	1	
1	**0**	0	0	0	0	0	1	= decimal 129
1	**0**	1	1	1	1	1	0	= decimal 190

With this information, we can say that the device with the IP address of 192.168.18.70 is on subnet 64, and 192.168.18.170 is on subnet 128. Notice that with a subnet mask of 255.255.255.192, a total number of 124 hosts is possible across both subnets—each subnet has 62. Comparing this value to the total number of hosts with a subnet mask of 255.255.255.0 is 254 ($2^8 - 2$), there has been a loss of available host addresses, but you have gained the ability to spread the addresses over two different networks.

As another example, let's see what happens when 3 bits of the fourth byte are used to create subnets.

Binary of Fourth Byte

~~00000000~~
00100000
01000000
01100000
10000000
10100000
11000000
~~11100000~~

The first and last lines are discarded because of the IP rules listed previously. Thus, using 3 bits, there are six possible subnets, $2^3 - 2$, where each subnet has a maximum of 30 hosts, $2^5 - 2$.

2^7	2^6	2^5	2^4	2^3	2^2	2^1	2^0	
128	64	32	16	8	4	2	1	
0	0	1	-	-	-	-	-	= subnet 32
0	1	0	-	-	-	-	-	= subnet 64
0	1	1	-	-	-	-	-	= subnet 96
1	0	0	-	-	-	-	-	= subnet 128
1	0	1	-	-	-	-	-	= subnet 160
1	1	0	-	-	-	-	-	= subnet 192

The possible host addresses for subnet 32 are

2^7	2^6	2^5	2^4	2^3	2^2	2^1	2^0	
128	64	32	16	8	4	2	1	
0	0	1	0	0	0	0	1	= decimal 33
0	0	1	1	1	1	1	0	= decimal 62

Subnet 64:

2^7	2^6	2^5	2^4	2^3	2^2	2^1	2^0	
128	64	32	16	8	4	2	1	
0	1	0	0	0	0	0	1	= decimal 65
0	1	0	1	1	1	1	0	= decimal 94

Subnet 96:

2^7	2^6	2^5	2^4	2^3	2^2	2^1	2^0	
128	64	32	16	8	4	2	1	
0	1	1	0	0	0	0	1	= decimal 97
0	1	1	1	1	1	1	0	= decimal 126

Subnet 128:

2^7	2^6	2^5	2^4	2^3	2^2	2^1	2^0	
128	64	32	16	8	4	2	1	
1	0	0	0	0	0	0	1	= decimal 129
1	0	0	1	1	1	1	0	= decimal 158

Subnet 160:

2^7	2^6	2^5	2^4	2^3	2^2	2^1	2^0	
128	64	32	16	8	4	2	1	
1	0	1	0	0	0	0	1	= decimal 161
1	0	1	1	1	1	1	0	= decimal 190

Subnet 192:

2^7	2^6	2^5	2^4	2^3	2^2	2^1	2^0	
128	64	32	16	8	4	2	1	
1	1	0	0	0	0	0	1	= decimal 193
1	1	0	1	1	1	1	0	= decimal 222

In summary, using a subnet mask of 255.255.255.224 produces six subnets of 30 hosts per subnet. Counting all the possible hosts across all six subnets, a total of 180 hosts is possible. Thus a subnet mask of 255.255.255.224 reduces the possible hosts of 254 with a standard Class C subnet mask to 180 hosts with a nonstandard subnet mask. But the gain is the ability to dispense IP addresses across six different networks. For example, 192.168.18.50 is on subnet 32, 192,168.18.70 is on subnet 64, 192.168.18.110 is on subnet 96, 192.168.18.140 is on subnet 128, 192.168.18.170 is on subnet 160, and 192.168.18.210 is on subnet 192. The CIDR notation for the IP network 192.168.18.0 with the subnet mask of 255.255.255.224 is 192.168.18.0/27.

PRIVATE NETWORKS

Another way to help with the IP address shortage is to use methods to reduce the number of Internet IP addresses needed by different companies. This would make it possible for more organizations to access the Internet. One way to reduce the number of needed Internet IP addresses is to use routers between private and public networks and only use the Internet IP addresses on the router's interfaces that connect to the Internet. This scheme is possible through the use of IP numbers designed for private networks in conjunction with routers.

Within the IP address space, there are addresses reserved for use on private networks. Private IP network addresses are typically used by companies, organizations, and individual networks where the systems do not have a presence on the Internet. In order to access the Internet, a router, or gateway, is used to funnel the requests from the private network to the public Internet. The router's interfaces to the Internet must have an IP address that is unique on the Internet, but the remaining machines on the private network do not need unique Internet-compliant addresses. Because of this design of multiple private networks interfacing with the public Internet, an organization, company, or individual does not need to have a lot of Internet-compliant addresses. That is, they may not need all 256 possible host addresses of a Class C address. The same holds true for Class B and Class A addresses. By applying a different, nonstandard subnet to a Class A, B, or C address, the resultant subnets can be used on different subnets of a company, organization, or personal network, or the subnet addresses can be used by different entities. This approach to subnet division between different, unrelated parties is typically used by Internet Service Providers (ISPs) to allow for many different people and organizations to access the Internet. The following range of IPv4 addresses is reserved for private networks:

- 10.0.0.0 through 10.255.255.255
- 172.16.0.0 through 172.31.255.255
- 192.168.0.0. through 192.168.255.255

In addition to alleviating the need for many Internet IP addresses on an organization's network, it is recommended that you use the reserved private network IP numbers on private networks. The primary reason for this recommendation is security. Routers, by default, will not allow traffic outside a private network to enter the private network unless it is in response to a request that was initiated by a system on the private network.

IPv6

With the great increase in Internet use and in the number of devices, the number of available addresses with the current 32-bit IPv4 address is rapidly approaching zero. With this is mind, IPv6 was developed. It is now a standard, and some software and hardware already support IPv6. But there are a lot of issues and devices across the Internet have to be replaced or upgraded to handle IPv6. You might want to investigate your school's or company's environment in your area to see if IPv6 is already in use for research or production. When IPv6 was first being proposed and developed, it was originally called IP Next Generation, or IPng. As the protocol was finalized, and to avoid confusion with products on the market, the official name IPv6 was assigned.

IPv6 uses a 128-bit address, which includes a network and host portion. According to some, with a 128-bit IP address, there are enough addresses to allow for more than 1500 IP addresses for each square meter of the entire surface area of the earth! The IPv6 address design also supports subnet masks, multicasts, and CIDR-type structures. The structure of the IPv6 header is very different from the IPv4 header and also encodes information into different, or extension, headers. IPv6 also contains support for video and audio data so that a high-quality path can be determined and used throughout a multimedia conversation.

There are three types of multilevel hierarchical addresses in the IPv6 address space: provider-oriented unicast, anycast, and multicast. The *provider-oriented unicast* address is assigned to individual devices and interfaces. To designate this type of address, the number starts with a specific prefix, 010. The format of an IPv6 unicast address is as follows:

| 010 | Registry ID | Provider ID | Subscriber ID | Subnet ID | Interface ID |

The Registry ID is the address registry of the authority that assigns the Provider ID value to ISPs. The providers can then designate portions of their address space to subscribers, which is indicated by the Subscriber ID. Each subscriber is assigned a specific subnet, which is indicated by the Subnet ID value. The Interface ID is the unique number assigned to a specific device or interface within the corresponding subnet. Some of the IPv6 prefix address assignments are as follows:

Prefix	Role
0000 0000	Reserved
0000 0000	Unassigned
0000 001	Reserved for NSAP allocation
0000 010	Reserved for IPX allocation
0000 0011	Unassigned
0000 1	Unassigned
0001	Unassigned
001	Aggregatable global unicast addresses

010	Unassigned
011	Unassigned
100	Unassigned
101	Unassigned
110	Unassigned
1110	Unassigned
1111 0	Unassigned
1111 10	Unassigned
1111 110	Unassigned
1111 1110 0	Unassigned
1111 1110 10	Link local use addresses
1111 1110 11	Site local use addresses
1111 1111	Multicast addresses

Anycast addresses apply to more than one device or interface but not to all interfaces on the network. These can be useful when information needs to be sent to all the interfaces and devices corresponding to a particular Provider ID value. The original implementation of anycast addressing was known as *cluster addressing*. *Multicast addresses* are used to address the members of a multicast group. Multicast addresses start with the hexadecimal value of FF or decimal 255.

An IPv6 address written in dotted decimal notation can be quite long. For example,

```
105.100.215.50.255.255.255.255.0.0.32.136.150.5.255.255
```

Instead of this format, IPv6 numbers are represented in colon hexadecimal notation, where each group of 16 bits is written as a hexadecimal value. Each hexadecimal number is separated by a colon. Using this format, the above number is expressed in colon hexadecimal notation as

```
6964 : D732 : FFFF : FFFF : 0 : 2088 : 9605: FFFF
```

Also, when more than two zeros occur together, two colons are used to represent the range of zeros. For example, the number

```
6964: 0 : 0 : 0 : 0 : 0 : 0: FFFF
```

can be represented as

```
6964 : : FFFF
```

This form of shorthand format for a contiguous range of zeros can only be used once in an IPv6 address.

There is a special format of an IPv6 address that can be used to encapsulate IPv4 addresses. This scheme is useful for transition phases between IPv4 and IPv6 networks. In this special IPv6 address, the first 80 bits of the 128-bit address are set to all zeroes. These are then followed by ones for the next 16 bits. This leaves 32 bits, which are used to encapsulate the 32-bit IPv4 address.

ASYNCHRONOUS TRANSFER MODE (ATM)

Asynchronous Transfer Mode (ATM) packets are fixed in size and are referred to as *cells*. Each cell consists of a 5-byte header and a 48-byte information field. This type of fixed packet size helps to make routing and packet delivery easier and more efficient. Devices on an ATM network follow the Network Service Access Point (NSAP) addressing scheme. This standard is specified by the International Standards Organization (ISO), and it was originally designed for the OSI ISO protocol stack. The length of an NSAP address is variable, ranging from between 7 bytes to 20 bytes. This means that the NSAP address can be potentially longer than an IPv6 address, which is 16 bytes or 128 bits. To provide flexibility of address assignment, the ISO assigns a unique ID to a naming authority for a particular country or region. This unique ID is referred to as the Authority and Format Indicator (AFI) value. The format of the authority ID assigned by the ISO indicates the name of the authority and the format for the remaining elements of the NSAP address. The naming authority then partitions portions of the address space into addressing domains. Each address domain is given a range of numbers it can use for the Initial Domain Identifier (IDI) field of the NSAP address. The Initial Domain Part (IDP) is composed of the AFI and IDI values and uniquely identifies an addressing domain across the entire ATM name space. Figure 6-9 illustrates the format of an NSAP address.

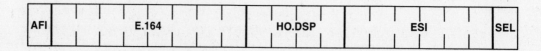

| AFI | E.164 | HO.DSP | ESI | SEL |

AFI   Authority and Format Identifier
HO-DSP   High-Order Domain Specific Part
ESI   End System Identifier (MAC address)
SEL   NSAP Selector

Fig. 6-9. NSAP address format.

The AFI and IDI fields on the NSAP address can be combined three different ways:

- **E.164 NSAP.** In this combination, the IDI field is an E.164 address; E.164 addresses are used on telephone networks. The E.164 NSAP style is designed to be used by ATM public network providers.

- **ICD NSAP.** This combination is designed for private networks. The AFI field identifies the British Standards Institution. The IDI field contains an international organization's code that has been assigned by the British Standards Institution.

- **DCC NSAP.** This combination is also designed for private networks. In this design, the AFI value identifies different countries. The ISO National Member in each country then assigns the IDI codes for organizations in the respective country.

The remaining portion of the NSAP address that is not part of the IDP is called the *Domain Specific Part* (DSP). The DSP is divided into high- and low-order parts. The high-order part, HO-DSP, is similar to the low-order portion of an IP network number. The high-order portion can also be used for subnetting. For each network defined, each device is assigned a unique *End-System Identifier* (ESI) value. The last element of the NSAP address, the *Selector field*, allows a single physical interface to host multiple logical network interfaces such as IP or ATM.

Name Resolution

As we mentioned previously in this chapter, humans typically refer to devices by names, but systems communicate with each other by addresses. Therefore, there needs to be some way to translate, map, or resolve names to addresses and vice versa. This is the role of name resolution services such as Domain Name Service (DNS) and Address Resolution Protocol (ARP). The details of DNS are covered in Chapter 8, so we will just briefly cover DNS in this section. Address Resolution Protocol will be discussed in depth later in this section.

Domain Name Service is an IP-based service that allows translation of a hierarchical system name to its corresponding IP address. For example, when you point your browser to www.packet-level.com, a DNS server resolves the name to the IP address 161.58.73.170. Similarly, the name www.packetsandpings.com resolves to 209.25.171.161. When the names are translated to the corresponding IP addresses, the various routers on the network and the Internet can properly forward and route the data to the appropriate networks. Once the packets get to the correct network, the next step is to find the correct device. This is handled by data-link, physical, or MAC addresses. To translate an IP address to the MAC address the ARP is used. Most IP-based systems run an ARP service by default, and resolved addresses are stored in memory for a short period of time to speed up the lookup process for subsequent queries. Figure 6-10 is an example of the contents of an ARP cache.

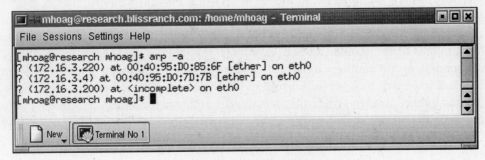

Fig. 6-10. ARP cache entries.

In order for two devices to communicate with each other, they must know each other's physical address. This is necessary because the physical network hardware does not understand logical or software addressing such as IP. When a computer or system is given an IP address, that address assignment is purely software based, and the IP number is used by software to identify devices and to work with services. But the hardware on the networked systems has no knowledge of any software addresses and must rely on physical, MAC, or data-link addresses to communicate. The process of resolving a logical address, such as IP, to a physical address occurs only on the local network. One device can only resolve the hardware address of another device if the devices are on the same network segment and there are no routers or network borders between them. A system will never resolve the hardware address of another device on another network. But devices on one network do communicate with other networks that are separated by routers. This functionality is handled by the routers and other packet-switching devices between the different networks. For example, in Figure 6-11 there are two devices on two different networks that need to communicate with each other. Between both of these systems are two routers.

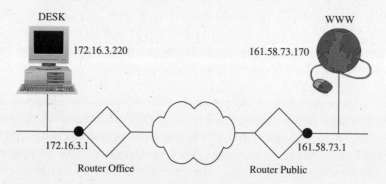

Fig. 6-11. Two devices on different networks separated by two routers.

When device 172.16.3.220 (DESK) gets ready to send a packet to system 161.58.73.170 (WWW), the sending device, DESK, places the destination device's IP address in the packet. The software on the DESK device realizes the destination is not on its network and knows the packet must travel through the router, Router Office. The DESK device then resolves the physical address of Router Office's interface, which is connected to the same network. On some environments, the term *gateway* is used to indicate the router that is used to go outside the local network. Once the DESK device has resolved the router's physical address, the packet is sent to Router Office. Router Office examines the packet and determines that the destination is for another network that is not directly connected to itself. Router Office knows that to send packets to another network the packets must go through Router Public. Router Office then resolves the physical address of Router Public's interface that is connected to the same network as one of the interfaces on Router Office. Router Office then sends the packet to Router Public. Router Public examines the packet it has received from Router Office and determines that the packet is destined for a device that is directly connected to one of its interfaces. Router Public then resolves the physical address of the destination device, WWW, and the packet is delivered to the WWW system. Notice that through this entire process the sending device, DESK, never knows the physical address of the destination device, WWW.

There are three methods in which address resolution can occur. The particular one that is used depends on the type of physical network, the vendor's hardware implementations, and the software. The three address resolution categories are *table lookup*, *closed-form computation*, and *message exchange*.

TABLE LOOKUP

In this technique, a table of each device's logical address and physical address is maintained. When a resolution request occurs, the table is searched to find the appropriate match. The form of the table is an array, and the host or unique portion of the software address is used as an index into the array to find the requested information. For example, in an IP network, the following address resolution array is stored in a device's memory:

```
Interface: 172.16.3.220 on Interface 0x5000006
Internet Address      Physical Address      Type
172.16.3.40           0-40-95-d0-7d-7b      dynamic
172.16.3.60           0-40-95-a6-3d-7e      dynamic
172.16.3.31           00-60-b0-28-0d-2c     dynamic
172.16.3.33           00-40-95-d1-7f-76     dynamic
```

When a request comes in to the device, the host portion of the address is used to find the appropriate match in the table. The network portion of the address is not involved in the lookup process because all the devices are on the same network and share the same network address.

The lookup approach in a one-dimensional array of hardware addresses becomes less efficient as the size of the network and the number of entries in the lookup table grows. To help improve the efficiency of the necessary computations, hashing or direct indexing are typically implemented. Direct indexing is slightly more efficient than hashing, but in order for it to work well, the software addresses need to come from a compact group of addresses.

CLOSED-FORM COMPUTATION

In this method, the software address used for each device is selected so that the physical address can be derived from the software address through some form of mathematical computation. This method of address resolution works well in environments where the physical addresses of devices can be set. With that capability, an administrator can construct a physical and software addressing scheme so the translation from software address to physical address is minimal and fast. In some cases, a portion of the physical and software addresses can be set to the same values, which makes translation even simpler. For example, the physical address or portion of the physical address could be set to be the same as the IP host number. The table below gives an example of this type of address assignment.

IP Address	Physical Address
172.16.3.4	00-00-00-00-00-04
172.16.3.6	00-00-00-00-00-06
172.16.3.31	00-00-00-00-00-1F
172.16.3.33	00-00-00-00-00-21

In this example, when a request for the physical address of the device with the IP number of 172.16.3.10 occurs, the environment immediately knows the physical address is 00-00-00-00-00-10.

MESSAGE EXCHANGE

Through the process of exchanging messages across the network, the devices determine the physical addresses. A device that needs the physical address of another system sends out a message asking for the device's address. Since the physical address is not known, this message-exchange system uses software addresses to request physical address information. There are two methods in which an address request through messaging can be resolved. The first approach is to use specific servers that handle all of the address resolution requests for the subnet. When a device needs to know the physical address of another device, it constructs a packet with its physical address and software address and sends the request to the address-resolution server. The server then returns a message to the requester with the physical address of the device in the resolution request reply.

The second approach specifies that each device is responsible for accepting address-resolution requests. The device that has the IP address contained in the request sends back a reply with its hardware address. In order for each device to participate in this scheme, the system that is asking for a device's physical address sends out a broadcast. A *broadcast* is a special type of packet that contains the physical address and software address of the sender and the software address of the requested device. Each device examines the broadcast packet, and if a device has the same software address as the one contained in the request portion of the packet, the device replies to the sender with its physical address.

Both of these techniques have their advantages and disadvantages. Dedicated address resolution servers can add expensive overhead and maintenance, but for large organizations this approach may be more efficient. As more and more devices are added to the network, the additional load of address resolution broadcast traffic may justify the addition of address resolution servers. But the ability of each device to resolve addresses makes it much easier for devices to be added and removed from the environment. In an address resolution server system, the information in the servers may need to be updated to reflect device changes on the network.

ADDRESS RESOLUTION PROTOCOL (ARP)

The IP protocol suite includes the Address Resolution Protocol (ARP) for devices to resolve IP addresses to physical addresses. The use of a protocol ensures that all devices can understand and handle the messages properly. The ARP protocol includes definitions for two types of messages: a request and a response message. The *request message* contains the IP address of the requested device in addition to the IP and physical address of the device initiating the request. The *response message* contains the IP and physical address of the requested device and the IP and physical address of the device that sent out the response message.

The ARP request that is sent out by a device is a broadcast packet, so it reaches all devices on the same network. When the system is found that has the requested IP address, the reply is sent back to the requester as a unicast or directed packet. Since the ARP request contains the IP and hardware address of the requester, the device replying to the request can send the message directly to the requester. This reduces the overall amount of traffic introduced in an ARP request-reply session. Figure 6-12 is an example of an ARP request sent out by a device, and Figure 6-13 is the corresponding ARP response message. One of the easiest ways to generate an ARP response-reply is to PING a device that is not in a system's local ARP cache.

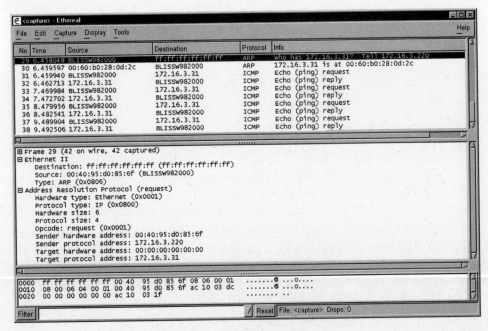

Fig. 6-12.   ARP Request Message.

There are a few important items in the ARP packets that we can see in the packet captures shown in Figures 6-12 and 6-13. Notice that in the ARP request packet, the frame type is the hexadecimal value 0x806. This is visible on the fifth line in the middle pane of both figures. In the ARP request packet, notice the destination address, the third line in the middle pane, is FF:FF:FF:FF:FF:FF. This is the hardware address of a local broadcast. In addition, notice in the ARP request, Figure 6-12, that the destination device's hardware address is a string of zeros. Look at the second to last line in the middle pane. This makes sense because the device sending out the ARP packet does not yet know the destination or target device's hardware address. In the ARP reply packet, the sender's hardware address in the ARP request packet is now the destination address in the ARP reply packet—the third line from top and second line from bottom in the middle pane of Figure 6-13. This shows that the response back to the ARP requester is a directed or unicast message and is not a broadcast message. Notice also that the hardware address of the requested device is contained in the source and sender hardware address sections of the reply packet—fourth line from the top and the bottom of the middle pane of Figure 6-13.

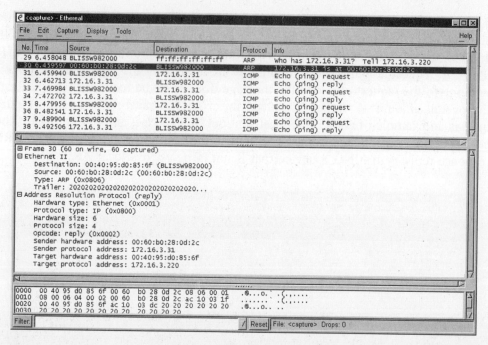

Fig. 6-13. ARP Response Message.

Most devices that participate in a messaging address resolution scheme maintain a cache of ARP entries in memory. The size of the cache and the lifetime of the entries is determined by the software implementation. On most operating systems, you can view the current, local, cached ARP table. On Windows and Linux/UNIX systems, executing ARP–A at a command line lists the current ARP table entries. Figure 6-10, shown previously in this chapter, shows the results of the ARP–A command on a Linux system.

REVERSE ADDRESS RESOLUTION PROTOCOL (RARP)

Reverse Address Resolution Protocol (RARP) is an IP protocol that resolves hardware addresses to an IP address. This type of situation arises with systems that do not have an operating system when they start up. But these devices have hardware addresses, and at boot time they send out a RARP message that essentially says, "I have this physical address. Does anybody know what my IP address is?" In a RARP configuration, RARP servers handle the RARP requests and reply back to the requester with the IP address. The requester can then communicate with a server or servers to receive an operating system so the device can continue to boot successfully.

When an RARP request goes out because a device is looking for its IP number, the destination address is set to all ones, which is the broadcast address. Since routers do not forward broadcasts on to other networks, a problem occurs if the

RARP server is on a different network than the device requesting its IP address. To overcome this problem, another protocol, called *BOOTP*, is used to deliver the RARP request from router to router until the RARP request reaches the RARP server. The BOOTP packets are directed packets, so broadcasts are not introduced on all the networks between the RARP requester and the RARP server.

ATM'S ADDRESS RESOLUTION PROTOCOL

In order for an ATM network to operate with IP networks, there needs to be some mechanism to resolve the IP address to the ARM hardware addresses. This is accomplished with a protocol called ATM'S Address Resolution Protocol (ATMARP), which is part of the Classical IP over ATM model. In this scheme, ATMARP uses an ARP server to handle the address resolution requests. This permits address resolution to occur without the need to support broadcasts.

Review Questions

6.1 Which of the following IP protocols uses a hierarchical addressing or naming structure?
  a. DNS
  b. ARP
  c. BOOTP
  d. LDAP

6.2 Write two examples of hierarchical naming and addressing.

6.3 How many octets are in an IPv6 address that does not contain any zeros?

6.4 What is meant by the term *addressing* in computer networks?

6.5 How can a device recognize that an incoming packet is an ARP request?

6.6 How many responses does the sender of an ARP broadcast request expect to receive?

6.7 Suppose that the definition of a Class B network uses 20 out of the 32 bits to define the network address. How many Class B networks are possible in this scenario?

6.8 What is meant by the term *naming* in computer networks?

6.9 What is a top-level domain?

6.10 How long is an Ethernet hardware address?

6.11 What is the name of the addressing standard used by telephones?

6.12 What is meant by the term *multi-homed*?

6.13 What is the reserved bit pattern of the first byte for a Class D address?

6.14 How many possible Class B networks are there?

6.15 What is the Initial Domain Part portion of an ATM address?

6.16 What is the destination physical address in an IP ARP request packet for device 192.168.44.64?

Problems

6.1   Explain what is meant by hierarchical addressing.

6.2   Do you think the current IP addressing scheme could be redesigned to use the device's hardware addresses instead of IP numbers? Explain your answer.

6.3   To provide more subnets, a Class B address is assigned the subnet mask of 255.255.240.0. How many hosts are possible per subnet?

6.4   Using the information in Problem 6.3, how many subnets are possible?

6.5   The ARP and RARP protocol in the IP suite perform similar address resolution functions. Describe at least one major difference between the implementation of the two protocols.

6.6   An organization wants to use the private network number 192.168.90.0 across four subnets. The maximum number of hosts that exist per subnet will be 25. What subnet mask would you use to solve this problem?

6.7   What are the IP addresses used or spanned by the CIDR address 192.168.10.0/20?

6.8   Define the role of a gateway in address resolution.

6.9   What is the purpose of the National Direct Dialing code?

6.10   What is the purpose of a subnet mask?

6.11   Define multicasting.

6.12   The IP network 192.168.130.0 is using the subnet mask 255.255.255.224. What subnet are the following hosts on?
192.168.130.10
192.168.130.67
192.168.130.93
192.168.130.199
192.168.130.222
192.168.130.250

6.13   Explain the closed-form computation method of address resolution.

Answers to Review Questions

6.1   **a. and d.** The hierarchical name structure is used by Domain Name Services (DNSs) for names of devices on a TCP/IP network. Another example of an IP protocol that uses hierarchical naming structure is Lightweight Directory Access Protocol (LDAP).

6.2   Two examples of hierarchical naming would be support.cisco.com and www.redcross.org. Two examples of a hierarchical address would be 172.16.3.4 and 512-555-1212.

6.3   An IPv6 address consists of 128 bits or 16 bytes. Octet is another term used for *byte*; therefore, this IPv6 address has 16 octets.

6.4 The process of assigning unique addresses to the different network devices is called *addressing*.

6.5 In an ARP request packet, the frame type is the hexadecimal value 0x806. Thus, when the device investigates the incoming packet, a frame type of 0x806 indicates the packet is an ARP request.

6.6 The sender of an ARP request message expects to receive only one response because only one device should have the IP number contained in the ARP request packet.

6.7 We can express the number of possible networks as the formula:

$$\text{Number of networks} = 2^N - 2$$

where N is the number of bits used for the network portion of the address. Therefore,

$$2^{20} - 2 = 1{,}048{,}572 \text{ networks}$$

6.8 Naming is the process by which devices are assigned, or receive, a unique network name.

6.9 A top-level domain is the first division for a name space. For example, if an authority decided to divide the name space by country and then by states or districts and then by cities, country would be the top-level domain in this example.

6.10 The Ethernet hardware address is a 48-bit, or 6-byte, address.

6.11 The standard for telephone numbers is referred to as ITU-E.164.

6.12 Devices on an IP network that have more than one interface or connection to the same or different networks are called multi-homed systems.

6.13 The bit pattern of the first byte of a Class D address is as follows:

Bit Pattern	Class							
1		1	1	0	x	x	x	x	D

6.14 For a Class B address, the number of bits that can be used for the network portion of the IP address is 14. Six bits from the first byte, and 8 bits from the second byte. Converting 2^{14} to decimal gives us 16,384. Therefore, there are a maximum of 16,284 Class B networks in the IP address space.

6.15 The Initial Domain Part (IDP) is composed of the Authority and Format Indicator (AFI) and Initial Domain Identifier (IDI) values and uniquely identifies an addressing domain across the entire ATM name space.

6.16 FF-FF-FF-FF-FF-FF is the destination physical address in an IP ARP request packet for the device 192.168.44.64. Since the sender does not know the physical address of the destination device, a broadcast packet is sent out with all ones in the destination hardware address field.

Solutions to Problems

6.1 The type of naming scheme that includes information about the location of a system is called hierarchical.

6.2   No, because there is no hierarchy in the hardware addresses and no common portion of the address that is common to all devices. Since there is no common portion of the MAC addresses to distinguish which network segment the devices reside on, the routing tables would have to include the addresses of all devices. This would make the tables very large and unmanageable.

6.3   4094 hosts. The subnet mask of 255.255.240.0 uses 4 bits in the third octet to create the subnets.

```
Binary  11111111.11111111.11110000.00000000
Decimal 255.255.240.0
```

Therefore, 12 bits are available for the host address—4 bits from the third byte plus 8 bits from the last byte.

$$\text{Number of hosts} = 2^{12} - 2 = 4094$$

6.4   14 subnets. The subnet mask of 255.255.240.0 uses 4 bits in the third octet to create the subnets.

```
Binary  11111111.11111111.11110000.00000000
Decimal 255.255.240.0
```

Therefore, 4 bits are used to create the subnets.

$$\text{Number of subnets} = 2^4 - 2 = 14$$

6.5   The IP ARP protocol uses the message method to perform address resolution. RARP uses RARP servers to provide the address resolution services.

6.6   255.255.255.192. To create four subnets for the network 192.168.90.0, at least 3 bits of the host address portion must be used to create the subnets. More than 3 bits could be used, except in order to support up to 25 hosts per subnet, the proper mask must be chosen to provide sufficient host addresses. The subnet mask of 255.255.255.192 produces the following:

$$\text{Number of subnets} = 2^3 - 2 = 6$$

$$\text{Number of hosts per subnet} = 2^5 - 2 = 30$$

6.7   The CIDR address 192.168.10.0/20 uses 4 bits of the third byte for sequential Class C IP addresses.

Decimal	Binary of Third Byte
192.168.10.0	00001010
192.168.11.0	00001011
192.168.12.0	00001100
192.168.13.0	00001101
192.168.14.0	00001110
192.168.15.0	00001111

Thus, the range of IP addresses is 192.168.10.0 through 192.168.15.0.

6.8   The border router in a subnet that interfaces to other networks is called a *gateway*. Whenever a device wants to send a message to another system outside its segment, it sends the message to the border router, which then sends it on to the destination network or route.

6.9 The term National Direct Dialing (NDD) is used to refer to the special telephone code used to access another area code.

6.10 When a packet arrives at a router, the router needs to be able to determine the IP address's network address. The subnet mask is used to determine which portion of the address is the network portion and which part is the host address. To accomplish this number separation, the router performs an AND operation of the IP address with the subnet mask.

6.11 Class D IP addresses are reserved for multicasting, which provides the ability to send a message to a group of devices that are members of the same multicast group.

6.12 The subnet mask 255.255.255.224, uses 3 bits of the fourth byte, so there are six possible subnets, $2^3 - 2$, where each subnet has a maximum of 30 hosts, $2^5 - 2$.

2^7	2^6	2^5	2^4	2^3	2^2	2^1	2^0	
128	64	32	16	8	4	2	1	
0	0	1	-	-	-	-	-	= subnet 32
0	1	0	-	-	-	-	-	= subnet 64
0	1	1	-	-	-	-	-	= subnet 96
1	0	0	-	-	-	-	-	= subnet 128
1	0	1	-	-	-	-	-	= subnet 160
1	1	0	-	-	-	-	-	= subnet 192

The possible host addresses for subnet 32 are

2^7	2^6	2^5	2^4	2^3	2^2	2^1	2^0	
128	64	32	16	8	4	2	1	
0	0	1	0	0	0	0	1	= decimal 33
0	0	1	1	1	1	1	0	= decimal 62

Subnet 64:

2^7	2^6	2^5	2^4	2^3	2^2	2^1	2^0	
128	64	32	16	8	4	2	1	
0	1	0	0	0	0	0	1	= decimal 65
0	1	0	1	1	1	1	0	= decimal 94

Subnet 96:

2^7	2^6	2^5	2^4	2^3	2^2	2^1	2^0	
128	64	32	16	8	4	2	1	
0	1	1	0	0	0	0	1	= decimal 97
0	1	1	1	1	1	1	0	= decimal 126

Subnet 128:

2^7	2^6	2^5	2^4	2^3	2^2	2^1	2^0	
128	64	32	16	8	4	2	1	
1	0	0	0	0	0	0	1	= decimal 129
1	0	0	1	1	1	1	0	= decimal 158

Subnet 160:

2^7	2^6	2^5	2^4	2^3	2^2	2^1	2^0	
128	64	32	16	8	4	2	1	
1	0	1	0	0	0	0	1	= decimal 161
1	0	1	1	1	1	1	0	= decimal 190

Subnet 192:

2^7	2^6	2^5	2^4	2^3	2^2	2^1	2^0	
128	64	32	16	8	4	2	1	
1	1	0	0	0	0	0	1	= decimal 193
1	1	0	1	1	1	1	0	= decimal 222

IP addresses 192.168.130.10 and 192.168.130.250 cannot be used on a 192.168.130.0 network with the subnet mask of 255.255.255.224. IP numbers 192.168.130.67 and 192.168.130.93 are both on subnet 64. IP numbers 192.168.130.199 and 192.168.130.222 are both on subnet 192.

6.13 In the closed-form computation method, the software address used for each device is selected so that the physical address can be derived from the software address through some form of mathematical computation. This method of address resolution works well in environments where the physical addresses of devices can be set. With that capability, an administrator can construct a physical and software addressing scheme, so the translation from software address to physical address is minimal and fast.

CHAPTER 7

Routing

As discussed in Chapter 6, the Network Layer is responsible for determining a path through an internetwork, whether the path is across the hall or across the Internet. Although there are many Network Layer protocols, such as IP, Novell's IPX, and Apple's AppleTalk, most Layer 3 protocols use similar methods to establish a path from the source to destination. And as you learned in Chapter 2, it is the router's job to determine the path and then forward the packets appropriately. This chapter focuses primarily on the Internet Protocol. With that in mind, there are a number of different tasks the router must perform.

Routing Information

The first thing a router must know is how many ports it has and what types they are. This information is typically discovered automatically by the router's operating system and does not require configuration. Figure 7-1 shows a router with an Ethernet port, a Token Ring port, and an ISDN port. It is common to see these abbreviated with a letter or two to designate the type of port, followed immediately by a number that the router uses to distinguish among many similar ports. Because most routers begin their port numbering at 0, the ports in Figure 7-1 would likely be described as e0, to0, and bri0, respectively.

The next piece of information the router must learn is the host address of each of its ports and what their network addresses are. This is almost always done by manually configuring the router. For IP, this information always includes the IP address and the subnet mask. In Figure 7-1, the 0 interface is given the IP address 10.1.1.1 and the to0 interface is given the IP address 10.1.2.5. This information is collectively called *Network Layer Reachability Information* (NLRI).

Note: The term *port* is generally used to describe a physical connector, whereas the term *interface* generally implies that it is a node with a valid address. For instance, it is common to say that bridges and switches have ports and routers and computers have interfaces. This is why NIC stands for *Network Interface Card*

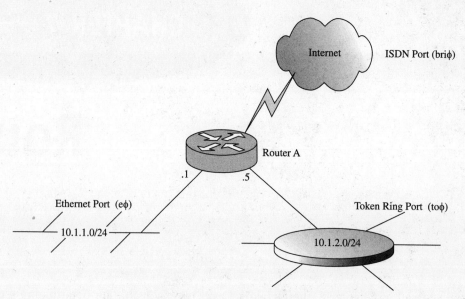

Fig. 7-1. Network routing ports.

instead of NPC. However, many people do use the terms *interface* and *port* interchangeably.

THE ROUTING TABLE

Once the router has these two pieces of information, it combines them into an entry that it places in a table in its memory that is commonly called the *routing table*. This table has at least two fields: Network Address and Next Hop, which can either be an interface, such as e0 or bri0, or it can be the IP address of a neighbor. This entry is commonly called a *route*. Thus, the router in Figure 7-1 would have the following two routes in its routing table:

Network Address	Mask	Next Hop
10.1.1.0	255.255.255.0	e0
10.1.2.0	255.255.255.0	to0

This table is used as a repository of all the NLR router knows so that the router has a single place to go to determine where it should send its packets. In large networks, this table can become quite lengthy. The table above represents the bare minimum information required to route packets. In practice, there are many more fields in the routing tables, and we discuss some of these later in the chapter.

THE ROUTING PROCESS

The next thing the router needs to know is how to identify the packets' destinations. Recall from Chapter 5 that in packet-switched networks, packets from many different sources and destinations can be multiplexed across the same link. There is no signaling process to establish a dedicated circuit as in circuit-switched networks. So to figure out where each packet is destined, the router must read each packet's IP header, which contains a destination address field as well as many other fields. The value in this field is the Network Layer address of the destination host. In this case, it is the IP address.

Once the router reads the destination field into memory, it compares this value with all the values in its routing table. If it finds the destination host's network in its routing table, it transmits the packet out the associated interface and its job is finished.

As an example, refer again to Figure 7-1. If the router receives a packet on its e0 interface with a destination address of 10.1.2.30, the router searches for a route that includes that address. When it finds the 10.1.2.0 route, it forwards the packet out the to0 interface to its destination.

Although that process is simple enough, consider Figure 7-2.

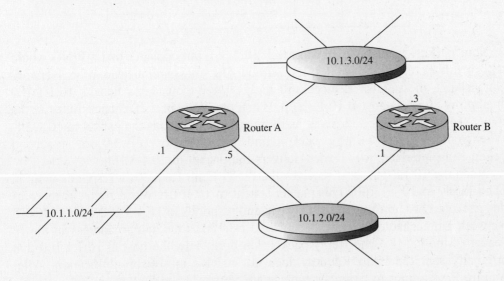

Fig. 7-2.   Network with two routes and ports.

In this network, router A's routing table would look like this:

Network Address	Mask	Next Hop
0.1.1.0	255.255.255.0	e0
10.1.2.0	255.255.255.0	to0

Router B's routing table would look like this:

Network Address	Mask	Next Hop
0.1.2.0	255.255.255.0	to0
10.1.3.0	255.255.255.0	to1

What would happen if a packet arrived on router A's Ethernet interface with a destination address of 10.1.3.15? Router A would search its routing table and conclude that no route to 10.1.3.15 existed and then return an ICMP Network Unreachable message to the source IP address, even though a path to that network clearly exists through router B.

The problem, of course, is that router A has not been configured with a route to that network, and has no way to discover it on its own. A simple solution would be to manually add the information for network 10.1.3.0 in router A's routing table. To get to network 10.1.3.0, router A should send its packets to 10.1.3.5, which is the to0 interface on router B. From there, we assume router B knows what to do with the packets. After this configuration, router A's table might look like this:

Network Address	Mask	Next Hop
10.1.1.0	255.255.255.0	e0
10.1.2.0	255.255.255.0	to0
10.1.3.0	255.255.255.0	10.1.2.5

Now, packets from 10.1.1.0 can reach 10.1.3.0, but consider that a PING would now result in the familiar Request Timed Out message instead of a Network Unreachable message or a successful reply. Why? Consider a host at 10.1.1.100 attempting to ping a host at 10.1.3.100. When the PING packet reaches router A, the router sees the network address in its routing table and sends the packet to 10.1.2.5. When router B receives the packet, it finds the entry for 10.1.3.0 out its second Token Ring interface, to1. It then delivers the packet to 10.1.3.100.

When the 10.1.3.100 host receives the PING Echo Request, it responds with an Echo Reply to 10.1.1.100. This packet is sent to 10.1.3.1. When router B receives this packet, it has no route to the network and responds to 10.1.3.100 with an ICMP Network Unreachable message because 10.1.3.100 is the source address in the IP header of the ICMP Echo Reply packet. Unfortunately, the host at 10.1.1.100 that originally sent the Echo Request does not receive any error notification. After waiting for its timer to expire, it reports a Request Timed Out error.

Thus, we can see that configuration to both routers is required. Unfortunately, real-world networks usually have hundreds or thousands of entries in the routing table and it is simply not feasible to enter all of this information by hand. Further, for the sake of redundancy, most networks are configured with multiple paths, which creates loops, much like those discussed in Chapter 3. To solve these problems, we use routing protocols.

Routing Protocols

Routing protocols are methods that routers can use to communicate NLR Information to each other. In other words, one router can share with another router information about the routes it knows. The goal of every routing protocol is to

- Reduce administration by automatically discovering networks that are reachable
- Identify a loop-free path through the network
- Identify the "best" path if there are multiple routes
- Ensure that all routers in the network agree on the best paths

There are many different routing protocols in use today. Each one has relative strengths and weaknesses. Some are open standards, governed by international standards bodies, like the IETF or ISO; others are proprietary to a single company. However, all of these routing protocols include a way for the routers themselves to communicate so that NLRI can be collected and, once collected, each protocol includes a way to digest the NLRI and process it in order to resolve any potential loops in the topology and identify the best path between various locations.

The method of communication is generally specified by the format of the packet used to carry information between routers. The method of digestion is called an *algorithm*. This is discussed in more detail as we delve into specific protocols in the next section.

In order to choose the best path, routing protocols use metrics. A *metric* is a numeric value that represents the priority or preference for a route relative to other routes to the same destination. Metrics can be based on many different things as you will see later, but they are only used when there are multiple paths to choose from, except in one notable case.

Practically, it is impossible for every router in the network to learn about a change in one part of the network (such as a link being disconnected) at the same time. Thus, there is some period of time where the routers are possibly in disagreement about what is the best path through the internetwork. Once the routers are all in agreement and no loops exist, the network is said to be *converged*.

There are two basic ways to categorize routing protocols. The first is based on the behavior of the routing protocol and the second categorization is administrative.

BEHAVIORAL–BASED PROTOCOLS

In practice today, there are two major routing technologies. These two share few traits. They are based on different algorithms, pass different information about their routes, use dramatically different methods of communicating with other routers, and employ different metrics.

The first group is known as distance vector routing protocols, and the second group is known as link-state routing protocols. In this section we compare the distance vector and link-state algorithms.

Distance Vector Protocols

The distance vector protocols are based on one of two algorithms known as the Bellman–Ford algorithm and the Ford–Fulkerson algorithm. The distance vector name comes from the fact that all distance vector algorithms identify routes in terms of a vector, which is the combination of a distance and a direction. The distance here is the metric, and the direction is the next hop to take in the path to the destination.

As an example, the vector for network 10.1.3.0 in Figure 7-2 from router A might be one router-hop away, via 10.1.2.5.

Another important aspect of distance vector protocols is that they learn information from a neighbor and then pass it on to another neighbor without any information about the originating router. This is called *routing by rumor*, and it can cause issues in a complex network.

Distance vector protocols are vulnerable to two kinds of loops. Protocols overcome loops between a pair of routers by employing a technique known as *Split Horizon*, and loops involving several routers are resolved with a technique called *Counting to Infinity*.

Note: Counting to Infinity is the one notable exception mentioned above where a metric is significant of itself and not relative to the metric of another route.

One last significant trait of distance vector protocols is that they use periodic updates and full routing updates. This means that on a regular interval (typically once every 30 or 90 seconds) they send their *entire* routing table to each neighbor. This can result in a very long convergence time.

To remove routes from a network when a link is disconnected or moved to another router, a router can stop advertising the route. Each RIP neighbor keeps a timer for each route. That timer is typically set to three or four times the update period. This allows three consecutive updates to be missed before the route is pulled from the routing table. This is important because Routing Information Protocol (RIP) uses the UDP protocol, so if an error occurs on the line, the update is lost. Unfortunately, on extremely busy networks, congestion commonly drowns routing protocol traffic until routes drop off. Once the routes drop off, the traffic stops (it has nowhere to go) and the routing protocol updates can once again be seen. The routers reconverge and the traffic picks up again, creating an ugly cycle. Some common distance vector protocols are as follows:

- Routing Information Protocol (RIP)
- AppleTalk's Routing Table Maintenance Protocol (RTMP)
- DEC's DNA Phase IV
- Cisco's IGRP

The most common distance vector routing protocol by far is RIP. RIP evolved from the Xerox Network Systems (XNS) protocol and was released by Berkeley Software for UNIX in 1982 as a daemon called *routed*. In 1988 RIP was formally standardized in RFC 1058.

Unlike the link-state protocols below, the operation of RIP is extremely simple. It uses UDP port 520 and the broadcast IP address 255.255.255.255 to advertise every route in its table once every 30 seconds, whether anyone is listening or not.

RIP uses hop count as its metric. This is a number between 1 and 16 that represents the distance to the destination in hops. Figure 7-3 shows how hops are counted.

In this illustration, you can see that directly connected networks are considered one hop away, and each additional gateway that must be traversed to get to the

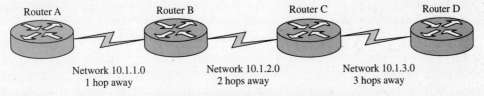

Network 10.1.1.0   Network 10.1.2.0   Network 10.1.3.0
1 hop away   2 hops away   3 hops away

Fig. 7-3. How hops are counted.

destination increments the count by one hop. It is important to remember that the hop count is always from a single router's perspective. For instance, for router A to get to network 10.1.3.0 is three hops, but from router B, it is only two hops.

To understand how RIP routers use the hop count, consider Figure 7-4.

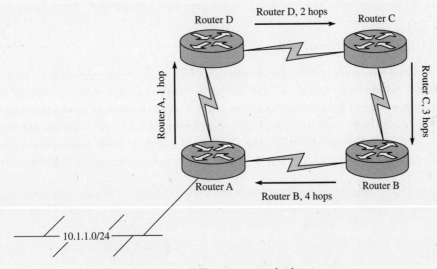

Fig. 7-4. How RIP routers use the hop count.

In this illustration, we have four routers—A, B, C, and D—that are all running RIP. Router A advertises its directly connected Ethernet network to router D with a hop count of one. Router D receives this route and realizes that from router D's perspective, it is two hops away. Router D then advertises this network to router C with a hop count of two. Router C, in turn, advertises it to B, and router B advertises it back to router A.

When the route arrives back at router A, router A believes that router B also has a connection to the same network. It has no way of knowing that router B is only advertising router A's own route fourth-hand. So router A must make a choice of which route to use. To make this choice, it compares the only metric it has, and determines that its directly connected route with a hop count of one is shorter than the route through router B with a hop count of five, so it ignores the longer route and uses the shorter route.

At the same time, however, router A also sends an identical broadcast toward router B. Router B forwards this broadcast to router C, which forwards it to router D, which forwards it to router A, exactly like the first route.

As routers B, C, and D each receive both routes, they compare the hop count from their perspective and choose the shortest path.

As you learned in Chapter 6, IP has a unique history due in part to its original organization of network classes (for example, Class A, B, C, etc.) and the subsequent move to classless behavior. Because RIP predates this classless restructuring, RIP version 1 is considered a *classful protocol*. The protocol is classful because, although the interfaces are always given subnet masks, these subnet masks are not sent in RIP version 1 routing updates. Therefore, a neighboring RIP router assumes that all network advertisements received on an interface use the same subnet mask as that interface.

To address this and other issues, a second version of RIP was created. RIP version 2 not only transmits the subnet mask, giving it support for Variable Length Subnet Masks (even though it is not truly classless), but it also supports authentication of routing updates via a shared secret password and a few other features.

Link-State Protocols

Compared to distance vector protocols, link-state protocols enjoy numerous significant advantages: First, all IP link-state protocols are fully classless, which means that not only do they include the subnet mask with routing updates but they also do not do route lookups based only on the major network. This allows them to be much more efficient and to conserve a great number of IP addresses.

Second, link-state protocols use an arbitrary metric. Consider the network in Figure 7-5.

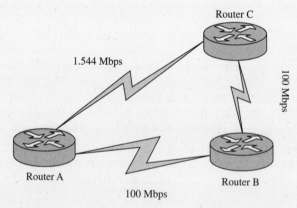

Fig. 7-5. Using a link-state protocol to improve network efficiency.

If routers A, B, and C were speaking RIP, then the preferred path from A to C would be the direct 1.544 Mbps link because it is only one hop away. However, the route through router B has almost 100 times as much bandwidth, even though it is two hops away. Many other link qualities can be factored into a distance vector metric, including the following:

- MTU size
- Reliability

- Delay
- Load

In fact, Cisco's proprietary distance vector protocol (IGRP) uses a composite metric that takes all of these qualities into account. Although this is certainly more useful than mere hop count, it still does not have the flexibility of an arbitrary metric. For instance, what if a Network Service Provider got paid more for traffic transported across an inferior link? As you can see, when a potentially infinite number of nontechnical factors are considered, an arbitrary metric can be very helpful.

Next, link-state protocols use event-driven updates rather than periodic updates. This is extremely important for a number of reasons. First, sending the entire routing protocol every 30 to 90 seconds is not only totally unnecessary, but it wastes bandwidth and processor and memory resources. Second, event-driven updates allow a network to converge much faster. See the example in Figure 7-6.

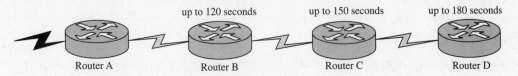

Fig. 7-6.   Using link-state protocol for an event-driven update.

If router A fails for some reason, it could take up to 120 seconds for the routes on router B to time-out. At router B's next update to router C, which could be up to 30 seconds later, it can send a route marked unreachable. Up to another 30 seconds later, router C, in turn, sends the route marked unreachable to router D. As you can see, 3 minutes is a very long time for accurate information to propagate through such a small network.

By contrast, link-state protocols send Hello packets at very short intervals; typically 10 seconds or less. When a neighbor doesn't respond, an update with just the relevant information is sent immediately instead of sending the entire routing table regularly. The link-state update is then flooded throughout the entire domain as fast as the router's processors can send it. This typically causes even larger link-state networks to reconverge in a matter of a few seconds.

Another major advantage of link-state protocols is that they do not route by rumor. Instead of sending a list of networks a router has heard about, a link-state router originates only updates about networks that it is responsible for and these updates contain the address of the originating router so there is no confusion. When a link-state router receives information from other routers, it floods those updates to all neighbors unaltered, instead of incrementing the hop count or other metric.

Once all the routers in the network have identical databases of updates, they run an algorithm called the *Dijkstra algorithm*. Because all routers use the same algorithm and start with the same information, they all arrive at the same picture of the network, which prevents the loops endemic to distance vector networks.

Last, link-state protocols form adjacencies with neighbors. This also has two primary benefits. The first is that these relationships allow them to unicast or multicast their updates instead of broadcasting them to everyone on the network.

Second, because they know exactly how many other routers are listening, they can receive acknowledgments instead of simply hoping for the best. Although Hello packets are not acknowledged, each packet containing routing updates is explicitly acknowledged and missing packets are resent, so no data is lost in transit.

Some of the popular link-state protocols are:

- ISO's Intermediate-System to Intermediate-System (IS-IS)
- Novell's NetWare Link Services Protocol (NLSP)
- Apple's AURP
- IETF's Open Shortest Path First (OSPF)

Because OSPF is the Internet Engineering Task Force's officially recommended routing protocol for IP networks, we discuss it briefly here. OSPF is specified in several RFCs, including

- RFC 1311
- RFC 1247
- RFC 2328

In addition to the advantages of link-state protocols described above, OSPF also offers the following:

- A hierarchical structure instead of a flat structure
- Support for load balancing traffic across multiple links
- Secure authentication of routing updates
- Route tagging

ADMINISTRATIVE CLASSIFICATION

Although the technical challenges of creating routing protocols that produced stable and efficient networks were certainly daunting, administrative challenges were no less so. As companies began to connect their networks together, and ultimately to the Internet, it became obvious that the policies and preferences and design of one network wasn't always compatible with that of another, even when they were using the same protocol. Each company or organization operates and is structured differently than other organizations and their networks must facilitate their unique needs. Decisions like the level and types of security become a concern when everyone is using the same single protocol, no matter which protocol it is. What is appropriate for a bank may not be appropriate for a university and vice versa.

Further, many of the protocols have practical limits to scalability that make them impossible to deploy on a global scale. An example of this is RIP's 16-hop count limit. So the solution was to create two classes of protocols: interior and exterior.

Interior Routing Protocols

The routing protocols previously discussed, such as RIP and OSPF, are considered *interior routing protocols*. These protocols are appropriate for a single organization, even if that organization's network contains hundreds or thousands of routers. The key differentiator is that the protocol is intended to be administered by a single person or group. For instance, the Network Support department of a large corporation may be responsible for all of that organization's routers worldwide. However, this administrative classification does not prohibit two different companies from connecting their networks using the same interior routing protocol.

Exterior Routing Protocols

By contrast, an exterior routing protocol's job is to connect interior routing protocols together. In order to accomplish this, the Internet has been divided into 65,535 different autonomous systems. Each of these systems has its own administration, and inside the autonomous system, each administration runs the interior routing protocol of its choice.

Figure 7-7 shows two autonomous systems, AS 100 and AS 200. Each system is using its own interior routing protocol, and the two autonomous systems are connected via an exterior protocol. Note that all the routers in AS 200 are speaking RIP internally, and only a single router is acting as a border gateway. Similarly, in AS 100, all routers are using OSPF to communicate internally, but a single router is identified as a border gateway.

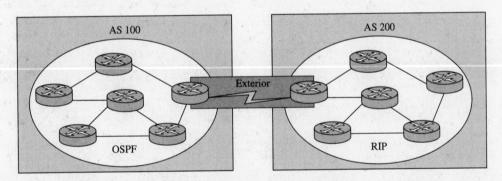

Fig. 7-7. Autonomous systems connected by an exterior routing protocol.

This architecture has a number of advantages. First, the interior routing protocol can be optimized for efficiency and speed without being encumbered by external restrictions. The interior routing protocol can be configured to meet the organization's needs without infringing on the needs of other organizations. At the same time, the exterior routing protocol excels at mapping the policies and preferences of one organization to another without impacting the performance of the internal network.

In fact, although one group handles the assignment of the autonomous system numbers for the Internet, just as a single group is responsible for registering IP addresses, no one group is responsible for managing the entire protocol. Instead, each organization administers only its own autonomous system. The other feature of the exterior routing protocol is that it is extremely scalable. Because it is hierarchical in nature, features like route aggregation and summarization can be used.

The aptly named *Border Gateway Protocol* (BGP) is the most common exterior routing protocol in use today. Recall that *gateway* is synonymous with the term *router*. Thus, this protocol manages the routers at the borders of an organization's network. BGP is a distance vector protocol, but instead of using network hops as its distance, it uses autonomous system hops called an *AS Path*. Figure 7-8 shows four autonomous systems. If router R1 in AS 100 advertises a route to its network via BGP to AS 200, a BGP router in AS 200 would see the AS path as 100. If AS 200 advertises this route to AS 300, then AS 300 would show the path as 200 100. When this route gets to R4 in AS 400, the path would show 300 200 100. Notice that the actual path is 10 hops between R1 and R4, but the AS path statement is much shorter.

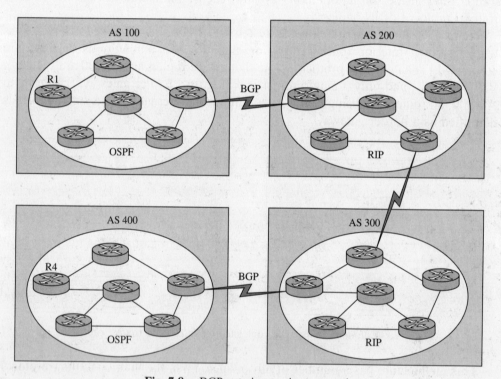

Fig. 7-8. BGP exterior routing protocol.

As an example of how BGP allows networks to scale and still retain local autonomy, consider that BGP dictates only which autonomous systems the packets will travel through. As a packet enters the autonomous system, however, only the local organization controls which path is used to get from one side of the AS to the other.

Although BGP is much more complex than other distance vector protocols such as RIP, it is still inherently vulnerable to the same routing loop problems caused by routing by rumor. To combat this, it uses the same methods, such as split horizon, as other distance vector protocols. The concept is fundamentally the same.

Hierarchical Routing

Hierarchical routing is a method of segregating the network that allows routing protocols to scale very well. An example of this is the relationship between interior and exterior routing protocols. Another example is the area structure of OSPF. In both these examples, one method in particular is used to gain the bulk of the efficiency. This method is called *summarization* or *route aggregation*. This section discusses summarization and a special case of extreme summarization: the *default route*.

SUMMARIZATION

Summarization is a technique used in routing to describe many networks in one route. To understand this concept and the need for this technique, consider the often-used analogy of America's streets and interstates. In this analogy a route is equivalent to a sign on the road that tells you (the packet) where to go. The casual observer who may have been driving his or her entire life may not have noticed, but there are differences between the signs you see at a street corner and signs on the side of the interstate.

First, the street signs are very explicit. They give the name of the street and typically the block address. They are also quite small. By contrast, signs on the freeway are very large because people traveling at a high rate of speed do not have much time to read and understand the sign. On interstate road signs there is typically only the name of an entire city or town and the distance in miles, or, at most, the name of a major street that connects to the interstate directly.

Pretend you're driving down the interstate and see a sign for the next city. The sign is 100 ft wide by 50 ft tall and has the name of every street in the entire city written in 6-in-tall letters. To use that sign, you would have to come to a complete stop and read for several minutes before continuing on your journey. Cars would pile up behind you for miles.

Data networks operate in exactly the same way. As branches come together, the information becomes less specific. If the routers on the backbone of the Internet knew the address of every single network on the whole planet, it would take days for them to figure out where to send your packets. Their solution, of course, is to aggregate the routes (see Figure 7-9).

Here, each router on the left (column A) has a single /24 network. Although these routers could advertise all these networks all the way to the right-most router (column D) so that it would see a total of 16 routes, ideally, we should summarize to make the process as efficient as possible, which would result in the right-most router seeing only two routes. The key to remember is that when you summarize, you lose information. Losing unimportant information is OK, but it is up to you, the network designer, to ensure that you don't lose important information.

To return to our interstate analogy, when you're 50 mi away from a city that has multiple exits off the interstate, you typically see a sign that simply says "Whoville 50 miles," but when you get to the city, you see that the signs include major roads,

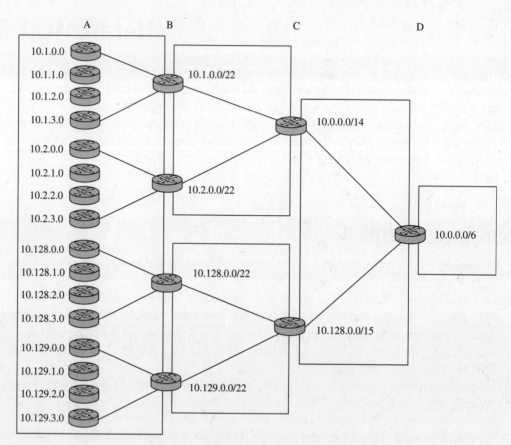

A   B   C   D

Fig. 7-9. Aggregating routes on a network.

such as "Whoville, Mainstreet 2 miles." If there were five exits that all went to Whoville and all the signs just said "Whoville," which one would you take? The more specific information tells you which route is closest to your destination. Most people, once they get to know an area, tend to take shortcuts and less-congested back roads. These more efficient routes are often lost in the summary of information found on road signs.

Now, we'll take a closer look at Figure 7-9. For a quick refresher, remember that the purpose of the subnet mask is to distinguish between the network portion and host portion of the address. The key to summarization lies in the subnet mask, although at first glance, the masks in the figure may not make sense. The reason is because they are in decimal. By converting to binary, summarization becomes intuitively obvious. In this case, the routers in the first group have the following network addresses in binary:

	Address	Mask
Router 1	00001010.00000001.00000000.00000000	11111111.11111111.11111111.00000000
Router 2	00001010.00000001.00000001.00000000	11111111.11111111.11111111.00000000
Router 3	00001010.00000001.00000010.00000000	11111111.11111111.11111111.00000000
Router 4	00001010.00000001.00000011.00000000	11111111.11111111.11111111.00000000

We use the notation /24 to indicate there are 24 "one" bits in the subnet mask. To summarize any given set of routes, you simply start at the left, and if all the bits in that position are identical, you set the bit in that position of the subnet mask to 1. Repeat this process for the next bit to the right and continue until you come to the first position where the bits are not identical. The comparison would look like this:

- Address: 00001010.00000001.00000000.00000000
- Address: 00001010.00000001.00000001.00000000
- Address: 00001010.00000001.00000010.00000000
- Address: <u>00001010.00000001.00000011.00000000</u>
- Mask: 11111111.11111111.11111100.00000000

Once the 1's are set in the subnet mask, it tells us what the network portion of the route is. As you can see, there are now 22 bits in the subnet mask and the network portion of the third and fourth octets are all 0's so the route is shown as:

`10.1.0.0 /22`

Of course, a /16 subnet mask, which is much more common, would also summarize those networks as follows:

- Address: **00001010.00000001.**00000000.00000000
- Address: **00001010.00000001.**00000001.00000000
- Address: **00001010.00000001.**00000010.00000000
- Address: **<u>00001010.00000001.</u>**00000011.00000000
- Mask: 11111111.11111111.00000000.00000000

This address would be shown as

`10.1.0.0 /16`

However, this is not the most specific route.

This entire process is repeated for the rest of the routers on the left, which results in four /22 networks. These networks are:

- 10.1.0.0 /22
- 10.2.0.0 /22
- 10.128.0.0 /22
- 10.129.0.0 /22

It is also important to note that the summarization is actually performed on the second column of routers. The routers in columns A and B know exactly where each network is. It is not until the router in column B advertises this route to the router in column C that summarization takes place.

The first router in column C receives two routes: 10.1.0.0 /22 and 10.2.0.0 /22. It then attempts to summarize these two routes and advertise them to router D. It does this as follows:

First it receives the following two routes:

Route 1

- Address: 00001010.00000001.00000000.00000000
- Mask: 11111111.11111111.11111100.00000000

Route 2

- Address: 00001010.00000010.00000000.00000000
- Mask: 11111111.11111111.11111100.00000000

It compares them and finds:

- Address: **00001010.0000000**1.00000010.00000000
- Address: <u>**00001010.0000001**0.00000011.00000000</u>
- Mask: 11111111.11111100.00000000.00000000

The summary network address advertised to router D is therefore:

- Address: 00001010.00000000.00000000.00000000
- Mask: 11111111.11111100.00000000.00000000

This address would be shown in dotted decimal notation as:

- 10.0.0.0 /14

It is worth noting that not only does this network summarize 10.1.0.0 /22 and 10.2.0.0 /22, but it also summarizes 10.0.0.0 /22 and 10.3.0.0 /22. Be careful not to accidentally include a network in your summarization that you did not intend to summarize, or you could direct traffic to the wrong location.

Likewise the 10.128.0.0 /22 and 10.129.0.0 /22 routes arrive at the lower router in column C and are summarized as a /14 to router D.

First it receives the following two routes:

Route 1

- Address: 00001010.10000000.00000000.00000000
- Mask: 11111111.11111111.11111100.00000000

Route 2

- Address: 00001010.10000001.00000000.00000000
- Mask: 11111111.11111111.11111100.00000000

It compares them and finds:

- Address: **00001010.1000000**0.00000000.00000000
- Address: <u>**00001010.1000000**1.00000000.00000000</u>
- Mask: 11111111.11111110.00000000.00000000

The summary network address advertised to router D is therefore:

- Address: 00001010.00000000.00000000.00000000
- Mask: 11111111.11111110.00000000.00000000

This address would be shown in dotted decimal notation as:

- 10.128.0.0 /15

Finally, router D receives the 10.0.0.0 /14 and 10.128.0.0 /15 routes and summarizes them as follows:

First it receives the following two routes:

Route 1

- Address: 00001010.00000000.00000000.00000000
- Mask: 11111111.11111100.00000000.00000000

Route 2

- Address: 00001010.10000000.00000000.00000000
- Mask: 11111111.11111110.00000000.00000000

It compares them and finds:

- Address: **00001010.**00000000.00000000.00000000
- Address: **00001010.**10000000.00000000.00000000
- Mask: 11111111.00000000.00000000.00000000

Which is coincidentally the natural mask of the Class A 10.0.0.0 network. In other words, 255.0.0.0 or /8. Now we can see that with proper summarization, router D has only two routes instead of 16 and because the networks are contiguous, the more specific information lost by summarization is irrelevant, because its presence would not lead to more optimal routing. At this point, we should discuss how the router itself chooses routes. Consider Figure 7-10.

In this figure we see that our networks are no longer contiguous. Two networks marked in bold have been swapped. However, the routers in column B still

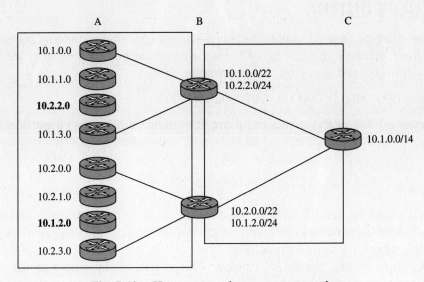

Fig. 7-10.   How a router chooses to route packets.

summarize as they did before, but they also include the more specific route to the network in bold.

Thus, the top router in column B advertises that it can reach 10.1.0.0 /22 when that is only partially true, and it advertises 10.2.2.0 /24. Similarly, the lower router in column B advertises that it can reach 10.2.0.0 /22 and 10.1.2.0 /24. When these four routes arrive at the router in column C, how does it choose to route its packets?

The answer to this is the concept of the longest match. If the router in column C receives a packet destined for 10.2.2.2, it checks all the routes in its table. It finds the following:
Destination

- Address 00001010.00000010.00000010.00000010

Route 1

- Address: 00001010.00000010.00000010.00000000
- Mask: 11111111.11111111.11111111.00000000

Route 2

- Address: 00001010.00000010.00000000.00000000
- Mask: 11111111.11111111.11111100.00000000

Note that both the 10.2.2.0 /24 and 10.2.0.0 /22 routes match the destination. In all cases, a router must choose the route with the longest mask. This is done because the longest mask is necessarily more specific than a shorter match; thus we infer that it is closer and more accurate. The router in column C would therefore send its packets to the top router in column B, which would deliver them to the correct location.

If you carry the concept of summarization to the most extreme case, you create what is called a *default route*. We discuss this in the next section.

DEFAULT ROUTING

The most extreme case of summarization is when every single route in existence is summarized. Because the first bit of the network could be anything, the first bit of the subnet mask, and every bit, for that matter, is 0.

- Mask: 00000000.00000000.00000000.00000000

Because all bits in the subnet mask are zero, there is no network portion of the address. It essentially captures *all* addresses. It is therefore most often displayed as

- Address 0.0.0.0
- Mask   0.0.0.0

This is called the *default route* because any other route that matches a destination address has a longer subnet mask and hence is more preferred. Only when there are no other options is a default route used.

An example of this can be seen below. This is part of the output of the "route print" command from a Windows 2000 command prompt. You may be surprised to learn that all hosts keep routing tables, just like routers. The reason they're not considered routers is that they don't forward traffic on behalf of other devices.

```
C:\>route print
Active Routes:
Network   Destination   Netmask          Gateway
          Interface     Metric
0.0.0.0                 0.0.0.0          192.168.1.1
          192.168.1.3   1
192.168.1.0             255.255.255.0    192.168.1.3
          192.168.1.3   1
192.168.1.3             255.255.255.255  127.0.0.1
          127.0.0.1     1
192.168.1.255           255.255.255.255  192.168.1.3
          192.168.1.3     1
255.255.255.255         255.255.255.255  192.168.1.3  1000002
          1
Default Gateway:        192.168.1.1
```

Here we see that by configuring a default gateway in the TCP/IP configuration dialog boxes, behind the scenes, Windows is actually placing a default route to the IP address of the default gateway you specified. Following the principle of the most specific match, we can see that if I ping my own 192.168.1.3 address, I would match the route:

```
192.168.1.3  255.255.255.255  127.0.0.1  127.0.0.1  1
```

This would cause my ping traffic to be sent across the software loopback, 127.0.0.1.

Anything sent to my local segment would go out my own 192.168.1.3 interface with myself as the gateway. Anything else would be matched by the

```
0.0.0.0    0.0.0.0    192.168.1.1    192.168.1.3    1
```

Again, this meets all network addresses possible and forwards the traffic out my 192.168.1.3 interface to the 192.168.1.1 gateway.

Practically, default routes are a necessity because it would be impossible to put routes to every network on the Internet into our local routing tables. Again, to get around this requirement, we simply use normal routing for local networks and then employ a default route pointing to the Internet's backbone. The Internet Service Provider aggregates and summarizes all their customer's routes. Then the network service providers summarize all their connected ISPs. This is the essence of hierarchical routing.

Multicast Routing

Multicast routing is special because of its need to reach many different clients with a single packet sent to a group address. Instead of sending a unicast packet to a single destination along a single path, multicast must send a packet to an arbitrary number of destinations, which necessarily means an arbitrary number of paths. To accomplish this, a number of special routing protocols can be used. These include:

- Distance Vector Multicast Routing Protocol (DVMRP)
- Multicast Open Shortest Path First (MOSPF)
- Protocol Independent Multicast (PIM)

Generally, multicast routers receive a multicast packet on one interface and then forward it out all other interfaces that are configured for multicast routing. If there are multiple paths through the network, this could generate a number of routing loops. So to avoid loops, multicast routing uses one of two distribution methods: *Source Tree* and *Shared Tree*.

SOURCE TREES

In the source tree distribution model, a tree diagram can be created to describe the path between each multicast source (for example, a streaming media server) and destination. The source and destination are typically represented with the following notation:

(S, G)

where:

- S = Source IP Address
- G = the Group IP Address

For example, Figure 7-11 shows the physical connectivity between a set of routers. All of these routers are participating in multicast routing. As you can see, there are many possible paths through the network to get from any one point to another.

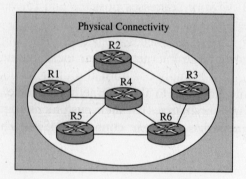

Fig. 7-11. Physical connectivity between six routers.

Note: In the wild, the (S, G) pair would appear as something like (192.168.1.1, 224.1.2.2) but for the sake of simplicity, we have replaced the source IP address with a router name in the examples in Figures 7-11, 7-12, 7-13, and 7-14.

Figure 7-12 shows the Source Tree (R1, 224.1.1.1), which is the shortest path between R1 and all nodes to which packets destined for the 224.1.1.1 multicast address are delivered.

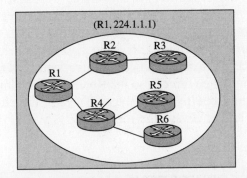

Fig. 7-12. Source tree R1.

Figure 7-13 shows the tree (R3, 224.1.1.1). Although the source is on the other side of the network, the tree looks very similar to (R1, 224.1.1.1). Notice the names of the routers have changed. It is not the same tree.

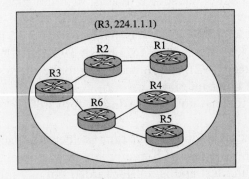

Fig. 7-13.   Source tree R3.

Figure 7-14 shows the tree (R6, 224.1.1.1). R6 has three physical connections instead of two, as do R1 and R3. This causes its tree to be broader and shallower.

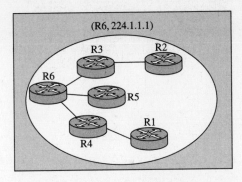

Fig. 7-14.   Source tree R6.

SHARED TREES

Unlike source trees, where every (S, G) pair has its own unique tree where the source is always the root of the tree, in the shared tree distribution model, there is only one tree shared among all sources. The notation for this is (*, G) because the source no longer matters.

Routers in a shared tree must know the source router, commonly called a *Rendezvous Point* (RP). When a multicast source sends its traffic to one of these routers, the router would then direct it to the Rendezvous Point, which would deliver it throughout the shared tree to all receivers. The RP, therefore, is responsible for determining the tree and is always the root.

REVERSE PATH FORWARDING

Most multicast routers use a technique known as *reverse path forwarding* to avoid loops. Because they are all using a tree model to ensure no loops exist, the algorithm used to forward traffic is relatively simple. Instead of basing decisions on lookups in a routing table, the router simply checks the packet to see if the interface it arrived on is on the reverse path to the source. If it is, then the packet is forwarded. If not, then the router knows that the packet has arrived from a nonoptimal route and should not be forwarded back toward the source. Figure 7-15 illustrates this concept.

The multicast packet arrives with a source of 192.168.1.1. Because it arrives on the interface that leads to 192.168.1.1, according to the shortest path tree, the packet is forwarded out the other interfaces.

Note: Multicast routers don't necessarily forward the packet out all other interfaces.

Figure 7-16 shows the opposite. This time an identical packet arrives on another interface. Because the shortest path tree points to a different interface, it fails the reverse path forwarding test and is not forwarded out any interface.

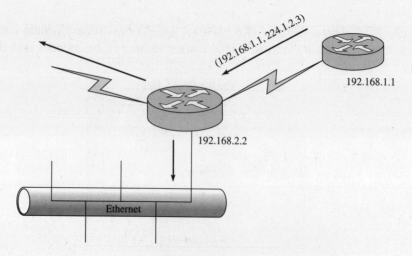

Fig. 7-15.   Using reverse path forwarding to avoid loops.

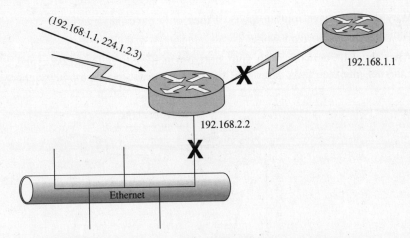

Fig. 7-16.   A packet failing the reverse path forwarding test.

Review Questions

7.1   A router has the following routes in its routing table.

```
Route            Outgoing Interface

0.0.0.0 /0    e1
10.0.0.0 /8   e0
10.0.0.0 /16 e1
10.0.1.0 /24 s0
10.1.1.0 /24 s1
10.1.0.0 /16 s0
10.1.0.0 /24 e1
10.1.1.1 /32 s2
```

A packet arrives at the router with a destination address of 10.1.1.1. Which interface will the router use to transmit that packet?

7.2   A router has the following routes in its routing table:

```
Route            Outgoing Interface
0.0.0.0 /0    e1
10.0.0.0 /8   e0
10.0.0.0 /16 e1
10.0.1.0 /24 s0
10.1.1.0 /24 s1
10.1.0.0 /16 s0
10.1.0.0 /24 e1
10.1.1.1 /32 s2
```

A packet arrives at the router with a destination address of 10.0.4.1. Which interface will the router use to transmit that packet?

7.3 Why do hosts have routing tables if they only have one interface?

7.4 How does split horizon work?

7.5 After the RIP network with split horizon in Figure 7-17 is converged, router A's Ethernet interface fails. How will the network react to this topology change?

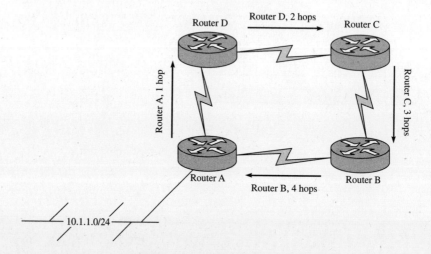

Fig. 7-17. RIP network with split horizon.

7.6 Why are the "all ones" and "all zeros" subnets not used?

7.7 How does a directed broadcast work, using the network shown in Figure 7-18 as an example.?

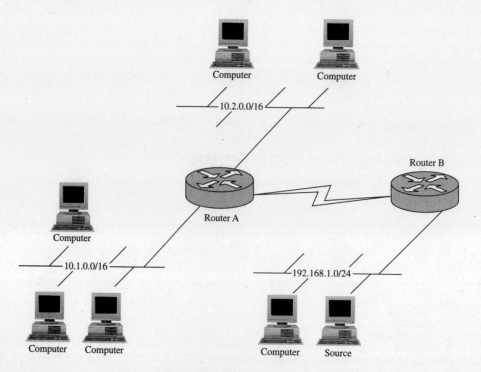

Fig. 7-18. A directed broadcast.

7.8 Given the shared tree multicast-enabled network in Figure 7-19, where router R6 is the rendezvous point, what path would be taken through the network for a client attached to router R8 to send multicast traffic to a client attached to R1?

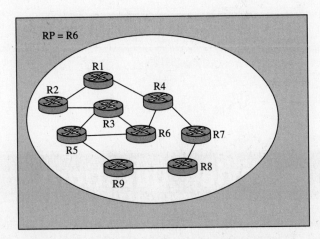

Fig. 7-19. Shared-tree multicast-enabled network.

7.9 If the network in Figure 7-19 was a source tree network, what path would be taken?

7.10 Using the network diagram in Figure 7-20, which path is preferred by RIP from R6 to R2?

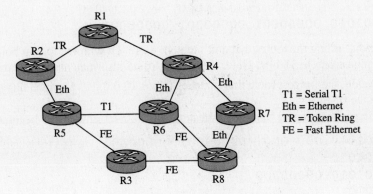

T1 = Serial T1
Eth = Ethernet
TR = Token Ring
FE = Fast Ethernet

Fig. 7-20. Network segments and links.

7.11 If the network diagram in Figure 7-20 was using OSPF instead of RIP, which path would be preferred from R6 to R2?

7.12 After manually changing the costs of the links in the previous question as shown in Figure 7-21, which path would be preferred between R6 and R2?

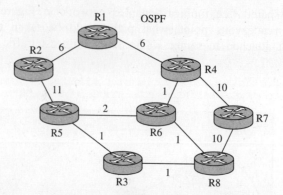

Fig. 7-21.   Revised link costs.

 Answers to Review Questions

7.1   s2. Remember that regardless of the order of the routes, the longest match is always taken. The /32 route is the longest, most specific match, so its outgoing interface of s2 will be used.

To see how this is calculated, first convert everything to binary. Here, the destination 10.1.1.1 and routes become:

```
00001010.00000001.00000001.00000001 <-Destination
00001010              ← !0.0.0.0 /8
00001010.00000000     ← 10.0.0.0 /16
00001010.00000000.00000001 ← 10.0.1.0 /24
00001010.00000001.00000001 ← 10.1.1.0 /24
00001010.00000001.    ← 10.1.0.0 /16
00001010.00000001.00000000 ← 10.1.0.0 /24
00001010.00000001.00000001.00000001 ← 10.1.1.1 /32
```

After discarding the routes that don't match, we're left with the four in bold. Of these, the longest one is 32 bits. Note, the default route also matches, but wasn't listed.

7.2   e1. Again, the longest route that matches this is 10.0.0.0 /16, which has an outgoing interface of e1.

After converting to binary, the destination 10.0.4.1 and routes become:

```
00001010.00000001.00000001.00000001 Destination
00001010     ← 10.0.0.0 /8
00001010.00000000     ← 10.0.0.0 /16
00001010.00000000.00000001 ← 10.0.1.0 /24
00001010.00000001.00000001 ← 10.1.1.0 /24
00001010.00000001.    ← 10.1.0.0 /16
00001010.00000001.00000000 ← 10.1.0.0 /24
00001010.00000001.00000001.00000001 ← 10.1.1.1 /32
```

Only two routes and the default route match the destination 10.0.4.1 and of these the /16 is the most specific.

7.3   The routing table on a host is still required to transmit packets. Not only does it tell the host where its default gateway is, but it also explicitly defines the broadcast address of the network as well as the loopback interface.

Hosts, such as PCs and servers, are typically found on multi-access broadcast networks. Here there may be hundreds or thousands of devices on the same IP subnet. It is also possible for hosts to have multiple gateways. Consider Figure 7-22.

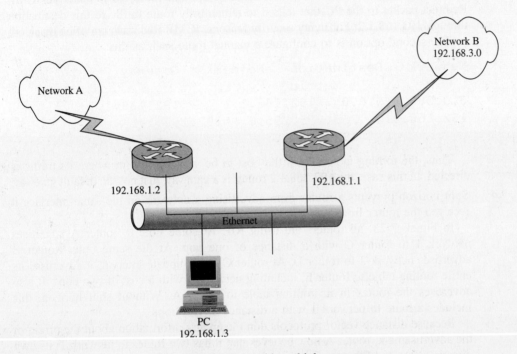

Fig. 7-22.   A host with multiple gateways.

Here there are two routers attached to the same network that a group of PCs are on. If the PC has a default gateway of 192.168.1.1 configured, it will have a route such as this in its routing table:

```
Network Destination Netmask      Gateway      Interface
           Metric
0.0.0.0 0.0.0.0      192.168.1.1 192.168.1.3 1
```

Of course, this means all traffic that isn't destined for the local network is sent to 192.168.1.1. As you can see, the result is suboptimal routing because traffic sent to network B first goes to the router 192.168.1.1, which then forwards the traffic to 192.168.1.2 before it is sent on to network B.

It is possible to add a second default route to router B such as this:

```
Network Destination Netmask      Gateway      Interface
           Metric
0.0.0.0 0.0.0.0      192.168.1.1 192.168.1.3 1
0.0.0.0 0.0.0.0      192.168.1.2 192.168.1.3 1
```

But this would only load-balance traffic or be used as a backup in case the first router fails, depending on the operating system running on the PC. The problem is that the PC has no way of knowing which router has the best path to network B because it is not participating in any routing protocol. In effect, our manual summarization (actually the result of *not* manually adding more specific routes) has left the PC with a loss of valuable information.

To resolve this problem, there are two options. The first is to enable ICMP Redirects. In this case, when the 192.168.1.1 router receives a packet destined for network B, it realizes that it is not the most optimal route, so it sends an ICMP Redirect packet to the PC that tells it to temporarily route traffic to this destination through 192.168.1.2. For many security reasons, ICMP Redirects are often disabled.

The second option is to configure a manual route such as this:

```
Network   Destination  Netmask    Gateway     Interface
               Metric
0.0.0.0 0.0.0.0   192.168.1.1     192.168.1.3   1
192.168.3.0  255.255.255.0   192.168.1.2
              192.168.1.3      1
```

Thus, the routing table allows the host to be very explicit in where its traffic is directed. In this case, the 192.168.1.2 router is a gateway, just not the default gateway.

7.4 Split horizon prevents a router from advertising a network on the same interface it received the router from.

In Figure 7-23, all routers are using RIP. At some time 0, router A advertises network 1 to router C with a distance of one hop. At the same time, Router B advertises network 1 to router D. At router C's next update interval, it advertises its entire routing table to router E, including network 1 with a cost of two hops. It also advertises the routes in its routing table to router A. Without split horizon, this includes a route to network 1 with a distance of two hops.

Because distance vector protocols don't keep any information about the origin of the advertisement, router A now believes that it has two routes to network 1: its own directly connected Ethernet interface and a two-hop route through router C. However, because its own interface is zero hops away, it discards this route.

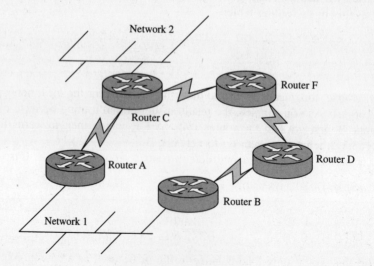

Fig. 7-23.   Split horizon.

A short while later, router D advertises network 1 to router E with a hop count of two and router E advertises network 1 to router C with a hop count of three. Router C discards this information because the path through router A is much shorter.

All is well until router A's Ethernet interface goes down. At the next update interval, router A sends an advertisement for network 1 with a hop count of 16 or "infinity" to indicate that it cannot be reached via router A. Unfortunately, before this can happen, router A receives an update from router C indicating that it can reach network 1 only two hops away. (Again, neither router has any idea that this path is actually through the interface that is now unavailable.)

At this point, a packet is sent from a host on network 2 destined for a host on network 1. Router C forwards the packet to router A. Router A examines the packet and forwards it to router C! Router C examines it and forwards it back to router A! This process continues until the time-to-live value of the packet expires.

Split horizon prevents this scenario by forbidding routers to advertise routes out the same interface on which they were received.

7.5 When router A realizes its Ethernet interface is down, it will begin looking for an alternate route. Because routers A and D are using split horizon, router D is not advertising network 10.1.1.0 back to router A so no loop will form. Or will it?

As the route to network 10.1.1.0 is passed throughout the network, it eventually reaches router B, which forwards it back to router A with a cost of four hops. Because router A no longer has the zero-hop route of its locally connected interface, it accepts this route and broadcasts it to router D with a hop count of five at the next update interval.

At this point, if a packet were sent to 10.1.1.100, router A would forward it to router B, which would forward it to router C, which would forward it to router B, which would forward it to router A. Router A would again forward it to router B, and again we have a loop! This packet continues circling the network until its time-to-live value reaches zero.

To prevent this type of loop from occurring, distance vector protocols use a technique called *Counting to Infinity*.

In this case, infinity is defined as 16 hops, which is why RIP is limited to 16 hops. The way this works is that router D receives the route to 10.1.1.100 from router A with the hop count of five, then it passes it along to router C with a hop count of six. Router C passes it to router B with a hop count of seven. Router B again passes it to router A with a hop count of eight. This process continues until router B finally advertises a route to router A with a hop count of 16.

The problem with this approach is that it can take several minutes for these routers to converge. This is why link-state protocols are so popular.

7.6 Originally there were four types of broadcasts.

- Limited broadcasts
- Directed broadcasts
- All-subnets-directed broadcasts
- Subnets-directed broadcasts

The limited broadcast is the familiar 255.255.255.255 form. This is called a *limited broadcast* because routers are not allowed to forward them.

The directed broadcast and subnets-directed broadcasts were originally intended to be different, but are now indistinguishable. That is, they're both the network address, with all "ones" in the host portion, for example, 10.255.255.255.

The all-subnets-directed broadcast was intended to be used to broadcast to all subnets of a particular classful network. For example, if your 10.0.0.0 network had 8 bits of subnetting, you might have an address 10.1.0.0 /16. Its subnet broadcast address would be 10.1.255.255. A broadcast to 10.255.255.255 would be sent to all subnets:

10.1.0.0
10.2.0.0
10.3.0.0
. . .
10.254.0.0

Unfortunately, the classful routing protocols, which did not submit subnet masks in their routing updates had no way of understanding the difference between 10.0.0.0 /16 and 10.0.0.0 /8. And if you were to use the "all ones" subnet, which would be 10.255.0.0 /16, and you sent a broadcast to 10.255.255.255, the router would have no way of knowing whether it was intended for all subnets or just as a directed broadcast to the 10.255.0.0 /16 network.

Thus, RFC 950, the document in which subnets were first defined, simply prohibited the use of the "all ones" and "all zeros" subnets.

Today, the all-subnets-directed broadcast isn't used, and our classless routing protocols can easily understand the difference between 10.0.0.0 /16 and 10.0.0.0 /8. So there's no technical reason not to use the "all zeros" or "all ones" subnet. However, many people prefer not to use them, as they tend to be confusing.

7.7 Consider the network in Figure 7-18.

If the computer labeled "Source" were to send a limited broadcast of 255.255.255.255, it would be received and processed only by the computers and router B on its local segment.

If this computer were again to send a directed broadcast to 10.1.255.255, it would be unicast to router B, which would be required to forward it to router A. Router A would then transmit this packet on the Ethernet interface containing 10.1.0.0 /24, where it would be considered a broadcast and subsequently received and processed by all hosts on that subnet.

If the same computer were to send an all-subnets-directed broadcast to 10.255.255.255, router B would be required to forward this packet to router A. Router A would be required to transmit the packet on both Ethernet interfaces containing the 10.1.0.0 segment and the 10.2.0.0 segment. This means that all hosts on these segments would receive and process this packet. Fortunately, these are no longer used.

7.8 First, the traffic is sent by R6 to the RP as shown in Figure 7-24. The path taken is R8, R9, R5, R6. Note that the path R8, R7, R4, R6 could also be taken. The former path was chosen arbitrarily.

Once the multicast packet is received by the RP, it forwards the traffic via the shortest path in its tree, which is R6, R4, R1. The tree and path are shown in Figure 7-25.

7.9 To determine this, the shortest path tree from R8 to R1 must be calculated. This is shown in Figure 7-26. Thus, the path is R8, R7, R4, R1 because source trees are always created from the point of view of the sender. The root of the tree is always the sender.

7.10 R2 would advertise its networks to R5 and R1 with a hop count of one.
R5 would advertise R2's networks to R6 with a hop count of two.
R1 would advertise R2's networks to R4 with a hop count of two.
R4 would advertise R2's networks to R6 with a hop count of three.

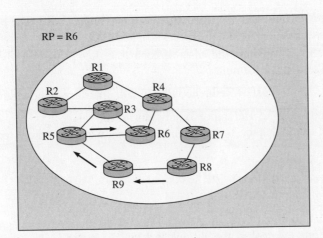

Fig. 7-24. Traffic sent by R6 to the RP.

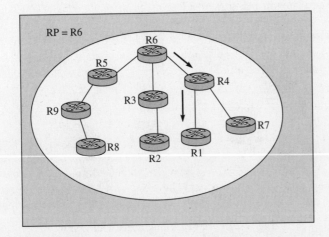

Fig. 7-25. The RP forwards traffic via the shortest path in its tree.

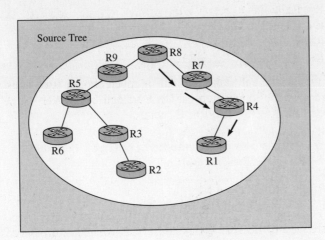

Fig. 7-26. The shortest path tree from R8 to R1.

Thus, R6 would take the shortest path of two hops via R5. The path would be R6, R5, R2.

7.11 Here, we must calculate the costs of each link. Recall that the default behavior of OSPF is to use the formula:

$$\text{Cost} = \text{Reference Bandwidth}/\text{Interface Bandwidth}$$

The default value of Reference Bandwidth is 100 Mbps.

Recall from Chapter 3 that the interface bandwidths for these technologies are as follows:

- T1 = 1.544 Mbps
- Ethernet = 10 Mbps
- Token Ring = 16 Mbps
- Fast Ethernet = 100 Mbps

Therefore, the cost of the T1 link is 100/1.544, or 65.
The cost of each Ethernet segment is 100/10, or 10.
The cost of each Token Ring segment is 100/16, or 6.
The cost of each Fast Ethernet segment is 100/100, or 1.
These are shown in Figure 7-27.

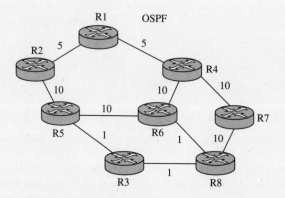

Fig. 7-27. Network link costs with OSPF.

To find the cost of a path, simply add the links in that path together as shown below:

- R6, R5, R2 = 75
- R6, R4, R1, R2 = 22
- R6, R8, R3, R5, R2 = 13
- R6, R8, R7, R4, R1, R2 = 33

Even though the path taken by RIP is much shorter (two hops versus four), the performance of the longer hop isn't constrained by the very slow T1 link and the high-speed path R6, R8, R3, R5, R2 wins.

7.12 After adding up the paths now, we get

- R6, R5, R2 = 13
- R6, R4, R1, R2 = 13
- R6, R8, R3, R5, R2 = 14
- R6, R8, R7, R4, R1, R2 = 33

Now we see a tie because two paths have an equal cost. In this case, both paths are taken. OSPF supports load-balancing of up to four paths of equal costs.

CHAPTER 8

Services and Applications

Different networking protocols provide a large collection of applications and services that operate at the upper layers of the OSI model. Some of these services are used frequently by many people, and others are used by a small section of the population. Throughout the history of networking, a protocol was usually designed and developed following a need by individuals to do a specific task on the network. This development model holds true today as rapid advances in areas such as transmission speed and content types continue to drive the evolution of new protocols and products. In this chapter, we cover some of the common services and applications in the IP protocol suite. The topics addressed in this chapter include only a very small subset of the available protocols but they are among the most commonly used. Other protocol suites, such as IPX and AppleTalk, include the same types of services and applications but usually have different names and function differently due to the variations in operating systems and Application Programming Interface (API) code.

File Transfer Protocol

File Transfer Protocol (FTP) is one of the oldest IP protocols around. It is the most popular protocol used on the Internet to transfer files between different systems. In fact, when you go to a Web site and download a file, the system may use FTP to transfer the file without your being aware of it. FTP was originally a part of the ARPANET protocols and was in use before both IP and TCP were developed. When the IP protocol suite was introduced, FTP was reworked to operate with the IP protocol suite. In the early days of the Internet, before the introduction of graphical elements, approximately one-third of all Internet traffic was FTP-related. Before we delve into the details of the version of FTP used today, let's examine some of the history and background of the development of a protocol for transferring files.

In the early days of computing, files were transferred between systems on some type of physical media. One of the most commonly used transfer media was magnetic tape housed on large reels that were similar to the reels used on contemporary reel-to-reel tape recorders. The files, or data, from one system were written to magnetic tape and then the tape was removed from the system by either humans or robotic arms. The tape was then transferred to another system, remounted on the remote system, and another application on the remote system would read the data from the tape. If the two systems were in different locations, then the tapes had to be mailed or transferred by courier. These steps to transfer files introduced a lot of delay, but at the time it was the most efficient method available. However, when networks were introduced and the different systems were connected, it became possible to transfer the data among the machines across the media resulting in a much faster transfer of information. Overall, networks made it possible to have the output of one program be the input of another program. But creating a system to transfer files across a network is not an easy task.

One of the first items to consider when designing a network file transfer protocol is coordination between the two systems. Administrators at both the sender and receiver side have to make sure that the systems are operational and the applications to send and receive the data are loaded and running. In addition, if the systems are running other services and/or other network activities are using bandwidth, the administrators must ensure that sufficient resources are available to handle the file transfer task. Another important consideration of direct output-to-input data transfer is the effects of a failure in the system. If the information from the application on one system is placed directly on the transmission media and the information is not saved to a file, then if there is a failure in the middle of the data transfer, the entire process must be started again from the beginning. One way to overcome this is to save the output from an application to a file and then send the file across the network. Using this model, the applications have to be modified to be able to read the input from a file and to place the output in a file.

Using files to store and transfer data has several benefits. If there is a failure in the transfer of information on the network, the files can be resent without the need for the application to rerun and regenerate the data. If there are several applications running, the administrator can stagger the transfer of files as necessary to ensure that sufficient bandwidth and other resources are available. In an environment that has direct output-to-input data transfer without storing the information to files, it may not be possible to stagger the times the applications run to reduce bandwidth demands. However, storing the data to files takes up storage space. While storage space is not a big issue today, at the time file transfer protocols were developed, storage space was very costly.

In order for a file transfer protocol to be useful, it must be able to transfer any type of file. If the software to transfer files was included in the application's code, then it could become proprietary and only allow the transfer of specific files. In addition, having each application include its own file transfer code adds more code baggage and management issues every time the application is modified. Using a protocol and external applications to handle just the file transfer piece alleviates these problems. However, placing file transfer details into a protocol introduces some other issues. Implementations of a file transfer protocol must be able to handle differences in how various operating systems store files. On some environments, there may be restrictions on filenames, such as the length of the name or the characters permitted in a name. In addition, different operating systems typically implement different security schemes, which are often tied to user accounts. The user initiating the file transfer from one system may not have an account on the recipient system. There needs to be some way for files to be sent to another system anonymously without creating any security risks on the systems. The file transfer software must be able to handle these differences without imposing any extra burden on the users of the application.

Depending on the user and application needs, files may need to be transferred as a batch process or with an interactive interface. Through the use of a scheduler, batch processes are convenient for transferring large files during off-peak hours. Interactive file transfer allows the user to send files whenever they need to. This mechanism provides immediate feedback so the user knows if the data transfer was successful or not. In addition, for small files, it is often more convenient to send files quickly without the need to work with a batch program and scheduler. The best implementations of file transfer applications provide for both interactive and batch file transfers.

IP's FTP protocol specifications provide for all of the items we mentioned above. It includes the capability to transfer files of any type between different operating systems. If the user initiating the transfer does not have an account on the destination system, FTP supports anonymous connections and the ability to control the actions of the anonymous user. FTP also includes the ability to handle interactive and batch file transfers. To provide for these features and functions, FTP operates as a client-server model. The system that accepts files runs an FTP service and the machine that sends and retrieves the files runs an FTP client software piece. Most implementations of an FTP service also include an FTP client piece so the device receiving files can also send files using FTP. When an FTP connection is created between a client and the server, the control connection does not actually transfer files. In addition, the FTP client does not send each keystroke to the server. If the command the user types at the FTP prompt does not require server interaction, the command is interpreted locally. Similarly, for commands that require the server's attention, the FTP client software constructs the necessary command syntax and sends that information to the FTP server. This type of information is sent on the control connection between the client and the server. When a file is transferred to or from the FTP server, a separate data connection for each file transfer is set up by the FTP server. When the file transfer is complete, the file transfer connection is closed. The FTP control connection is maintained until the user or the FTP server closes the FTP session. To avoid confusion between these two operations—control and file transfer—a different IP protocol port number is assigned to each. Port 21 is the IP protocol port used for the FTP control connection and port 20 is used for file transfers. Using two different ports and connections for control and data has several advantages. First, the implementation is much simpler and FTP commands do not interfere with the data and vice versa. This also allows the user to interact with the system while a file transfer is taking place. For example, the user can abort and cancel the file transfer. Another benefit is the end of the file can be used to indicate when the file transfer port is closed. Using this procedure means that any size file can be transferred and there is no need in advance to specify file sizes. When the end of the file is reached, the file transfer is done.

The FTP protocol specifications do not include any details on the user interface. Whatever features are available in your chosen FTP client and server applications depend on what the vendor has decided to include in its software. Fortunately, most FTP implementations support all of the above features, and the interfaces are remarkably similar. Most common vendors use the same command names, switches, and parameters that were present on early FTP implementations. This makes it easier to move between different operating systems without having to relearn a whole new set of commands. Graphical interfaces can vary quite a bit but the popular ones all have very similar interfaces. Furthermore, most current Web browsers support FTP, which makes it easy to transfer files without the need to install additional software.

The FTP command line interface supported on many systems uses similar commands to perform various tasks. Figure 8-1 is an example of the available commands on a FreeBSD UNIX system.

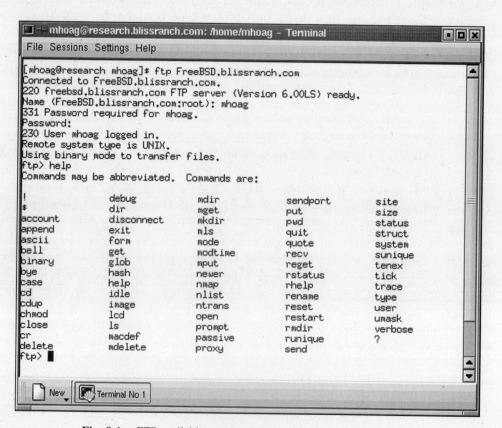

Fig. 8-1. FTP available commands on a FreeBSD UNIX system.

Figure 8-2 illustrates the FTP commands available on a Linux system. Notice the Linux and UNIX systems are essentially identical, which makes sense when you take a look at the development path of Linux.

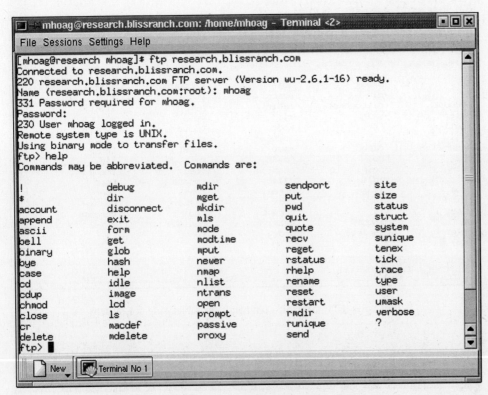

Fig. 8-2.   FTP available commands on a Linux system.

Novell NetWare servers have supported FTP services for many years, and Figure 8-3 shows the available FTP commands on a NetWare 5.1 server.

Most Windows server operating systems include the ability to provide FTP services. Figure 8-4 illustrates the available commands on a Windows 2000 Advanced Server.

Many of the FTP commands accessible at a command prompt are very rarely used, and new users to FTP do not need to feel overwhelmed by the number of commands. An example of an obscure command is tenex. TENEX was the name of an early operating system that contained a version of FTP. However, the file format used by Unix and TENEX were different so the tenex command was created to assist in handling these file differences.

There are two ways to create a connection to an FTP server. One method is to place the name or IP number of the FTP server after the ftp command. For example:

```
ftp research.blissranch.com
```
or
```
ftp 172.16.3.6
```

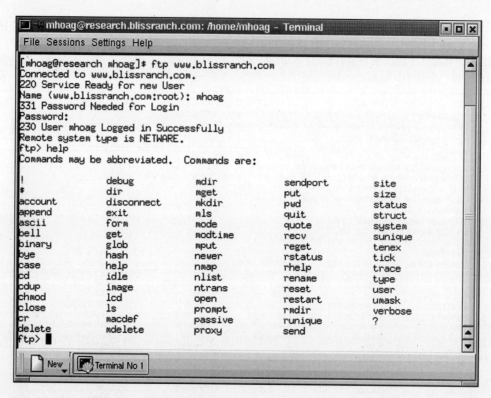

Fig. 8-3. FTP available commands on a NetWare 5.1 system.

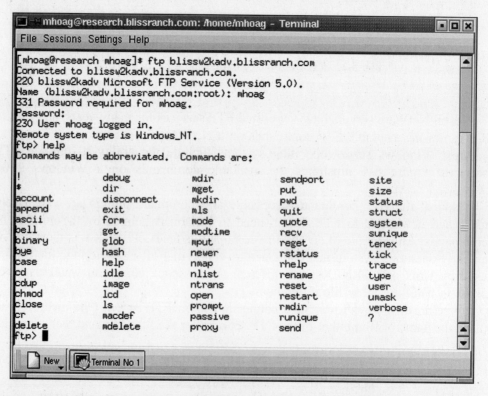

Fig. 8-4. FTP available commands on a Windows 2000 advanced server system.

The second method uses the FTP open command in the FTP application. For example

```
ftp> open ftp.blissranch.com
Connected to ftp.blissranch.com.
220 Service Ready for new User
User (ftp.blissranch.com:(none)):
```

The text above in bold indicates the command entered, and the remaining text is the information echoed back when the open command was executed. Once connected to the FTP server, the command prompt is located at the default directory specified by the FTP server configuration. In order to progress further you will need to log in to the system as either a registered user or as anonymous. Anonymous access allows users to connect without the need to set up user accounts and passwords. This is useful when the FTP server is designed to primarily provide download support. On some systems when you connect as an anonymous user, your e-mail account for the password is required. Depending on the security configuration for the anonymous and user accounts, you may or may not be able to upload or place files on the FTP server.

To view the contents of the directory on the FTP server, the ls command can be used. For example:

```
ftp> ls
200 PORT Command OK
150 Opening data connection
winstuff
linuxstuff
working
ethereallinux
bookstuff
apache
etherealw2k
Fonts
226 Transfer Complete
ftp: 85 bytes received in 0.06Seconds 1.42Kbytes/sec.
ftp>
```

To get some help about the commands, enter help followed by the FTP command name at the ftp> prompt. For example, to obtain information about the ls command:

```
ftp> help ls
ls              List contents of remote directory
ftp>
```

You can also use the dir command to view the contents of the default FTP server directory:

```
ftp> dir
200 PORT Command OK
150 Opening data connection
total 0
```

```
d  [RWCEAFMS]  admin                                   512 Oct 01
         17:35winstuff
d  [RWCEAFMS]  admin                                   512 Oct 01
         17:36 linuxstuff
d  [RWCEAFMS]  admin                                   512 Oct 01
         17:36 working
d  [RWCEAFMS]  admin                                   512 Aug 08
         11:42 ethereallinux
d  [RWCEAFMS]  admin                                   512 Oct 01
         17:36 bookstuff
d  [RWCEAFMS]  admin                                   512 Oct 01
         17:36 apache
d  [RWCEAFMS]  admin                                   512 Jul 28
         23:13 etherealw2k
d  [RWCEAFMS]  admin                                   512 Jul 26
         10:07 Fonts
226 Transfer Complete
ftp: 606 bytes received in 0.17Seconds 3.56Kbytes/sec.
ftp>
```

To transfer a copy of a file to an FTP server, the put, send, or mput commands are typically used. The put and send commands will transfer one file, and the mput command can be used to transfer several files at a time. The put and send commands are used with the name of the file to place a copy of the file on the FTP server. Wildcard characters such as * for all matches or ? for positional matches can be used with mput to copy more than one file to the FTP server. Figure 8-5 is an example of using the put command to copy a file called motif to an FTP server.

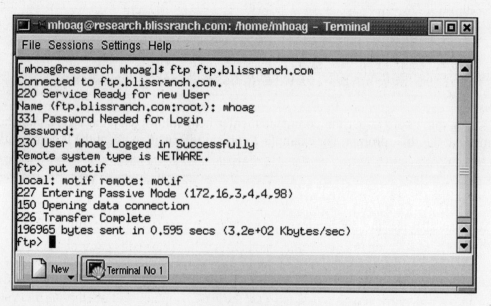

Fig. 8-5.   Example of the FTP put command.

To retrieve a copy of a file from the FTP server, the get command is used. To copy multiple files, use the mget command. As with the put and send command, the get command is followed by the name of the file. mget is similar to mput in that wildcard characters can be used to download multiple files. Figure 8-6 is an example of the get command used to retrieve a copy of a file called scribble.kil.

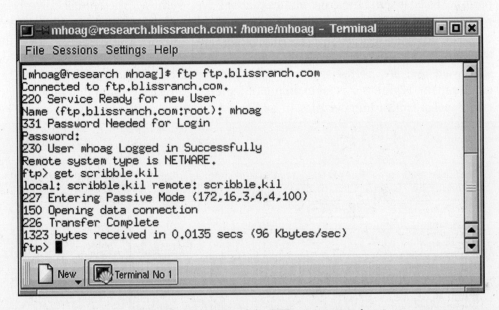

```
[mhoag@research mhoag]$ ftp ftp.blissranch.com
Connected to ftp.blissranch.com.
220 Service Ready for new User
Name (ftp.blissranch.com:root): mhoag
331 Password Needed for Login
Password:
230 User mhoag Logged in Successfully
Remote system type is NETWARE.
ftp> get scribble.kil
local: scribble.kil remote: scribble.kil
227 Entering Passive Mode (172,16,3,4,4,100)
150 Opening data connection
226 Transfer Complete
1323 bytes received in 0.0135 secs (96 Kbytes/sec)
ftp>
```

Fig. 8-6.   Example of the FTP get command.

When using FTP to move files among different operating systems, sometimes the syntax of the filenames in one system may be incompatible with the naming structure in another system. For example, in some systems only lowercase may be used for the alpha characters used in filenames. Most FTP implementations support the case command, which allows toggling of the case of the alpha characters used in filenames. Some other commands that are helpful when using FTP at a command prompt include the pwd command. This echoes back the directory path on the remote system that your FTP session is connected to. The cd command allows you to change to the directory specified in the path used after the cd command. To move up one directory in the remote systems hierarchy, the cdup command can be used.

Another item to consider is that the types of files transferred between systems may be different. In order to provide the maximum flexibility to accommodate all the different file types used across different operating systems, FTP supports two types of file transfer: ASCII and binary. The ASCII option is used for transferring text files, and binary is for everything else. If you are not sure of the file type or if an operating system does not use the standard ASCII set or adds extra characters, try the binary file transfer type. The binary choice does a bit-by-bit copy and does not perform any translation on the file. If the file is text and the systems used two different character sets to represent text, the ASCII option will attempt to translate between the different character sets.

Another FTP command you may find useful is the verbose switch. If you look at Figures 8-5, 8-6, and 8-7, illustrating FTP commands, notice that the beginning of some lines contains a three-digit number. This number indicates the type of message. For example, in Figure 8-6, the number 226 indicates that the file transfer was complete. When these message numbers are visible in the output, verbose mode is enabled. To suppress these message numbers, enter verbose at the FTP command prompt. To enable the message numbers again, type verbose. The command verbose acts as a toggle between the display and no display of the message numbers.

There are many graphical FTP applications that provide a different interface for transferring files between systems. Most of these applications are either free or shareware and are useful for users who are more comfortable with a graphical environment. Figure 8-7 is an example of a graphical FTP program that provides an easy mechanism to transfer files in addition to supporting the ability to send FTP commands.

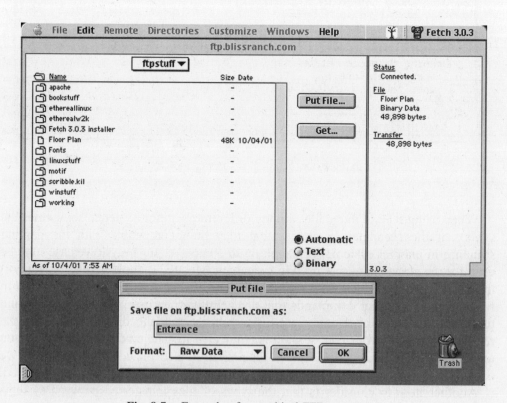

Fig. 8-7.   Example of a graphical FTP program.

TFTP

The IP protocol suite also includes another file transfer protocol called Trivial File Transfer Protocol (TFTP). One of the big differences between FTP and TFTP is the underlying IP protocol. FTP uses TCP, and TFTP uses UDP. Recall that TCP is a connection-oriented protocol that provides reliability while UDP is not connection-oriented so it does not provide reliability. TFTP does not allow for user authentication, the contents of remote directories cannot be displayed, and only file transfer is supported for files that permit global access. While all these features make TFTP sound inferior, TFTP does have important uses. For example, diskless or operating systemless computers need to find a BOOTP server to download an operating system. TFTP can provide this type of file transfer service quite well without the need for a lot of configuration.

Domain Name System

In Chapter 6 we briefly mentioned Domain Name System (DNS) services and how DNS assists in resolving the names of devices or services to their corresponding IP number. The assignment of friendly names to systems and services helps humans interact with the network. When the different devices communicate with each other, IP addresses and physical (MAC) addresses are used to transfer the information among the senders and receivers. It is much easier for people to remember a string of words or characters rather than a string of numbers. Therefore, in order to provide convenience to the user but allow the systems to communicate, there needs to be a mechanism to translate the friendly names to the corresponding IP addresses. DNS is one of the services and mechanisms available in the IP protocol suite that provides this service.

DNS services are spread across many different server systems to provide name resolution on the Internet. No single DNS server maintains a complete list of the registered domain names found on the Internet. Instead, the different DNS servers maintain a database of certain names and addresses. A good example of distributed DNS services is how Internet Service Providers (ISPs) handle DNS requests. When you access the Internet through an ISP, your system is usually configured to use a DNS server maintained by the ISP or another company or organization. When you make a request to access a Web site, the DNS server that your system is set up to use is queried to resolve the name. If the information is not in the DNS server's database, the DNS server becomes a client and passes on the request to another DNS server. This process continues until a DNS server is found that can resolve the name to its IP addresses. This type of action to find a source that can resolve the address is called a *recursive query*. Before we go into the details of DNS, let's examine the structure and syntax of system names for IP networks. Note that DNS names are not the same as the types of names used by some operating systems to refer to systems on the network. Device names used on IP-based networks to communicate with other systems are not dependent on the operating system. Systems communicating on a network may or may not have the same operating system; and on the Internet, many different types of hardware and operating systems are present.

The Domain Name System is hierarchical. A DNS name for a device or service consists of alphanumeric characters separated by dots (periods). Each item between the dots specifies the name of a group or organization of systems. The left-most item in a DNS name is the name of the device or service, and the right-most item is the name of the top of the hierarchy and is called the most significant segment of the name. The names are not case sensitive and each segment can be up to 63 characters. The overall length of the complete domain name cannot exceed 255 characters. The only part of the name that has specific names is the most significant segment. Any other segment in the name is the choice of the individual or organization. However, in order to maintain unique names on a public network, the upper-level names of DNS names are registered. Any names to sublevels or devices below the registered name are optional. Some of the top-level domain (TLD), most significant segment, names are listed below:

TLD	Purpose
com	Commercial organizations and companies around the world.
edu	Educational institutions, covering all levels of education.
gov	Reserved exclusively for the U.S. government.
int	For organization established through international treaties.
mil	Reserved exclusively for the U.S. military.
net	Network provider, support, ISPs, or other network-related services around the world.
org	Noncommercial organizations and nonprofits, such as the American Red Cross, around the world.
XX	XX refers to a two-letter country code. For example, UK refers to the United Kingdom.

There are also some new top-level domains that have recently been made available. Others have been proposed and may possibly appear in the future. These are:

TLD	Purpose	Available for Registration
biz	Business around the world	Yes
info	Unrestricted use	Yes
name	For registration by individuals	Yes
aero	Air transport industry	No
coop	For cooperatives	No
museum	For museums	No
pro	For accountants, lawyers, and physicians	No

The next sublevel typically seen below the TLD is the domain name that represents the organization, company, or organizational entity. For example, a fictitious company called Texas Stars makes decorative and ornamental stars. To attract people to their products and to find out more about the company, the organization has decided to develop a Web site. They have chosen the domain name of texas-stars and since they are a commercial organization, they plan to use .com as the TLD name. The domain name, along with the TLD name, must be registered by an Internet registration authority. For our example, the name texas-stars.com, would be registered by our fictitious company. The company is planning to have a Web server accessible to the public and to make it easy for users the company wants to use www.texas-stars.com. In order to support this, the name of the server hosting the Web site is called www and the entire DNS name, www.texas-stars.com is registered and entered in the DNS name space. Once the domain name for the company is registered, the company can create any subdomains below as they wish. For example, the Texas Stars company plans on dividing the name space into two major divisions: retail and wholesale. To accommodate these categories, two subdomains could be created: .retail.texas-stars.com and .wholesale.texas-stars.com.

In the retail area of the company there is a database that is accessible from a Web browser. In this example, the DNS name of the database server might be something like inventory, and the complete DNS name of the database server would be: inventory.retail.texas-stars.com.

If the database server will not be accessible from the Internet, then the name does not need to be registered and made accessible in the Internet name space. The company could implement private, internal DNS servers to resolve names of systems in the company that are not accessible from a public network.

DNS SERVER HIERARCHY

As we mentioned previously, there is no single DNS server on the Internet that maintains a list of all the systems and services on the Internet. Instead, a hierarchy of DNS servers exists across the Internet, and the top of the name space hierarchy is maintained by a group of servers called the *root servers*. These servers do not contain information about all the systems for a domain but know another DNS server to contact to pass on the request. There are 13 current root servers for the Internet:

ROOT-SERVERS Name	IP Number	Org	City	Type
A.ROOT-SERVERS.NET.	198.41.0.4	NSI	Herndon, VA	US com
B.ROOT-SERVERS.NET.	128.9.0.107	USC-ISI	Marina del Rey, CA	US edu
C.ROOT-SERVERS.NET.	192.33.4.12	PSInet	Herndon, VA	US com
D.ROOT-SERVERS.NET.	128.8.10.90	U of Maryland	College Park, MD	US edu
E.ROOT-SERVERS.NET.	192.203.230.10	NASA	Mt. View, CA	US usg
F.ROOT-SERVERS.NET.	192.5.5.241	Internet Software C.	Palo Alto, CA	US com
G.ROOT-SERVERS.NET.	192.112.36.4	DISA	Vienna, VA	US usg
H.ROOT-SERVERS.NET.	128.63.2.53	ARL	Aberdeen, MD	US usg
I.ROOT-SERVERS.NET.	192.36.148.17	NORDUnet	Stockholm	SE int
J.ROOT-SERVERS.NET.	198.41.0.10	NSI (TBD)	Herndon, VA	US com
K.ROOT-SERVERS.NET.	193.0.14.129	RIPE	London	UK int
L.ROOT-SERVERS.NET.	198.32.64.12	ICANN	Marina del Rey, CA	US org
M.ROOT-SERVERS.NET.	202.12.27.33	WIDE	Tokyo	JP edu

Note that the names of the servers end with a dot (period). The reason is that the top-most object in the DNS name space is root and that is represented by a dot (period). Thus, the name of the Web server for our fictitious company should be written as www.texas-stars.com. However, most Web browsers and other software that use DNS names do not require the trailing dot because the DNS root object is assumed.

DNS servers below the root servers may maintain the information for a geographic region or for a company or for any type of divisional boundaries. Furthermore, DNS servers can maintain the name information for the domain they are physically located in or for other domains or subdomains. Companies that elect to support DNS services within their organization may decide to use just one DNS server or several DNS servers. For small companies, a single DNS server will probably suffice and provide all the necessary name resolutions. However, a single server does introduce a single point of failure. Therefore, even for small companies, it may be better to have at least two DNS servers in case one fails. Larger companies may find the two servers are not enough to handle the load, or they wish to reduce the traffic and the latency for resolving names across their WAN. In these environments, the organizations may decide to place several DNS servers sprinkled throughout the organization based on the WAN infrastructure. When multiple DNS servers are used across an environment that contains subdomains, the servers must be configured with the following information:

- Each DNS server in a domain must know the DNS servers for each of its subdomains. For example, the DNS server for the .texas-stars.com domain must know the DNS servers for the .retail.texas-stars.com and .wholesale.texas-stars.com domains.

- Each DNS server is configured to know the location of at least one root server. Most implementations of DNS servers provide the complete list of all 13 DNS root servers in their configurations.

- Each DNS server will support at least one domain or subdomain. A DNS server cannot be configured to support only a portion of a domain or subdomain. However, the DNS server can be configured to support multiple domains and/or subdomains.

The overall goal of maintaining the above information for each DNS server is to provide continuity in the hierarchical DNS name space. There are no gaps in the name resolution structure so a name will be resolved by some DNS server in the hierarchy.

When a client needs to resolve an address, it runs, or accesses, resolver software to perform the request to a DNS server. On most operating systems that support the IP protocol, the resolver software is a component of the operating system or software library call that applications can use. The client is also configured with the IP address of at least one DNS server, and the request is sent to the DNS server configured on the client workstation. Figure 8-8 shows some of the details of a DNS request packet. The DNS resolver software sends the request as a UDP packet. Notice the name of the requested system, blissmac.blissranch.com, is contained in the Queries section of Figure 8-8.

If the DNS server contains the information for the requested name, a DNS reply message is sent back to the requester. Figure 8-9 shows some of the details of a DNS reply packet.

Notice that the DNS reply contains the original query, the results of the query, and details about the DNS server.

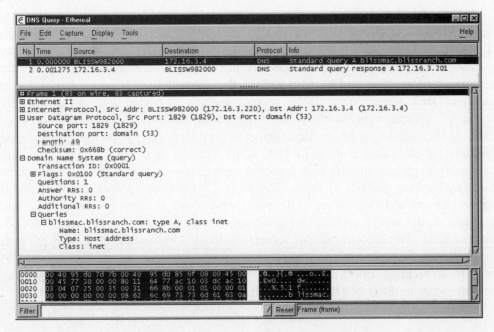

Fig. 8-8. Example of a DNS request packet.

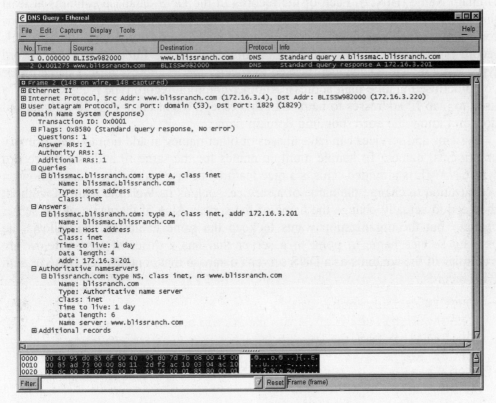

Fig. 8-9. Example of a DNS reply packet.

As you can probably deduce, there may be a considerable number of queries sent out by DNS servers to resolve names that are not contained in their own databases. If you take DNS servers used by ISPs as an example, there are many, many addresses that users will request that are not in their databases. In order to help improve performance and to help reduce the amount of DNS server lookups to another DNS server, most DNS servers include a cache that stores recently requested addresses in memory. In some configurations, the time-to-live of an entry in the cache may be on the order of several days and/or on the frequency of lookups for the same names. In fact, some heavily used DNS servers maintain extremely large and/or specialized caches to maintain a lot of DNS information in memory for long periods of times. The second method to improve performance is replication of a DNS server. The root servers on the Internet are replicated throughout the world in different geographic locations to provide better access. For example, if replicas of the root servers are located in Canada, then DNS requests in the same geographic region can receive a faster response than if the request was sent to a location on the other side of the world. In addition to improving performance, replicas of DNS servers also provide a level of fault tolerance.

STRUCTURE OF DNS DATABASE RECORDS

The structure and syntax of DNS records follow a standard called Berkeley Internet Domain Name (BIND). Each of the records in the DNS database contains at least three items: domain name, record type, and a value. The record type A, which stands for address type, specifies the domain name and the corresponding address. This record type is probably the most commonly used on the Internet. Another record type, MX for Mail eXchanger, is used to specify the IP address for the name of the computer used in an e-mail address. Another common record type is PTR, which is used to map IP addresses to names. In this case, a client knows the IP number but does not know the corresponding domain name.

Systems and services can have aliases or other names in addition to their primary or principal names. To handle multiple names for the same IP address, the record type CNAME is provided. This is a nice feature because supporting aliases allow an organization to change the name of a service, such as its Web site address, without the need to actually change the name of the server. Also, if the name of the server changes but the organization wants to keep the same name, an alias allows the existing service name to point to a server that has a different name. Below are examples of the contents of a DNS server's database that contains A, CNAME, and PTR records.

```
$ORIGIN blissranch.com.
@INSOAwww.blissranch.com. root.blissranch.com. (
2001061413; Serial
10800; Refresh
3600; Retry
604800; Expire
86400 ); Minimum
$ORIGIN com.
```

```
blissranchINNSwww.blissranch.com.
$ORIGIN blissranch.com.
apacheINA172.16.3.11
BlissMACINA172.16.3.201
BLISSW2KADVINA172.16.3.21
FreeBSDINA172.16.3.10
ftpINCNAMEwww.blissranch.com.
MelDesktopINA172.16.3.220
netservicesINA172.16.3.2
researchINA172.16.3.6
wwwINA172.16.3.4
```

Notice the A records with their corresponding IP addresses and the CNAME record with the name of the aliased object.

```
$ORIGIN 3.16.172.IN-ADDR.ARPA.
@INSOAwww.blissranch.com. root.3.16.172.IN-ADDR.ARPA. (
2001100404; Serial
10800; Refresh
3600; Retry
604800; Expire
86400 ); Minimum
$ORIGIN 16.172.IN-ADDR.ARPA.
3INNSwww.blissranch.com.
$ORIGIN 3.16.172.IN-ADDR.ARPA.
2INPTRnetservices.blissranch.com.
4INPTRwww.blissranch.com.
6INPTRresearch.blissranch.com.
```

In the above example, notice the PTR records with the host portion of the IP address on the far left and the corresponding DNS name on the right. The NS entry identifies the name of the authoritative, or master, name server for the domain indicated in the database.

Dynamic Host Configuration Protocol

As you will recall, each device on an IP network needs to have a unique host number so it can communicate properly. For large and/or changing networks, manually assigning numbers to each machine can be a daunting task. Fortunately, Dynamic Host Configuration Protocol (DHCP) provides an option to assigning IP numbers and other IP information dynamically to systems. Using a service to assign IP numbers is useful in environments with mobile systems, such as laptops and notebooks that travel among different networks. DHCP also provides the ability to assign permanent numbers to specific systems, such as servers, so the IP number will remain the same and not change when the systems are rebooted.

DHCP works as a client server model where a system that does not have an IP address makes a request to a DHCP server for an address. This process is typically performed when a system is booted so it can get an IP address to access the network and other resources. Since the system does not have an IP address when it is started, the device must first send out a DHCP Discover (DHCPDISCOVER) message to find a DHCP server. This DHCPDISCOVER message is sent out as a broadcast using the special IP address of 255.255.255.255. When DHCP servers receive this message, they reply back to the requester indicating that they are available to provide DHCP services. The requester chooses one of the DHCP servers (usually the first that responded to the discovery message) and sends a request for an IP address. The DHCP server checks in its database to see if the information from the requester, such as the physical address, is configured for a permanent IP address. If there is no permanent assignment, the DHCP server looks in its pool of available addresses it can assign and picks the next number that is not currently in use. The DHCP server sends the IP address back to the requester and the requester uses the IP address. Note that the DHCP protocol is an extension of the BOOTP protocol.

Figure 8-10 is an example of a DHCP reply message sent back to the requester. Notice on the bottom line of the figure that the IP address assigned to the requester is specified.

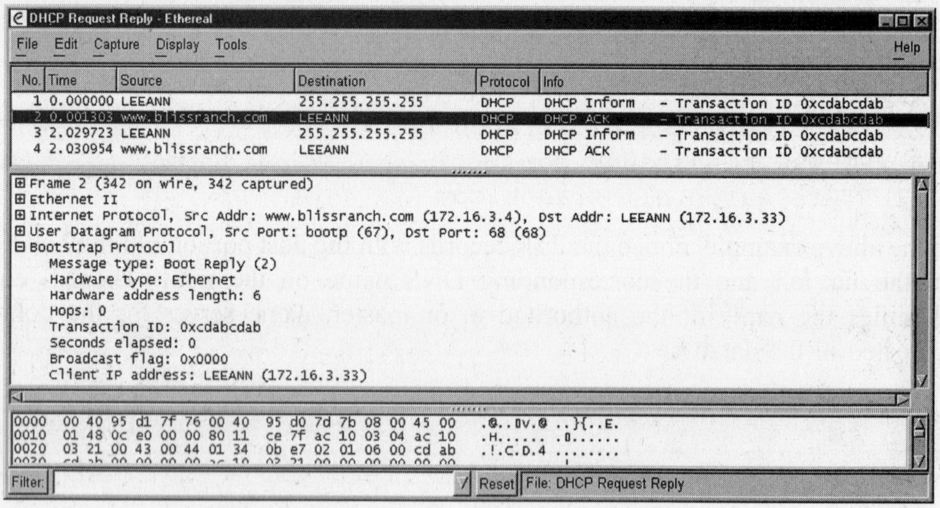

Fig. 8-10. Example of a DHCP server reply message.

In some networks, it is not feasible to have a DHCP server on each subnet. However, placing DHCP servers on networks that are different from the DHCP requesters poses a problem. Since the DHCPDISCOVER packet is sent out as a broadcast, routers will not pass these packets on to other networks. In order to allow DHCP servers to exist on different networks than the requesters, the routers run a relay agent that directs DHCPDISCOVER packets to the DHCP server or to the next router that can pass the request on. The relay agent sends a directed or unicast message and does not pass the DHCPDISCOVER broadcast on to other networks.

When the DHCP server is reached, the server sends a unicast packet back to the requester.

IP addresses assigned dynamically, that is, not permanent addresses, are available for use for a lease period. When the time nears the halfway point into the expiration period of the lease, the system using the IP address sends a request to the server asking for an extension of the lease. If the DHCP server says no or the DHCP server cannot be found, the system will continue until half of the remaining expiration time has elapsed. The DHCP client will send out another request to extend the lease. If a DHCP server does not respond to the request, the client again waits for half the remaining time to elapse. This process of asking for an extension and waiting for the DHCP server to reply continues until either a lease extension is returned or the time has run out. When the time runs out, the device using the leased address must release the IP address.

In order to reduce the amount of traffic that can result when a lot of machines that need to find a DHCP server are booted at the same time, the DHCP requests are sent out at random intervals. This design helps to stagger the requests over a wider time frame. The second approach to improving performance is to store some DHCP information locally on the client. When a system successfully discovers a DHCP server, it saves the IP address of the DHCP server. In addition, when a system has successfully obtained an IP address from the DHCP server, the IP address is also saved in the requester's system. The next time the system starts, it uses the previously saved IP address and the address of the DHCP server to see if the previous IP address can be used. This process cuts down on the amount of traffic generated when a system on a DHCP network is first booted.

DHCP can deliver other IP-based information besides the IP number and subnet mask. For example, the default gateway or router and the IP addresses of DNS servers can be delivered to systems using DHCP. There are over 90 different possible IP protocol-based items that can be delivered to a system through DHCP.

Simple Network Management Protocol

Simple Network Management Protocol (SNMP) is a protocol that can be used by software and hardware that are designed to monitor various network and system components. For example, some network management tools provide the ability to send alerts when utilization reaches a certain value or when the temperature inside a server system reaches a certain point. In addition to noting failures or problems, system and network administrators may want to monitor activities over a period of time to look for trends and/or changes in the environment. These type of items, and many more, can be captured or trapped through the use of the SNMP protocol.

Network management software ranges widely in capabilities and in price. The basic structure includes a software piece called a *manager*, which collects all the information and acts on the data. The other components are *agents*, which run on the different network devices and send information to or accept directives from the manager. The *SNMP protocol*, which runs on top of UDP, specifies the syntax and format of the information passed between the agents and manager components. For each possible request and reply, SNMP specifies the exact meaning of these messages. Information passed between the managers and agents is encoded using the Abstract Syntax Notation (ASN.1) standard. Figure 8-11 is an example of the SNMP manager piece of the product called HP OpenView. Notice that under the Identifier header, the ASN.1 object ID for the corresponding Management Information Base (MIB) variable is indicated.

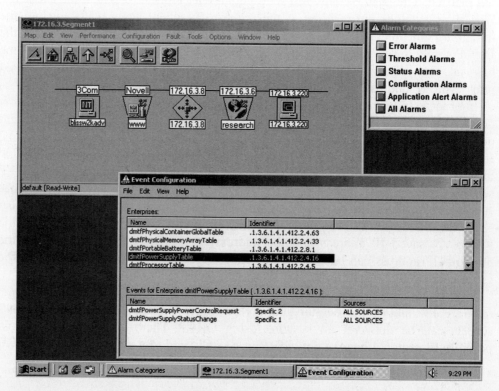

Fig. 8-11.   Example of HP OpenView that uses SNMP.

The commands defined by SNMP for manager-agent interaction are not extensive. The table below gives a brief description of the SNMP message types:

SNMP Message	Description
get-request	Used to request the value of a variable or variables
get-next-request	Used to request the next variable in reference to the current variable
get-bulk-request	Used to request the contents of a table
set-request	Changes the value of a variable or variables to the value(s) in the message
inform-request	This message is used between SNMP managers to describe the MIB
snmpv2-trap	This message is used between the agents to the manager when a trap has occurred

The messages function as fetch-store operations where *store* is used to pass information, such as values, to a device and *fetch* is used to retrieve information or values from devices. For example, an object could be defined to count the number of times CPU utilization goes above a certain value. The SNMP manager could then retrieve and accumulate the information so an administrator could determine when the events occurred and how often. In order to collect information from the proper devices and to keep track of the information from the different devices, each object has to have a unique name. In addition, both the manager and agent pieces must agree on the same names and on the definitions of the different store and fetch operations. The objects can then be accessed by SNMP through the MIB. The SNMP protocol does not define a MIB but instead specifies the format of messages and how they are encoded in the MIB. The ASN.1 standard mentioned above gives each object a long prefix to make sure the names are unique within an SNMP environment. When SMNP objects are referred to in messages, an integer is used to represent each portion of the long object name. Because of the simplicity of SNMP, variables that represent objects can be created and used as needed in the MIB. This allows new hardware and/or software items to be monitored that were not in existence when SNMP was first designed. Over the course of time, there have been many MIB variables created that correspond to various protocols of the IP suite and networking hardware. Some of the common MIB variable types are as follows:

- TCP
- UDP
- IP
- ARP
- ICMP
- EGP
- Ethernet hardware
- Token Ring hardware
- FDDI hardware
- Routers
- Switches
- Bridges
- Printers

MIB variables can hold either single values or an array of values. For example, the router table maintained by a switch is essentially an array and the switch's table could be associated as an array with a MIB variable. Because ASN.1 does not include an indexing function, the system requesting information from a MIB variable that is an array must know how the information is stored.

Electronic Mail

Electronic mail, or e-mail, is probably the most common type of traffic to travel the Internet and other networks. When it was first developed, e-mail was designed to emulate the office paper memo. Messages could be sent to other individuals and they could reply to the messages. Since then, e-mail implementations have evolved to applications and, in some cases, products where even the hardware can send e-mails. In some systems, users can send messages or e-mail to applications, and the application will respond in the form of an e-mail.

Before an individual can use e-mail, he or she must have at least one electronic mailbox. A mailbox is usually a designated area of disk storage on a server that can only be accessed by the mailbox owner. In most implementations of e-mail, mailboxes are associated with user accounts so on each system where a user has an account, he or she may also have a mailbox. In order for mail to be sent properly from mailbox to mailbox, each mailbox must have a unique e-mail address. The e-mail address is a multipart hierarchical address. The first portion of the address indicates the user or mailbox account. The latter portion of the e-mail address indicates the location of the mailbox. To separate the two components of an e-mail address, most environments use the @ (at sign) symbol. On some systems, the first portion of the address may be something simple like the user's first name initial and last name. For example, a user by the name of Bob Bliss working at the Texas Stars company may be assigned the e-mail address of bbliss@texas-stars.com.

On other systems, entire names separated by periods are used, for example, bob.bliss@texas-stars.com.

If Bob Bliss worked in the research division of the retail section of the Texas Stars company, his address might be bob.bliss@research.retail.texas-stars.com.

E-MAIL MESSAGE FORMAT

The structure of an e-mail message is very simple and consists of two parts that are separated by a blank line. The first part of the e-mail message is a header that contains information about who is sending the message, who is/are the recipient(s), the data, and the format of the message content. In order for the e-mail message to be properly processed, the header must contain certain keywords. Within the header there must be a line that begins with the keyword *To* followed by a recipient or list of recipients. Another line beginning with *From* is required and is followed by the e-mail address of the sender of the message. The remaining lines in the header are optional but most e-mail programs include the Date and Subject header keywords. Any other items in the e-mail message header may be added by the e-mail program and it's up to the designers to decide what optional items to place in the header. In addition, the software programs receiving the e-mail messages must be able to understand and interpret the items in the header to properly handle the e-mail messages. Below is a list of generic header keywords that are typically found in e-mail messages traveling around the Internet.

Keyword	Purpose
To	E-mail address of the recipient or recipients
From	E-mail address of the sender of the mail message
Date	The date the e-mail message was sent by the sender
Subject	The message's topic. The content is determined by the sender
CC	E-mail address or addresses to send carbon copies of the mail message

BCC	E-mail address or addresses to send blind carbon copies of the mail message
Reply-to	The e-mail address of where a reply to the message should be sent
Charset	The type of character set used. For most e-mail messages this is ASCII
Mailer	The name of the e-mail software used to send the message
Sender	This is the same as the e-mail address of the sender of the message
Face	An encoded image of the sender's face

Notice the use of the term *carbon copy*. This term refers back to the office metaphor for e-mail. That is, when an office or individual wanted to send the same paper memo to several people, a copy of the memo was made by placing a piece of carbon paper between the sheets of paper in the typewriter. Thus, two or three (but probably not many more) copies of the memo were created at the same time. As office machinery developed, the mimeograph machine and the copier made it easier to produce multiple copies of paper documents. In the concept of e-mail, a carbon copy simply means that every e-mail address listed on the CC line receives a copy of the e-mail message. The term *blind carbon copy* means that all the recipients receive a complete copy of the e-mail except they do not see any other e-mail addresses listed on the BCC line. In order to distinguish between carbon copies and blind carbon copies, some e-mail programs add a piece of information in the body of the message that indicates messages that are sent as blind carbon copies.

Below is an example of an e-mail message created by a simple e-mail program called PINE on a Linux system. Notice the various keywords used in the header portion of the e-mail message and the blank line between the header section and the contents of the message. For your information, the two e-mail accounts reside on the same system.

```
From mhoag@research.blissranch.com Fri Oct 5 11:17:02
        2001
Return-Path: <mhoag@research.blissranch.com>
Received: from localhost (mhoag@localhost)
        by research.blissranch.com (8.11.2/8.11.2) with
        ESMTP id f95GH1o11558
        for <bbliss@research.blissranch.com>; Fri, 5 Oct
        2001 11:17:02 -0500
Date: Fri, 5 Oct 2001 11:17:01 -0500 (CDT)
From: Melanie Hoag <mhoag@research.blissranch.com>
To: Bob Bliss <bbliss@research.blissranch.com>
Subject: Lunch Meeting?
Message-ID: <Pine.LNX.4.33.0110051115290.11556-
        100000@research.blissranch.com>
MIME-Version: 1.0
Content-Type: TEXT/PLAIN; charset=US-ASCII
How about getting together today for lunch and talk about
        some new
projects. I suggest we meet at the BBQ place in Hutto.
        Let me know by
11:00 if you can go.
Mel
```

The original intent of e-mail was to send only text messages, but people quickly realized that it would be useful to send other types of information and file formats. To send binary information as mail messages, the binary data is encoded in ASCII format so it can be sent as an e-mail message. The recipient then converts the message back to its binary form. There are many possible encoding schemes that could be used to encode and decode data. In order to provide compatible systems, the Internet Engineering Task Force (IETF) developed the Multipurpose Internet Mail Extensions (MIME). The MIME specifications do not define just one technique for encoding binary data. MIME allows the sender and recipient to choose an encoding format that they both understand and that is readily available. The header of a MIME-encoded message includes additional information to indicate that the body of the message is in MIME format. The body of the message contains additional information that specifies the encoding scheme used and the type of data. MIME also allows a message to be divided into parts, and each part can use a different encoding technique. From the perspective of the user who is sending a message with a binary attachment, such as a graphic image, the role that MIME plays is transparent. The user's e-mail application will display the text portion of the message the sender included with the attachment. The e-mail program will then either display the attachment or prompt the user for a location to save the file. When the attachment is saved or displayed within the e-mail program, the application performs the appropriate decoding of the attachment. Below is the top and bottom portion of an e-mail message that contains a binary file attachment.

```
From mhoag@research.blissranch.com Fri Oct 5 13:00:27
       2001
Return-Path: <mhoag@research.blissranch.com>
Received: from localhost (mhoag@localhost)
       by research.blissranch.com (8.11.2/8.11.2) with
       ESMTP id f95IONd11784
       for <bbliss@research.blissranch.com>; Fri, 5 Oct
       2001 13:00:23 -0500
Date: Fri, 5 Oct 2001 13:00:22 -0500 (CDT)
From: Melanie Hoag <mhoag@research.blissranch.com>
To: Bob Bliss <bbliss@research.blissranch.com>
Subject: Background Design Idea
Message-ID: <Pine.LNX.4.33.0110051258220.11780-
       101000@research.blissranch.com>
MIME-Version: 1.0
Content-Type: MULTIPART/MIXED; BOUNDARY="279709187-
       251511497-1002304822=:11780"
  This message is in MIME format. The first part should be
       readable text,
  while the remaining parts are likely unreadable
       without MIME-aware tools.
  Send mail to mime@docserver.cac.washington.edu for more
       info.
--279709187-251511497-1002304822=:11780
```

```
Content-Type: TEXT/PLAIN; charset=US-ASCII
Bob,
I've attached a graphic file as an idea for the Web site
        background. Let
me know what you think when you get a moment.
Mel
--279709187-251511497-1002304822=:11780
Content-Type: APPLICATION/octet-stream; name=motif
Content-Transfer-Encoding: BASE64
Content-ID:
        <Pine.LNX.4.33.0110051300221.11780@research.
        blissranch.com>
Content-Description:
Content-Disposition: attachment; filename=motif
Qk02AAMAAAAAADYAAAAoAAAAAAEAAAABAAAABABgAAAAAAAAAwASC
        wAAEgsA
AAAAAAAAAA////////////////////////////////////////////
        /////
.
.
.
////////////////////////////////////////////////////
        //////////
////////////////
--279709187-251511497-1002304822=:11780-
```

Notice the reference to MIME at the top of the message, and the four lines below the text of the message indicate the type of encoding used.

E-MAIL TRANSFER

When e-mail messages are sent around the network, there are usually two components involved: user agent and message transfer agent. Users interact with an e-mail interface program that provides the tools to compose and reply to e-mails. When the user chooses to send the e-mail, the message is placed in a queue that is either on the user's computer or on a server. The second component, the mail transfer software, monitors the queue and when a message arrives, the mail transfer program takes on the role of a client. The mail transfer program contacts the server that contains the recipient's mailbox and sends a copy of the mail message to the remote mail server. The remote mail server software delivers the mail to the mailbox of the recipient.

The connection between the sending mail transfer program and the receiving mail transfer program is accomplished through TCP and another protocol called SMTP. Simple Mail Transfer Protocol (SMTP) handles the connection establishment, transfer of information, and connection closure. In order to provide reliability, the sender maintains a copy of the e-mail message until the receiver has indicated the received message has been saved to a storage system. Thus, if the message is lost or arrives damaged, the sender can resend the message until it arrives intact and is safely stored. SMTP is not a trivial protocol, despite its name. For example, it includes the ability to query another mail server for the existence of a mailbox before mail is sent.

Many software e-mail programs can create lists of addresses that are grouped together as a mailing list. This allows the user to send a message out to several people at one time without the need to add each address to the To portion of the e-mail. Mailing lists are assigned names and are treated like another e-mail address. For example, the Texas Stars company wants to send an e-mail out to all the employees in the shipping department. The e-mail administrator creates a mailing list called ShippingStaff and adds all the e-mail addresses of all the shipping employees to the list. When a message needs to be sent to all of the shipping department employees, the address used in the To portion of the e-mail is shippingstaff@texas-stars.com. When the e-mail system receives an e-mail addressed to a mailing list, it sends the message to all members of the mailing list. This type of program that sends e-mail to each entry in a list is called *mail exploders* or *mail forwarders*. This type of activity can be very resource intensive so specialized systems are typically used to handle these large amounts of mail transfers. Systems that are dedicated to sending and forwarding mail are often called *mail gateways* or *e-mail relays*.

Maintaining the entries in mailing lists can be very tedious. To make this task easier, a type of program, called a *list manager*, can be used to add and remove addresses from mailing lists. When an address needs to be added to the mailing list, the appropriate command is contained in an e-mail directed to the list manager. The same concept holds true for removing addresses from a mailing list. The list manager receives an e-mail with the command to remove the e-mail address contained in the message from the mailing list.

In some implementations, to make e-mail addressing easier and more intuitive for users, the e-mail addresses assigned to users use the name of the e-mail gateway instead of the name of the mail server. For example, Blake Thurman works in the testing facility of the Texas Stars company and his e-mail address is blake@testing.research.retail.texas-stars.com.

Lee Ann Bliss, who works in the marketing department, has the e-mail address of labliss@marketing.texas-stars.com.

Using different naming styles for the user names and the different e-mail server systems makes it more difficult for users to remember e-mail address. However, if the e-mail gateway server called texas-stars.com is used, and a naming standard is used for the account names, then the two employees' addresses could be something like bthurman@texas-stars.com.

The e-mail gateway server maintains a database of all the e-mail gateway addresses mapped to the actual e-mail server mailboxes. When mail is addressed to the e-mail gateway, the system searches the database for the actual mailbox address and sends the message to the proper place. This type of system also helps to mask nonfriendly e-mail names, such as strings of numbers, from users.

In order for a system to create and maintain electronic mailboxes, the computer must be running mail server software. For users who want to create and receive mail at their desktops, it is impractical for each system to run an e-mail service. In addition, if users want to use different computers to read and send their e-mail, there must be only one copy of their electronic mailbox. The best solution to overcome these issues is to place the mailboxes on dedicated servers and allow other systems to remotely access the mailboxes. In order to provide coordinated access and standards, the IP suite includes the POP3 protocol to handle remote mailbox access. Post Office Protocol (POP3) runs as an additional service on a server and is usually running on the same system as the e-mail server software. The POP3 protocol includes features such as requiring users to authenticate before they can remotely access a mailbox. It also includes the ability to perform queries such as retrieving a list of mailbox contents. A nice feature of POP3 is that a persistent connection between the POP3 client, the user requesting access to a remote mailbox, and the POP server does not have to be maintained. This is particularly useful for dial-up or occasional network access.

A more sophisticated remote mailbox access protocol is available with Interactive Mail Access Protocol (IMAP). This is particularly useful for users who have, or use, multiple computers to access the same mailbox. With IMAP, the e-mail maintains a central location for the mail. This is in contrast to POP3, where once e-mail is accessed from one system it is not available on another system. POP3 copies the mail to the machine the user is accessing the mailbox from and then the e-mail server deletes the mail from the server. IMAP does not delete the mail from the mailbox when the mailbox is accessed or read. The user must explicitly delete the mail from the mailbox.

World Wide Web

The World Wide Web (WWW or Web) is one of the many services available on the Internet and on private networks. It began at the European Center for Nuclear Research (CERN), in March 1989. Approximately 18 months later, the first text-based prototype was functional and in December of 1991 the first public demonstration was given in San Antonio, Texas. In February 1993, the first graphical user interface, called Mosaic, was released. Mosaic became so popular that its developer from the National Center for Supercomputing Applications (NCSA) left to form his own company called Netscape. In 1994 the World Wide Web Consortium (W3C) was organized to develop standards and encourage participation among the different Internet sites. Information about the W3C can be found at http://www.w3.org. Since its beginnings in 1989, the Web has changed dramatically and is continuing to develop and evolve. Through the use of an application called a browser, users can access large repositories of information stored on servers throughout the world. Browsers can either be text-based or graphical and allow the user to navigate through the information. Graphical browsers usually employ the use of a mouse or other pointing device to traverse the content and to select items. The whole effect of Web services is to provide an interactive environment for the user to access, manipulate, and navigate through information.

Originally the Web was a hypertext environment that consisted of a series of documents containing text. You navigate around and between the text documents through the use of links. Links are pointers to locations of other documents and include the name and path of the document. As the use of the Web grew, many other types of files were made accessible, and the Web is now thought of as a hypermedia system. One great advantage of the Web is the availability of information housed on a single system or a few systems that is accessible to anybody who can get on the Internet. Companies and organizations can provide information to the public about their products and services to anybody who wants it on a 24/7 basis and not just to conventional marketing locations. Communities, towns, and cities can post important and current information. You are probably already aware of the vast amounts and types of information accessible on the Internet.

The file on a server containing the Web content is called a page and the system that stores and delivers Web pages to browsers is called a Web server. When you go to a Web address, the initial content you see on your browser when the information is retrieved is called the homepage. The format of the page, the content specifications, and the syntax are governed by the standard called HyperText Markup Language (HTML). The concept of a markup language is that the language itself does not include environment-specific formatting instructions. Instead, the language uses levels of importance or emphasis to produce the desired effect. For example, instead of specifying the actual size of the font, such as 48 point, the number 5 represents a larger font size than the number 3. This way the author of the HTML document can specify display guidelines while the user's browser decides the details to use in the actual presentation of the page.

HTML

In this section, we cover a brief overview of HTML and its structure. There are many books available and a lot of information is on the Internet about HTML. An HTML document is divided into two sections or parts: a head and a body. The head contains details about the document, such as the title of the document, that are viewed in a browser. The body of the HTML document contains the majority of the information.

The HTML language is like other programming languages in that there are special words or phrases that are used to specify actions and variables. HTML uses tags to provide structure for the document and to indicate actions. Tags that specify the start of formatting instructions or an action appear as a name surrounded by the less than and greater than symbols. To indicate the end of a tag, a less than symbol (<) and a slash symbol (/) are used before the name of the tag, and a greater than symbol (>) is used after the name of the tag. Below is an example of a very simple HTML page that contains some text, graphics, a table, and a horizontal line.

```
<!doctype html public "-//w3c//dtd html 4.0
        <transitional//en">
<html>
<head>
    <meta http-equiv="Content-Type" content="text/html;
        charset=iso-8859-1">
```

```
      <meta name="Author" content="Melanie Hoag">
      <meta name="GENERATOR" content="Mozilla/4.75 [en]
           (Win98; U) [Netscape]">
      <title>You're a Grand Old Flag</title>
</head>
<body>
<center>
<h1>
<font color="#3333FF"><font size=+4>You're a Grand Old
           Flag</font></font></h1></center>
<center>
<p><br><img SRC="Big Flag.JPG" height=100
           width=172></center>
<ul>
<li>
<font size=+2>Red</font></li>
<li>
<font size=+2>White</font></li>
<li>
<font size=+2>Blue</font></li>
</ul>
<center><img SRC="usflag.gif" height=50
           width=68></center>
<p><br><b></b>
<br> 
<table BORDER COLS=3 WIDTH="10%" HEIGHT="10%" >
<caption><b><i><font color="#FF0000"><font
           size=+1>Notices</font></font></i></b></caption>
<tr>
<td></td>
<td></td>
<td></td>
</tr>
<tr>
<td></td>
<td></td>
<td></td>
</tr>
<tr>
<td></td>
<td></td>
<td></td>
</tr>
</table>
<center>  <a
           href="www.packetsandpings.com">PacketsAndPings</
           a>
```

```
<br>
<hr SIZE=5 WIDTH="100%"></center>
</body>
</html>
```

At the top and bottom of the document, the pair of tags:

```
<html>
</html>
```

indicates that the content between the tags is HTML code. At the top of the document, the head tags identify the header portion of the HTML code. The body tags identify the section of the HTML document that is the body. We mentioned above that instead of specifying a particular font size, numbers are used to represent levels of importance or emphasis. The following line, taken from the example above, uses the tag h1 to indicate the highest level.

```
<h1>
<font color="#3333FF"><font size=+4>You're a Grand Old
     Flag</font></font></h1>
```

Since HTML is text, any graphics or non-ASCII characters that you want to include in the document are handled by specifying the file, and the user's browser will load the image from the file. The following two lines from our example HTML document each specifies a graphic image followed by the name of the file. The size of the transparent rectangle enclosing the graphic can also be specified.

```
<img SRC="Big Flag.JPG" height=100 width=172>
<img SRC="usflag.gif" height=50 width=68>
```

A horizontal line, or rule, that goes across the entire width of the page is specified with the following code:

```
<hr SIZE=5 WIDTH="100%">
```

The size specification indicates the height or thickness of the line. In the list below, some of the other elements of the sample HTML document are identified:

- *br:* A line break. The   following the br tag indicates a carriage return.
- *center:* Align the text between the tags with the middle of the page.
- *font color:* Specifies the color of the text between the tags.
- *li:* Each item in a list begins with this tag.
- *table:* Specifies a table.
- *td:* A data cell in a table.
- *title:* Text that is displayed in the browser's window title bar.
- *tr:* A table row.
- *ul:* An unordered bulleted list. The term *unordered* means the browser does not have to sort the items in the list before displaying the list.

You can refer to another document on the same Web server or another Web site through the use of an anchor. The tags <a> and </a> act as a bracket around the document or location reference. When presented in a browser, the contents between the anchor tags appear as an item that can be selected or clicked on with the mouse. In the example HTML code above, the following anchor references another Web site and the text displayed in the browser is PacketsAndPings.

```
<a href="www.packetsandpings.com">PacketsAndPings</a>
```

HTTP

HyperText Transfer Protocol (HTTP) specifies the rules for communication between browsers and Web servers. The HTTP requests are sent as ASCII text and there are several keywords that permit different types of actions. The get command is used to request a document or item from the server. Figures 8-12 and 8-13 show examples of two different operating systems using different browsers accessing the same information on the same Web server. Notice the information sent to the server from the browser when an HTTP get command is delivered.

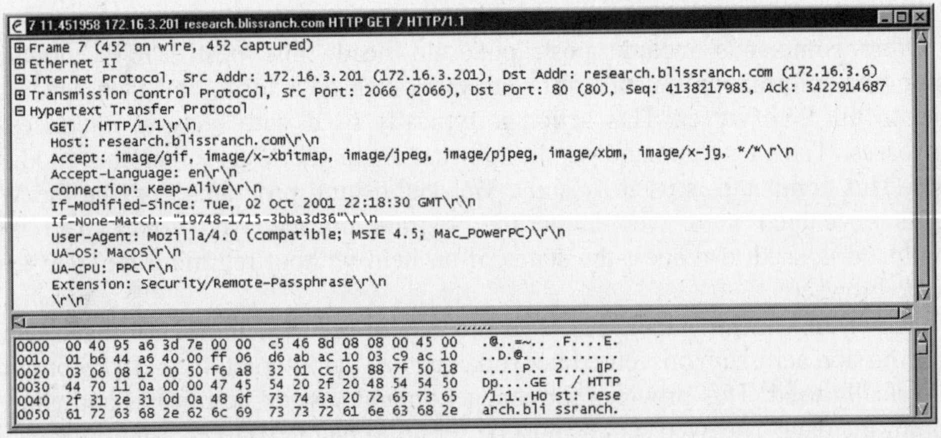

Fig. 8-12. HTTP get command sent to a Web server from Internet Explorer on a Macintosh system.

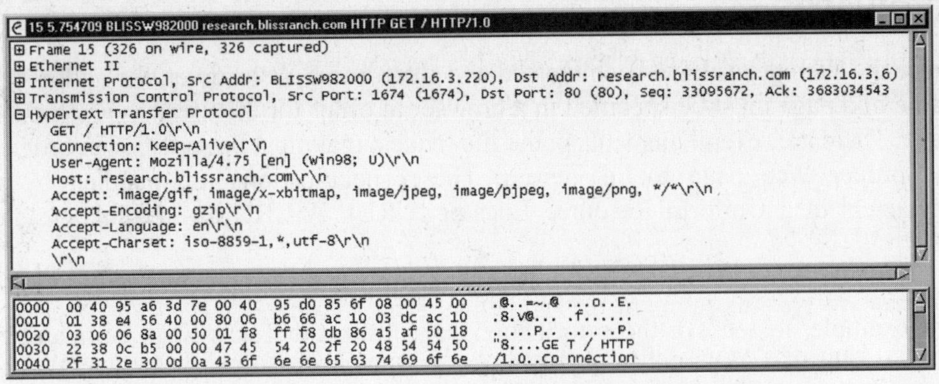

Fig. 8-13. HTTP get command sent to a Web server from Netscape on a Windows 98 system.

The information returned from a get command by the server includes a header that contains status information, a blank line, and then the item itself. Figure 8-14 is an example of the information sent back to a browser in response to a get command.

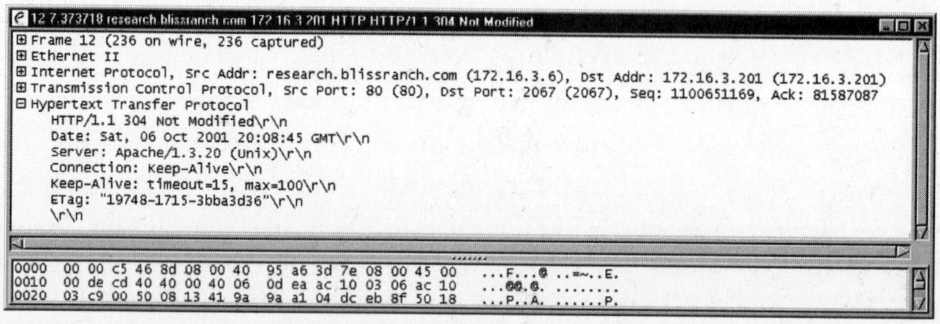

```
12 7.373718 research.blissranch.com 172.16.3.201 HTTP HTTP/1.1 304 Not Modified                    _ □ X
⊞ Frame 12 (236 on wire, 236 captured)
⊞ Ethernet II
⊞ Internet Protocol, Src Addr: research.blissranch.com (172.16.3.6), Dst Addr: 172.16.3.201 (172.16.3.201)
⊞ Transmission Control Protocol, Src Port: 80 (80), Dst Port: 2067 (2067), Seq: 1100651169, Ack: 81587087
⊟ Hypertext Transfer Protocol
    HTTP/1.1 304 Not Modified\r\n
    Date: Sat, 06 Oct 2001 20:08:45 GMT\r\n
    Server: Apache/1.3.20 (Unix)\r\n
    Connection: Keep-Alive\r\n
    Keep-Alive: timeout=15, max=100\r\n
    ETag: "19748-1715-3bba3d36"\r\n
    \r\n

0000  00 00 c5 46 8d 08 00 40  95 a6 3d 7e 08 00 45 00   ...F...@ ..=~..E.
0010  00 de cd 40 40 00 40 06  0d ea ac 10 03 06 ac 10   ...@@.@. ........
0020  03 c9 00 50 08 13 41 9a  9a a1 04 dc eb 8f 50 18   ...P..A. ......P.
```

Fig. 8-14. HTTP get response sent from a Web server to a browser.

Notice that just below the heading "Hypertext Transfer Protocol" in Figure 8-14, the code 304 indicates that the requested page was not modified. The Web server did not send the page to the browser since it has not been modified.

Other commands include post, put, and head. The post HTTP command assembles information entered on a browser, such as a form, and then sends the data to the Web server. This action is typically used with browser interfaces to databases. The put command sends information to the Web server that modifies files. This command is used by some Web publishing programs to place the Web pages developed in a Web authoring program on the Web server. The head command is used to request the status of an item without returning the item itself to the browser.

One of the concerns about HTTP is the lack of security. In order to have secure transmission across an unsecured network, such as the Internet, the HTTPS protocol is typically used. This provides for connection and session certificates and encryption of the data. The Web server must be set up to handle HTTPS, and information transfers take a little longer because of overhead added by the security protocols.

BROWSERS

Once the Web pages have been created and stored on a Web server, the address and name of a page must be specified in a browser in order for the user to view the Web page. There are several elements in the file request that must be specified in order for the proper Web page to be viewed. These specifications are handled by the characters in a Uniform Resource Locator (URL). A URL has a generic syntax which is:

```
protocol://name-of-server/path-and-or-document-name
```

For example, to retrieve the information page from the Texas Stars company, the URL would be:

```
http://www.texas-stars.com/information.html
```

If the Web server is not using the standard port, 80, for Web pages, the URL can also include the port number. The syntax for including a port number is:

```
protocol://name-of-server:port-number'path-and-or-
          document-name
```

Depending on the services supported by the Web server and the browser, different protocols can be used to access information. For example:

- *file:* Specifies a file or directory that is usually on the local system.
- *ftp:* This sends the request to retrieve the information using ftp.
- *https:* SSL retrieval of an HTML document.
- *mailto:* Can be used to send mail.
- *news:* Access a system that is running a news server.
- *nntp:* Access a system that is running a news server.
- *telnet:* Used for establishing a telnet connection to the destination.

If the browser and server support other services and protocols, such as FTP, the browser can be used to work with those protocols. Figure 8-15 is an example of access to an FTP server within a browser.

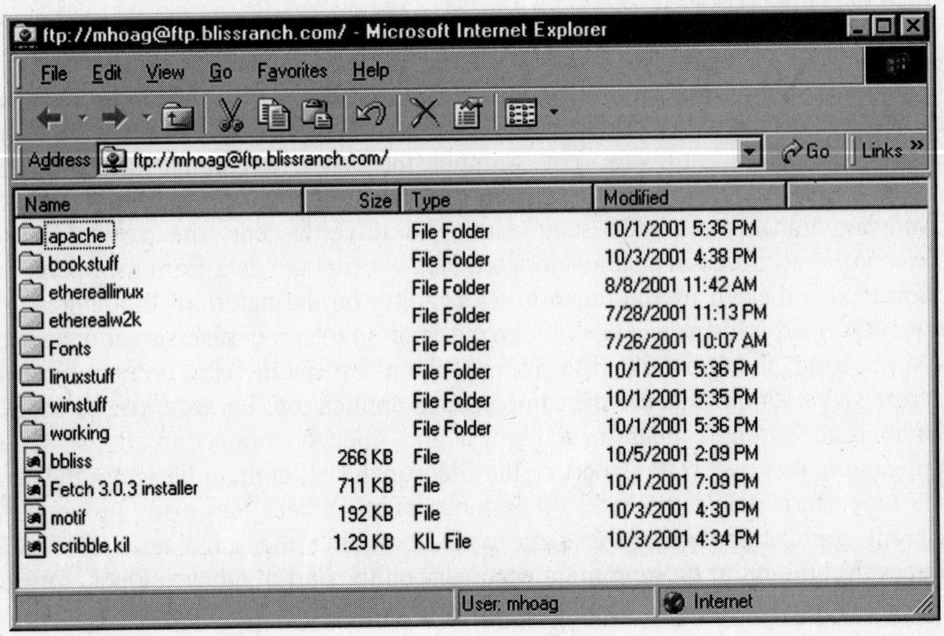

Fig. 8-15.   FTP access within a browser.

To improve the performance of the browser when accessing information on a remote system, browsers include the ability to cache information. The cache is a location on the user's local drive that stores pages and associated items when the page is first accessed. When a user makes a request to revisit the page, the browser looks first for a copy in stored cache. If the document is present locally, the browser loads the page from cache instead of contacting the server. Most browsers include the ability for the user to specify cache settings such as the amount of disk space that can be consumed by cached Web pages. In addition, the HTTP specifications include time information with the document. Thus, cached pages can have an expiration time and if the user requests a cached page that has expired, the browser will contact the server to get a current copy of the page.

OTHER MARKUP LANGUAGES

With the growth of the Internet and information types, more protocols are being developed to access and manipulate information from a browser. Some of these include Wireless Access Protocol (WAP) that is used by portable devices, such as cell phones and pagers, to interact with Web-based services. Extensible Markup Language (XML) has become very popular for the manipulation and interaction of data among different types of data stores such as databases.

RPC and Middleware

The majority of services that run on an IP network employ some action on the client side and other actions and functions on servers. This is the basic style of client-server structures and software. For example, the client may collect data from the user, assemble it into proper format, contact and establish a connection with the server, and transmit the request or data. The server accepts the request for the connection if all necessary parameters are met, accepts the data from the client, and performs as indicated by the requests. Depending on the nature of the request, the server may send information back to the client or on to some other server or service.

Applications that are created to run in a client-server-type environment typically perform some actions that are the same in each application. For example, to transfer data to a server, the client must request and open a connection to the server. Applications that use TCP as part of the file transfer all contain basically the same code to perform the same tasks. It is more efficient and less error prone if the different applications share the same code for doing the same tasks. This also reduces the amount of programming necessary on the part of the developers for each application. Furthermore, if there is an error or bug in the common code, the repair only needs to be made once in the shared code instead of in all the applications that include the similar piece of code. This style of software development that relies on common shared libraries of codes is called the Remote Procedure Call (RPC) mechanism. Procedures are defined to perform specific, small tasks and interaction with them is handled through parameters. These parameters specify details related to the procedure, such as maximum or minimum values. When developers use the procedures in their code, they use arguments to pass values in for the parameters expected by the procedure.

However, there is one drawback to this style of procedural programming. Different operating systems use different code to produce the same results. Thus, compiling the program on one computer platform does not allow the application to run on a different architecture. To help overcome these type of problems, there are programming languages available that produce code independent of the operating system or hardware. These generally run on top of an engine or interface that is specific for different operating systems. An example of this style of platform-independent code is Java. The different Java classes and applets are platform-independent and the Java run-time engine provides the interface to different platforms and operating systems. This style of platform-independent coding allows client software running on one type of platform to interact with server software running on another type of platform.

The RPC architecture and design also need to account for differences in the way data is stored on different systems. Different platforms may specify the left or right portion of a byte of data as the most significant byte. If there is no adjustment for these types of differences, the data exchange between the different systems is useless.

Middleware is the term used to represent software development tools that provide a collection of procedures and interfaces to develop client-server-type applications. The concept of developing programs by accessing shared code bundled into separate pieces, or objects, is referred to as *object-oriented programming*. An object contains a set of operations or methods that operates on defined data items. Depending on the goal of the application, some of the object code may reside on a server and some on the client. Through method invocation and data values, the control of the object's behavior is specified.

Sun Microsystems developed one of the first RPC mechanisms that was used quite a bit. It was called Open Network Computing Remote Procedure Call and was often referred to as Sun RPC. The environment defined a data standard known as eXternal Data Representation (XDR). The Sun RPC development system used IP protocols and allowed the programmer to use either TCP or UDP. Another object environment was developed by the Open Software Foundation, and it was called Distribute Computing Environment (DCE). As with Sun RPC, DCE uses IP and the developer can either use UDP or TCP. Microsoft released its own version of RPC technology under the name Microsoft Remote Procedure Call (MSRPC). MSRPC is derived from DCE but defines its own Interface Definition Language (IDL) and its own protocol used for client and server software code pieces, or stubs, to communicate. Since then, Microsoft has developed another version of MSRPC (MSRPC2) or Object RPC (ORPC), which differs significantly from the original MSRPC. Microsoft released another object environment called Component Object Model (COM), released in 1994, and Distributed Component Object Model (DCOM), was released in 1998. Another well-known object-oriented middleware development environment is Common Object Request Broker Architecture (CORBA). In the CORBA system, the software creates a proxy at run time when it is needed.

Review Questions

8.1 What is the port number used by FTP to transfer data?
  a. 21
  b. 22
  c. 20
  d. 19

8.2 What is a mail exploder?

8.3 What is SMTP used for?

8.4 What commands can be used to download files from an FTP server?

8.5 What FTP command can be used to view the files on the remote FTP server?

8.6 What does the int top-level domain refer to?

8.7 What is the DNS MX record type used for?

8.8 What is the IP address used for when a DHCP client sends out a discover message to locate a DHCP server?

8.9 What is MIME used for?

8.10 What is the purpose of HTML?

8.11 What is HTTP?

8.12 Define the term *middleware*.

Problems

8.1 You need to transfer a sound file between two different systems using FTP. Which file type would you specify for the file transfer?

8.2 How can a client on one network find a DHCP server on another network?

8.3 In the topics covered in this chapter, which service or protocol uses the ASN.1 standard for names and values?

8.4 What is an advantage of defining e-mail addresses using the e-mail gateway system instead of the actual machines storing the electronic mailboxes?

8.5 Give an example of a good use for TFTP.

8.6 What is the main purpose of DNS services?

8.7 Melissa's Pink Doll Factory is planning on setting up a Web site to sell its products. Give an example for the name of a Web server that would be easy for users to remember.

8.8 What are the three things that must be configured for each DNS server?

8.9 What is a MIB?

8.10 What is meant by an electronic mailbox?

8.11 What are the two required keywords in an e-mail header?

8.12 What is an HTML tag?

8.13 Give some examples of protocols that can be specified in a URL.

8.14 Define what is meant by RPC in the client/server development environment.

Answers to Review Questions

8.1 **c.** Port 20 is used for file transfers. Port 21 is the IP protocol port used for the FTP control connection.

8.2 A mail exploder is a type of program that sends e-mail to each entry in a mailing list.

8.3 The connection between the sending mail transfer program and the receiving mail transfer program is accomplished through TCP and another protocol called Simple Mail Transfer Protocol (SMTP). SMTP handles the connection establishment, transfer of information, and connection closure.

8.4 To retrieve a copy of a file from the FTP server, the get command is used. To copy multiple files, use the mget command.

8.5 The pwd command echoes back the directory path on the remote system that your FTP session is connected to.

8.6 The top-level domain int is used for organizations established through international treaties.

8.7 Mail eXchanger (MX) is used to specify the IP address for the name of the computer used in an e-mail address.

8.8 This DHCPDISCOVER message is sent out as a broadcast using the special IP address of 255.255.255.255.

8.9 MIME provides the ability to specify the encoding schemes used to encode nontext data in an e-mail. The Internet Engineering Task Force (IETF) developed the Multipurpose Internet Mail Extensions (MIME). The MIME specifications do not define just one technique for encoding binary data. MIME allows the sender and recipient to choose an encoding format that they both understand and that is readily available.

8.10 The format of the page, the content specifications, and the syntax are governed by the standard called HyperText Markup Language (HTML). The concept of a markup language is that the language itself does not include environment-specific formatting instructions. Instead, the language uses levels of importance or emphasis to produce the desired effect.

8.11 HyperText Transfer Protocol (HTTP) specifies the rules for communication between browsers and Web servers.

8.12 *Middleware* is the term used to represent software development tools that provide a collection of procedures and interfaces to develop client/server-type applications. The concept of developing programs by accessing shared code bundled into separate pieces, or objects, is referred to as object-oriented programming.

Solutions to Problems

8.1   Binary. FTP supports two types of file transfers: ASCII and binary. The ASCII option is used for transferring text files and binary is for everything else. If you are not sure of the file type or if an operating system does not use the standard ASCII set or adds extra characters, try the binary file transfer type. The binary choice does a bit-by-bit copy and does not perform any translation on the file.

8.2   Relay agents. To allow DHCP servers to exist on different networks than the requesters, the routers run a relay agent that directs DHCPDISCOVER packets to the DHCP server or to the next router that can pass the request on. The relay agent sends a directed or unicast message and does not pass the DHCPDISCOVER broadcast on to other networks. When the DHCP server is reached, the server sends a unicast packet back to the requester.

8.3   SNMP. Information passed between the managers and agents is encoded using the Abstract Syntax Notation standard, or ASN.1.

8.4   To make e-mail addressing easier and more intuitive for users, the e-mail addresses assigned to users use the name of the e-mail gateway instead of the name of the mail server. Using different naming styles for the user names and the different e-mail server systems makes it more difficult for users to remember e-mail addresses. However, if the e-mail gateway server is used and a naming standard is used for the account names, then addressing is easier for users. The e-mail gateway server maintains a database of all the e-mail gateway addresses mapped to the actual e-mail server mailboxes. When mail is addressed to the e-mail gateway, the system searches the database for the actual mailbox address and sends the message to the proper place. This type of system also helps to mask nonfriendly e-mail names, such as strings of numbers, from users.

8.5   For example, on diskless or operating systemless computers that need to find a BOOTP server to download an operating system. TFTP can provide this type of file transfer service quite well without the need for a lot of configuration.

8.6   DNS is one of the services and mechanisms available in the IP protocol suite to translate the friendly names of devices to their corresponding IP addresses. Its primary use is to make it easier for users to interact with the network and its services.

8.7   Because Melissa's Pink Doll Factory is a commercial organization, the top-level domain the company will use is .com. An example of a name for their Web site might be www.melissa-pink-dolls.com.

8.8
- Each DNS server in a domain must know the DNS servers for each of its subdomains. For example, the DNS server for the .texas-stars.com domain must know the DNS servers for the .retail.texas-stars.com and .wholesale.texas-stars.com domains.

- Each DNS server is configured to know the location of at least one root server. Most implementations of DNS servers provide the complete list of all 13 DNS root servers in their configurations.

- Each DNS server will support at least one domain or subdomain. A DNS server cannot be configured to support only a portion of a domain or subdomain. However, the DNS server can be configured to support multiple domains and/or subdomains.

8.9   The objects that can be accessed by SNMP are known as the Management Information Base (MIB). The SNMP protocol does not define a MIB but instead specifies the format of messages and how they are encoded in the MIB.

8.10 An electronic mailbox is usually a designated area of disk storage on a server that can be accessed only by the mailbox owner. In most implementations of e-mail, mailboxes are associated with user accounts so on each system where a user has an account, he or she may also have a mailbox.

8.11 Within the e-mail header there must be a line that begins with the keyword To, followed by a recipient or list of recipients. Another line beginning with From is required and is followed by the e-mail address of the sender of the mail message.

8.12 The HTML language is like other programming languages in that there are special words or phrases that are used to specify actions and variables. HTML uses tags to provide structure for the document and to indicate actions. Tags that specify the start of formatting instructions or an action appear as a name surrounded by the less than and greater than symbols. To indicate the end of a tag, a less than and a slash symbol are used before the name of the tag and a greater than symbol is used after the name of the tag.

8.13 Depending on the services supported by the Web server and the browser, different protocols can be used in a URL to access information. For example:

- file: Specifies a file or directory that is usually on the local system.
- ftp: This sends the request to retrieve the information using ftp.
- https: SSL retrieval of an HTML document.
- mailto: Can be used to send mail.
- news: Access a system that is running a news server.
- nntp: Access a system that is running a news server.
- telnet: Used for establishing a telnet connection to the destination.

8.14 This style of software development that relies on common shared libraries of codes is called the Remote Procedure Call (RPC) mechanism. Procedures are defined to perform specific, small tasks and interaction with them is handled through parameters. These parameters specify details related to the procedure, such as maximum or minimum values. When developers use the procedures in their code, they use arguments to pass values in for the parameters expected by the procedure.

CHAPTER 9

Security

The term *security* brings to mind all sorts of items and issues that refer to data protection and prevention of unwanted access. Furthermore, there is no single definition for the term *network security*. What is important are the items and assets an organization or company deems are crucial for successful operations and to keep those safe. Each network, company, and organization must be considered on a case-by-case basis. Once all the data is collected on what items and/or services are important, only then can a security policy be developed and implemented. Security policies do not come in generic flavors. Once the needs are determined, an organization can start building on security policies modeled after existing implementations but the policies will need to be tweaked and modified to fit the specifics of the organization.

Another aspect of network and systems security involves how to plan for extended power outages or loss of physical facilities such as the result of a fire. In these types of situations, the physical devices, computers, and software may be destroyed so procedures need to be in place for disaster recovery. According to Gartner Research, a division of Gartner Inc. that conducts analysis of business and technology issues, trends, and current events, two out of five enterprises that experience a disaster will go out of business in five years. Enterprises can improve those odds—but only if they take the necessary measures before and after the disaster.

The topic of disaster recovery for networks and computing services is not within the scope of this book. However, there is a lot of information available on the Internet about disaster recovery planning from government and private sources.

This chapter addresses some of the issues and techniques involved in securing network activities. The items covered here by no means address all the possible areas of concern for networks. However, the topics included provide a good foundation for understanding some of the concerns and techniques that are currently being used to address some of the issues. Staying on top of network security topics, new threats, and mechanisms to discover and squash new and old threats is an ongoing process. Many organizations have entire departments and teams for securing assets and managing network security issues and policies.

Threats

Threats to a network may be very obvious or they may come disguised as unsuspecting activities or actions. Organizations typically have data that is private to the company and not for public consumption. In some environments, some of the data is for public access whereas the remainder is not. In these situations, there needs to be clear barriers to prevent unauthorized access from the public side to the private side. Securing a network involves physical security and software security. The physical aspects include controlling physical access to the equipment. An organization needs to determine who can walk into their facilities and into what areas they are permitted access. For example, the individual who delivers the newspaper very early in the morning should not be allowed to walk into the server room or phone connection closet. On the other hand, the server and telecommunications administrators need to have access to the server and/or the phone connection closet but restricted access to other areas that do not involve their jobs' responsibilities. Gaining access to the physical equipment makes it much easier for an individual to gain unauthorized access or just plain steal the hardware for later scrutiny. No matter how many software protection schemes are in place, if physical security is weak or lacking, software cannot overcome physical security holes.

There are many different types of people who can threaten a network. The term *hacker* is often used for individuals who attempt to gain, or do gain, unauthorized access to a network or systems. In the early days of computers a hacker was not a person committing illegal acts but an individual who was attempting to figure out how to construct the correct code to make something work. The term *cracker* was used in the media for a short time as an attempt to distinguish a hacker performing illegal activities and a hacker doing legal tasks. Now, however, the term *hacker* refers to the illegal activities of individuals trying to break into a network.

To gain access to a network, the hacker will typically perform a port scan to determine what ports are open. If a port scan is done poorly, it is easy to determine when one is occurring. If you see a systematic set of packets sent to each port in order, that is a pretty good sign a port scan is being attempted by an inexperienced hacker. The more experienced hacker will perform a port scan but will either stagger the ports randomly and/or test the ports over a period of time for as long as a few days. An experienced hacker wants to prevent a pattern from occurring so it will not be detected by monitoring software or by administrators. Once the hacker gains access to a network, the damage that can be done will depend on the reasons he or she broke in to begin with. Some hackers claim to be experimenting or testing the system, and others are there to steal proprietary, government, or military information.

Another potential threat to a company's network are former employees who were dismissed under nonfavorable conditions. As soon as an employee is notified of termination, all access to company accounts should be frozen so the disgruntled employee cannot get into the system and do damage or steal information before leaving the premises.

A further area of concern is inside threats. According to some security experts, the major cause of data theft and electronic vandalism is employees. This is not to say, of course, that the majority of employees are stealing your data but that in cases of stolen information, the majority of the perpetuators are employees. Security policies need to address internal access to information and equipment to prevent accidental or intentional loss of data or improper access to data. Once a security policy is in place, it must be applied to all individuals no matter what their job function is. Although the CEO may find it inconvenient to change her or his password every 30 days, if an exception is made to make it more convenient by extending his or her password frequency, then there is no security policy. If the security policy states that all employees must change their passwords every 30 days then that applies to *all* employees regardless of their job function.

Once data or information is stolen, lost, or modified beyond repair, there are other cost factors that occur after the incident. For example, if the information must be re-created and/or entered back into the system, the people cost of that activity has to be considered. For example, will additional employees need to be hired to get the job done? Will existing employees be taken from other job functions to restore the information? The salary, benefits, and time away from regular duties all have a monetary value for whomever ends up putting the data back. Then, there is also the cost of loss or degradation of business during the period of time the data is unavailable. For example, if a company has lost its inventory database and customers are wanting to buy products, the company may not be able to fulfill orders until the database is back on-line. In the meantime, the customers may look elsewhere for another company that can provide the products in a timely fashion. When that occurs, customers may never come back because they perceive the company as being unreliable. In addition to the customers' experience, you also have word of mouth and today, with the speed of e-mail and the Internet, word of mouth can be very fast and far reaching. Another concern with data that has been tampered with is liability issues. If the information is incorrect and other processes depend on the data, an error at one point can greatly modify the outcome of another process. For example, if an automated ordering system that is used to maintain the proper level of machine lubricant orders the incorrect amount of replacement fluid because the inventory database was incorrect, the machinery may have to be shut down or it may become damaged, which would result in loss of business.

SECURITY POLICY ISSUES

As we have stated above, there is no one single security policy for all networks and information systems. However, there are a few common issues that are of concern for most organizations and companies that manage information. Below are some items to keep in mind when designing a security policy.

- *Authorization:* Implementing a security policy means that somebody is in charge. Security levels must be set and modified as needed. In some environments, it may not be a good idea to have only one person who is authorized to set and change security policies. What would happen if the individual became incapacitated and could no longer perform his or her duties? Or, worse, the individual died or was the very criminal that the security policy was guarding against. Most security policies involve multiple individuals with different levels of authorization so no one person has the keys to the entire kingdom.

- *Accountability:* Most security policies include the ability to audit events and activities. When auditing is implemented, there needs to be an individual or group of individuals accountable for the audited information. For example, if a suspected activity occurs, who gets contacted, in what time frame, and so on.

- *Data Availability:* Users need to know they will have access to the information when they need it. For organizations that are on a 24/7 basis, this can be an especially challenging issue.

- *Data Integrity:* Users must be comfortable that the information they require is the same as what is stored on the network. Measures must be in place to make sure that the data is not modified during delivery between communicating systems. In earlier chapters we covered techniques to help ensure data arrived at the recipient intact and undamaged. Parity bits, checksums, and Cyclic Redundancy Checks (CRCs) all help to provide mechanisms for the data to arrive undamaged or to notify the system that packets are damaged. However, these methods do not guarantee that the data arriving at the recipient actually came from the reported sender. You cannot rely on these mechanisms for this type of data integrity because an unauthorized individual can capture the packets off the transmission media; modify the contents and the parity bit, checksum, and/or CRC values; and place the modified packets back on the transmission media. To the unsuspecting receiver, the data looks good because the parity bit, checksum, or CRC says so. Furthermore, using the sender's hardware and/or IP addresses to verify the identity of the sender is not reliable. It is very easy to spoof these addresses so that packets sent from the hacker contain the addresses of the actual sender. Once again, the recipient is unaware that anything is amiss because the sender's addresses, parity bits, checksums, and CRCs all check out okay.

- *Data Confidentiality:* Users who request information for their eyes only, or for a group of authorized users, must be comfortable that the information is inaccessible to unauthorized individuals.

- *Privacy:* In some systems, it is important that the identity of a user remain anonymous. In some environments, personal information must be properly secured and treated with respect so an individual's private information is kept confidential.

DENIAL-OF-SERVICE ATTACKS

The primary purpose of a Denial-of-Service (DoS) attack is to flood your service or network with so many unwanted packets that the affected systems are put out of commission. If a DoS attack hits your company's public Web server, then users will be unable to access the Web site, which then generates a whole host of other problems. The most common form of a DoS attack is the SYN attack. The name is based on the packet used when a Transmission Control Protocol (TCP) connection is established. The attacker sends a flurry of SYN packets to a system, which then spends all of its time trying to satisfy all the requests to set up TCP connections it thinks are occurring. A properly configured firewall can be used to help stop or notify the administrator that a suspected DoS attack is in progress. For good information and sample trace files of a DoS attack, check out www.packet-level.com.

PROTECTION TECHNIQUES

Techniques need to be put in place to reduce the impact of security threats on networks and systems. Although we cannot cover all the techniques available (plus the ones that have yet to be invented!), there are some common procedures to consider. One area involves protecting data integrity. We already mentioned using parity bits, checksums, CRCs, and sender hardware and IP addresses as not being reliable methods for determining data integrity from intentional damage. Data encryption/decryption and signature techniques are the most effective means of ensuring that the data is understood only by the intended recipients and that the senders of the information are actually who they say they are.

Another common technique that is used to protect access to information is the use of accounts, passwords, and access control. *Accounts* mean that in order for an individual to gain access to the system, he or she must have a digital identity that has been set up by the appropriate department or individuals. Secondly, the accounts must have passwords that are not easily compromised. Once these are in place, the environment must make sure that the users' passwords are not sent across the transmission media in a form that can be easily picked up and deciphered by an unauthorized individual. By the way, it is very easy to snatch packets off the transmission media and uncover their contents.

Encryption/Decryption

One way to prevent unauthorized viewing of information as it travels across a network is to make the contents of the messages unreadable except by the intended recipient. This can be accomplished by encoding the message using cryptographic hashing mechanisms. The term *cryptology* is used to refer to the science of creating and breaking ciphers. *Cryptanalysis* is the term for breaking ciphers.

Cryptography is an old science, and it was in existence well before the advent of computers and electronic technology. Historically, encrypting messages has been used as far back as Julius Caesar who used a simple form of cryptography to protect his messages from his enemies. Military and diplomatic organizations have long used, and are still using, cryptography to keep information unreadable by the other side's eyes. Even people who write diaries or lovers who exchange messages use cryptography to protect the contents from spying eyes.

In cryptography, the message that is to be encrypted is known as *plaintext*. This term is used because the information is easily read by anyone. The algorithm to encrypt the plaintext is parameterized by a key. The plaintext message that has been encrypted by the function and key is known as *ciphertext*. Encryption, which involves a mathematical manipulation of the data, is generically referred to as message authentication code (MAC). Historically, there are two categories of encryption methods: *substitution ciphers* and *transposition ciphers*.

SUBSTITUTION CIPHERS

A substitution cipher is simply a scheme where one character or symbol is used in place of the actual character. For example, below is a very simple substitution cipher for the lowercase letters of the English (U.S.) alphabet:

```
plaintext   a  b  c  d  e  f  g  h  i
            j  k  l  m  n  o  p  q  r
            s  t  u  v  w  x  y  z
ciphertext  Z  X  C  V  B  N  M  A  S
            D  F  G  H  J  K  L  Q  W
            E  R  T  Y  U  I  O  P
```

The plaintext message of:

```
thisweekendisaholiday
```

would be the following in ciphertext using the above cipher:

```
RASEUBBFBJVSEZAKMSVZO
```

This example uses a 26-letter key that can produce about 4.03×10^{26} different possible combinations. By the way, 4.03×10^{26} is a really big number! This may seem like an impossible code to break, but it can be quite simple when you take into account the behavior and patterns of the underlying plaintext contents. For example, in the English (U.S.) language, the following letters are found most frequently in words and sentences. The list is sorted with the most frequent letters at the top:

- e
- t
- o
- a
- n
- i

There are also common two-letter combinations, called *digrams*, such as:

- th
- in
- er

- re
- an

And there are common three-letter combinations, called *trigrams:*

- the
- ing
- and
- ion

An individual attempting to break the code would use these common letter facts to determine which of the ciphertext characters occurs most frequently. To that value, the letter *e* would be assigned. Then the next most frequent letter would be assigned *t*, and so on down the list. Next, the common patterns of two- and three-letter combinations would be searched. In our simple example above, the letter *B* occurs the most number of times in the ciphertext—three times. Using our knowledge of English, we could start breaking the code and guess that *B* is actually the letter *e*. As a matter of fact, *B* is the substitution cipher for *e*.

TRANSPOSITION CIPHERS

Even though a substitution cipher hides the actual characters themselves, it does nothing to hide the frequency or patterns of characters in the plaintext. In a transposition cipher, the actual characters of the plaintext are retained but the characters are reordered. To accomplish this, a key of nonrepeating characters is used in conjunction with an array ordering of the plaintext. To begin creating the ciphertext, each letter of the key is placed as the header of a column. For example, we will use the key NETWORK and we will be creating a columnar transposition cipher, which is quite common. Figure 9-1 illustrates the arrangement of the key and the columns.

N	E	T	W	O	R	K

Fig. 9-1.   Columnar transposition cipher—step 1.

Next the letters in the key are assigned a number based on their alphabetical order. For example, in NETWORK, the letter *E* occurs first in the alphabet when compared to all the other letters in the key. The letter *K* is next, and so on. Figure 9-2 illustrates the number position assignment of the key NETWORK.

N	E	T	W	O	R	K
3	1	6	7	4	5	2

Fig. 9-2. Columnar transposition cipher—step 2.

Then the plaintext is placed in the rows below the letter and number headers. The plaintext is entered to fill the cells in the array from left to right. Figure 9-3 is an example of the filled array for our plaintext example of

```
thisweekendisaholiday
```

N	E	T	W	O	R	K
3	1	6	7	4	5	2
t	h	i	s	w	e	e
k	e	n	d	i	s	a
h	o	l	i	d	a	y

Fig. 9-3. Columnar transposition cipher—step 3.

The last step is to start at the column that contains the 1 (lowest value) and write down the letters in the column. When the first column letters are written down, go to the column that contains 2 and append that column of letters to the first column of letters. The entire process continues until all the contents of the array have been rewritten as the ciphertext. Figure 9-4 shows the end result of stringing all of the column contents together to produce the following ciphertext:

```
heoeaytkhwidesainlsdi
```

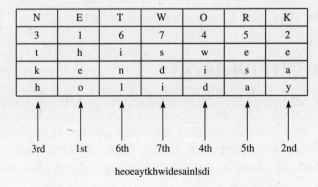

Fig. 9-4. Columnar transposition cipher—step 4.

A transposition cipher is harder to break because, to begin with, the code breaker must know it is a transposition cipher and not a substitution cipher. But by looking at the frequency of certain letters and patterns, the code breaker can determine if it is a transposition or a substitution cipher. The next hurdle is to determine the number of columns that are used. To attempt to find this piece of information, the hacker could look for a phrase that might be contained in the message. If this can be determined, then the number of columns could be deduced. The final challenge is the order of the columns. If the hacker does not know the keyword, he or she will need to resort to pattern matching in an attempt to determine the column order.

DATA ENCRYPTION STANDARD (DES)

Data Encryption Standard (DES) was a cipher developed by IBM that was adopted by the U.S. government in January 1977 for unclassified information. The cipher was also used a lot in public and private organizations and companies. The basic concept behind DES is that the plaintext is substitution encrypted in blocks of 64 bits and is parameterized by a 64-bit key, of which only 56 bits are actually used for the key.

The original version of DES is no longer secure, but DES has gone through some modifications to improve the security. One method used to improve on the original DES is called *DES chaining*. In this scheme, a block of plaintext is exclusively ORed with the ciphertext block immediately preceding it in the stream of encrypted data. The resulting XORed plaintext block is then DES encrypted. One of the hot encryption techniques used in current product is BLOWFISH essentially arose as a block cipher, and is a better technique than DES.

RSA

RSA is named after its three inventors: Rivest, Shamir, and Adleman. RSA typically uses a 512-bit key, which requires a lot more computational power than DES does. The security of RSA is based on the factoring of large numbers. Because of the necessary computational horsepower and time required to encrypt (and decrypt) with RSA, it is very hard to break. RSA is typically used in systems to generate the public and private keys used by key encryption systems.

PUBLIC KEY CRYPTOGRAPHY

One way to encrypt information is to use a secret key that is only known to the sender and the receiver. The level of secrecy possible with keys is based on the length of the key. If a key can use only decimal numbers, then a two-digit key has 100 possible combinations. If the key is lengthened to three digits, the number of possible combinations rises to 1000, and at six digits, the number reaches 1,000,000.

When the sender gets ready to send a message to the receiver, the sender encrypts the data with the secret key and sends the packets over the transmission media. The receiver decrypts the sender's messages with the secret key and is then able to read the contents. The decryption of the message at the recipient's end involves applying another mathematical process to unscramble the information. The idea behind this strategy is not to attempt to secure the connection but to make the data unreadable by unauthorized individuals who snag the packets off the transmission media. Only the holders of the matched secret keys can decipher each other's messages. Because a sender may communicate with several recipients, each system may hold several secret keys.

Public key encryption is probably one of the most heavily used methods to prevent unauthorized individuals from reading information that is not intended for them. It was developed by Diffie and Hellman, and their scheme uses a secret key process with an interesting variation. An encryption scheme that uses just one key for both the sender and the receiver can be easily compromised. If the secret key were to get into the wrong hands, then the entire mechanism would be useless. In the Diffie-Hellman key scheme, two keys are used by each communicating entity.

In Public key cryptography, there are two pairs of keys involved—a public key and a private key. The encryption/decryption scheme is designed so that one key cannot be derived from the other key. In other words, if an individual has one of the pair of keys, she cannot figure out the missing key and break the code. The sender and recipient each hold two keys, one of which is known to both of them, while the other is not. The common key is the public key, and this key is available to anyone who wishes to communicate with the sender. The private key is unique for each system and is known only to the specific system. When a device wants to send a message to a recipient, the sender encrypts the message with the public key and sends the encrypted message to the recipient. To decrypt the message, the recipient has to use the private key. The recipient cannot decrypt the message with the public key. When the recipient wants to send a message back to the sender, the recipient encrypts the message with the public key and sends it to the sender. The sender uses his private key to decrypt the message. The sender cannot use the public key to decrypt the message.

This type of double-key encryption/decryption makes it very hard for an unauthorized party to decrypt the message. The public-private key sets that are used by the sender and receiver are specific and cannot be used on another message from a different system. For example, if system BrowserAlexa is communicating with server WebServer, the public key used by both systems is designed to work only with the secret keys assigned to the BrowserAlexa and WebServer pair. To elaborate, we'll call the public key PubAlexa, and the private key held by BrowserAlexa we'll call PrivAlexa, and the private key of the Web server is PrivWebAlexa. When BrowserAlexa gets ready to send a message to WebServer, the message is encrypted with the PubAlexa key. When WebServer receives the message, it uses the PrivWebAlexa key to decrypt the message. When WebServer is ready to send a message back to BrowserAlexa, WebServer encrypts the message with the PubAlexa key and sends the information to BrowserAlexa. BrowserAlexa uses the PrivAlexa key to decrypt the message. If WebServer receives a message from a different system than BrowserAlexa, WebServer cannot use the PrivWeb-Alexa key or the PubAlexa key to decrypt the message. Using two keys where one is private and the other part of the set is public is safe because the encrypt and decrypt functions have a one-way property. Either key can be used to encrypt or decrypt a message, but either key by itself cannot perform both functions on the same message.

A very critical element in public key cryptography is how the keys are delivered to the proper systems. If I send you the public key and your private key, then anybody can capture our packets and get both keys. Furthermore, because I sent you your private key, I am also probably retaining a copy of your private key. If my system is compromised, your private key is no longer private. To facilitate the proper exchange of keys and to generate the keys, a Certificate Authority (CA) is involved. In some references, the CA is referred to as the trusted *key distribution center* (KDC).

The CA is either an internal or an external entity that is responsible for verifying who the sender and receiver are, generating the public-private key sets for the two entities, delivering the public key to both parties, and delivering the private keys to their respective owners. An example of an external CA is Verisign. Many network and server operating systems have the ability to provide CAs internally, and some also work with external CAs. In addition to creating the keys, the public keys must be exchanged between the two entities, and each device must know for sure that the other entity is who it says it is. The Diffie-Hellman key exchange protocol is used to allow two entities that do not know each other to exchange keys safely.

To distribute public keys to individuals, digital certificates are commonly used and are often encountered in browsers and secure e-mail systems. A certificate is issued from a CA, which basically says that the public key contained in the certificate actually belongs to the individual or company indicated in the certificate. Over the course of time, a user may accumulate a number of certificates from different organizations. The X.509 standard specifies the format and type of information contained in a certificate. The information is either mandatory or optional, and all certificates must include the following information:

- The name of the organization, company, or entity that the public key is for
- The public key of the same organization, company, or entity stated in the certificate
- The name of the Certificate Authority for the public key
- A digital signature

A common optional specification in a certificate is an expiration date. Figure 9-5 is an example of a certificate in a browser used for accessing a Web site.

DIGITAL SIGNATURES

An encryption/decryption scheme can also be used to authenticate the message's sender. If I sent you a message and I signed it "From Santa Claus," how would you know if the message was really from Santa Claus or not? But, if we use the public key scheme again with a little variation, messages can be digitally signed, and the recipient knows the message source is authentic. To accomplish this, both public and private keys are used. One of the two keys can be used to encrypt a message, and the other key has to be used to decrypt the message. In the case of a digital signature, the message is encrypted with the sender's private key, and the recipient decrypts the message with the public key. Because only the sender has the private

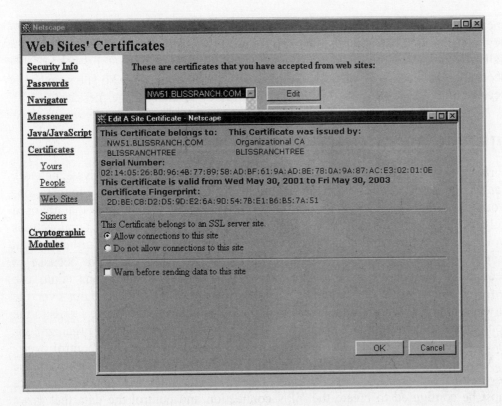

Fig. 9-5.   Example of a digital certificate.

key, if the recipient can decrypt the message with the public key of the sender, then the recipient knows the sender is authentic.

A common authentication protocol used in digital signature implementations is Kerberos. The name comes from a Greek mythological multiheaded dog that guards the entrance to Hades. Another protocol that is used to sign plaintext documents is Message Digests. This method is based on a one-way hash function that is called the *message digest*. The idea behind a cryptographic hash is to map a large message into a small fixed-length number. You can think of the hash as being like a cryptographic checksum on the message. The hash needs to be at least 128 bits long so the messages cannot be extracted from the packets. Probably the most widely used modification of the original message digest is MD5, which is named after the fifth in a series of hash functions designed by Ron Rivest. Another message digest algorithm is Secure Hash Algorithm (SHA), which is a government standard and is also used by companies that conduct business with the government.

PUBLIC KEY CRYPTOGRAPHY AND DIGITAL SIGNATURES

Combining digital signatures and public key cryptography, you can deliver messages that are confidential and at the same time verify that the sender is authentic. To accomplish this, the message is first encrypted with the sender's private key to provide the digital signature. Then the encrypted message is encrypted again with the public key. The recipient must first decrypt with his private key, and if this is successful, then we know the message was delivered confidentially. Then the recipient decrypts the second time with the public key. If this decryption is successful, then the recipient knows the sender is who she says she is because only the sender has the proper private key to encrypt the message.

VIRTUAL PRIVATE NETWORKS (VPN)

Virtual Private Networks (VPN) provide the ability to create a private network connection across a public network. Without this type of technology, organizations would have to lease or set up communication lines between each other that are used only by them. For most companies, the cost of leasing or installing such connections would be so expensive that it would be out of their financial range. Furthermore, it may be physically impossible to install dedicated transmission links because of geographic boundaries or available space in conduits. Organizations could use wireless and satellite connections, but because the signals are sent out over the airways, anybody within range could pick up the signals and thus have access to the companies' transmitted data. Virtual Private Network can be used by organizations that need to communicate across networks they do not own or have control over.

Virtual Private Network is software that is run by both organizations on the devices that are used to connect to each other across the Internet. The VPN software must be configured to create the VPN connection and control the data that flows across the VPN connection. The VPN software acts like a packet filter in that it only allows data to travel from it to the other VPN device the VPN software is configured for. The second task VPN performs is encryption of the data before it is transmitted across the VPN link. The encryption makes the data unreadable to individuals who are outside the VPN connection if, by some means, they are able to tap into the VPN connection.

TUNNELING

In our previous discussions of encryption and decryption for public key and VPN applications, only the message or data portion of the transmitted packet is encrypted. The header sections of the packet are not encrypted, so the addresses can be read by the devices to determine if the packets are for them or not. It is not practical to encrypt the addressing portion of a packet that will be traveling across a public network. If the address information was encrypted, then each device the packet could encounter on its journey across the Internet would have to decrypt the packet just to read the address information. If the devices can decrypt the header information, they can also decrypt the data portion of the packet, so encrypting the packet to prevent unauthorized access would be wasted effort. Therefore packets sent across a public network must have their addressing information unencrypted. But the data portion of the packet can be encrypted. As the data-encrypted packets travel across a public network, unauthorized individuals can pick the packets off the wire and read addressing information. Although they cannot read the contents, their access to the IP (logical) and physical addresses makes it possible for unscrupulous individuals to spoof packets so they appear to be coming from another source. For example, a Human Resources staff member is sending a message to Payroll to go ahead and print the paychecks for the week. When these packets are sniffed off the transmission media, the physical and logical addresses of both the Human Resource staff's machine and Payroll system are now known. The hacker could then put his or her own packets on the transmission media with the source address of the Human Resource system in place of the hacker's address information. Then, when the spoofed packets arrive at the Payroll system, the Payroll system thinks the packets are from the Human Resource staff member. To prevent this type of activity, the addressing and other nondata information in packets needs to be secured from unauthorized eyes. The technique that provides this capability across a public network, such as the Internet, is known as *tunneling*.

Tunneling creates an IP-in-IP tunnel and also uses a VPN to establish a private connection across the network. The entire outgoing packet at one end of the VPN is encrypted—header and all. To this packet is added an unencrypted header that contains the addressing information of the sending VPN system (router) and the receiving VPN router at the other end. No other machine addresses or IP numbers are present inside this added header except for those of the two VPN machines. The receiver end decrypts the encrypted portion of the packet and then forwards it on to the network attached to the VPN. This scheme is called tunneling because the only known packet addresses are the addresses of the two ends of the VPN tunnel.

Firewalls

Encryption technology helps to provide secure transmission of private information over a public network. But it does not provide any means to keep out unwanted traffic from your network. Ideally, the traffic that crosses from the Internet to a company's private network should just be traffic that is only for the private network and not all the other traffic that is on the Internet. Furthermore, a hacker could find out the IP number of the address of a system on the company's private network and send a constant stream of packets to the system. Depending on the nature and content of the unwanted packets, the result may be to render the system useless and create a crash. If the address the unauthorized individual discovered is a server, causing the server to crash may cause any number of other problems within the company. To make matters worse, if the hacker is able to send executable code or commands to the server or cause the server to execute some process, the results may be disastrous. So, in addition to making the information in data packets secure, you want to protect your systems from useless and potentially harmful traffic. To filter out unwanted traffic, firewalls need to be installed and configured.

The concept of a network and system firewall is to allow only permitted traffic to enter the system from outside the network. The term *firewall* as used in networks is fashioned after physical firewalls used in buildings. The idea of installing a firewall during building construction is to keep a fire from passing from the source of the fire to beyond the firewall. In apartment complexes, for example, if each unit is separated by a firewall, then a fire in one apartment would not be able to spread as easily to other units because of the firewalls. Note that in order to make firewalls effective, a firewall must be in place at every boundary to the outside world. The same holds true for networks. Wherever a private network has an interface to a public network, a firewall needs to be in place and configured according to the organization's security policy. If one boundary is left unprotected, the entire network is unprotected.

To be effective, network firewalls must meet certain minimum standards and provide basic prevention schemes. The idea of firewalls is to create a secure perimeter around the network that prevents unauthorized access and interference with private network activities. One of the first important tasks of a firewall is that the firewall itself must be secure. If the firewall can be compromised, then there is no effective firewall in place. There are quite a number of firewall products on the market, and typically their major differences in functions (and price) include what OSI layers are protected, the granularity of preventing and permitting access, and any known weaknesses, such as how easy it is to get around the firewall. Most security experts agree that one way to secure firewalls is to use dedicated systems for the firewalls. In other words, don't run the firewall software on the same system as the company's Web server, database server, or any other application or service. One of the reasons for this approach has to do with IP port numbers.

Every service running on an IP-based environment has at least one port number assigned to the service so another service cannot use the same port number. For example, Web servers use port 80 for nonsecure HTTP connections and port 443 for secure connections to browsers. If a vendor decided to write its gaming software to use port 80, then when you went to use your browser to access a Web site, you might end up accessing the gaming system and not the Web site. To keep track of which services use which ports, the ports used by applications can be registered with Internet Assigned Numbers Authority (IANA). Yet not all of the possible IP port numbers can be registered. The port numbers are divided into three ranges:

- *Well-Known Ports.* These port numbers are assigned by the IANA, and on most systems these numbers can be used only by processes or services that operate at a privileged level in the operating system. The number range for well-known ports is 0 through 1023. Some common examples of well-known ports are shown in Table 9-1.

- *Registered Ports.* These ports are registered with IANA and can be used by most applications and users. The range of registered ports is from 1024 through 49151.

- *Dynamic and/or Private Ports.* These ports can be used by anything and anybody. These are typically used by clients accessing a service because the number of the port used on the client side is not relevant because the client is not running a service.

To get the most recent list of port numbers, go to www.iana.org/assignments/port-numbers.

Now that we have a little background about port numbers and which services use which ports, how are these important when it comes to a firewall? A firewall should be configured to have open ports only for the services that are used on the private

Table 9-1   Common Well-known Ports

Port Number	Purpose
20	FTP control
21	FTP data
23	Telnet
25	SMTP
69	TFTP
80	HTTP
110	POP3
119	NNTP
123	NTP
137	NETBIOS Name Service
161	SNMP
162	SNMPTRAP
443	HTTPS

network that permit connections from the outside. For example, if the only service accessible to Internet users is the company's Web site, then only port 80 needs to be open on the firewall. If the Web server also supports secure HTTP connections, then port 443 would also need to be open. If HTTPS is not used, port 443 does not need to be open. One of the biggest places where threats and unauthorized access occurs is with open, unused ports. Some software vendors leave many ports open, assuming that the system or another system will be running the related services. To see how unused open ports can be hazardous to your network, let's look at an example.

An administrator may think that even though an FTP server is not running on her network, then what harm can there be if the FTP ports are left open because there is nothing present to respond to FTP requests? But an unscrupulous individual can use an open, unused port to send all sorts of stuff through that has nothing to do with FTP. You can think of a firewall that has open, unused ports as a house that has all the doors and windows locked except for the small ventilation window near the roof of the house. It may take some doing to get to and through the unlocked window, but if it is there, somebody will try it. It is essential that administrators keep an eye on what ports are open on the firewalls and keep only the bare minimum open. Unauthorized individuals will issue port scans on all sorts of systems in an attempt to find open ports. By the way, it is relatively easy to detect when certain types of port scans are in progress. Some firewall software products include the ability to recognize some types of port scans. For a good reference on how to detect port scans and sample port scan packet traces, check out www.packet-level.com.

In addition to making sure the firewall is itself secure, there are some other important criteria that must be met:

- All of the traffic coming from the Internet, or from another network that is not maintained by the organization, must go through the firewalls. In addition to individuals attempting to gain unauthorized access to information on the company's private network, viruses, worms, Trojan horses, and other things can enter a network from the outside.

- All traffic that goes out from the private network onto another network or the Internet must go through the firewalls. This feature is important so an organization can determine which locations and services on the Internet are appropriate and necessary for conducting business.

- Any unauthorized traffic coming in to the private network or going out from the private network must be rejected by the firewall. Most firewalls have some level of logging or auditing of unauthorized traffic so the administrators can determine the sources of the attempts and other information. Make sure that if your firewall product performs logging or auditing, that you check to make sure that the port hits you want monitored are included. For example, a common trick to enter a firewall is by using port 53 set as the source address. Port 53 is used by DNS, and some firewalls allow it to pass on through because the source port appears as if it is the result of a DNS query initiated from the private network. Port 161, which is used by Simple Network Management Protocol (SNMP), is a common port that an unauthorized individual would check to see if it is open. If it is, a lot of information about the system and environment can be retrieved from the SNMP database. Also be aware that some desktop administration software uses SNMP. For example, the HP JetDirect Remote management software uses SNMP.

A final note about firewalls and cable modems, DSL, or other always-on Internet access from your home: Use a firewall on the device that connects to the Internet and/or run a firewall on all of your PCs, Macs, Linux/Unix, or other machines that have access to the Internet. If you are already running a personal firewall, then you are probably aware of the type of unauthorized activity you have seen against your system(s). If you do not have a personal firewall in place, you should install one ASAP before more information about your systems is discovered or unauthorized access to your system(s) is successful.

PACKET FILTERING

One of the primary mechanisms by which a firewall functions is by filtering packets. That is, packets that are not permitted to enter the private network from the Internet are rejected at the firewall and are filtered out of the packet stream. Similarly, packets that are not permitted to leave the private network are blocked at the firewall, and the traffic reaching the Internet is filtered by passing through a firewall. The main process by which packet filtering works is that the firewall examines the header information in the packets. Firewalls can examine the source and destination IP addresses, and if the numbers or networks are on the permitted lists, the packets can pass through the firewall. Packet filtering of IP addresses operates at the network layer, or layer 3, of the OSI stack. This type of filtering by itself does not a firewall make. Another type of filtering that a firewall can perform is protocol and application layer filtering.

APPLICATION GATEWAY

The firewall can examine the packet header and determine the IP protocol or higher OSI level of service contained in the packet. This level of filtering in conjunction with the layer 3 filtering can provide a much better firewall. For example, on an e-mail gateway server, the firewall could be configured to reject all packets coming into the e-mail gateway except those needed by the e-mail gateway software. Thus any Web traffic, FTP traffic, or anything that is not permitted in e-mail traffic could not enter the private network through the firewall. In another example, protocol filtering can also apply to outgoing traffic. For example, in a public library, the administration wants to make sure the three Internet computers available for the public can access the Internet but not other services. The firewall could be configured to check that the packets going out to the Internet match the addresses of the three Internet machines. If the HTTP protocol is not included in the packet, the packet is rejected at the firewall. Thus users attempting to use the library's Internet machines to access a game server would be denied access because the game packets would not be allowed to leave the private network. Firewalls that provide upper OSI layer filtering are sometimes called *application-layer gateways* or *proxies*. Figure 9-6 is a conceptual illustration of a firewall that both incorporates packet filtering and contains an application gateway.

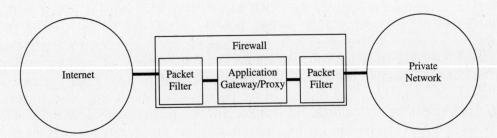

Fig. 9-6. Concept illustration of a firewall with packet filtering and an application gateway.

IP Security

IP Security (IPSec) is an IP protocol suite standard that was developed to address some of the security limitations of IPv4. Its design provides three main features and functions:

- *Modularity.* The security administrators can choose an encryption algorithm and security protocols.
- *Security services.* There are a number of security services the administrators can choose from. These include access control, message integrity, authentication, replay protection so packets cannot be resent from an unauthorized party, and privacy.

- *Level of detail of security services application.* Administrators can choose to place a restriction on all packets meeting a specific criteria or on a subset of those packets based on other factors.

IPSec is composed of two protocol elements that specify two header types that can be used together or separately. One of the two header protocols, IP Authentication Header (AH), provides access control, authentication, connectionless message integrity, and replay protection. The other protocol, IP Encapsulating Security Payload (ESP), offers the same support as AH with confidentiality added. The administrator has the option to use either one of these protocols, or both can be put in place. The second major component of IPSec is Internet Security Association and Key Management Protocol (ISAKMP). One of the major roles of this component is to provide support for the management of keys. IPSec specifies Internet Key Exchange Protocol (IKE) as the key management protocol.

The two major pieces of IPSec are bound together by way of the Security Association (SA), which is used to establish the simplex (one-way) connection between two communicating parties. For example, an SA may exist between a client and a router or gateway, between a client and server, or between two routers or gateways. Because the binding is simplex, to provide two-way conversations, two pairs of SAs must exist—one for each direction. If both AH and ESP are supported between two entities exchanging information, then four SAs will be needed.

When a connection is made from one device to another, the SA at the receiving system is assigned a Security Parameter Index (SPI). This value is placed in the header of the AH and/or ESP packets that are transmitted by the sender. The receiver examines the incoming packets and uses the SI value to determine who that packet is coming from and what algorithms to use to properly interpret the packet. The ISAKMP specifies the settings and configurations of the SAs. These parameters include the procedures and formats of the packets to establish, negotiate, modify, and delete security associations. Internet Security Association and Key Management Protocol is also involved in key exchange, but it does not specify any specific key exchange protocol that must be used. A common key exchange protocol that is used is IKE.

The principal role of the authentication header is to ensure that the integrity and origin of the data are authentic. It also prevents the replay of packets so an unauthorized user cannot resend the packets in an attempt to confuse systems or to repeat particular activities. The AH protocol can be used with IPv4 or IPv6 packets. Figure 9-7 illustrates the conceptual structure of the IPSec AH. The fields of the IPSec AH are outlined in Table 9-2.

NextHdr	PayloadLength	Reserved
SPI		
SeqNum		
AuthenticationData		

Fig. 9-7. IPSec Authentication Header.

Table 9-2   IPSec AH Fields

Field	Role
NextHdr	Identifies the type of the next payload after the authentication header
PayloadLength	This is the length of the authentication header expressed in 32-bit words or 4-byte units. The number two (2) is then subtracted from the length to produce the PayloadLength value.
Reserved	The value is set to 0, and this field is reserved for future use.
SPI	This is the unique value that identifies the security association for the packet (datagram). The unique value is produced by combining the destination IP address with an arbitrary 32-bit value.
SeqNum	This counter value increases for each datagram, and it is designed to protect against replay of the packet.
AuthenticationData	This is a variable-length field that contains the message integrity code for the packet. There can be different message digest algorithms used to produce the integrity code. For example, DES and MD5 can be used.

The ESP protocol's main functions are to provide choices of security services that can be used with either IPv4 or IPv6 datagrams. Depending on the implementation, ESP can be used with or without AH. When ESP is used, the ESP header is placed after the IP header and before the upper-layer protocol in the packet. If a secure tunnel is used between the two communicating devices, the ESP header is placed before the encapsulated IP header. The different security features that can be used are defined at the time the SA is established between the two parties. The available security options include authenticity of the data's source, integrity of the data, confidentiality, and replay protection. The format of the ESP header is outlined in Figure 9-8. The fields of the IPSec ESP are outlined in Table 9-3.

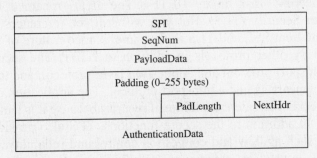

Fig. 9-8.   IPSec Encapsulating Security Payload header.

A common implementation of the IPSec ESP protocol is to create an IPSec tunnel between two routers across a public network.

Web Security

When the Web was first created, the designers had no concept of its growth and the type of information that would be traveling across the Internet today. As companies

Table 9-3   IPSec Encapsulating Security Payload Fields

Field	Role
SPI	This is the unique value that identifies the security association for the packet (datagram). The unique value is produced by combining the destination IP address with an arbitrary 32-bit value.
SeqNum	This counter value increases for each datagram, and it is designed to protect against replay of the packet.
PayloadData	This field contains the data that is described in the NextHdr field. If the environment has chosen to use encryption, then the contents of the PayloadData field will be encrypted by whatever method was decided upon.
Padding	This field is necessary, and the amount will vary depending on what encryption method was used for the PayloadData field. The padding ensures the ciphertext ends on a 4-byte boundary.
PadLength	This field contains the value of the padding added by the Padding field.
NextHdr	This field identifies the type of the next payload after the ESP header.
AuthenticationData	This is a variable-length field that contains the message integrity code for the packet. There can be different message digest algorithms used to produce the integrity code. For example, DES and MD5 can be used.

placed their Web front on the Internet, it became clear that there needed to be protocols and procedures in place to protect the transfer of sensitive information, such as credit card data, social security numbers, and other personal identification information within a browser. The first popular solution to provide authentication, integrity, and privacy for Web transactions was Secure Socket Layer (SSL). Secure Socket Layer was originally developed by Netscape, and it is now managed by the Internet Engineering Task Force (IETF). The IETF renamed the protocol to Transport Layer Security (TLS). But you will still see references to SSL, and, in general, you can treat SSL and TLS as the same. A nice feature of SSL/TLS is that it can be used by other protocols in addition to HTTP. The secure protocol sits between the transport protocol and application layer protocol, and to the upper layer services, TLS appears as just a transport protocol. The application does not need to do anything special to create the additional security because it is handled by a lower-layer protocol. In addition to the secure functions, TLS also provides all the TCP-type functions such as flow and congestion control and reliability.

When HTTP is used in conjunction with TLS, it is referred to as HTTPS for Secure HTTP and is specified as such in a URL. For example, to connect to the Texas Stars Web server with a secure HTTP connection, the URL would be

```
https://www.texas-stars.com
```

Note the use of "https" instead of "http." The HTTPS connection uses a different IP port than the standard HTTP connection at port 80. By default, HTTPS will use port 443. A very nice benefit of using a secure protocol that is independent of upper-layer protocols and applications is the ability to support real-time, interactive secure transmissions. To provide for interactive secure conversations, TLS is divided into two parts—a *handshake protocol* and a *record protocol*.

The TLS handshake protocol is used to negotiate and set up the parameters for the communication connection. Some of these setup parameters include items such as the session keys and encryption algorithms. If the connection parameters specify the use of certificates, the handshake protocol handles the exchange of certificates. If you have ever accessed a secure Web site that uses certificates, your browser will notify you of a certificate offer.

This certificate ensures the recipient will obtain a reliable copy of the other party's public key. Once the certificate is installed in the user's browser, the Web server can verify messages from the user with its private key.

The record protocol does the actual data transfer of the HTTPS connection. It handles the procedures necessary for carrying out the message fragmentation or assembly of the application layer messages. In addition, the data can be delivered in a compressed format. Compression does not add any security, but it may assist in speeding up data transfer.

The TLS protocol provides the ability to resume a session. This is particularly useful for Web transactions where different information types are delivered to the user. As you will recall, TCP will create a new connection for each file transferred. Thus, if a Web page contains links to several graphic elements, a separate TCP data transfer connection will be opened for each graphic image. With TLS, establishing a new session for each file transfer would take a lot of time and resources. Instead, if the server still has an active session with the same user, the same session ID will be used for all of the file transfers to the browser.

The Computer Incident Advisory Capability (CIAC) of the Department of Energy has some very useful information on its Web site that addresses Web security. The following is extracted from a document titled "J-042: Web Security" (located on-line at http://ciac.llnl.gov/ciac/bulletins/j-042.shtml). Note that the material contains references to items specific to certain operating systems, and when implementing these practices, you would need to make the corresponding adjustment for your Web server platform.

Following are some best practices in managing Web server security:

- Place your Web server(s) in a DMZ. Set your firewall to drop connections to your Web server on all ports but http (port 80) or https (port 443).

- Remove all unneeded services from your Web server, keeping FTP (but only if you need it) and a secure log-in capability such as secure shell. An unneeded service can become an avenue of attack.

- Disallow all remote administration unless it is done using a one-time password or an encrypted link.

- Limit the number of persons having administrator or root-level access.

- Log all user activity and either maintain those logs in an encrypted form on the Web server or store them on a separate machine on your Intranet.

- Monitor system logs regularly for any suspicious activity. Install some trap macros to watch for attacks on the server (such as the PHF attack). Create macros that run every hour or so that would check the integrity of passwords and other critical files. When the macros detect a change, an e-mail should be sent to the system manager.

- Remove *all* unnecessary files such as phf from the scripts directory /cgi-bin.

- Remove the default document trees that are shipped with Web servers such as IIS and ExAir. Apply all relevant security patches as soon as they are announced.

- If you must use a GUI interface at the console, remove the commands that automatically start the window manager from the .RC startup directories and then create a startup command for the window manager. You can then use the window manager when you need to work on the system, but shut it down when you are done. Do not leave the window manager running for any extended length of time.

- If the machine must be administered remotely, require that a secure capability such as secure shell is used to make a secure connection. Do not allow telnet or nonanonymous ftp connections (those connections requiring a username and password) to this machine from any untrusted site. It would also be good to limit these connections only to a minimum number of secure machines and have those machines reside within your Intranet.

- Run the Web server in a chroot-ed part of the directory tree so it cannot access the real system files.

- Run the anonymous FTP server (if you need it) in a chroot-ed part of the directory tree that is different from the Web server's tree.

- Do all updates from your Intranet. Maintain your Web page originals on a server on your Intranet and make all changes and updates here; then push these updates to the public server through an SSL connection. If you do this on an hourly basis, you can avoid having a corrupted server exposed for a long period of time.

- Scan your Web server periodically with tools such as ISS or nmap to look for vulnerabilities.

- Have intrusion detection software monitor the connections to the server. Set the detector to give an alarm upon detecting known exploits and suspicious activities and to capture these sessions for review. This information can help you recover from an intrusion and strengthen your defenses.

E-mail Security

When you send an e-mail message to an individual at a different location, the message passes through several routers and network equipment to get from you to the recipient. At any location in the pathway, your message could be picked up by somebody else and the contents read. Furthermore, the unauthorized individual picking up your message might put it back on the transmission media in a modified form and/or may respond to you in such a manner that you think the response is legitimate and comes from the actual intended recipient. To provide an environment that makes e-mail more difficult to understand when it is captured by a hacker, individuals and products use encryption techniques to encrypt the e-mail messages. Two systems that are in use include Pretty Good Privacy (PGP) and Privacy Enhanced E-mail (PEM).

PRETTY GOOD PRIVACY (PGP)

Pretty Good Privacy (PGP) can be used to encrypt any type of data—not just e-mail. This system was developed by Phil Zimmermann, and it provides the following functions and features:

- Privacy
- Authentication
- Digital signatures
- Compression

The PGP software and accompanying code are free, it is available for most operating systems, and it can be downloaded from the Internet. There are also some commercial products that use PGP. The structure of PGP is based on RSA, International Data Encryption Algorithm (IDEA), and MD5 technologies. When a user first implements PGP to send a message, PGP hashes the message using MD5 and then encrypts the results with the user's private RSA key. The encrypted hash and original message are incorporated into a single message and compressed using ZIP. ZIP uses the Ziv-Lempel algorithm to compress data. The PGP program on the sender's system prompts for some random input. Using the random input and the typing speed of the sender, IDEA is used to produce a 128-bit message or session key. The message key is then used to encrypt the compressed sender's data. Finally, the message is encrypted again with the recipient's public key. The two components resulting from the PGP manipulation are converted to Base64 and sent as a MIME format message. The recipient reverses the Base64 bit encoding and decrypts with their private key. The information is decompressed, and the plaintext is extracted from the encrypted hash. The encrypted hash is decrypted using the sender's public key. The recipient performs the MD5 computation on the plaintext, and if it agrees with the hash sent with the message, then the recipient knows the message is correct and the sender is authentic.

Pretty Good Privacy provides support for three different RSA key lengths depending on the organization type that is using PGP:

- *385 bits.* This key length is designed for casual use and should not be used by organizations or companies that will be exchanging sensitive information.
- *512 bits.* This key length is designed for commercial use, and it could be broken by organizations or individuals with deep pockets—that is, a lot of money and/or resources.
- *1024 bits.* This key size is designed for the military and is essentially impossible to break within somebody's lifetime.

PRIVACY ENHANCED E-MAIL (PEM)

Privacy Enhanced E-mail (PEM) is an early Internet standard defined by RFCs 1421 and 1424. The concept is similar to PGP, but the technique is different. A PEM message is first converted to a canonical form so that all the messages have the same format for white spaces, carriage returns, and line feeds. MD5 or MD2 is used to generate a hash of the message. The original message and hash are concatenated and encrypted by using DES. The encrypted message is encoded with Base64 coding and sent to the recipient as a MIME format e-mail message.

Keys used in PEM are managed by certificate authorities, and the certificates conform to the X.509 standards for key certificates. The ASN.1 standard is used to define the layout, and X.400 is used to define the names. Even though PEM is an Internet standard and PGP is not, PGP is used much more than PEM is.

Threats (Revisited and Updated)

Now that you have a background of some of the topics surrounding network security, you will find the following information from the SANS Institute interesting and very important. The report is titled "Twenty Most Critical Internet Security Vulnerabilities." More in-depth information, details, and links to other security-related Web sites are available at the SANS Web site at www.sans.org:

Top Vulnerabilities That Affect All Systems:

- Default installs of operating systems and applications
- Accounts with no passwords or weak passwords
- Nonexistent or incomplete backups
- Large number of open ports
- Not filtering packets for correct incoming and outgoing addresses
- Nonexistent or incomplete logging
- Vulnerable CGI programs

   Top Vulnerabilities to Windows Systems:

- Unicode vulnerability
- ISAPI extension buffer overflows
- IIS RDS exploit (Microsoft Remote Data Services)
- NETBIOS-unprotected Windows networking shares
- Information leakage via null session connections
- Weak hashing in SAM (LM hash)

Top Vulnerabilities to Unix Systems:

- Buffer overflows in RPC services

- Sendmail vulnerabilities
- Bind weaknesses
- R commands
- LPD (remote print protocol daemon)
- sadmind and mountd
- Default SNMP strings

Review Questions

9.1 According to Gartner's research on disaster recovery and companies' probability of recovery, which of the following statements is correct?
  - **a.** Two out of ten enterprises that experience a disaster will go out of business in 2 years.
  - **b.** One out of five enterprises that experience a disaster will go out of business in 1 year.
  - **c.** Three out of five enterprises that experience a disaster will go out of business in 5 years.
  - **d.** Two out of five enterprises that experience a disaster will go out of business in 5 years.

9.2 Which of the following activities might be considered a possible source of threat to a company's network?
  - **a.** The daily courier service personnel who drop off and pick up packages.
  - **b.** Former employees who left the company because of downsizing.
  - **c.** An employee traveling on company business to a conference in another city.
  - **d.** The building management company where an organization has its offices has decided to install a fire sprinkler system to help reduce the spread of fire.

9.3 What is meant by spoofing?

9.4 What is a substitution cipher?

9.5 What is a transposition cipher?

9.6 In a public key cryptography system, a sender has encrypted a message with the recipient's public key. What key does the recipient use to decipher the message?
  - **a.** The recipient's private key
  - **b.** The recipient's public key
  - **c.** The sender's private key
  - **d.** The sender's public key

9.7 When a digital signature is created, which key is used to encrypt the signature?

9.8 What is a common authentication protocol used for digital signatures?

9.9 In one sentence, describe a firewall.

9.10 What is meant by an application gateway?

9.11 What does IPSec AH provide?

9.12 What does IPSec ESP provide?

9.13 What is the default port used by HTTPS?

Problems

9.1 List six items that should be addressed by security policies.

9.2 Describe a DoS attack.

9.3 Describe why parity bits, checksums, and CRCs do not provide security.

9.4 What is one major problem with substitution ciphers?

9.5 Briefly describe DES.

9.6 Briefly describe RSA.

9.7 What are the four required fields that must be defined in an X.509 security certificate?

9.8 What is the advantage of using digital signatures and public key cryptography together?

9.9 Briefly describe how a Virtual Private Network (VPN) functions.

9.10 Briefly describe tunneling for secure data transmission.

9.11 What are the three types of IP ports?

9.12 Briefly describe packet filtering.

9.13 What are the three primary features of IPSec?

9.14 Briefly describe the IPSec SA?

9.15 What is the main purpose of a browser certificate?

9.16 What are the four features provided by Pretty Good Privacy (PGP)?

9.17 Briefly describe the Privacy Enhanced E-mail (PEM) process.

Answers to Review Questions

9.1 **d.** "Gartner estimates that two out of five enterprises that experience a disaster will go out of business in five years. Enterprises can improve those odds—but only if they take the necessary measures before and after the disaster."

9.2 **a, b, c, d.** All of the choices could create the right conditions to threaten the network. The regular daily courier person is familiar to employees, so they may not notice anything is wrong should a delivery person walk into the server room. Even with handsome severance packages and benefits, employees who lost their jobs due to downsizing may be disgruntled. An employee's traveling to another location may not create a threat, but if the employee has a laptop computer that contains private information or the Web browser has saved passwords, if the laptop is stolen, a hacker has a powerful tool to access the network. Installing a sprinkler system to help reduce the spread of fire is a good idea. But, if the system ever went off and a company's servers, computers, and other equipment were damaged by fire or water, the company might or might not be able to recover from the disaster.

9.3 Spoofing refers to the modification of packets' source address information so it appears that the packets were sent from another source.

9.4   A substitution cipher is simply a scheme where one character or symbol is used in place of the actual character.

9.5   In a transposition cipher, the actual characters of the plaintext are retained but the characters are reordered.

9.6   **a.** When a message is encrypted with a public key, the only key that can decrypt the message is the private key of the same set. Thus only the recipient can decrypt with his or her private key when the message has been encrypted with the recipient's public key.

9.7   In the case of a digital signature, the message is encrypted with the sender's private key, and the recipient decrypts the message with the public key. Because only the sender has the private key, if the recipient can decrypt the message with the public key of the sender, then the recipient knows the sender is authentic.

9.8   A common authentication protocol used in digital signature implementations is Kerberos.

9.9   The concept of a firewall is to allow only permitted traffic to leave the network and only permitted traffic to enter the network from the outside.

9.10   Firewalls that provide upper OSI layer filtering are sometimes called application-layer gateways or proxies.

9.11   AH or IP Authentication Header provides access control, authentication, connection-less message integrity, and replay protection.

9.12   IP Encapsulating Security Payload (ESP) provides access control, authentication, connectionless message integrity, replay protection, and confidentiality.

9.13   By default, HTTPS will use port 443.

Solutions to Problems

9.1   The six items that all security policies should address are
- Authorization
- Accountability
- Data availability
- Data integrity
- Data confidentiality
- Privacy

9.2   A Denial-of-Service (DoS) attack floods the network with so many unwanted packets that the affected systems are put out of commission. The most common form of a DoS attack is the SYN attack. The attacker sends a flurry of SYN packets to a system, which then spends all of its time trying to satisfy all the requests to set up TCP connections it thinks are occurring.

9.3   Parity bits, checksums, and CRCs do not guarantee that the data arriving at the recipient has actually come from the reported sender. You cannot rely on these mechanisms for this type of data integrity because an unauthorized individual can capture the packets off the transmission media, modify the contents and the parity bit, checksum and/or CRC values, and place the modified packets back on the transmission media.

9.4 Substitution ciphers hide the actual characters of the message, but they do not hide the frequency or patterns of characters in the message.

9.5 The basic concept behind DES is that the plaintext is substitution encrypted in blocks of 64 bits and is parameterized by a 64-bit key of which only 56 bits are actually used for the key.

9.6 RSA typically uses a 512-bit key, which requires a lot more computational power than DES does. The security of RSA is based on the factoring of large numbers. Because of the necessary computational horsepower and time required to encrypt (and decrypt) with RSA, it is very hard to break.

9.7 The following fields are required in an X.509 security certificate:
- The name of the organization, company, or entity that the public key is for
- The public key of the same organization, company, or entity stated in the certificate
- The name of the Certificate Authority for the public key
- A digital signature

9.8 By combining digital signatures and public key cryptography, you can deliver messages that are confidential and verify that the sender is authentic.

9.9 Virtual Private Network is software that is run by both organizations on the devices that are used to connect to each other across the Internet. The VPN software acts like a packet filter in that it allows data to travel only from one VPN device to the other VPN device that the VPN software is configured for. The second task VPN performs is encryption of the data before it is transmitted across the VPN link.

9.10 Tunneling creates an IP-in-IP tunnel and uses VPN to establish a private connection across the network. The entire outgoing packet at one end of the VPN network is encrypted—header and all. To this packet is added an unencrypted header that contains the addressing information of the sending VPN system (router) and the receiving VPN router at the other end. No other machine addresses or IP numbers are present inside this added header except for the two VPN machines. The receiver end decrypts the encrypted portion of the packet and then forwards it on to the network attached to the VPN.

9.11
- Well-known ports: These port numbers are assigned by the IANA and on most systems they can be used only by processes or services that operate at a privileged level in the operating system. The number range for well-known ports is 0 through 1023. Some common examples of well-known ports are:
- Registered ports: These ports are registered with IANA and can be used by most applications and users. The range of registered ports is from 1024 through 49151.
- Dynamic and/or private ports: These can be used by anything and anybody. These are typically used by clients accessing a service because the number of the port used on the client side is irrelevant because the client is not running a service.

9.12 The main process by which packet filtering works is the firewall examines the header information in the packets. Firewalls can examine the source and destination IP addresses, and if the numbers or networks are on the permitted lists, the packets can pass through the firewall. Packet filtering of IP addresses operates at the network layer, or layer 3, of the OSI stack.

9.13 IPSec provides three main features and functions:
- Modularity: The security administrators can choose an encryption algorithm and security protocols.

- Security services: There are a number of security services the administrators can choose. These include access control, message integrity, authentication, replay protection so packets cannot be resent from an unauthorized party, and privacy.
- Level of detail of security services application: Administrators can choose to place a restriction on all packets meeting a specific criteria or on a subset of those packets based on other factors.

9.14 The two major pieces of IPSec are bound together by way of the Security Association (SA) that is used to establish the simplex (one-way) connection between two communicating parties. For example, an SA may exist between a client and a router or gateway, between a client and server, or between two routers or gateways. Because the binding is simplex, to provide two-way conversations, two pairs of SAs must exist—one for each direction. If both AH and ESP are supported between two entities exchanging information, then four SAs will be needed.

9.15 A browser certificate ensures the recipient that she has obtained or will obtain a reliable copy of the other party's public key.

9.16 Pretty Good Privacy (PGP) provides the following features:
- Privacy
- Authentication
- Digital signatures
- Compression

9.17 The Privacy Enhanced E-mail (PEM) message is first converted to a canonical form so that all the messages have the same format for white spaces, carriage returns, and line feeds. MD5 or MD2 is used to generate a hash of the message. The original message and hash are concatenated and encrypted by using DES. The encrypted message is encoded with Base64 coding and sent to the recipient as a MIME format e-mail message.

APPENDIX A

Glossary

10Base2

802.3 Ethernet on thin coaxial cable. The 10 specifies a bandwidth of 10 Mbps, the Base specifies that it's a baseband transmission, and the 2 indicates a maximum segment length for this cable type of 200 m (the actual limitation is 185).

10Base5

802.3 Ethernet on thick coaxial cable. The 10 specifies a bandwidth of 10 Mbps, the Base indicates that it's a baseband transmission, and the 5 indicates a maximum segment length for this cable type of 500 m.

10BaseT

802.3 Ethernet on twisted-pair cable. The 10 specifies a bandwidth of 10 Mbps, the Base indicates that it's a baseband transmission, and the T indicates that the medium is twisted-pair.

active hub

The central hub in a network that retransmits the data it receives and can be connected to computers or to other hubs.

Address Resolution Protocol (ARP)

A protocol in the TCP/IP suite that correlates logical network addresses with physical addresses.

analog

A signal transmission technology used on broadband networks. This type of signal creates analog waveforms from digital data for transmission and requires a digital-to-analog converter (d-to-a) to reverse the conversion. A device called an analog-to-digital converter is required to convert the signal back into digital data.

Application layer

The uppermost layer of the OSI Reference Model for networking. This layer provides a consistent interface to the network for all computer software. The interface is commonly referred to as an Application Programming Interface (API), which allows for a program to be written once, without regard to the type of network involved, and then used on any network, regardless of the protocol in use.

Application Programming Interface (API)

The building blocks for software applications, which include routines, protocols, and tools.

Asynchronous Transfer Mode (ATM)

A networking technology based on the transfer of fixed-size packets, or cells. The fixed size of the cells stabilizes transmission, which is especially useful for large transmissions such as video or audio data.

attenuation

The weakening of a signal as it is transferred across a communications medium.

bandwidth

The amount of data that can be transferred across a communications medium.

baseband

A signal transmission technology for transferring digital signals across a communications medium. Baseband signals are made up of varying voltage levels to indicate binary 1's and 0's.

baseline

A network's normal performance measurements over time that can be used to diagnose or troubleshoot network problems.

Border Gateway Protocol (BGP)

A part of the TCP/IP protocol suite that enables communication of routing information between routers.

bridge

A hardware networking device used to connect two LANs or LAN segments. A bridge operates at the Data-Link layer of the OSI Reference Model.

broadband

A signal transmission technology for transferring analog signals along multiple channels of a communications medium simultaneously.

bus topology

A network design in which all computers on a LAN are connected to a central network cable, or backbone.

Carrier Sense Multiple Access (CSMA)

A network channel access method in which devices on the network send an intent-to-transmit message before actually sending data, to attempt to avoid a collision with other network transmissions.

Carrier Sense Multiple Access/Collision Detection (CSMA/CD)

A version of CSMA in which network devices are able to sense a collision on the network and wait a random amount of time before retransmitting.

Carrier Sense Multiple Access/Collision Avoidance (CSMA/CA)

A version of CSMA in which network devices "listen" to the network medium to make sure the line is clear before transmitting data.

Classless Interdomain Routing (CIDR)

A scheme for IP addressing that replaces the Class A, B, and C addressing system. CIDR allows for one IP address to be used to designate additional unique IP addresses. A CIDR IP address looks like a standard IP address with a slash followed by a number appended to the end; for example: 206.224.65.194/12.

Data-Link layer

Layer 2 of the OSI model, the Data-Link layer packages data from the upper layers into frames and then transmits them onto the media. To do this, it must define a set of rules for flow-and-error control and assign physical addresses to each device on the link. To this end, layer 2 is commonly split into two sublayers: Logical Link Control (LLC) and Media Access Control (MAC).

Domain Name Service (DNS)

A translation service that correlates domain names into IP addresses.

Dynamic Host Configuration Protocol (DHCP)

A part of the TCP/IP protocol suite, DHCP dynamically assigns IP addresses to network devices.

Ethernet

A networking technology developed in the 1970s which is governed by the IEEE 802.3 specification.

Fast Ethernet

The high-speed version of Ethernet that supports data transfer rates of 100 Mbps.

Fiber Distributed Data Interface (FDDI)

A network architecture that uses fiber-optic cable and two counter-rotating rings to transmit data at 100 Mbps.

frame

The basic package of bits that represents data sent from one networked computer to another. A frame includes the sender's and receiver's network addresses plus control information at the head and a CRC at the tail as well as the actual message contents.

frame type

One of four standards that defines the structure of an Ethernet packet: Ethernet 802.3, Ethernet 802.2, Ethernet SNAP, or Ethernet II. Most networks can identify the frame type automatically.

hops

The number of routers a message must pass through to get to its intended recipient.

hub

The central concentration point of a star network.

impedance

The resistance of a cable to the transmission of signals; impedance is what accounts for signal attenuation.

Integrated Services Digital Network (ISDN)

A digital communication method that can transmit voice and data at high speeds.

interference

The crossover that occurs when one type of signal or emission impinges on another, and either distort or diminishes it.

Internet Protocol (IP)—IPv4 IPv6

TCP/IP's primary network protocol, which provides addressing and routing information.

internetwork

A logical network that consists of two or more physical networks.

Internetwork Packet Exchange/Sequenced Packet Exchange (IPX/SPX)

The set of protocols developed by Novell that is most commonly associated with NetWare, but is also supported in Microsoft networks.

IP address

The four sets of numbers, separated by decimal points, that represent the numeric address of a computer attached to a TCP/IP network, such as the Internet.

Lightweight Directory Access Protocol (LDAP)

Part of the TCP/IP protocol suite, LDAP is a set of protocol for accessing information directories.

local area network (LAN)

A collection of networked devices, including computers, printers, etc., that fits within the scope of a single physical network.

Logical Link Control (LLC)

One of the two sublayers of the Data-Link layer of the OSI model. LLC moves packets onto and off of the network.

loopback address

An IP address with 127 in the first octet that cannot be used as the host address on a network. It is used to test the TCP/IP protocol stack within a computer without sending information out onto the network.

media

The actual cable (or radio or microwaves in wireless networking) used to transmit data over the network.

Media Access Control (MAC)

One of the two sublayers of the Data-Link layer of the OSI model. MAC moves packets onto and off of the network.

mesh

A hybrid topology in which all computers are connected to each other to provide fault-tolerant connections throughout a network.

Network Access Point (NAP)

A part of the Internet backbone where Internet service providers (ISPs) share routing and addressing information in a peering arrangement.

Network layer

Layer 3 of the OSI networking model that is responsible for assigning a globally unique address to every device and providing directions from any point on the network to any other point. To achieve this, routed and routing protocols operate at this layer.

network operating system (NOS)

A software collection that allows a computer to communicate on a network.

Open Shortest Path first (OSPF)

A part of the TCP/IP protocol suite, OSPF is a link-state routing protocol that determines the best path for a packet through an internetwork.

OSI (Open Systems Interconnection) Network Reference Model

A standard that specifies a conceptual model called the Open Systems Interconnection (OSI) Network Reference Model (OSI Standard 7498), which breaks networked communications into seven layers: Application, Presentation, Session, Transport, Network, Data-Link, and Physical.

packet

Data destined for network transmission that is specially organized and formatted.

packet switching

A transmission method in which packets are transmitted over a networking medium that maintains several paths between sender and receiver.

peer-to-peer

A form of networking in which all computers on the network act as both clients and servers.

Physical layer

The bottom layer of the OSI model where data is transmitted across the actual network medium.

Point-to-Point Protocol (PPP)

A part of the TCP/IP protocol suite, PPP has many options and features, including IP address management and authentication multiplexing and management features, such as configuration, testing, error detection, etc. It is commonly used by PCs with modems to dial either the Internet or a corporate network.

Presentation layer

Layer 6 of the OSI model that translates data into a standard format.

Protocol Data Unit (PDU)

A unit of data that consists of a header, which is defined by the protocol in use, followed by various application data.

redirector

A software component in a protocol suite that intercepts requests from applications and determines whether the service is local or remote.

repeater

A hardware device used to strengthen signals being transmitted on a network.

Reverse Address Resolution Protocol (RARP)

A part of the TCP/IP protocol suite that translates a physical address into an IP address.

ring topology

A network topology that consists of computers connected to one another in a closed circle.

router

A Network layer device that connects networks with different physical media and translates between different network architectures, such as Token Ring and Ethernet.

Routing Information Protocol (RIP)

A part of the TCP/IP protocol suite, RIP establishes communication between routers to share routing information.

Session layer

Layer 5 of the OSI model that establishes, maintains, and terminates sessions across the network. This layer manages name recognition, synchronization, and some access features, such as when a device can transmit and how long it can transmit.

Simple Network Management Protocol (SNMP)

A part of the TCP/IP protocol suite, SNMP monitors remote hosts over a TCP/IP network.

star topology

A networking topology in which the computers are connected via a central connecting point, usually a hub.

subnet

A segment of a network.

switch

A networking device that manages networked connections between devices on a star network.

time slice

A CPU cycle. Time slicing grants CPU cycles to processes and limits the amount of time that a process can have exclusive use of the CPU.

Token Ring

A network architecture developed by IBM that uses token passing in a logical ring topology.

Transmission Control Protocol/Internet Protocol (TCP/IP)

The most widely used protocol suite in the world, and the standard for communication on the Internet.

Transport layer

Layer 4 of the OSI model that prepares data for transmission across the network.

wide area network (WAN)

A network that is spread across a large geographic area. Often a distance of 2 or more miles is used to define a WAN.

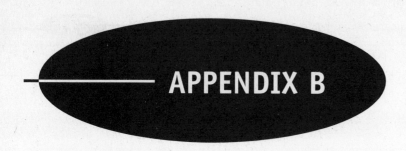

Online Internet and Networking Standards

This appendix lists some of the most important standards for networking and the Internet and the URLS where more information is located.

- **IEEE 802.x standards**—These standards, which include Ethernet, Token Ring, FDDI, LLC, and more, can be downloaded in PDF format for free from `www.ieee.org`.

- **RFCs**—All Requests For Comments (RFCs) can be found at `www.faqs.org`.

- **Cabling standards**—Go to the EIA and TIA Web sites: `www.tiaonline.org` and `www.eia.org`.

- **Internet Drafts and Working Groups**—These can be found on-line at `www.ietf.org`.

- **Telecommunication Standards**—`www.itu.int/home/index.html`.

- **Association for Computing Machinery**—`www.acm.org/`.

- **American National Standards Institute**—`www.ansi.org/`.

- **International Organization for Standardization**— `www.iso.org/iso/en/ISOOnline.frontpage`.

- **Official Internet Protocol Standards**— `www.rfc-editor.org/rfcxx00.html`.

- **Internet Assigned Numbers Authority**—`www.iana.org/`.

- **Gartner**—`www3.gartner.com`—Security and analysis of network issues.

- **Computer Incident Advisory Capability (U.S. Department of Energy)**— `www.ciac.org/ciac/`.

- **The SANS Institute**—`www.sans.org`—security.

- **packet-level.com**—`www.packet-level.com/`.

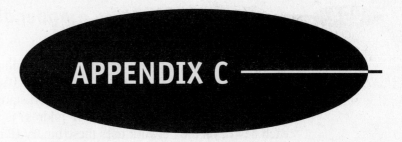

APPENDIX C

Binary Arithmetic and IP Address Calculation

Devices that communicate on an IP network must have a unique IP number so there is a distinction between the different entities. The IP number is a system's identity and when packets are transmitted by a device, the IP address of the device is included in the packet. If the recipient's IP address is known to the sender, the recipient's address is also included in the packet. The sender's IP address is like the From name on an e-mail message and the recipient's address is similar to the To address portion of an e-mail message. If the recipient's address is not known, packets may be addressed to a broadcast address or multicast address. The broadcast address is sent to all devices on the same network and a multicast address is sent to all systems in a group.

Humans tend to interact with IP systems by their user-friendly names, such as www.lanwrights.com, but there is an IP number that is used by devices on the network. People usually see the IP number as four decimal numbers separated by periods, such as 206.224.65.194. This number uniquely identifies the machine and includes the network and host address. The network address is the portion of the IP number that is the same for all devices on the same network or subnet. The host portion of the IP address is unique for each device on the subnet. The combination of the network and host address in one IP number makes the IP number unique for each system. Computer software and hardware do not use friendly names or IP numbers but work with the binary number equivalents. On the outside, software and hardware may appear to use names and decimal numbers but that is to provide an interface to humans. At the computational level, everything boils down to bits. A *bit* is the smallest unit of information or data and each bit can exist in one of two states: a 0 (zero) may indicate the bit is off and a 1 (one) means the bit is on. A system that has two states is represented by using *bi* in the name. For example, *bicycle* means "two cycle." To indicate we are working with numbers, the word *nary* is used. Thus, *binary* means two numbers: 0 and 1. Any number and mathematical calculation can be represented and performed by using only 0's and 1's.

At the computational level, routers, workstations, servers, packets, etc., all work with information in bits. Thus, an IP address is actually a string of 0's and 1's, and each device on the network uses these binary IP numbers to work with each other on the network. Since people can't remember long strings of 0's and 1's very well, we translate the binary numbers to decimal numbers and then sometimes associate these numbers with names. Thus, to truly understand topics such as:

- What makes up an IP decimal number?
- Why do Class A addresses have only so many networks?
- What is the purpose of a subnet mask?

we need to get down to the binary level.

Binary Arithmetic

Since you were a child, you learned to count by tens. That is, when the numbers 0 through 9 were used up, you started putting them together to get numbers larger than 9. And for each extra column added to the number, you used the terms 10s place, 100s place, 1000s place, and so on. Figure C-1 illustrates the decimal number expansion for the number 205.

1000	100	10	1
	2	0	5

$$205 = 100 + 100 + 0 + 1 + 1 + 1 + 1 + 1$$

Fig. C-1.   Decimal number expansion for the number 205.

Then, when you were introduced to adding numbers and the sum of numbers in a column was larger than 9, the stuff to the left of the 9 was carried over to the next column and added to those values. Figure C-2 illustrates the carry concept of decimal addition.

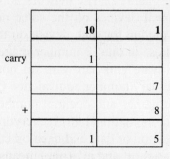

	10	1
carry	1	
		7
+		8
	1	5

$$15 = 10 + 1 + 1 + 1 + 1 + 1$$

Fig. C-2.   Carry concept for decimal addition.

A similar concept was used when you began taking away or subtracting numbers. What happened when you had to subtract the numbers 1 through 9 from a 0 in the same column? You borrowed one from the adjacent column on the left. You may be wondering why we have gone down arithmetic memory lane. The reason is these same concepts you use for decimal or base 10 arithmetic holds true when you have only two numbers to work with.

When you have two numbers or bits to work with, you have four possible states or combinations as shown in Figure C-3.

1 bit	1 bit
0	0
0	1
1	0
1	1

Fig. C-3. Four possible states for 2 bits.

But how do you represent the decimal number 2 with only 1's and 0's? One way is to use more than one 0 and one 1. For example, you could use a 1 and a 0 together to represent 2, and you can use a 1 and 1 together to represent 3. Figure C-4 illustrates the four possible states for two bits and the decimal equivalents. If you take three bits and look at all the possible combinations, you generate eight possible states as shown in Figure C-4.

1 bit	1 bit	1 bit	Decimal
0	0	0	0
0	0	1	1
0	1	0	2
0	1	1	3
1	0	0	4
1	0	1	5
1	1	0	6
1	1	1	7

Fig. C-4. Eight possible states for 3 bits.

Binary numbers are added and subtracted just like decimal numbers—carry and borrow. For example, what is the result of adding 11001101 and 00000011? Since we only have 1's and 0's, adding two 1's together results in 10. That is, $1 + 1 = 0$ and carry the 1 to result in 10. Figure C-5 illustrates the addition of two binary numbers.

carry				1	1	1	1	
	1	1	0	0	1	1	0	1
+	0	0	0	0	0	0	1	1
	1	1	0	1	0	0	0	0

Fig. C-5. Binary addition.

What happens when you subtract binary numbers? Again, the same processes you use for decimal numbers apply to binary numbers. Binary 0 minus 0 equals 0, binary 1 minus binary 1 is also 0, and binary 1 minus 0 is 1. However binary 0 minus 1 means you have to borrow a 1 from the next position to yield binary 10 minus 1 which equals 1. Figure C-6 shows an example of subtracting 00000011 from 11001101.

borrow						1		
	1	1	0	0	1	1->0	0	1
–	0	0	0	0	0	0	1	1
	1	1	0	0	1	0	1	0

Fig. C-6. Binary subtraction.

When you observe the progression of numbers as the state increases by another bit, the decimal values increase by a factor of two. You can represent the decimal equivalent of a binary value by taking the number 2 and raising it to the power of the column number where the first column in numbered zero. For example, with just 1 bit, the decimal equivalent is 2^0, which is equal to decimal 1. 2^2 is equal to the decimal value of 4, and 2^3 is equal to the decimal value of 8. Figure C-7 shows this concept for 8 bits.

2^7	2^6	2^5	2^4	2^3	2^2	2^1	2^0
128	64	32	16	8	4	2	1

Fig. C-7. Decimal equivalents of the power of twos.

To represent a binary value using 8 bits, we use a 0 to indicate that the corresponding bit is not set, or used, and a 1 to indicate that the value is set, or used. For example, to translate the binary number 10100101 to decimal, put the binary number in the chart as shown in Figure C-8, and you can quickly convert to the decimal value of 165.

2^7	2^6	2^5	2^4	2^3	2^2	2^1	2^0
128	64	32	16	8	4	2	1
1	0	1	0	0	1	0	1

128 + 32 + 4 + 1 = 165

Fig. C-8. Decimal equivalents of the binary number 10100101.

IP Address Calculation

In computer technologies, 8 bits of numbers are commonly grouped together to form what is called a *byte* or an *octet*. An IPv4 number consists of 4 octets or bytes that are separated by dots (periods) and the form of the number is called dotted decimal notation. When the IP number is used by the different networking devices, it is used in its 32-bit binary form. For example, we can take the IP decimal number of 206.224.65.194 and represent it in its binary form as follows:

Decimal	Binary
206.224.65.194	11001110.11100000.01000001.11000010

The numbering scheme used for IPv4 addresses is a 32-bit number that incorporates a two-part hierarchical structure. The IP number contains a network portion that is shared by all devices on the same network segment, and a unique number for each interface. The design of the IP addressing scheme divides the addresses into five classes, A, B, C, D, and E. This separation of the address space into classes is referred to as *classful IP addressing*. To distinguish the different classes, specific bit patterns are used to indicate the class of the address. The bit pattern in the first portion of the first byte of the four-byte address determines the IP address class. In the table below, the bit pattern of the first byte is listed for each class. Note that in the table, an *x* indicates that either a 1 or 0 can be used because this portion of the IP number has no impact on the classification of the IP address.

Bit Pattern	Class
0 x x x x x x x	A
1 0 x x x x x x	B
1 1 0 x x x x x	C
1 1 1 0 x x x x	D
1 1 1 1 0 x x x	E

Another component of the class definition involves the division of the IP address to represent the common network portion and the unique interface, or host, number. All of the devices on the same portion of a network must all use the same network number. The second portion of the IP address must be different for all devices, or hosts, on the same network. Again, the designers of the IPv4 addressing scheme defined the following specifications:

Class	Number of Network Bits	Number of Host Bits
A	8	24
B	16	16
C	24	8

Notice that Class D and Class E are not included in the above table. The reason is that these two classes are not used for assignment to specific devices. Class D addresses are used for multicasting, and Class E is reserved for special and research uses.

Taking into account the number of bits for network and host portions of the IP address, we can also say that the first byte of a Class A address is the network number, the first two bytes of a Class B address are the network number, and the first three bytes of a Class C address are the network number. If we take into account the bit pattern in the first byte and the number of bits for the network address, we can list the network address ranges for the first byte in each class of IP addresses.

Class	Beginning Address	Ending Address
A	0	127
B	128	191
C	192	223
D	224	239
E	240	255

To determine these address ranges, we need to look at the binary values. For a Class A address, the first bit of the first byte must be a 0, which limits the maximum value of the end network address.

2^7	2^6	2^5	2^4	2^3	2^2	2^1	2^0	
128	64	32	16	8	4	2	1	
0	0	0	0	0	0	0	0	=decimal 0
0	1	1	1	1	1	1	1	=decimal 127

For a Class B address, the range of network numbers for the first byte is also limited due to the reservation of the first 2 bits in the first byte.

2^7	2^6	2^5	2^4	2^3	2^2	2^1	2^0	
128	64	32	16	8	4	2	1	
1	**0**	0	0	0	0	0	0	=decimal 128
1	**0**	1	1	1	1	1	1	=decimal 191

The Class C available network address for the first byte is restricted because the first 3 bits are set aside for the class definition.

2^7	2^6	2^5	2^4	2^3	2^2	2^1	2^0	
128	64	32	16	8	4	2	1	
1	**1**	**0**	0	0	0	0	0	=decimal 192
1	**1**	**0**	1	1	1	1	1	=decimal 223

If you take into account the remaining three bytes and the number of bits used for the network portion of an IP address, the number of available networks for Classes B and C are greater than a Class A address. You can determine the number of maximum networks for each class by counting the number of bits in the network portion of the address and then raising that value to the power of two. For example, for a Class A address there are 7 bits that can be used for the network address. Since the first bit must be a 0, we cannot manipulate that bit, which leaves 7 remaining bits in the first byte. When you convert 2^7 to decimal, the value returned is 128. Thus, in the total IP address space, there is a maximum of 128 Class A networks. Extending this to a Class B address, the number of bits that can be used for the network portion of the IP address is 14—6 bits from the first byte and 8 bits from the second byte, because a Class B address uses the first two bytes as the network address. Converting 2^{14} to decimal gives us 16,384. Therefore, there are a maximum of 16,284 Class B networks in the IP address space. In the Class C network, there are a maximum of 2^{21} or 2,097,152 possible networks. This is calculated by the 5 bits in the first byte plus the 16 bits in the second and third byte to give us 21 usable bits for the network address. Note that there are some values that are not permitted, but we are not considering these at this point.

Class D IP addresses are reserved for multicasting, which provides the ability to send a message to a group of devices that are members of the same multicast group. In the Class D addresses scheme, 28 bits are available for specifying multicast groups. This means there are over 268 million, or 268,435,456 to be exact, possible multicast groups. There are two types of multicast groups that are supported by the Class D address rules. *Permanent* multicast groups always exist and do not have to be set up or configured. The other type of multicast groups are *temporary*, and they must be created before they can be used by any device. Once the group is defined, the multicast implementations can include procedures for hosts to ask to join a multicast group and to leave a multicast group. When all members of a multicast group leave the group, the temporary multicast group is no longer available.

The host, or unique portion of the IP address, is the bits that are not used for the network address. For a Class A address, the last three bytes of the IP address are available for host assignments. To determine the maximum number of hosts you can use on a particular class address, count the number of bits available for the host portion of the address and raise that value to the power of two. For example, in a Class A address, there are 24 bits available for the host address. The value 2^{24} translates to 16,777,216 decimal. This means that each Class A network can have a maximum of 16,777,216 hosts on the same network. A Class B network can have 2^{16} or 65,536 hosts per network and a Class C network can have 2^{8} or 256 hosts per network. Note that there are some values that are not permitted, but we are not considering these at this point.

Another element in the IP addressing scheme is a subnet mask. When a packet arrives at a router, or any device, the device needs to be able to determine the IP address's class. To efficiently determine this, an IP address is associated with a subnet mask. The subnet mask is used to determine which portion of the address is the network portion and which part is the host address. To accomplish this number separation, the router performs an AND operation of the IP address with the subnet mask. Each class of addresses has a default subnet mask and these are listed in the table below:

Class	Subnet Mask
A	255.0.0.0
B	255.255.0.0
C	255.255.255.0

Converting the subnet masks to their binary equivalent reveals the following patterns:

Decimal	Binary
255.0.0.0	11111111.00000000.00000000.00000000
255.255.0.0	11111111.11111111.00000000.00000000
255.255.255.0	11111111.11111111.11111111.00000000

With both the IP address and the subnet mask, the routers can determine which portion of the IP address is the network address and which section is the host number.

SUBNETTING IPV4 NETWORKS WITH STANDARD SUBNET MASKS

In the early days of IPv4 usage, environments that were using Class A and Class B addresses rarely used all of the available host numbers possible for their network addresses. Instead of using another IP network address and waste unused host addresses, the concept of subdividing or subnetting a network address to be used across networks was proposed. The first implementation of this was to use a Class C subnet mask with a Class B address, and a Class B subnet mask with a Class A address to produce more subnetworks. To see how this works, let's take a look at the Class B network address 172.16.0.0 and examine how a Class C subnet mask can produce subnets. Note that when an IP number ends with a zero, the IP number is referring to an IP network. So, for example, 172.16.0.0 refers to the network 172.16 and the 0.0 indicates the portion of the address that is used for host addresses. The Class A network, 10.0.0.0, shows that the last three bytes are available for host addresses. Before we delve into subnetting 172.16.0.0, let's first list some of the possible IP addresses using the standard Class B subnet mask of 255.255.0.0.

Network	Subnet Mask	Example IP Addresses
172.16.0.0	255.255.0.0	172.16.1.5
		172.16.1.46
		172.16.2.5
		172.16.2.46
		172.16.52.8
		172.16.52.72
		172.16.52.100
		and so on for a total of 65,536
		possible host numbers

By applying the Class C subnet mask, 255.255.255.0, you can divide the Class B network 172.16.0.0 into 256 possible subnets and each of those subnets would have a maximum of 256 hosts. The following table shows some examples of possible subnets and IP addresses.

Network	Subnet Mask	Subnet	Example IP Addresses
172.16.0.0	255.255.255.0	172.16.1.0	172.16.1.5
			172.16.1.46
			and so on for a total of 256
			possible host numbers

172.16.2.0	172.16.2.5
	172.16.2.46
	and so on for a total of 256 possible host numbers
172.16.52.0	172.16.52.8
	172.16.52.72
	172.16.52.100
	and so on for a total of 256 possible host numbers

Notice that we used the same example IP addresses as in the previous table but now with the Class C subnet mask we have three different subnets using the same range of numbers. You can also apply this concept to a Class A address. That is, you can use either a Class B or a Class C subnet mask with a Class A address. The mask you decide to use depends on the maximum number of hosts you will be supporting on each subnet. If you have more than 256 hosts on some or all of the subnets, then you will need to use a Class B subnet mask. Using a Class B subnet mask with a Class A address gives you 256 subnets with each subnet supporting the 65,536 possible hosts. Using a Class C subnet mask with a Class A address allows for 65,536 possible subnets with 256 hosts per subnet.

SUBNETTING IPV4 NETWORKS WITH NONSTANDARD SUBNET MASKS

Over the last several years, the proliferation of systems and users on the Internet has grown to the point where all Class A and Class B addresses are in use and very few Class C addresses remain available. Because of this shortage of available addresses, the various IPv4 task force members implemented the use of nonstandard IP subnet masks to allow for more possible subnets. The use of nonstandard subnet masks is also referred to as *classless addressing*. To demonstrate the use of nonstandard IP subnet masks, we will use the Class C address of 192.168.44.0 to provide more than one subnet. Recall that the standard subnet mask of a Class C address is 255.255.255.0 and the last, or fourth byte, is available for host addresses. By applying a nonstandard subnet mask to 192.168.44.0, some of the bits in the host portion can be used to create additional subnets. For example, let's say that we need to provide different subnets for the 192.168.44.0 address. If we use the two left-most bits of the fourth byte, we can produce four different subnets. Once again, we need to refer to the binary values and in this example we are only concerned with the last byte.

Binary of 4*th* Byte

00000000
01000000
10000000
11000000

Using 2 bits to create subnets leaves 6 bits that can be used for host addresses. That is, 2^6 or 64 hosts per subnet. In reality, not all of the possible numbers can be used for IP addresses. We have mentioned this briefly, so let's cover some of the rules at this point. The rules are important to know when it comes to designing an IP subnetting scheme for production networks.

1. The network 127.0.0.0 cannot be assigned to a network. Typically, the address 127.0.0.1 in the 127.0.0.0 network is used to refer to the interface or device itself. 127.0.0.1 is also called the local host number or loopback address.

2. A network address cannot consist of all bits set to zeros. When zeros are used in the network portion of the address, the IP number refers to the host number on the local network. For example, 0.0.0.68 means host number 68 on the network the device resides on.

3. A host address cannot consist of all bits set to zeros. When zeros are used in the host portion of the address, the IP number is referring to the network address. For example, 192.168.18.0 is referring to the network 192.168.18. Similarly, 10.0.0.0 is referring to the Class A network 10.

4. A host address cannot consist of all bits set to ones. When ones are used for the host portion of the address, the IP address is referring to all hosts on the network. For example, 192.168.18.255 means all hosts on network 192.168.18.0.

5. The number 0.0.0.0 refers to this host on this network.

6. 255.255.255.255 is a broadcast address and means all hosts on the local network. An early implementation of BSD UNIX used the IP address format of all zeros in the host portion as a broadcast. This form is referred to as the *Berkeley broadcast*. Some systems are designed to accept both address forms for broadcasts.

7. Taking these rules into account, we need to revise the actual number of subnets and hosts available on a network. For example, in the following table of possible IP subnet numbers, both the first and last entries are not valid:

Binary of 4th Byte

~~00000000~~
01000000
10000000
~~11000000~~

The reason that the first and last entries cannot be used is the bits that will be used to produce the subnets are either all 0's or 1's. This, using 2 bits of the fourth byte produces only two subnets. We can express the number of possible subnets as a formula:

$$\text{Number of subnets} = 2^M - 2$$

where M is the number of bits used to define the subnet or the number of masked host bits. In our example, there are 2 bits that are used to define the subnets. Thus,

$$\text{Number of subnets} = 2^2 - 2 = 2$$

So now the number of legal subnets left when 2 host bits are used to produce subnets are:

Binary of 4*th* Byte

01000000
10000000

We can also calculate the number of hosts per subnet with a similar formula:

$$\text{Number of hosts per subnet} = 2^U - 2$$

where U is the number of remaining host bits or unmasked host bits. In our example, there are 6 bits available for the host addresses, so:

$$\text{Number of hosts per subnet} = 2^6 - 2 = 62$$

Because we have used two bits of the last byte to create two subnets, the subnet mask is no longer the following:

```
Binary    11111111.11111111.11111111.00000000
Decimal   255.255.255.0
```

Instead, the subnet mask is:

```
Binary    11111111.11111111.11111111.11000000
Decimal   255.255.255.192
```

We can also specify the subnet mask by using a classless interdomain routing (CIDR) naming notation. CIDR notation appends the number of bits used for the network address to the end of the IP address. A forward slash separates the IP number from the number of network address bits. For example, using the subnet mask of 255.255.255.192 with the network IP address of 192.168.44.0, the CIDR address is 192.168.44.0/26.

Another item we need to define is the number of each subnet and the available host numbers on each subnet. Examining the binary value of the last byte of a Class C IP address where the subnet mask is 255.255.255.192:

2^7	2^6	2^5	2^4	2^3	2^2	2^1	2^0
128	64	32	16	8	4	2	1
0	1	–	–	–	–	–	–
1	0	–	–	–	–	–	–

reveals that we have subnet 64 and subnet 128. For subnet 64, the range of host numbers is:

2^7	2^6	2^5	2^4	2^3	2^2	2^1	2^0	
128	64	32	16	8	4	2	1	
0	**1**	0	0	0	0	0	1	=decimal 65
0	**1**	1	1	1	1	1	0	=decimal 126

For subnet 128, the range of host numbers is:

2^7	2^6	2^5	2^4	2^3	2^2	2^1	2^0	
128	64	32	16	8	4	2	1	
1	**0**	0	0	0	0	0	1	=decimal 129
1	**0**	1	1	1	1	1	0	=decimal 190

With this information, we can say that the device with the IP address of 192.168.18.70 is on subnet 64 and 192.168.18.170 is on subnet 128. Notice that with a subnet mask of 255.255.255.192, a total number of 124 hosts is possible across both subnets—each subnet has 62. Comparing this value to the total number of hosts with a subnet mask of 255.255.255.0 is 254 ($2^8 - 2$), there has been a loss of available host addresses but you have gained the ability to spread the addresses over two different networks.

As another example, let's see what happens when 3 bits of the fourth byte are used to create subnets.

Binary of 4*th* Byte

~~00000000~~
00100000
01000000
01100000
10000000
10100000
11000000
~~11100000~~

The first and last lines are discarded because of the IP rules listed previously. Thus, using 3 bits, there are six possible subnets, $2^3 - 2$, where each subnet has a maximum of 30 hosts, $2^5 - 2$.

2^7	2^6	2^5	2^4	2^3	2^2	2^1	2^0	
128	64	32	16	8	4	2	1	
0	0	1	–	–	–	–	–	=subnet 32
0	1	0	–	–	–	–	–	=subnet 64
0	1	1	–	–	–	–	–	=subnet 96
1	0	0	–	–	–	–	–	=subnet 128
1	0	1	–	–	–	–	–	=subnet 160
1	1	0	–	–	–	–	–	=subnet 192

The possible host addresses for subnet 32 are:.

2^7	2^6	2^5	2^4	2^3	2^2	2^1	2^0	
128	64	32	16	8	4	2	1	
0	**0**	**1**	0	0	0	0	1	=decimal 33
0	**0**	**1**	1	1	1	1	0	=decimal 62

For subnet 64:

2^7	2^6	2^5	2^4	2^3	2^2	2^1	2^0	
128	64	32	16	8	4	2	1	
0	1	0	0	0	0	0	1	=decimal 65
0	1	0	1	1	1	1	0	=decimal 94

For subnet 96:

2^7	2^6	2^5	2^4	2^3	2^2	2^1	2^0	
128	64	32	16	8	4	2	1	
0	1	1	0	0	0	0	1	=decimal 97
0	1	1	1	1	1	1	0	=decimal 126

For subnet 128:

2^7	2^6	2^5	2^4	2^3	2^2	2^1	2^0	
128	64	32	16	8	4	2	1	
1	0	0	0	0	0	0	1	=decimal 129
1	0	0	1	1	1	0	0	=decimal 158

For subnet 160:

2^7	2^6	2^5	2^4	2^3	2^2	2^1	2^0	
128	64	32	16	8	4	2	1	
1	0	1	0	0	0	0	1	=decimal 161
1	0	1	1	1	1	1	0	=decimal 190

For subnet 192:

2^7	2^6	2^5	2^4	2^3	2^2	2^1	2^0	
128	64	32	16	8	4	2	1	
1	1	0	0	0	0	0	1	=decimal 193
1	1	0	1	1	1	1	0	=decimal 222

In summary, using a subnet mask of 255.255.255.224 produces six subnets of 30 hosts per subnet. Counting all the possible hosts across all six subnets, a total of 180 hosts are possible. Thus, a subnet mask of 255.255.255.224 reduces the possible hosts of 254 with a standard Class C subnet mask to 180 hosts with a nonstandard subnet mask. However, the gain is the ability to dispense IP addresses across six different networks. For example, 192.168.18.50 is on subnet 32; 192,168.18.70 is on subnet 64; 192.168.18.110 is on subnet 96; 192.168.18.140 is on subnet 128; 192.168.18.170 is on subnet 160; and 192.168.18.210 is on subnet 192. The CIDR notation for the IP network 192.168.18.0 with the subnet mask of 255.255.255.224 is 192.168.18.0/27.

Private IPv4 Networks

Within the IP address space, there are addresses reserved for use on private networks. Private IP network addresses are typically used by companies, organizations, and individual networks when the systems do not have a presence on the Internet. In order to access the Internet, a router, or gateway, is used to funnel the requests from the private network to the public Internet. The router's interfaces to the Internet must have an IP address that is unique on the Internet but the remaining machines on the private network do not need unique Internet-compliant addresses. Because of this design of multiple private networks interfacing with the public Internet, an organization, company, or individual does not need to have a lot of Internet-compliant addresses. That is, they may not need all 256 possible host addresses of a Class C address. The same holds true for Class B and Class A addresses. By applying a different, nonstandard subnet to a Class A, B, or C address, the resultant subnets can be used on different subnets of a company, organization, or personal network or the subnet addresses can be used by different entities. This approach to subnet division between different, unrelated parties is typically used by ISPs (Internet Service Providers) to allow for many different people and organizations to access the Internet. The following range of IPv4 addresses is reserved for private networks:

- 10.0.0.0 through 10.255.255.255
- 172.16.0.0 through 172.31.255.255
- 192.168.0.0. through 192.168.255.255

IPv6

IPv6 uses a 128-bit address that includes a network and host portion. According to some, with a 128-bit IP address, there are enough addresses to allow for more than 1500 IP addresses for each square meter of the entire surface area of the earth! The IPv6 address design also supports subnet masks, multicasts, and CIDR-type structures. The structure of the IPv6 header is very different from the IPv4 header and also encodes information into different, or extension, headers. IPv6 also contains support for video and audio data so that a high-quality path can be determined and used throughout a multimedia conversation.

There are three types of multilevel hierarchical addresses in the IPv6 address space: provider-oriented unicast, anycast, and multicast. The provider-oriented unicast address is assigned to individual devices and interfaces. To designate this type of address, the number starts with a specific prefix, 010. The format of an IPv6 unicast address is as follows:

| 010 | Registry ID | Provider ID | Subscriber ID | Subnet ID | Interface ID |

The Registry ID is the address registry of the authority that assigns the Provider ID value to ISPs. The providers can then designate portions of their address space to subscribers, which is indicated by the Subscriber ID. Each subscriber is assigned a specific subnet and that is indicated by the Subnet ID value. The Interface ID is the unique number assigned to a specific device or interface within the corresponding subnet. Some of the IPv6 prefix address assignments are as follows:

Prefix	Role
0000 0000	Reserved
0000 0000	Unassigned
0000 001	Reserved for NSAP allocation
0000 010	Reserved for IPX allocation
0000 0011	Unassigned
0000 1	Unassigned
0001	Unassigned
001	Aggregatable global unicast addresses
010	Unassigned
011	Unassigned
100	Unassigned
101	Unassigned
110	Unassigned
1110	Unassigned
1111 0	Unassigned
1111 10	Unassigned
1111 110	Unassigned
1111 1110 0	Unassigned
1111 1110 10	Link local use addresses
1111 1110 11	Site local use addresses
1111 1111	Multicast addresses

Anycast addresses apply to more than one device or interface but not to all interfaces on the network. These can be useful when information needs to be sent to all the interfaces and devices corresponding to a particular Provider ID value. The original implementation of anycast addressing was known as *cluster addressing*. Multicast addresses are used to address the members of a multicast group. Multicast addresses start with the hexadecimal value of FF or decimal 255.

Writing out an IPv6 address in dotted decimal notation can be quite long. For example:

```
105.100.215.50.255.255.255.255.0.0.32.136.150.5.255.255
```

Instead of this format, IPv6 numbers are represented as colon hexadecimal notation where each group of 16 bits is written as a hexadecimal value. Each hexadecimal number is separated by a colon. Using this format, the above number is expressed in colon hexadecimal notation as:

```
6964 : D732 : FFFF : FFFF : 0 : 2088 : 9605: FFFF
```

Also when more than two zeros occur together, two colons are used to represent the range of zeros. For example, the number:

```
6964: 0 : 0 : 0 : 0 : 0 : 0: FFFF
```

can be represented as:

```
6964 : : FFFF
```

This form of shorthand format for a contiguous range of zeros can only be used once in an IPv6 address.

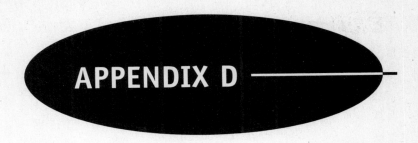

APPENDIX D

Bibliography

This appendix lists some great networking resources in print.

- *Computer Networks*, 2nd edition, Larry L. Peterson and Bruce S. Davie, Academic Press, 2000, ISBN 1558605142
- *Computer Networks*, 3rd edition, Andrew S. Tanenbaum, Prentice Hall, 1996, ISBN 0133499456
- *Computer Networks and Internets*, Douglas E. Comer, Prentice Hall, 2001, ISBN 0130914495
- *An Engineering Approach to Computer Networking*, S. Keshav, Addison-Wesley, 1997, ISBN 0201634422
- *Guide to Networking Essentials*, 2nd edition, Ed Tittel and David Johnson, Course Technology, 2001, ISBN 0619034505
- *Local & Metropolitan Area Networks*, 6th edition, William Stallings, Prentice Hall, 2000, ISBN 0130129390
- *MCSE Networking Essentials Exam Cram Personal Trainer*, Ed Tittel, The Coriolis Group, 2000, ISBN 1576106446
- *Networking with NetWare for Dummies*, 4th edition, Ed Tittel, Earl Follis, and James E. Gaskin, Hungry Minds, Inc., 2001, ISBN 0764502816
- *The Switch Book*, Rich Seifert, John Wiley & Sons, 2000, ISBN 0471345865
- *Windows 2000 Networking for Dummies*, Ed Tittel and James Michael Stewart, Hungry Minds, Inc., 2001, ISBN 0764508113

INDEX